LONG
TIME
GONE

LONG TIME GONE

THE AUTOBIOGRAPHY OF DAVID CROSBY

David Crosby

Carl Gottlieb

Doubleday

NEW YORK LONDON TORONTO SYDNEY AUCKLAND

Published by Doubleday, a division of
Bantam Doubleday Dell Publishing Group, Inc.
666 Fifth Avenue, New York, New York 10103

DOUBLEDAY and the portrayal of an anchor
with a dolphin are trademarks of
Doubleday, a division of Bantam Doubleday Dell
Publishing Group, Inc.

Library of Congress Cataloging-in-Publication Data

Crosby, David.
Long time gone: the autobiography of David Crosby/David
Crosby/Carl Gottlieb.—1st ed.
p.   cm.
1. Crosby, David.   2. Rock musicians—United States—Biography.
I. Gottlieb, Carl.   II. Title.
ML420.C935A3   1988
784.5'4'00924—dc19

[B]   88–23744
                                                    CIP
                                                     MN

Book design by Tasha Hall
Photo insert design by Julie Duquet

For my wife, Jan, and all my friends who helped.

(With thanks to Bill Wilson and Dr. Bob)

INTRODUCTION

···

Is there anything you want to know, just ask me
I'm the world's most opinionated man
I'll give you an answer if I can
Catch one passing through
That's right for you

"Anything at All,"
Words and Music by David Crosby

T his is how I remember my life. Other folks may not have the same memories, even though we might have shared some of the same experiences. They can write their own books; several of them already have. I know I have an ego—opinions differ as to its health, size, and value. When the research is done and the last friend or enemy has spoken his or her piece into the microphones that record our lives, what's left is my side of the story, events and emotions drawn from my memory bank, a personal chronicle of experience and recollection. I've lived only one life and more than half of it was spent in the public eye, like a cinder; the pivotal moments and central events will always be the same, regardless of who asks and no matter how many times I tell some stories.

I was always a show-biz kid. My father won one of the first Academy Awards for cinematography in 1931 for a movie called *Tabu*. He shot that in black-and-white on a Tahitian island, developing the negative himself at night. I've seen the film; the silver nitrate blacks-and-whites show a world that was lost before I was born. In 1968 I bought a wooden schooner and sailed her across the Caribbean and through the Panama Canal up to California and across the Pacific. I sailed that boat on voyages of personal discovery and eventually traded my owner's stateroom for a cell in Huntsville State Prison in Texas. I served a year in a variety of jails and prisons after a conviction that was eventually overturned by the Supreme Court of the State of Texas. I was drug-free when I was released and I've stayed that way so far. I had good friends, I lost them, and some came back when I came back. I'm married to the woman who shared the seven-year downward slide and made a parallel recovery.

I've spent my life playing, singing, and making music. My motivations (when I could articulate them) were sometimes simple, sometimes complex, and always a mystery. I always knew how to sing; it was the extra dimension of accompaniment that transformed me into a performer. I've always said that I picked up the guitar as a shortcut to sex and after my first joint I was sure that if everyone smoked dope there'd be an end to war. I was right about the sex. I was wrong when it came to drugs. But who knew? There wasn't any instruction book. Life comes without an operator's manual and in the end all we can do is try to see it as it is.

By an accident of birth and adolescent choices motivated by pure hormonal rush, I was caught up in a cultural revolution. Sex, drugs, and rock 'n' roll—I was in the middle of it from the beginning. I chased perpetual pleasure and got a full measure of pain as a payback. I was twenty-eight before I could commit my life and love to one woman, only to suffer her unexpected death after a freak auto accident. Later, others overdosed, crashed, and burned. And always there was dope—the best grass, pharmaceutical cocaine in factory-sealed brown glass bottles, and psychedelics cooked in the lab of Owsley Stanley, the Master Chef himself, the man whose very name was synonymous with quality LSD. I never thought of my life as driven by drugs—not at first and not for years.

An autobiography is an opportunity to describe my life the way I think I lived it, a chance to correct the record, or to create a record where none existed before. Toward that end, this book speaks with several voices. First, there's me, delivering the first-person account of the guy who's done the crime and served the time. That's this text.

> Slightly indented, like this, is the more or less objective view of the coauthor, who writes from the perspective of a worldly friend who has collected the data and collated the research. In English class they called it an Omniscient Voice and the authors agreed that a third-person narrative would be appropriate to present credentials and explain sources. The indented text will also set the stage, supply background information, and introduce characters who add alternative views of what happened. For example, our editor was David Gernert, a tall blond man with two black shoes and a beard. He had this to say about the pictures we assembled for the book:

DAVID GERNERT: *The photos are in what Lucy and I feel is the best order, to follow both a general chronology and the book's narrative. It will be possible to add a couple more photos—depending on the designer's space allotment—for about another two days, after which this will be in the hands of the printers (the inserts get printed separately and first). If you want to add a couple of key pictures, we need them ASAP.*

> Lucy Herring is David Gernert's assistant. There are a number of other voices, contradictory passages, and comments from third parties, some of them not friends of David Crosby. The authors have included alternative versions to correct any imbalance that might've crept into Crosby's otherwise perfect account of a confused and chaotic life.

I'd like to thank the many friends and acquaintances who gave generously of their time and memories and responded to our requests for interviews, documents, and photos. My wife, Jan, gave me her tireless support and constant companionship and since I can't thank her enough, ever, I'll start by telling her here that I love her—then, now, and always.

Maryann Zvoleff spent a large part of her life caught up in the details of my life and her dedication and commitment have made her our researcher, assistant, and friend. She has experienced the worst and knows the best. David Gernert waited patiently for pages that seemed never to come and Marcia Jacobs transcribed miles of tape, most of it recorded under difficult conditions: at sea, in bikers' cabins in California's Central Valley, and in noisy bars, airports, and restaurants. Nena Callaghan moonlighted away from her desk at my partner's office at Universal Studios and Bill Siddons and Debbie Meister took hours and days that might have been better spent managing my career and spent them supporting the incomprehensible demands we made as we tried to meet a variety of contractual and self-imposed deadlines. Mark Hurst pored over every word on every page and is a much-appreciated copy editor and fan.

Al Lowman was the agent who represented the book with great energy and ability in New York and Larry Grossman, the coauthor's agent for twenty years, represented Gottlieb's interests in prolonged, complicated, and hard-fought negotiations. Both men delivered contracts to the authors that would've earned David and Carl a fortune if they could've sold them by the pound.

CARL GOTTLIEB: *To the tireless and selfless gnomes, trolls, princes, and ladies who sweated out the transformation of this manuscript into a book, we extend our eternal gratitude.*

For everyone who loved the music and wondered how one guy could screw up his life so completely and still survive, this book's for you.

—David Crosby

P R O L O G U E :
M E D I C A L
P A P E R W O R K

....

<u>ROSS GENERAL HOSPITAL</u>
11-22-83

<u>PATIENT:</u>	CROSBY, DAVID
<u>IDENTIFICATION:</u>	42-year-old, single, white male, rock musician.
<u>REVIEW OF SYSTEMS:</u>	Patient describes chills and sweats five to six times a day beginning 24 hours after the admission and says he "feels bad all over."
<u>HEENT:</u> (Head, Eyes, Ears, Nose, Throat)	Describes ringing in the ears and a dull headache in the frontal and occipital areas. The headache is not accompanied by visual symptoms or unilateral weakness. He describes a low grade tinnitus but can hear well.
<u>GI:</u> (Gastrointestinal)	He has stomach ache with nausea but no vomiting. He notes increased bowel rumbling without gas or belching. He has had constipation chronically. His last bowel movement which was hard and dry was approximately two days ago.
<u>GU:</u> (Genito-urinary)	He denies currently any history of urinary hesitancy or obstruction or pain but does state that he periodically notices a left pain in the costovertebral angle so that a question of urinary tract obstruction on a periodic or intermittent basis should be considered.
<u>NEUROLOGIC:</u>	There is a past history of seizure on one occasion when he was in an apartment with friends. This was apparently a witnessed grand mal tonic clonic seizure and may have been related to drug intake, but is not known.
<u>PHYSICAL EXAMINATION:</u>	Reveals a disheveled man who appears his stated age and is slightly obese.
<u>HEENT:</u>	Reveals long hair which is in need of shampooing, scalp has some plaque build-up, but no psoriasis is evident. External canals and tympanic membranes are intact. The nasal septum is perforate with some purulent material,

dried and old on either side. Mouth exam reveals four teeth which are broken and badly carious, left upper, lower and right lower. The tongue is normal as is the pharynx.

EXTREMITIES: Reveal multiple pigmentation in the lower legs from dependent edema and hemorrhage of small capillary vessels with subsequent hemosiderin staining. There are no active signs of lymphangitic streaking and there is only 1+ to trace edema bilaterally in the ankle or pretibial areas. The skin of the feet is wrinkled and dry. On the upper extremities, his skin is characterized by healing staphylococcus lesions which are pink, macular and slightly depigmented. There are these lesions as well as multiple burns on the fingertips of his right hand, more than left hand, where he has apparently suffered some flash fires handling the freebase unit needed to produce his cocaine for inhalation. This skin is not infected but is rather dry and will soon slough to be replaced by normal dermis. There are several open draining wounds on the neck with staph purulent exudate not apparent since he has been on Dicloxacillin 48 hrs.

DIAGNOSTIC IMPRESSION: Chemical dependency, opiate and cocaine.

Chronic staphylococcal neurodermatitis.

Perforate nasal septum.

History of lower urinary tract obstruction and urinary retention with gross hematuria secondary to probable renolithiasis and colic.

Fixed tissue eruption to tetracycline.

Hemosiderin straining of both lower extremities.

DISPOSITION: The patient will be treated for chemical dependency. Phenothiazines, such as Loxitane 5-10 mg. q. 8-12 h. will be used for severe anxiety with Librium 25-50 mg. q. 6 h. for minor to moderate anxiety. Darvocet N 100 will be used for excessive muscular pain. He will be encouraged to participate in group activities, to begin a program of self care physically by washing and shampooing and then to move into daily exercises, group therapy, and stress management.

Patient subsequently admitted to
Gladman Memorial Hospital, Oakland,
California, for additional
psychological testing. Gladman is a
locked facility.

GLADMAN MEMORIAL HOSPITAL

NAME: CROSBY, DAVID V.C.
AGE: 42 YEARS
DATE: DECEMBER 16, 1983
TESTS ADMINISTERED: Rorschach
Thematic Apperception Test (TAT)
Projective Figure Drawing Test
Memory Designs Test

REASON FOR REFERRAL: Differential Diagnosis

BEHAVIOR DURING TEST PROCEDURE:

This large framed, moderately obese 42 year old male
patient was at initial contact only minimally cooperative
and obviously also very tense and apprehensive. He
responded, however, favorably to persistent
encouragement by the examiner and subsequently became
more voluble and certainly sufficiently cooperative to
give acceptably productive response records.

RORSCHACH INTERPRETATION:

The presence of a chronic and recurrent agitated
depression that has kept on varying in intensity in a
characterologically poorly integrated, emotionally
tempestuous, intrinsically restless, and impulsive man,
is revealed by this test record.

The indications are that this patient has used drugs over
the years to contain his agitations and his depressions --
although he, himself, may not be fully aware of this. His
restlessness is very pervasive, and there are strong
suggestions that even as a youngster he has not coped well
with external strictures imposed upon him or with rules
and regulations in general.

At this moment, the test findings go on to show, he feels
very much embittered -- particularly by what he considers
to be an unjust confinement -- and he has also become more
agitated and irascible.

THEMATIC APPERCEPTION TEST (TAT):

Patient's TAT associations underscore the unintegrated
nature of his character structure, his intrinsic
impulsiveness and tempestuousness, his enormous
restlessness, and also his long struggles with a recurrent
agitated depression.

But in addition, these test results describe him as a
basically intelligent, sensitive, affection and
attention-seeking person who has, however, always been
afraid of establishing closer relationships with others
or of making a commitment that would be a prerequisite for
such relationships.

In recent years, he has felt increasingly lonely,
alienated, and embittered.

Diagnostically, therefore, these results corroborate
emphatically the Rorschach test findings.

PROJECTIVE FIGURE DRAWING TEST:

Once again, this patient's underlying restlessness,
agitations, anxieties and tensions, and recurrent
depressive moods are all clearly reflected in the quality
of his test performance here.

But here, also, he is described as an intrinsically
intelligent-- though not disciplined-- and sensitive man
who has, however, never found peace with himself nor
gratification in his relationships with others.

Diagnostically, then, these results continue to support
the other findings.

DISCUSSION:

The currently obtained psychodiagnostic test results
point to the chronic presence of a recurrent agitated
depression (non-psychotic) in an intrinsically
intelligent and sensitive, but characterologically
poorly integrated and emotionally highly tempestuous and
impulsive man.

No significant organic finds were brought to light in
spite of a long history of drug abuse.

In addition, then, to whatever medication might be
indicated, this patient should be able to derive benefit
from a carefully structured and at this point essentially
support-supplying course of psychotherapy. It must be
noted, however, that he feels very much embittered at this
time and that at least in the initial phases,
psychotherapeutic progress is therefore likely to be very
slow. Also, in spite of the absence of positive organic
findings, it will be imperative to persuade him to
terminate resolutely all further drug abuse since there
are strong suggestions that-- contrary to his intentions-
- such is likely only to exacerbate his agitations and his
restlessness.

Finally, it must also be noted that his current
embitteredness and sense of despair are related to his
lifelong inability to cope with externally imposed
confinement. It is in this context, then, that suicidal
attempts cannot be ruled out should he be forced to spend a
significant time in jail.

David Crosby went to jail twice in the next two years, eventually spending a total of more than a year in prison. He was paroled from the Texas Department of Corrections Prison in Huntsville, Texas, in August of 1986. During the intervening period he had not only done jail time, but had managed to tour both as a solo artist with his own band and as a member of Crosby, Stills, and Nash for two national tours. When David surrendered to the FBI in Florida in December of 1985, he was heavier, dirtier, sicker, and more addicted than when he was examined at Ross General Hospital and at Gladman in 1983. He and his girlfriend, Jan Dance, were consuming approximately seven grams (a quarter of an ounce) of cocaine a day, as well as half a gram of heroin, mostly by smoking the vapors in a glass pipe. They had no money, his home was being seized for payment of back taxes, and he had sold all his possessions or pledged them to dealers for more drugs. The money to get David and Jan from Marin County in Northern California to Florida came from the sale of his last remaining possession of any substance, a grand piano.

At the time of his surrender, he has shaved his mustache and bought some cheap wigs in a pitiful attempt to disguise his distinctive appearance. Jan weighed less than ninety pounds, hadn't washed her hair in more than a month, and was increasingly catatonic and withdrawn. Both of them smelled bad, looked worse, and were without true friends. Their families had written them off. They were sleeping on the floors of only slightly "safe" houses owned by nervous dealers in the Miami area. Speaking to an auditorium full of well-fed, perfectly groomed students at Beverly Hills High School in 1987, David talked about his drug experience. Beverly Hills High School is probably the only high school in the United States that has a producing oil well on its campus and certainly the only high school in the United States that doesn't need an oil well on the athletic field any more than most high schools need a five-story garage for student parking. David was clear-eyed and engaging, his charm captured on a student videotape of that appearance.

I told them I had all the advantages, like most of them. I came from a nice family. I had a happy childhood, a reasonable situation with good schools, neither of my parents was an alcoholic, and they didn't beat me with baseball bats. Still, I wound up in a cell in a Texas prison. We're not talking the drunk tank here. We're talking serious business: barbed wire, machine-gun towers, and a three-hundred pound guy with no neck and a cowboy hat saying, "Hey, rock star, git over here, boy." The only thing that saved my life was being physically, forcibly separated from my stash. It had to be taken, out of my control. The way they do that is to sentence you to do time, then detoxify you. This is how they detox you in prison: they lock you in a steel box that's about five feet by nine feet, they feed you through a hole in the door, and they don't let you out at all. You get a little shower and a shitter and that's it. You don't leave. If you get a phone call, the guard hands you a telephone receiver through the slot. You beg people in the hall to bring you books and the food is part of the punishment. After I told them all that, a student asked me, "Were you ever onstage stoned?" The answer to that is that never once, until I got out of prison, did I ever record, perform, or do anything any way except stoned. I did it all stoned.

LONG
TIME
GONE

O N E

·············

How far back do you want to go in tracing the roots of David Van Cortlandt Crosby? My grandfather was the great-great grandson of Professor Ebenezer Crosby, a surgeon on George Washington's staff during the American Revolution. There's a William Floyd who signed the Declaration of Independence and there's a Van Cortlandt Park in New York City, named for Jacobus Van Cortlandt, who was the mayor of New York City from 1710 to 1719. None of them raised me, however, so if there's any genetic legacy, it's a tendency to identify with underdogs and outlaws and a firmness of purpose which my best friends call stubborn ego and which my enemies call . . . stubborn ego. My father was Floyd Delafield Crosby, my mother was Aliph Van Cortlandt Whitehead, my brother was christened Floyd Crosby, Jr., called Chip, and eventually changed his name to Ethan. I'll call him Ethan from now on. He's four and a half years older than I am and he'll be pleased to read that he was a musician before me—because it's true and not often mentioned. As a matter of fact, in the beginning I learned a great deal of what I knew from him.

My father was born just before the turn of the century in

3

1899 in New York City, the son of Frederick Van Schoonhoven Crosby and Julia Floyd Delafield. He was was born at 23rd Street and Lexington Avenue, which was a nice residential area in 1899. It must've been nice. My paternal grandfather Frederick was the treasurer of the Union Pacific Railroad and my grandmother Julia was the daughter of Francis Delafield, a famous New York physician and surgeon. My father left an oral history at the American Film Institute in 1973. When his widow, Betty, was interviewed for this book, she donated that history. I didn't know it existed until we started doing this book. The pages of my father's taped recollections are an insight into the life of a gifted cinematographer, a man who was at the same time a dedicated perfectionist, a political progressive, and a father distanced from his sons, worried that we were out of his control. My father died in the fall of 1985 before I went to prison. It's my great regret that he didn't live to see me free from drugs.

Floyd Crosby was raised in upper-class New York, secure in his place in society. He "prepped," as they used to say, at St. Paul's School in Concord, New Hampshire. He was in the fifth form when the United States entered the Great War in Europe in 1917 and by 1918, when he was old enough, he left just before graduation to enter the United States Naval Academy in Annapolis, Maryland. The war ended shortly afterward, with the signing of the armistice in 1918, and Floyd was able to leave the military academy without putting further time in the service. My father served with honor in the second of two world wars that occurred in his lifetime.

Floyd was forty-two when I was born and he had already lived through events like the deadly influenza epidemic of 1917. In the twenties he sailed to Haiti on a four-masted schooner and went on photographic and film expeditions around the world, from Tahiti to the Mato Grosso jungle in Brazil and from Honduras to the Russian Orthodox monastery in Mount Athos, Greece. Why did the son of the treasurer of the Union Pacific Railroad go to such exotic locales? Because he wanted to and because he had already tried doing it the straight way. After graduating from St. Paul's, my father tried Wall Street, clerking at the Bankers Trust Company. The job lasted six months and when it ended he went into the cotton business in South Carolina. He returned to New York to go into a brokerage house, didn't much like any of the jobs, and never thought of himself as adept at any of them, which is just as well. He went on a world cruise in 1925, took a lot of pictures, and had the good fortune to meet William Beebe, a prominent explorer and scientist, one of the men who pioneered the underwater bathysphere, which took men deeper into the ocean than they had ever been before. I must have inherited his taste for diving. Floyd enrolled at the New York Institute of Photography, where he discovered an abiding love for the photographic image. Beebe took him on his next expedition to Haiti, along with Ilya Tolstoy, grandson of the Russian novelist. Beebe and Tolstoy were directors; my father was the cameraman. It was 1927 and they made underwater shots with Dad wearing an old Miller-Dun diving helmet and a set of weights, standing on the bottom, shooting the action—shark fights, giant sea turtles, whatever they could scare up to swim through the frame.

After that my father went to Hollywood with a letter of introduction to an executive at MGM. He hung around the studio for a few months in 1928, met a few people, and eventually had the good fortune to link up with the man who would define the documentary film, the great Robert Flaherty. Flaherty's reputation began with a stark documentary he shot in the Arctic, *Nanook of the North,* a film that's still shown in university film classes as the archetype of the genre. When he went to the Pacific to shoot a silent epic, *White Shadows in the South Seas,* he took my father to Tahiti as a general assistant.

FLOYD CROSBY: *Flaherty tried to get Metro to hire me and they wouldn't do it. So he said, "Come back tomorrow. I'll try again." So I went one morning about ten o'clock and he'd been to a champagne breakfast and was feeling fine . . . So he said, "Tell you what you do. You get on that boat tomorrow for Tahiti and I'll see you get a job when we get down there." This was in Culver City, my clothes were in Hollywood, I had no car, I had to leave from San Francisco the next day at two o'clock, and I had no passport.*

After firing off telegrams to Washington and San Francisco, making a flurry of last-minute arrangements, and catching the night train north from L.A. to San Francisco, Floyd found himself with only a passport clerk between him and the boat. The clerk hadn't gotten the okay back from Washington about issuing a passport to the young man, but even before the Depression, the country was crazy about the movies. Floyd remembers the guy saying, "Look, if I give you a passport and lose my job, will you get me a job in the movies?" To which my father answered, with breezy authority, "Sure, no problem." The clerk gave him his passport, he got his visa from the French, made the sailing time of two o'clock, and eventually landed in Tahiti. There he went to work on a big Hollywood feature for fifteen dollars a week. He watched everything, learned everything, and even developed film prints in their local lab when the regular technician got drunk and disappeared into the jungle for a few days. Going on location with a film company in French Polynesia was a great way to break into Hollywood and start in the movies.

In 1929 Flaherty got another picture to codirect, also in the South Seas. This time he was working with another great director, a German named F. W. Murnau, on a project to be shot in Tahiti. It was a movie that by today's standards would be called a docudrama. It combined authentic portrayal of Polynesian island tribal life with a fictional story and my father was asked to shoot it. He couldn't; he had another job. When he returned, he wired Tahiti to see if the job was still open and it was—he sailed immediately for French Polynesia and took over photography on *Tabu*, shooting by day and developing the negative himself at night. Forty-odd years later, I was able to send my father and stepmother to Tahiti, where they met my schooner and got to sail around the islands, revisiting the sites Floyd photographed for *Tabu*. Betty Cormack Crosby, my stepmother, has great memories of that trip:

BETTY CROSBY: *Dave gave us a trip to Tahiti. Bud Hedrick was the captain and we picked up the schooner in Papeete. On one of the islands Floyd showed me where they did the shooting of* Tabu *and we saw one old man there, toothless, and he was cutting something in his yard and as it turns out he was one of the boy dancers in that film! When he saw Floyd he got hysterical and when Floyd saw him he got hysterical . . . Even now, [when]* Tabu *is shown in Tahiti, all the Tahitians go to see Grandma or Grandpa or whatever and they cry because they're now dead or gone or something, but they show it and they all love it. It's such a beautiful picture. Does Dave still have it? You know, Floyd made a print for him. I hope he does.*

BUD HEDRICK: *We got a telegram that said* BETTY AND FLOYD ARE ARRIVING. SHOW THEM AROUND. *It didn't make sense. And then, when they got there, we realized it was Floyd Crosby and all—David's father! We sailed them around to all the islands and wherever we went people came out of the woodwork and said, "You don't remember me, but I was the little boy in the movie."*

I was able to reassure Betty that I do have my father's print of *Tabu* and it's the same work of art now as it was then. The original nitrate print has been converted to modern safety film and I've got a video copy as well; technology changes, pictures stay the same. I expect my daughter Donovan will someday have her old father's material transferred to some as-yet-unimaginable storage medium, probably a nonvolatile digital bubble memory on a mini-micro-teeny chip of ninth-generation silicon surrogate. That's how I'll be remembered. When my father returned to the Mainland, he met and married Aliph Van Cortlandt Whitehead. My daughter, Donovan Anne Crosby, might qualify as a Daughter of the American Revolution—if the DAR takes rock 'n' roll kids born in special circumstances.

During the thirties, my father pursued an active career as an outdoor cameraman, specializing in documentary and nature photography, and returned to New York City. The business was the same then as now in many respects; the motion picture craftsmen who worked regular hours in the big Hollywood studios under steady employment contracts made the big bucks, while the documentarians who worked endless hours in the field were paid a lot less—in 1932 Floyd made a total of fifteen hundred dollars in income and Aliph worked as a salesgirl at Macy's to make enough money for them to live. Robert Flaherty's brother showed up in New York with a young director named Fred Zinnemann; Floyd helped them with a photo essay they were shooting in Times Square on New Year's Eve. In 1934 Floyd and Aliph moved back to Hollywood. He hadn't done much shooting of studio interiors yet and his Oscar was for a feature that was shot entirely out of doors, so he waited around to get a break at the studios, watching and learning how things were done. He shot second-unit work on King Vidor's film *Our Daily Bread*, got involved in early Technicolor, and by 1936 he was the first to shoot three-strip Technicolor underwater. The event got my father published in *American Cinematographer* in an article titled "Shooting Technicolor on the Sea Bottom."

My brother Ethan was born in 1937. The economy wasn't exactly booming at the time, so Floyd took steady work with the United States Government. Under the Roosevelt Administration and the National Recovery Administration, there was government work for artists as well as hod carriers. Documentarians like Pare Lorentz, Joris Ivens, and Robert Flaherty were making stunning and memorable films and my father was photographing them, traveling all over the country. I was born on August 14, 1941.

ETHAN CROSBY: *He's a Leo with Aries rising and he just can't not have a big ego trip going.*

8

On December 7, 1941, the Japanese bombed Pearl Harbor, America entered the war, and Floyd went into the Army Air Corps, assigned to the Overseas Technical Unit of the Air Transport Command. The world was learning new ways to make war from the air and the science of high-altitude bombing evolved with the Allied development of the Norden bombsight. However, in order to get the Norden bombsight to the target, there had to be a way to guide the planes over unfamiliar territory, both friendly and enemy-held. Part of that is simply navigation. The other part was where my father proved invaluable. It was his job to satisfy the military's need for accurate photo reconnaissance. The Air Corps would take the machine gun out of the nose of a fast bomber and Floyd and his cameras would tuck into the Plexiglas bubble. My father, on his own, replaced the Plexi with plate glass to get better pictures. Like all great cameramen, he'd do anything to get a good shot; he ignored the fact that if plate glass ever took a bullet hit or shrapnel, he would've been hamburger. The modified planes would make dry runs to the target, flying unarmed without fighter escort, frequently over hostile territory. Dad's job was to shoot landmarks in order to make a photographic strip map and a briefing film of the route that fighter pilots would follow later. The young pilots, without any knowledge of the geography of the target and its approaches, would rely on my father's pictures to check their navigation and get their planes to the mission.

V-J Day, the day the war with Japan ended, was on my fourth birthday and World War II was over, atom bombs and all. My father was discharged and you'd think that after being away for four years, most of my life and half of my older brother's, he'd stay home and get reacquainted with his family, but he never stopped traveling. In 1946 he went off to make *International Ice Patrol,* working on ships and icebreakers in the North Atlantic. When he came back, he settled down. We moved into a house on the west side of Los Angeles in the community of Westwood. Floyd made some cultural films, shooting for a producer named

Irving Reis: *Heifitz* about the amazing violin virtuoso, *Rubinstein* about the pianist, and a series called *Of Men and Music.* The classical influence in my life was already starting. I started going to school at University Elementary School, run by the University of California, Los Angeles, for bright or advantaged children. We lived in a modest modernist house with a view of the Veterans' Cemetery—the family joke was "We have very quiet neighbors." Now it looks typically fifties, then it was progressively, tastefully hip. The family was even photographed for a Sunday newspaper house-and-garden supplement, "Cinematographer and Family at Home," and there we all are, posed and formal, Ethan with his guitar, Floyd with his mandolin, me with a recorder.

The first music I ever heard that I liked was stuff my mother brought home: ten-inch long-playing records of folk music, with Josh White, the Weavers, and a South African folk duo called Marais and Miranda. We also had a stock of 78 r.p.m. records of the classics on shellac and lots of classical music on the radio every Sunday. Then I started hearing my brother's jazz, which was in the fifties and, lucky for me, another golden age—Chet Baker, Gerry Mulligan, Dave Brubeck, Kai Winding and J. J. Johnson, Errol Garner, and Stan Kenton. As a matter of fact, when rock 'n' roll came in during that era and the Age of Elvis possessed America, I wasn't into it. By mid-American and Santa Barbara standards we were relatively sophisticated when it came to music. I wasn't isolated from contemporary pop—you couldn't escape Top 40 AM radio airplay hits like "Blueberry Hill" and "Blue Suede Shoes," but the first real honest-to-*Billboard* popular music that grabbed my attention and wouldn't let go was a tune I can still sing all the way through, the way I did then, the Everly Brothers' "All I Have to Do Is Dream" and then some of the other popular tunes. It was the harmonies that got to me. They tell me I was singing harmony when I was six years old and I'm not the one to contradict them because the experience that sticks in my memory is the way my family would sing at home. My father would play the mandolin, my older brother the guitar, and my mother sang. I'd do the harmony parts, all of us singing from a book called *The Fireside Book of Folk Songs.* There were two editions. We had both and sang all the songs in them, from sea chanteys to ethnic music, little knowing then that the classic folk song of the Mexican Revolution, "La Cucaracha," mentions marijuana.

And even before that, when I was very young, practically preschool, my mother took me to a live performance of a symphony orchestra and it was the most intense experience I can remember from my early life. I remember all the elbows bent the same way, moving at the same time, all the hands fingering the instruments, everything working together. It looked impossible, but there it was. I could hear the sound washing over me like a wave and the thing that struck my child's mind with such intense clarity was that all these separate people, playing different instruments of all sorts, were working together to produce one big music. It was like being a very small child standing in very big surf. It crashed over me and took me totally. I was completely open to it, without dissent or filter or censors, and I knew there was something about it being all those people doing it together. I didn't put it together then because I wasn't old enough, but the information was there and it jelled as I got older and the idea of cooperative effort to make something bigger than any one person could ever do was stuck in my head. That's why I love being a harmony singer, why I love being in a group. My favorite comic book as a child was the one of a bunch of kids that got together in a group. They were all orphans and they all got together in a little gang to save this farm and there was an old guy and they all worked together and it was my favorite comic book. It was a one-shot that got torn up because I got caught reading it with a flashlight under the bedspread. All gone now. The comic book and seeing the orchestra, along with the musical experience, I shared with my family, made me want to make music with other people, rather than be a solo artist or a lead singer. If there's anything to the educational theory of imprinting, it's lucky I was in front of that orchestra at that moment. If I had been taken to see a concert of a different sort, who knows what might have happened to my career? I could have been to see the massed pipes and drums of the Scottish Highlanders or a polka band with lots of accordions, but it didn't turn out that way.

So I fell in love with harmony and by the age of six I was taking on different parts as the family sang at home. The first harmony I ever sang that I can clearly recall was a second part to "The Erie Canal" and I loved it because it was the principal source of whatever warmth and closeness we ever shared. My father, for all his many virtues, was neither a demonstrative nor an emotional man and I can't remember that he ever said the words "I love you" to me or anyone else in the family. He was not real articulate, you know. That's why he used to tell jokes. He wanted to be liked; he wanted to be friendly; but he really didn't know how. He didn't know how to talk to you, so he would tell you a joke because he could remember the joke. But if you tried to have a conversation with him about something, it was real difficult for him. At home, if he had strong opinions, he didn't express them. The family was run, pretty much, by my mother, who ran it with intelligence and a lot of love. And with a lot of imposed guilt. My father's mother was a very cold person, which is probably what did it to my father. But she was from another century. When I sang with my family, I could experience harmony. There weren't many other times I felt it.

David was six years old when the House Un-American Activities Committee began the first of its Hollywood witch hunts. It was 1947 and Floyd Crosby was guilty by association, even though he didn't know it. Joris Ivens, a Dutch national and a socially conscious and politically progressive documentary film director, was also a man who had made films in the Soviet Union as early as 1929, invited by the Russian genius Pudovkin. Ivens made films in China that were critical of Chiang Kai-shek. He made films in Loyalist Spain and about strikes by Belgian miners. Even though he worked for the U.S. Government in making documentaries, even though he worked on *The Story of G.I. Joe* and *Action Stations!*, he also made *Our Russian Front.* By 1947 he had left the United States for good and was making films in Poland and East Germany, countries behind the Iron Curtain. And Floyd had worked for Ivens.

Despite several important credits on major motion pictures, David's father discovered in 1954 that he was "unemployable" when his old friend Fred Zinnemann tried to get him hired to shoot second unit on *From Here to Eternity.* Someone at Columbia Pictures spilled the beans: Floyd couldn't be used at Harry Cohn's personal studio because he was on "the List."

FLOYD CROSBY: *It was the first I'd heard about it, but then I realized that a number of times when it looked as though I was going to get a job, at the last minute I wouldn't get it . . . So I made an affidavit, which I filed with the union and with Columbia, saying that I had been a member of a group . . . which wanted to make documentaries or pictures about important subjects and it was considered a Communist group . . . and I said I had never been a Communist and I never intend to be and I was on secret orders for the Air Corps all during the war and this kind of stuff. After that I didn't have much trouble.*

Floyd never named names; he simply stated the truth of his position.

FLOYD CROSBY: *[In the 1930s] capitalism was in a lot of trouble and I think it was perfectly normal for people to be interested in—and investigating—other forms of government. I know I was interested. I never became a party member, but I was interested. I used to go to some of the groups that were trying to find out about communism. And because people were interested in finding out about another system, to blacklist them and not let them work was completely the action of reactionaries who had a big financial investment in the system, even though it was working badly; they were scared to death of anything else happening.*

In 1951, when work was scarce, Floyd got his big break in Hollywood, shooting *The Brave Bulls* for director Robert Rossen, and then, immediately after, Floyd shot what is to modern viewers his most impressive achievement—*High Noon*. For that, he won a Golden Globe for Best Black and White Photography of a feature film in 1952. Later, he would get involved for a brief period with Orson Welles on a project titled *My Friend Bonito*. After that experience, still smarting from the scarcity of work during the blacklist years, Floyd Crosby never turned down another job. As Ethan and David struggled to finish elementary and junior high school, their father worked the killingly long hours that are still standard in the kind of low-budget exploitation features that were the elder Crosby's speciality. He amassed credits on more than seventy-five feature films and dozens of early television films and episodes, working frequently for schlockmeisters and hustlers and putting his name on such features as *Reform School Girl, Rock All Night, Shack Out on 101, Suicide Battalion, She Gods of Shark Reef, Hell Canyon Outlaws,* and *War of the Satellites.*

My father actually became rather well known and respected for his amazing color photography on Roger Corman and American International Pictures horror films like *The Raven, Tales of Terror, Haunted Palace, The Fall of the House of Usher,* and *The Pit and the Pendulum.* He made twenty-three films with Roger Corman and later, while I was playing rock 'n' roll on the Sunset Strip for real, my father was filming teen classics like *Bikini Beach, How to Stuff a Wild Bikini,* and *Beach Blanket Bingo.* Talk about a generation gap. It was embarrassing.

ETHAN CROSBY: *I remember the day David was born and stuff like that, but when he and I began to actually relate was quite a bit farther along. There's one thing that I remember that's been in my mind about our upbringing that may partially explain why he strives so hard. David always ended up with second-best. He always had the room that wasn't the groovy room. That was important. In two houses, that was the case: the one in Westwood and the one in Carpinteria. At the time I said, "Great, I'll take the good room."*

Looking back on it now, that sucked. But that's the way it was.
That's the way things were done. David's always been fighting au-
thority. He's been a troublemaker in a lot of ways, he's been fighting
anybody having control over him, he was always getting kicked out
of school, crashing cars, and even getting arrested for burglary.
There was a trial and I was there when he went to court and so on
and he was absolutely defiant.

We tried to find out some more about that adventure, but my
court records as a young housebreaker are protected by
California's juvenile offender statutes. The cops knew who we
were because one of our guys had gotten popped and blabbed. He
tried it without the rest of us and without the system and got
busted. After they caught him, they started picking up the other
people, so I just went and turned myself in. They put me in jail
for a couple of days. I went to court and the court said, "Well,
he's underage. Put him on probation." My father was pissed and
it's probably significant that I was willing to travel that far along
the outlaw trail, even before sex, drugs, and rock 'n' roll.

TWO

·················

Most people who knew David as a child describe him as a unique and rebellious kid who kept his own counsel, an intriguing loner with a pervasive and ingrained distaste for authority. His mother, Aliph, raised two sons by herself. She's remembered as a gentle, large-boned woman with a soft voice and an excessive sweetness to her disposition. The family background practically dictated a genteel upbringing and a first-class private school education for Ethan and David. They were far enough apart in age to never attend the same schools at the same time and Ethan seems to have never been able to give David the benefit of his experience. By the time David would be old enough to go to a school Ethan might've attended, the family would've moved. Despite all the Van Cortlandt and Van Schoonhoven lineage, the generations of unbroken gentility and Episcopalian stability, Floyd and Aliph moved a lot and even scuffled for an income.

Eventually, Aliph's relatives chose her husband as an administrator of one of the family trust funds. For simply having his name on a piece of paper at a bank somewhere, Floyd could count on an additional stipend of $2,500 a year to start. By the fifties this sum had grown to $9,500 a year. That's probably the money that kept David in the exclusive old-line private and prep schools he attended in Santa Barbara. David was enrolled in the Crane School, an exclusive and rigorously academic grammar school set on pastoral parklike grounds in a small, exclusive, and wealthy community called Montecito, just south of Santa Barbara. Not as old as the private Eastern prep schools where Floyd went, Crane and Cate are as old and exclusive as you can get outside of the original Thirteen Colonies and the old Confederacy.

I remember my first school: University Elementary School in Los Angeles. It was the UCLA experimental and teacher training school and because it was that, we got things before other people. We got advanced teaching, it was an excellent school, and it wasn't very expensive, just hard to get in because everybody wanted their kids in it. You had to sign up years ahead of time. Ethan didn't go there. He was already in junior high school by the time I started and then he went away to Verde Valley School in Arizona. We moved out of Los Angeles, north to Santa Barbara. There I went to private school.

When I was eleven years old, my parents did one of the brightest things they ever did, as far as I was concerned. It involved sailing, which was then a rich man's sport. One of the things that a kid in Montecito did in those years was to sail in Santa Barbara Harbor, usually in a little boat called a Sea Shell, which was an eight-and-a-half-foot dinghy with one sail. My parents said if I earned half the money for one, they'd come up with the other half, which sounded great to me. I earned the money feeding chinchillas and helping with the place in Carpinteria, where we had some lemon trees. We had five and a half acres of lemons and three and a half acres of avocados, which we raised from seeds to seedlings and planted and grafted. I learned how to prune and graft and plant and all that jazz because I loved it. And because I earned the Sea Shell and got into the Sea Shell club. Somewhere I used to have a trophy for second place in a Sea Shell race; I eventually got real adventuresome with it and they finally said they didn't want me in the club anymore because I used to sail outside the harbor and beyond the outer marker. It evolved into my usual problem with authority. What can I tell you?

David continued sailing, making time during the long summers to go down to the yacht harbor and the piers off downtown Santa Barbara, finding time to fall in love with those most lovely of classic sailing craft, schooners. Berthed there was the boat that would eventually become Sterling Hayden's *Wanderer*, a schooner called the *Gracie S.* Another favorite was a schooner called *Rejoice*, designed by the great naval architect John Alden. From the time he was eleven, David would hang out around the shipyards and the docks at the marina: figuring out the rigging, begging rides on bigger boats, meeting kids from school who had boats of their own, spending time on the water with them, and learning the basics of seamanship. Most of his friends (and there weren't many) were students at the Crane School. The curriculum at Crane was traditional, the teacher-student ratios were enviably low, and teaching and administrative staffs were dedicated, probably happy in their work, and geographically situated in one of North America's pleasantest suburban enclaves. They still are and David's daughter is a student at Crane as this is written. The natural progression from Crane is to Cate, which was a private boys' boarding secondary school. David made the jump with both feet.

Cate was the best school I ever went to and it gave me a wonderful education. It was also the only discipline to which I ever willingly subjected myself. There was a wake-up bell in the mornings and then a second bell that meant it was time to go to breakfast. The second bell meant you had five minutes before they would close the doors to the dining room. I could jump out of bed at the second bell and be in the dining hall before they closed the doors, in a sports jacket and a tie, knotted. It was a civilizing influence because I had to bounce off all those other people. It was a fairly strict school and I'm sure they remember me as being just short of a cross between a comet and a tornado ricocheting around the halls. It was good, I liked it, and it got me away from my parents and started getting me used to the idea that I wanted to be out in public life on my own.

DAVID CROSBY

At Cate, you never were in a class with more than ten kids. The teachers were as good as money can buy. They were the best. Cate graduates go to Harvard, Yale, Stanford, Princeton, MIT, and all the Ivy League colleges and do very, very well. I'm very grateful for having gone there. When I got out of Cate, after two years, I knew more than most kids did in their senior year in high school. I coasted on those two years through the next two years of local public high schools without ever having to do a thing. I left Cate because I was a disruptive influence and a troublemaker. They didn't expell me, they just said, "Well, maybe you better not come back next year." Since I already was farther ahead than the seniors in the public school system, it worked out fine. The bottom line is that if you want an education, read. Read. Read. Read some more and then read some more. After that, get a few more books and read them. You can learn anything—they wrote it all down! Most of the values I learned I picked up from books like *The Catcher in the Rye,* from Shakespeare, from Thurber and White, out of *The New Yorker,* and from Dickens and Hemingway. That's why they call it required reading. Besides that, I soaked up huge amounts of science fiction by the masters of the genre: Heinlein, Asimov, Arthur C. Clarke, Philip K. Dick, Bradbury, and the rest.

David's classmates were kids with the same last names as the local streets and boulevards, Santa Barbara first families who liked what they saw and conferred their family names on any avenue, ridge, or hill that didn't already have the name of a Catholic saint. Fr. Junipero Serra's Franciscan missionaries loved the land here so much they tamed the local Indians and built the missions that still stand along the Camino Real. The adobe walls, towers, and arches are echoed everywhere, from the Santa Barbara Civic Center and county court house to the local homes, the ones with five-car garages and stables. The stocky kid with the moviemaking father and the doting mother moved into prep school with an attitude that would be surprising now; in those years it was absolutely guaranteed to mark him as a rebel and a loner. Like most rebels and loners, David began as a wimp and a nerd, as

19

those terms are used in the eighties. Bill Arens was, for a while, his roommate at Cate.

BILL ARENS: *Well, if you want an experience, take a look at the Cate yearbook for 1957 and there's a picture of the freshman class there. At the end of one row, I guess, you've got these two guys, little guys standing next to each other. We're all in blue blazers and gray slacks except this one rather roly-poly-looking fellow, who's in a gray suit, looks kind of out of place. And next to him is this little wimpy kid with blond hair, short butch-style blond hair with big blue eyes, and that's me. I looked about three years younger than the rest of the class. I'm this little midget in the picture. It's funny—I was the oldest in the class, but I was also the smallest, so David and I were basically the class wimps. David was about five-foot-two and round. Not a fatty, just round. Sophomore year we became roommates and there was a large room at the end of the schoolhouse that we shared. A terrific room, since we had a fireplace. Now, at Cate, kids all usually had their own private rooms and suddenly I have a roommate. In fact, my parents weren't terribly happy about it because they weren't sure that David Crosby was a good influence on me. They figured out that he wasn't a real good student and at that time in his life Crosby didn't have great charisma—when David walked into a room, people normally did not just suddenly start applauding. It was quite the opposite. There was a great deal of antipathy toward him. People always had very negative things to say about Dave, whether they knew him or not.*

To the normal preppies and jocks who populated Cate in the closing years of the Eisenhower Decade, Crosby was an abrasive and arrogant punk with an air of superiority and detachment that set him forever apart from the close-order drill of what was then considered an exemplary secondary school experience. He was bright and quick, with an easy aptitude for both hard work and learning—when the subject matter interested him. If it didn't, there wasn't a lot anyone could do to make him take interest. Stanley Woodworth came to the Cate School in 1948. As assistant headmaster, responsible for student discipline, he got to know young Crosby. He also had David in his Latin class. Latin? Yes, Latin. Though not normally included in the rock 'n' roll curriculum, it was required at Cate.

STANLEY WOODWORTH: *I taught, as I often did, a section of second-year Latin. We had a test every Friday and on the basis of that test on Monday we would change the seating. Students were seated in the order in which they ranked on the exam, from first through tenth. David sat in that tenth seat every week, with a smile which even then I equated with the smile on* La Gioconda, *the* Mona Lisa, *no more and no less. Whenever I went to Paris and looked at the* Gioconda *in the Louvre, I thought of David Crosby because he had this sort of benevolent smile, noncommittal. "You do your silly little thing and kindly allow me not to get involved and I'll do my little thing" was how it seemed. He never argued and I would always call on him. I always acted as though yesterday hadn't happened. I'd say, "David, what do you make of this next sentence?" And Crosby would respond in a small voice, "I couldn't make anything of it." He never opened his book, except to kill flies. I once asked him to bring his book up to show me something and there were ten flies all over the page that we were doing. Every Monday, of course, we'd have the ceremonial changing of the position and no one ever noticed that he was always Number Ten because there was so much bitterness and rancor about who was Number One. I would always act as though there was some surprise involved and I'd say, "Stay where you are until someone needs your seat." But it was always obvious that nobody was going to be in his seat.*

Woodworth recalls that David just didn't buy into the system. A sophomore in prep school, he was already detached and aloof. Later, frustrated adults who were responsible for his education or behavior would make the same observation, as would his peers and contemporaries. To people his own age, Crosby's attitude was unique. At that time, kids weren't defying their parents or ignoring authority figures. It just wasn't done, not in Santa Barbara, California. That kind of conduct was expected from ill-bred kids from the wrong side of the tracks. Crosby was behaving like some disadvantaged ethnic minority teenager from the slums or a farm kid from the agricultural communities that ring Reagan's Refuge. He was clearly not living up to his potential, whatever that was for a slightly chubby, bright-eyed, quick-minded kid with a respectable pedigree and a nerd's affection for science fiction.

Somehow, because I went to Cate School, I wound up on the "eligible" list—some roster kept by social forces beyond my understanding. It was probably a catalog of local young men who came from good families, with the right pedigree and the possibility of a lot of old money. Once on that list, you got to go to the debutante parties, which in Santa Barbara in the fifties was a big deal—black-tie formal for the men, the women in ball gowns. In some regards they were actually thrilling—each party was happening at some place like the Montecito Country Club, or someone's big old house, or the Coral Casino, the Valley Club, places like that. They'd set up tents and pavilions and hire orchestras—the I. Newton Perry Orchestra, as I recall, was the band of choice—and to my ears they were a bunch of drunk old guys playing "Nola" and "The Mexican Hat Dance" and "The Bunny Hop." Nothing they did ever said "music" to me. Not compared to what I had been brought up with at home.

The exposure to music at home had its effect and even before Cate, while still at Crane School, David demonstrated a surprisingly polished and preternaturally clear tenor voice. In a faded yearbook, there's a picture of the future felon of rock wearing satin kneepants, a tricornered hat, and the epaulets of the Victorian British Navy—that's right, Gilbert and Sullivan. In *H.M.S. Pinafore*, Crosby sang the role of First Lord of the Admiralty, the Right Honorable Sir Joseph Porter, K.C.B. The young boy sang in a voice that startled the parents and teachers gathered in the audience. Not only was he good, he had stage presence. Nobody knows where that came from, but there it was. Stanley Woodworth was there:

STANLEY WOODWORTH: *I very distinctly remember the first time that I saw him at Crane School at a commencement. That would be '55, but he would have been in seventh or eighth grade. He played the Captain of the Queen's Navy in the production of* Pinafore. *I usually consider elementary school dramatics as part of the cross that parents have to bear and so I sort of went. It was a chore, I thought, since I was a Gilbert and Sullivan fan myself and had sung in all the roles when I was a kid. I didn't look forward to this experience at all. I thought I'd be sitting there in the hot sun and David just blew me out. I've never been so impressed with an amateur performance in my life. I went home and couldn't stop talking about it. I didn't even know he existed! It was before I had him in my class at Cate. He had so much presence and he just carried everybody! The production was mediocre, but he was just fantastic. I was really happy to hear that he was coming to Cate. What did I know?*

BILL ARENS: *I discovered his unbelievable whistle. Did you ever hear any Al Jolson records? Ever heard him whistle? Crosby could probably put him to shame. At the age of fifteen or sixteen, Crosby could whistle any tune beautifully, like an instrument, and it was fabulous —the guy was really good. We were both in the glee club, by the way, so I knew he could sing, but this whistle, it was fantastic.*

I was never an academic giant. I was very good at English. I was good at languages, although I was as lazy as my Latin teacher says. I was better at French. The only things I was ever really good at were singing, which meant glee club, choir, and the lead in a musical revue that a guy who taught there wrote for us to perform. That and the rifle team were the only things at which I excelled. Singing and shooting. To this day I'm still good at singing and shooting. And causing trouble. The show was important to me because I had a good role and it was a chance for me to be good at something. I got some applause, instead of disapproving lectures about "Why can't you behave?" I achieved some stature with my peer group and that was important. It mattered to me because it confirmed that this might be a way to get what I want. One good performance and everybody liked me. I liked being liked. I also liked the feeling of knowing how to do something well. It was easy because I wasn't self-conscious about it. There's a feeling that happens to you if you are lucky enough to be comfortable doing something in front of people. If I got up there and I forgot the words, I would be scared to death, but I didn't forget the words. I was, have been, and still am totally comfortable onstage. I'm one of those lucky people who found out early in his life what he really wanted to do. Because my dad was in movies, I thought, "Hey, I've got an entry into the movies, maybe I should do that." The truth is that music has always been the direction I was headed. When I succeeded at school, they were all so amazed that I could do anything right that they probably were more positive about it than they needed to be. I got a lot of reinforcement at Crane, and at Cate.

At Cate, Crosby's principal extracurricular activity was music. He didn't play any sports. He was cast in a school revue called *Cuttin' Capers*. The show was preserved in a recording that was sold to parents and friends of the school and the performances are still audible. Listening to the scratchy old monophonic custom-pressed long-playing record, it's easy to hear how David surprised both his friends and his detractors. His old roommate remembers:

BILL ARENS: *There were three leads in* Cuttin' Capers *and he was far and away the best natural musical talent in the play, which absolutely blew everybody away because nobody had known it. When he sang, I can remember the surprise that a lot of people had. I took him aside and I said, "You ought to learn to play the guitar . . . you have the most fabulous voice and you could go on the road and could be very successful at music." And David just looks at me in a blasé sort of way and with his thumb and his forefinger grabs himself just at the skin of the Adam's apple and kind of wiggles it and says, "I don't need to play the guitar, I have the best instrument there is right here." Such humility. It's an absolutely true story. He knew he was good.*

David knew he was good and he knew he could be bad too. Closeted with science fiction and escapist novels, he rarely participated in anything except misadventure. Later, David would learn to drive and would escape in cars, driving aimlessly, like generations before and after. Before he was old enough to drive, while he was still a boarder at the Cate School, trapped in the preppie dormitory lifestyle, rebellion took other forms.

BILL ARENS: *At prep school your life is run by bells. You get up in the morning to a bell. You take a shower to a bell. You go to breakfast to a bell. You leave breakfast to a bell. You come back and clean your room and then you go to chapel to a bell and when chapel is over and the bell rings and you go to class and when all is said and done at the end of the day the bell rings and you go to sleep. One of the songs in* Cuttin' Capers *is "Hell's Bells." Crosby might've sang it, I don't remember, but there was a line in it about hell's bells being jangled and your nerves getting mangled. David and I were sitting around one day trying to figure out how to make some mischief and we wondered what would happen to this school if the bells didn't ring one day. Our four eyes lit up and so we started figuring out how we could turn off the bells. Well, there's a big clock down across from what used to be the study hall in the schoolhouse. And that, we discovered as we investigated, was what ran the bells.*

The system was run off a great clock with a punched paper roll that carried the information that programmed the electric bells that ran throughout the school. The paper tape would run over metal rollers with electric contacts, much like a player-piano roll. When it made the right connections, bells would ring. The whole deal was sequestered behind a locked door in the room that held the clock. Without a background in practical wiring, we couldn't figure out how to interrupt the current to the bell-timing mechanism—the wires ran unbroken by any switching circuitry.

Arens and I weren't deterred. We traced the lines to a basement utility bay, where the master fuse circuits and switches for the entire school were located. Access was by a ventilation shaft that ran under the main schoolhouse.

BILL ARENS: *If we started over by the McBean Library, there was an area where we could go under and crawl the whole length of the schoolhouse and drop into that cellar area. So we set all our plans and one night, in the middle of the night, at about three o'clock in the morning, we got up and snuck out and I crept the whole length of the schoolhouse on all fours, while David and another kid stayed up above as lookouts. I couldn't figure out which switch was the one to pull because there were so many of them, but there was one that was real big, like in the movies, so I just pulled that one. Sparks flew. Everything went out instantly.* Everything *was out. "Ohhh ohh ohh, we did it! We did it!" And then back all the way down, underneath the schoolhouse and out the other side. That took care of the class bells, but we still had to get rid of that damn bell on top of the kitchen, so we went up to the kitchen, we got a ladder, we climbed up, we had a couple of wire cutters, we clipped that thing off, we slung it into the cactus, we'd done it. We went back to our rooms silently and waited, knowing that at a quarter to seven, that damn bell wasn't going to ring. We were going to throw the whole school off schedule.*

By throwing the Big Switch, we not only shorted out the bells, we killed the juice to the kitchens, the maintenance sheds, and most of the equipment at the school. Some bells were gotten working by midmorning, but the noxious kitchen bell was silent all day. At lunch, Francis Parkman, the headmaster (we called him Parky) made the usual lunchtime announcements and concluded with an instruction that after the meal he would see me and Arens in his office. As it turned out, security around the Great Bell Caper was loose. The school had no secrets and everyone knew who was responsible. It's even possible someone snitched on us. The discipline was severe. It's probably one of the reasons I was eventually asked not to return to Cate. As direct punishment for that prank, we were both turned over to the prefects (senior boys with absolute authority over lower grades). For tampering with the system, we were made slaves to the bells.

BILL ARENS: *Every day for a week within thirty seconds of every bell that rang, David Crosby and I had to run from whatever part of the campus we were on and report to the senior prefect's dormitory room and in the morning, at wake-up time, we had to march down every dormitory hall singing "Hell's Bells," just to wake everybody up.*

Marching through the dormitory corridors at Cate, singing at the top of my voice as a walking alarm clock, was probably the only time that I didn't enjoy singing or attention. Not long after the "miracle of the bells," we were visited by a science display that utilized the Mr. Wizard format. Mr. Wizard was a character on children's television in the fifties who would entertain a boy or girl by demonstrating natural phenomena in a show-business sort of way—static electricity displays that made your hair stand on end, dry ice that would bubble and fume in water—the kind of junior chemistry and physics displays that are supposed to intrigue young viewers and get them hooked on more serious science, like dissecting frogs and building windmills for science fairs. At Cate, the visiting professor chose to demonstrate the inert gas helium. I was selected from the audience as a volunteer to participate in the experiment.

BILL ARENS: *Crosby goes up and, of course, none of us has any idea of what's coming and this Mr. Wizard guy says, "I would like you, Mr. Crosby, to put this little tube in your mouth and just breathe it in and just hold your breath and I'll tell you what to do after you do it."*

For students of any school of psychiatry that says childhood experiences are meaningful, this is a pivotal moment for me.

Twenty years before anyone knew there ever was such a thing as freebase cocaine or "crack," I'm being asked to take up the same smoking paraphernalia. There's some lab stuff and a rubber tube from which I'm supposed to inhale deeply. Of course, this is twenty years before my first hit, but listen to what happened after I took a long pull at the tube:

BILL ARENS: *David takes a long deep breath and, of course, David loves science and science fiction and stuff like that and the guy takes the tube and says, "David, I'd like you to say, 'I want to go to the moon.'" And so David looks out at the audience and says in that high squeaky voice you get when you speak with a lungful of helium, "I-want-to-go-to-the-moon." One hundred boys, off their chairs, on the floor, the whole place absolutely exploded because it was Crosby saying it. Mr. Wizard could not have picked a better person for the demonstration because the whole school knew that David was a science fiction reader and kind of a nerd. God, it was hilarious. Probably one of the funniest events in the four years I was at Cate. I've never seen anything get that big a laugh. They were laughing for ten or fifteen minutes. They just couldn't stop. They were howling, screaming with laughter, and David was loving it. He was center stage.*

> Floyd Crosby was working steadily in Hollywood and getting remarried to an attractive and sympathetic script supervisor named Betty Cormack. Betty became David's stepmother, but didn't see him much. Floyd was persona non grata in Aliph's world. David's father was never seen and not often mentioned. Aliph, according to those who knew her, continued to present a consistently sweet and pleasant face to the world.

By the time I was a senior in high school, we were living in Montecito in a series of places. We moved a lot because my mother had to make do with not too much money. My father had already married my stepmother and didn't come around to see us. After the divorce, I was a wild child and a definite problem. The minute I had a car, I was gone. In the meantime, my mother would do the best she could to try and keep influencing me along the path of righteousness. In spite of being an Episcopalian, she behaved like a stereotypical Jewish mother: lots of love, a fair measure of tears, and guilt-inspiring lines like "What have I done to deserve this?" She was concerned about my wildness and she didn't have much other leverage than to be hurt and express pain when I did the wrong thing, so she used the weapons that mothers have used since the beginning of time. She was a sweet and wonderful woman and what needs to be said here is that my mother was a poet, a good one. She used to write poetry all the time and that was an influence on me. She was a splendid singer, sang in choirs all the time, and loved the process. My mother was the one who got us all singing folk songs together. She loved classical music and played it in our house constantly.

When my father left, my mother was resentful. That was clear to me and Ethan—abundantly clear. She thought she gave him the best years of her life and she felt hurt, desperately hurt, although she tried to keep up a good face. My mother hated Betty and was angry with my dad and portrayed him to us as a bad guy. It's all standard; everybody does it. It took me a long time to realize that she was just defensive and hurt and that my dad was not a villain. In high school, however, I bought it at face value. I said, "Well gee, my dad's bad." At the same time, Ethan was trying to mature into being a young man and he tried to be a good older brother to me. He was. Ethan gave me my first guitar and taught me a lot about singing and playing. He was generous with his time to the extent that he could be; he was a good brother and I love him for it. Ethan was never much of a bad example, either —he never got in trouble or wound up in jail, nobody talked him into getting into fights or getting drunk. He was a pretty good guy.

My reaction was interesting . . . I started having terrible headaches. Probably migraines because I'd have them on one side of my head—so bad that one eye would be full of tears while the other would be clear. They may have been emotionally generated, I might've had an aneurysm, but in any case, they went away and I got well. I didn't see any good way to accept what was going on at home, I didn't want to be in a family, I wanted to get out and get loose and get laid and explore the world. I've always been an insatiably curious adventurer.

David didn't react well to the life at home and Aliph was unable to discipline him or get him to stay in when he wanted to go out. Ethan was already working around town as a musician, playing Santa Barbara's only jazz club, and on occasions when there were no debutante parties to attend, David and his friends would take their fake driver's licenses and go to some bar to watch Ethan play. Jazz was the hipster's music then and young David liked that world. David drank rum and Coke; everyone did, unless they were having a Seven and Seven (Seagram's 7 Crown and 7Up), a preppie version of a rye and ginger that was easy to order. One of David's friends, David Hopkins, remembers:

DAVID HOPKINS: *I recall myself coming back from school, summer vacations, and discovering at some point that David was already partying around, off in a corner doing something stupid with cough syrup or whatever the hell it was. That's what we did in those days. That was the big pastime in the summers. The girls would come out and there would be a slew of girls' parties and we'd go to those parties all summer long.*

It probably doesn't matter whether David passed Latin or not, since that fall he began attending public high schools in Carpinteria and in Santa Barbara, where he finally graduated from Santa Barbara High School. Not in the June ceremony like everyone else—he had cut too many classes and flunked too many courses to get to stand around in a rented cap and gown and throw his mortarboard in the air. David finished by correspondence during the summer, eventually getting a high school equivalency diploma that satisfied his parents' minimal expectations that he conclude his secondary education. Bill Arens stayed on at Cate, got another roommate, and graduated from the school.

BILL ARENS: *I can't remember anything athletic that David ever did. He wasn't particularly cleanly. He wasn't big on showers. He tended to be kind of slovenly and he had a rather gross sense of humor, by the definitions of those days. He told dirty jokes constantly and in many respects, when it came to sexual matters, he was very very much more sophisticated than the other boys. Much more knowledgeable. He had made a real study of it. What was funny was that we had a nickel bet on who would get the first piece of ass. He won, but that shows you the level of maturity at that time. We bet one nickel. My parents by this time were not happy with David and they forced the school to change my roommate situation and David was moved someplace else.*

I know I was over sixteen when it finally happened because I had a driver's license and it was the same year I broke my arm in a car wreck. I was still living in Carpinteria and the girl was someone who I had been dating a long time. It wasn't a spur-of-the-moment deal; it took planning. It was arranged for a time when I knew my mother would be out of the house. Finally, we were alone and we inexpertly did it. When it was over, we were both glowing. My mother came home later and I am positive she read the glow from across the room, although she never said anything about it. She was much too well-bred for that. When I didn't go back to Cate, she cried. She did a lot of that. David Hopkins was sent to boarding school in the East and Jeffrey Palmer became my new running mate. Jeffrey was friends with me and Ethan.

JEFFREY PALMER: *I met David at Santa Barbara High School. I didn't know his previous history, but we were both oddballs and sort of gravitated together and fell into a kind of interesting social circle. Everyone had a car and most of them were late models—I remember David had a Fiat 600 and after that an Austin Sprite. That was part of where we stood on the issues. Everyone had hot rods and we were in sports cars. There was this handsome Italian guy who came into local society by marrying the last sane heir of an oil fortune. It was part of the Mountain Drive culture, which was the center of hip in Santa Barbara. The wealthy of Montecito were always very bored and always looking for stimulants. The guy bought this nine-acre walled villa in Montecito with all these beautiful stone houses on the property: gatehouse, gardener's house, that kind of thing. It had a garage with a dozen stalls, full of race cars and fast motorcycles; it was "Oh yeah, take the Ferrari down and buy some beer, Jeff." The culture vibrated from there to the debutante parties in Montecito, to the yacht harbor, the sports car racing garages, and a few theater-coffeehouse places in between.*

According to Palmer, the compound was an early attempt at creating a lifestyle that Hugh Hefner later made famous. It might've been more innocent, but the elements seem a little less than savory, what with the mysterious Italian passing himself off as a count and inviting the bored and beautiful teenagers of Santa Barbara to make the place their clubhouse. It was a lifestyle of the rich and infamous and the locals who belonged to the scene apparently loved it. It was also the scene in which David had his earliest real drug experience, courtesy of a local wayward teenage girl.

JEFFREY PALMER: *It was just sort of a circle and it included people like the Ehrlich girls, who had brought in Trini Lopez to play at their debutante party, which was big-time back then. They had circus tents and we partied till four in the morning, after which time it was full-on breakfast and champagne when the sun came up. And there was a nymphet named Kathy, who went to a girl's school called Bishop in La Jolla and brought back the information that if you drank as much of a certain brand of cough syrup as you could and overdosed to the max on some ingredient they used to put in there, you could get really wrecked. We did this all in black-tie formal, which was very far out if you're sixteen.*

It's true. We tried that. If you drank about four bottles of that cough syrup, you got really out of your tree. I got sick, but I got high. I also ate morning glory seeds, Heavenly Blue morning glory seeds. It was supposed to be some sort of psychedelic, although nobody knew that word then. I think the active ingredient in morning glory seeds is belladonna or strychnine and I remember coming home and thinking, "Well gee, that stuff didn't really work too well" and then being in my room, getting up naked and looking at myself in the mirror in the bathroom and seeing all of my musculature, all of my circulatory system, all of my bones, and all of my nerves. I could see everything in my body right through my skin, so I must've been really out there. That was my first psychedelic experience, but cough syrup doesn't really qualify as a psychedelic. I got loaded on it, but it was kind of a woozy high. We wanted to be crazy. We didn't know anybody who had marijuana. If we did, we would've smoked it.

David had discovered women, he had a car and a driver's license, his mother couldn't keep him at home, and his father was rarely seen, since apparently there were no visitation rights included in the divorce agreement between Floyd and Aliph. He found himself fascinated by one of the most beautiful and exotic students in his class. Not a debutante or a rich kid, she was a local girl with intriguing eyes and long black hair, perceived by everyone as full-blooded Mexican, although in reality she was half Native American. Either way, she was definitely in the minority in the Santa Barbara-Montecito teen scene. Maria was dedicated to the dance department at Santa Barbara High School, then run by a noted modern dancer, June Lane. Maria met David in theater arts class. By this time, he liked the limelight and if he had any career goals at all, it was to become an actor—good pay, short hours, a chance to pick up girls, and he had a father in the business in Hollywood. In the end, it was Maria who moved to Hollywood and found work as an actress in films and television and it's Maria who still pursues that demanding and unrewarding profession.

MARIA CORDERO: *I met him in a theater arts class at Santa Barbara High and I guess he'd been kicked out of one of the schools that he went to. He was sort of proud of his reputation—kicked out of all the*

best and worst schools or something like that—and he was ambiva-
lent about private schools. He didn't like being thought of as a snob,
but he was a bit of a snob or else he wouldn't have mentioned it in
the first place. I walked in and sat down and he said, "Hi." And I
didn't know him from anyone, so I turned around and I was a very
shy person, so I turned around and looked at him and said, "Hello."
And later on he told me it was the coldest hello that he'd ever gotten
from anybody and that it had frosted his eyelashes. One of the first
things he said to me was "I'm a pink monkey and you're a pink
monkey and they don't like us because of that—they're all brown
monkeys." Well, that was very flattering and basically true, but he
didn't go out of his way to get on with brown monkeys. He went out
of his way to make himself a nuisance and a pest.

There was a bit I remembered from a book by Robert A.
Heinlein, about monkeys. It seemed like the truth as I knew it; if
you put a pink monkey in with the brown monkeys, the brown
monkeys will tear it to shreds. To avoid that, you just paint it
brown. That was another part of me being an outcast: I had a
Mexican girlfriend. But if the truth be told, it just didn't matter
what she was or where she came from, Maria was beautiful. She
was lovely and sensitive and bright and funny and she laughed a
lot. Maria had glossy black hair that had red highlights in it when
the sun really hit it. I've never seen anything like it before or
since.

All it took to get David's attention was startling beauty and
indifference to him; the combination of desirability and challenge was irresistible. He set out to become friends with Maria and they eventually sought each other out and became
steady companions. Maria worked as a waitress at a coffeehouse called the Io-Pan (after the two Greek gods). The Io-
Pan was a three-story house off Micheltorena and Chapala in
downtown Santa Barbara near the State Theater. Downstairs there was the usual menu of coffee, tea, cider, and
espresso and upstairs were rooms where the owners lived and
where staff could crash. Visiting performers who played the

room would also be given quarters upstairs when they appeared there.

It was a warm and happy environment. It was one of the new forms of nightlife, matched by only a few clubs in the area, among them the Noctambulist (translation: sleepwalker). Ethan was playing bass and congas down the block on lower State Street at a place called the Boom-Boom (no translation necessary). Maria and I would go down to hear Ethan. Jazz was still a new treat, the Boom-Boom club had a liquor license, and it was a racy and adult thing to do. Ethan was still trying to straighten me out, teaching me to play guitar, accompanying me on his stand-up bass, showing me what it was to perform on small stages in smoke-filled rooms, breaking the high school kid into the world of music. Once he showed me an E-minor chord and an A-major chord, I was off and running. Those were my two favorite chords for a long time. It just naturally stuck with me; it was the most natural thing that I could remember. Some people, the first time their hands touch a football, they know that they're supposed to play football. Some people hear a call from God and they know they're supposed to be preachers. I started playing guitar and singing and I never stopped. I knew that was it. It felt right. Soon enough we played as a duo, Ethan and David. We did the standard folkie repertoire of the period, since this was the age of the Kingston Trio, the Limeliters, Odetta, Joan Baez, Josh White, Bud and Travis, and Sonny Terry and Brownie McGhee. I played at the Io-Pan when it first opened: solo guitar and folk songs. There were people playing there like Van Dyke Parks and his brother Carlton (they called themselves the Steeltown Two) and Joe and Eddie, a pair of traveling black folk artists, all of whose paths would cross mine in the future. Travis Edmonson would eventually give me my first joint, but that was later.

As the fifties wound down, the local scene was relatively drug-free—the jazz musicians who played the Boom-Boom were true to the stereotype and Ethan remembers there was heroin and grass on the scene, none of which he or David enjoyed; the guys who used were just too far out and not a cool example. One of the owners of the Io-Pan smoked weed, but in Santa Barbara in 1959 and 1960 people who smoked marijuana kept it a secret and musicians who sniffed or injected heroin didn't tell *anyone* about their habits—the image of Frank Sinatra writhing and sweating in withdrawal in *The Man with the Golden Arm* was still most peoples' idea of what getting high was all about. Staying out late, playing coffeehouses, and singing and taking long drives in the Santa Barbara moonlight with Maria or some other high school sweetie was enough to get David high and it kept him nodding every day in class.

MARIA CORDERO: *He didn't play by any of the rules. He smoked and you weren't supposed to smoke on campus. He'd fall asleep in class and it seemed as if he was always about to be kicked out of school. I'm not saying he patterned himself after James Dean, but he was always the tortured rebel, always in a lot of pain because he was different. He took an enormous amount of pride in that, of course. And he was sophisticated. That's what was interesting about him. His car was a Sprite and that was interesting. There were very few people in those days who had their own cars, let alone a little bug-eyed jobbie. I don't know if I'd say he was a ladies' man. I'd say he was a bit too weird, too strange to be a ladies' man. I'm sure he was attractive to lots of the girls. He used to pull out his guitar and people would gather around.*

From playing in coffeehouses I found out that I knew just enough songs that I could get away with singing. I could play guitar almost well enough to do it and sing at the same time. Most especially I found out that I could get the attention of girls and right around that time I loved it. Truly loved it. Got me off. The music got me off. I used to play it down, but I was entranced with it. The minute I started to really sing and have songs to sing and be able to do it and be any good at it, I knew that's what I wanted to do. I didn't want to be an actor anymore. I didn't want to do any of that stuff. I've been telling people for years that I took up the guitar to get laid and that was a convenient line and it got a lot of laughs, but the truth is I just say that to downplay what the real deal was. The Real Deal was that I flat loved it. It was absolutely joyous to me. I absolutely loved it from the first time I did it. I loved it clear back to when I was a little kid singing in grade school and being in Gilbert and Sullivan plays and doing that show at Cate, *Cuttin' Capers,* and anything else. I loved it then. I always loved it. I always will love it. And I did get laid.

It was the beginning of the Crosby carnal obsession. "I followed my unit the way a caboose chases a train," he would say much, much later. It was true. This was one oddball high school senior who had his priorities very much in order: everything except music would take a backseat to sex and that's probably because music was a way to get girls into the backseat for sex. He even discussed marriage with Maria, since the times required that kind of commitment for young couples to "do it"—the Pill wasn't out yet. Jeffrey Palmer, David's constant companion in those days, recalls Maria as "a shadow that would loom in and out of all this, definitely a witch." Palmer's memories begin to sound like a Stephen Sondheim song from *West Side Story:* "Maria, exotic Maria. David was always in lust with Maria." She remembers:

MARIA CORDERO: *We were going to get married at one point, mostly because sex was such a big fucking deal and everything would have been fine if it hadn't been for our parents. We could have arranged everything and wouldn't have had to talk about marriage or anything like that, but I did want to get married to him and, as a matter of fact, he was the first of the male gender that I was ready to give up everything for. I had a lot of potential as an actress and a dancer and June wanted me to go to New York and audition for the Graham troupe and my acting teacher wanted me to go on acting and all of that stuff, but I just wanted to be David's wife and had all the wonderful fantasies about a house and raising children. David sort of backed out. It was all arranged that we would go on tour. We wanted to be together, but as it turned out, David decided not to. And what was his reason? "I don't know, babe. I just have to go my own way. I'm a loner." That kind of stuff, I think it was. Which wasn't any big surprise, but it was very disappointing, so I just went out on tour with the Bishop's Company—and that's another story.*

The Bishop's Company was basically a traveling Protestant church drama club, touring the United States in a couple of station wagons (one for the cast, the other for the stage manager and the scenery). Touring in that little theatrical troupe with Maria would've been impossible for David. Their only connection with ecclesiastical hierarchy was the name and that came from one of the founders, Phyllis Bishop. If David had made that tour, his life might've been different. As it was, he stayed around to play guitar and get laid. Maria Cordero has the definitive analysis of David's coffeehouse performances during those days:

MARIA CORDERO: *His melancholy pose so permeated everything he did that it became a bit of a drag sometimes. When he played at the Io-Pan, people would come in for a cider or something, a mocha "hold-the-whipped-cream," whatever, and they'd be having a good time when David would come on and do his set, one depressing song after another. "I'm a drifter, I'm a loner, I seen every city and town, I'll pass by here or I'll die here and be some stranger," it just went on and on and slowly but surely people would stop drinking and start staring at the floor. Then the waitress would come by and say, "Can I get you anything?" and they'd say, "How about a razor?" It was awful. Sometimes people would leave and the owners would say, "You know, we've got to get rid of David. He's driving the customers away." But he loved it and there he was, all that "I'm really horrible, everybody hates me, I'm different, isn't it neat, I can get attention this way and self-destruct in the end."*

Now it's true that Maria had this prophetic insight many years later, when she was familiar with the rest of David's life, and the skeptical memories might be one-sided. But there's a final epilogue to David's relationship with the woman Jeffrey Palmer called "the exotic, the beautiful Maria."

MARIA CORDERO: *Eventually, I just lost track of David and heard that he was in Los Angeles and singing. Then I heard he was playing in the Byrds, but by that time I was living with another man and was actually in a band and we were playing around and heard that the Byrds were playing at the Whisky a Go Go. We went to see David and visited during the break and drove around in Peter Fonda's beautiful station wagon—silver, I believe it was—and did some joints. Later, I was living in an apartment on Laurel Canyon, right near Sunset, and we went up to McGuinn's house and listened to a tape together and it was fun to be with him just because he was doing well and we'd had enough time between us to feel comfortable. He knew that I was deeply in love with this other man, so there was no question of divided loyalties, so we just spent time together. We were driving along, we were at a stop sign, and we clasped each other's hands very strongly and felt something pass between us—it was sexual and it was emotional and there was a lot of love and that was all. I think it's one of the nicest things that ever happened between us. I didn't see him again after that.*

THREE

....

I never made a clean move away from home and into the big city. There wasn't even the traditional punctuation mark of a formal high school graduation. I was going to school, then I wasn't. I began a lifelong fascination with cars. With Jeffrey Palmer or David Hopkins, we'd borrow or steal any car we could get and cruise the back roads and teen hangouts of Santa Barbara. I'd lie to my mother about having some errand to run downtown so that she'd give me a ride into the city when she went to a movie. With my extra key, we'd take off in Mom's car. Driving around, cruising Main, that was the ticket. In my mother's car, Hopkins's mother's car, his aunt's car, my aunt's, anybody's car, didn't matter. All it had to do was run. David Hopkins's father had a T-Bird, a pink '56 Thunderbird. We used to steal that and go cruising and every girl we knew would sit in the back, with their feet in the well, and we'd cruise Montecito singing "Poison Ivy." I guess the Hopkinses didn't find out about that. My first car was a 1950 Ford coupé with twin pipes and a column shift

4 0

and a Ford V-8 flathead engine. My second car was a 1952 Ford two-door column shift, flathead, twin pipes. My third car was a Fiat 600, which my dad got for me because it was the cheapest car there was. Good old Dad, always a class act. Then I saw the Sprites and they were inexpensive little sports cars, so I convinced my parents that I was going to work and save and scrimp and wash the dishes. I'd do anything if I could trade the Fiat in on the Sprite. I told my father, "It was only just a little bit bigger payments, Dad, and I promise to feed the lemon trees." I promised the moon and I got a Sprite. It was fun. The best thing about the Sprite was that the diameter of the exhaust pipe was the right size to take an extension tube from a vacuum cleaner. I would slide it right up in there and cut the muffler off completely. Made it a very loud car, which I drove everywhere. I loved it.

I moved out of the house as soon as I could and when I wasn't living at home I'd find a couch or a mattress on the floor at some friend's pad. After I got my high school certificate, I started at Santa Barbara City College, a junior college that's part of the extensive California system of not-much-higher education. Junior colleges in California are like junior high schools, in that their function is to provide a transition from one level of education to another. They're local schools, without dormitories, which gave me a solid excuse to get my mother to help with the rent on a place "closer to campus" (and farther from home and Mom). Junior colleges serve another function, which is to provide some education for students lacking the qualifications to get them into the large, prestigious state universities like UCLA and Berkeley or the smaller institutions at Santa Cruz, Santa Barbara, Chico, Davis, and beyond. Kids seriously intent on getting a college education can improve their grade-point average and student activities at the junior college level and transfer upon graduation. Kids without ability or ambition can get a minor associate degree. Kids who don't want to go to college can attend long enough to find a goal or major and to satisfy parental expectations, which is what I was doing when I got arrested for the first time in my life.

There wasn't a lot do in Santa Barbara for excitement. Playing at the Io-Pan and the Noctambulist, either solo or with Ethan, was fun. So was going to hear jazz and folk music performed locally in concert. But that wasn't stuff you could do every night of the week. A couple of local boys named Tom Bowser and Billy Martin collaborated with me on an alternative evening activity. It wasn't quite as glamorous or as organized as being in a teen burglary gang, which is what I've said in past interviews. Basically, Billy, Tom, and I were housebreakers. Prowlers. We had a system. We'd go out in the county where there would be only one police force to deal with, outside the city limits. We'd get a radio tuned to the county sheriff's frequency. Easy to do. I didn't know all their codes, but they had to say the address. If they got a burglary or housebreaking complaint, they'd have to at least say the street name to send a car and by that time we'd be long gone. We would go up to Montecito and look for a good place. We'd check for the classic invitations: old newspapers, dusty cars or locked garages, drawn curtains, or day-burning porch lights. There was a girl with us, I forget her name, who'd knock on the door. If nobody answered, we'd break in. You could crack a back door or a patio french door with nothing more complicated than a glass cutter and a roll of masking tape to hold the fragments quietly in place. Once we were inside, we'd wander around, look through private places, make a drink, steal a bottle, and lift any fancy souvenir that we liked. It wasn't real exotic booty: family silver, cameras, portable radios . . . the usual. This was before catalog shopping, so there were a lot fewer goodies to tempt us. Everything was so much more traceable in those days. One of the other boys got caught and named names and gave addresses. Dropped a dime on his pals, ratted us out. I gave myself up, like I said. My father was pissed.

Santa Barbara City College suspended me. My parents paid for some professional counseling and I went to see a therapist. That satisfied the court that I was repentant and mindful and my mother persuaded the college to take me back. I found something

I liked: semantics and communications. I began studying. I studied mass media communications, I studied language, I studied sociology as it applied to communications. I studied demographics a little bit, I studied sampling and statistics, even a little bit of cybernetics, as it applied. It seemed to me that most of the ills in the human condition were problems of communication and so, little idealist that I was, that's what I wanted to aim myself at, like a missile. I wanted to knock off communication problems because if you've got people starving on one part of the world and farmers being paid not to grow food on the other, you got a communications problem. If you've got war, you've got a major communication problem. War doesn't happen between two people who are talking to each other. You don't shoot someone you're talking to, you shoot a person that somebody else tells you is an ogre, an inhuman ogre who wants to kill you and your family, someone you've never spoken to and probably can't even see as you bomb him. You don't shoot somebody in the middle of a conversation. Guys don't say, "Let's work this thing out . . ." *Blam!* That isn't how it works.

I have had and still have a feeling that communication, mass media communication in particular, is as close as we get to having a tool to defeat the essential human illness: greed for power. Power corrupts, yes, and absolute power corrupts absolutely. People who get power want more power. They revel in power. They wallow in power, it seems to convince them, in some way, that they were supposed to have it all along and that it's obvious that God wants them to be powerful because they are all-wise and they know what they're doing and we don't and this is a bunch of bullshit. Now the interesting thing is that a few people with guitars and access to tools can point the finger at that crap in a major way. How? Why?

Because the record industry was designed to sell millions of copies of "White Christmas" and get songs played on the radio for millions and millions of people. Doing anything else, anything with some meaning and some serious intent, is like sneaking nuggets of truth into the shit stream. Folk music was a key because if you heard the Weavers sing "Wimoweh," it wasn't long before you heard "If I Had a Hammer" and "This Land Is Your Land." I was raised on Woody Guthrie and the Weavers and there's no question that they affected my values. That's one of the reasons I thought we were fortunate to be able to blow ourselves loose from the fifties. In the fifties we were totally self-centered and unconcerned with the rest of the world: isolationist, smug, and full of crap. I remember listening to Josh White's "Strange Fruit" and saying, "Mommy, I don't understand. What's that about?" And she said, "Well, dear, it's an awful thing." She explained, "I don't know if you're old enough to understand this, but there are people who don't like black people." I was a little kid; I knew there were black people. I didn't know anybody didn't like them. She told me how they used to lynch black people. That had to be explained to me—hanging people from a tree. That's what Josh White wrote that song about. My mother said, "It's very brave of him to put that on a record," and it came as a huge shock to me.

Years later, I heard Bob Dylan at Gerdes Folk City, singing "Blowin' in the Wind," and that affected me very strongly, only I didn't like him or his vocal quality because everybody loved him and I wasn't as big as him and I was jealous as hell. Besides, I thought vocals should be pure and choirboyish. Like me. I thought I was what was happening. But there he was, expressing the value systems that I respected and doing it marvelously. The early stuff—"Maggie's Farm," "Chimes of Freedom," and "Times They Are A'Changin' "—smacked me in the mouth. I said, "Holy shit. Let me at it!" And then there was "Tambourine Man." Dylan affected me. No question about it. The man was one of the major poets of our time. There was just no way around it.

The words Woody Guthrie drew on his guitar were as relevant to David Crosby as they were to Bob Dylan and Phil Ochs. Guthrie, a legendary folksinger and songwriter, was singing about many of those same images and events that

Floyd Crosby had photographed decades earlier. When Woody Guthrie burned THIS MACHINE KILLS FASCISTS into his instrument and into his art, he foreshadowed a generation of musicians and artists who found their voices while Nixon debated Krushchev, Fidel Castro consolidated the Cuban revolution, while the Student Nonviolent Coordinating Committee organized sit-ins and boycotts and freedom riders started for the South. The new activists were young and they spoke to their peers directly, as equals.

I used to tell a story about the dinosaurs and the little furry guys. There was a huge race of dinosaurs and there were these little tiny furball guys and the dinosaurs used to eat them when they saw them, step on them when they didn't, and not really care much about them. "No big deal, another squashed furball." The furball guys didn't dig this, but it went on that way for a long time until one of the furballs said, "Hey, I know what to do." He led the furballs out and they ate the dinosaur eggs. While the dinosaurs were off tromping around and crushing the jungle, the little guys would go in and steal their eggs and eat them. Shortly thereafter, there were no dinosaurs, while the furball guys did well and prospered. One of the things I've tried to be in my life is an egg thief. A deliberate, conscientious egg thief. Because I don't want greed and greed for power to prevail. I don't want them to win.

Early on, I saw that the only way you can have a revolution here is to affect the value system. Now, what is the value system? The value system is what matters to you. Does life matter to you? Do people matter to you? Does money matter to you? What matters? *That's* your value system. If you take the children of the Establishment, you steal the eggs, so to speak. If you take the long view, then you go to the children before they grow up into the value system. You offer them an alternative, a value system that's positive, one that's high and happy and joyful and creative and focused on birth and growth and human values. If you do that, then you can steal those children, steal them right away. You don't actually abduct them. You offer them an alternative way and hope they'll choose it themselves.

LONG TIME GONE

That's what we started out trying to do and in opposing us the power structure made its mistake. They didn't take us seriously. Yet, ideas are the most powerful forces for change! The big guys didn't ever see what we were, how we were affecting things, because they wouldn't look past their noses. The kids, me included, all grew up and the values changed. It was no longer glamorous and glorious to go to war. John Wayne was no longer right. We did that.

Before David could go out and steal dinosaur eggs and change the world, he had to leave Santa Barbara. Maria Cordero had left to go with another man and David moved to Los Angeles to study acting, actually boarding briefly during the summer of 1960 at the Pasadena Playhouse, where he apprenticed. Floyd and Betty Crosby kept an apartment in Los Angeles. (They had moved to nearby Ojai, about twenty miles south of Santa Barbara.) David moved into the same building after being evicted from his first Los Angeles apartment—the noise of late-night guitar playing, partying, and seductions proved too much for the neighbors. Living in proximity to his father and stepmother wasn't the answer, so the new kid in town moved around a lot. Eventually, he found a place in Laurel Canyon that he could share with Ethan when his brother would come to town.

In Hollywood, still toying with the idea of being an actor, David "took class" (as they say) with a noted acting coach, Jeff Corey, himself a blacklisted performer who took David into his class at Floyd Crosby's request. Acting lessons with Corey didn't last. Betty Crosby recalls that Jeff finally threw David out of class, since the young man couldn't (or wouldn't) show up for class on the regular and punctual basis that Corey demanded of his students (and does to this day). It was an uncanny replay of David's attendance in high school. Ethan moved to Los Angeles too and he and David played the folk clubs that dotted the city: the Unicorn, the Ash Grove, Ledbetter's, and, in far-off Pasadena, the Ice House. The commitment to playing music was beginning to take hold and a fledgling folkie was taking his first steps outside the nest, his round cheeks still downy and Santa Barbara soft. Only the voice was truly strong.

In those years, there was a two-tier structure to folk music: at the top were the major acts that sold millions of records, toured successfully, and spawned commercial clones. Below them were the "ethnic" folkies, who collected Folkways albums and read *Sing Out* magazine and studied Alan Lomax's Library of Congress folk music field recordings for new ways to sing "Silver Dagger," "Michael, Row the Boat Ashore," and "Roll On, Columbia." Sometimes a folk act would succeed commercially; a singer named Vince Martin had a hit with the Tarriers called "Cindy Oh Cindy." During the fifties, folk music had begun as the almost private preserve of a hundred people with guitars who met every Sunday in New York at the circular fountain in Washington Square Park in Greenwich Village. By 1961 and 1962, folk acts like the Limeliters were making successful college and concert tours, selling lots of albums, and even making the *Billboard* magazine pop charts with both albums and singles. A backup player for the Limeliters was a young guitarist named Jim McGuinn. Other acts on the circuit included the Highwaymen, the Kingston Trio, and Joan Baez.

JEFFREY PALMER: *One night Joan Baez came to town and this was every beginning hippie's heartthrob—Joan Baez! She had toes as long as most people's fingers and she was playing at the Lobrero Theater. Afterward we all went over to a coffeeshop together and somehow Joan Baez ended up there and came and sat at the same table with us. As I recall, David handed her a rose. I don't know where he got it from, he probably stole it from the table next to us, and it was all very romantic and I was so teenage-maled-out that I couldn't even talk, I was just petrified, but David was very cool about it.*

In Greenwich Village and across the country, the folk axis gathered strength and momentum. Noel Stookey, who would become Paul in Peter, Paul, and Mary, was the funniest and best-paid stand-up comic on the coffeehouse circuit (he anchored the lineup at Manny Roth's Cafe Wha? on Bleecker Street). The population density in New York and the nightlife tradition in the Village meant that the area could support dozens of venues. In one small neighborhood, half a hundred clubs and coffeehouses presented live entertainment every night, rotating acts, changing the lineups, providing almost everyone with a place to play. The permutations and combinations were staggering. Bill Cosby could open for Phil Ochs, who could trade licks with Bob Dylan, who would try them in front of NYU students and commuting teenagers from the Bronx and Queens with black tights and white lipstick. In Boston, their cousins from the Ivy League and the Boston college complexes would stay up until dawn at the Hays-Bickford Cafeteria, elbowing art students for choice tables. In Philadelphia and Chicago, similar scenes were spontaneously generating, like mushrooms, in the fertile climate for new ideas.

In California, the same things were happening at the same kinds of places: Berkeley, San Francisco, Palo Alto, West Hollywood (the Strip), and in Venice at the beach. Things were more spread-out and you had to have a car, but that wasn't a problem—VW vans and old Detroit iron that never rusted in the California sunshine could be had for a hundred dollars and gas was twenty-one cents a gallon. David commuted up and down the coast, meeting people like Gibson and Camp (Bob Gibson and Bob Camp), and Bud Dashiel and Travis Edmonson (the folk duo Bud and Travis). It was Travis Edmonson who turned David on to grass—the kid's first joint! David wasn't a strong enough act to get paid for solo performance, although his voice was remarkably pure and clear. He had no repertoire to speak (or sing) of and was doing songs like George Gershwin's "Summertime." It showed off his voice, but it wasn't what anyone would call "folk music." (Years later, Janis Joplin would make the same choice and offer the classic show tune to her rock 'n' roll audiences.)

Travis Edmonson and I and the bass player and drummer, two black guys that he was working with, were riding in my '52 Ford out to the house of some people who had come to the club and liked Travis and had asked us out for dinner. We were driving along the freeway and the guys in the back were saying, "Come on, Trav, light it up. Come on, light it up. Come on, man. Man, we only got five minutes befo' we be there. Light that joint, man. Shit, the kid don't matter. Come on. If he ain't smokin', it's time he did." Travis said, "Uhhh," then I said, "Are they talking about what I think they're talking about?" And he said, "Yeah, only you can't tell nobody now." I said, "I ain't gonna tell anybody. Light it up!" So he lit it up and passed it over. I took a couple of puffs and all of a sudden I felt like I was doing about a hundred miles an hour and I was actually doing about forty. I said, "I get it. Yeah, okay." And I loved it. I loved it from the very first.

John F. Kennedy created the Peace Corps and then approved the CIA-sponsored Cuban invasion at the Bay of Pigs, freedom riders left Washington, D.C., for New Orleans, and the first Miami-bound jetliner was hijacked and diverted to Havana, Cuba. In 1960 the Food and Drug Administration finally approved general consumer use of birth control pills and doctors started to write prescriptions for the little one-a-day precursors of the sexual revolution. Unfortunately for David and a girl with whom he was living, the Pill wasn't yet a part of their lives. Ethan remembers:

ETHAN CROSBY: *She came up to the club I was working at and laid the trip on me. "Hey, I'm knocked up and David's disappeared and what do I do?" So I went with her when she told her parents that my little brother had knocked her up. I thought I was going to get killed.*

I split. I said, "Hey, now's the time for me to become Woody Guthrie," so I went to Arizona and got a job there singing in a coffeehouse and then I went to Colorado. That's really the beginning of my actual independence, when I hit the road and started to do that. Until then, everything was still close. My mom was a couple of hours' drive up the coast and I could call home for money if I ran out. I did that lots of times when I was young. When I got to Boulder, I found a typically small and grubby folk club called the Attic because it was in a basement. Joe Loop, the owner-booker, hired me for an extended run and winter came early that year. Boulder was very, very cold and luckily I was always good at finding a place to stay. This time I found some college guys who were sharing a big old house. It kind of matched the big old overcoat I bought, a surplus Air Force greatcoat that reached down to my ankles. I lived in that coat, never came out. I lived in the basement of this old house near the furnace because that was the warmest room in the house. It was freezing out there! People used to go to the University of Colorado for the skiing; that's how cold it was. The college guys were making home-brewed beer; I was able to sneak bottles of the stuff out of wherever it was they kept it to age. I also took food from their refrigerator. I wasn't proud. I was a cold and hungry folksinger.

The girl he left behind never pursued him, but David was enjoying the life of the itinerant musician, traveling with a guitar case and a big overcoat, living by his wits, his music, and an occasional money order wired from home. Floyd or Aliph could always be counted on to come up with a plane ticket or some small sum to get him from one town to the next if pickings were slim. The standard pay scale for playing coffeehouses in those days was five or ten dollars a night—if you were a regular. If you just stopped in or if it was a "hoot night," when performers would sign up for a slot and take their chances, the waitresses would pass a basket to the patrons and people would contribute what they wanted; the proceeds were pooled and more or less evenly divided among all the performers at the end of the evening. It wasn't a way to make big money—or any money at all. It was a place to play, to learn new songs, meet new people, build a following, and seduce locals. Scoring grass was somewhat of a problem, since the drug was still a clandestine experience. People who smoked didn't let on. When one wanted to know if someone else got high or not, the axiom was "If you have to ask, don't ask."

From Boulder David traveled to New York to Greenwich Village, where a folksinger could make a living, see the big city, and explore the fabulous ferment that kept Bleecker and MacDougal steaming and bubbling all year 'round. Rent-controlled apartments could be found for less than fifty dollars a month in the East Village (which in those days was St. Marks Place and not much more) and similarly cheap quarters could be had in the West Village. Some of the clubs are still there, others have long disappeared, but the circuit was a ten-block loop that ran from West Broadway and Bleecker (the Bitter End, the Dugout, Cafe Rafio, the Village Gate) to MacDougal Street (Cafe Wha?, Gaslight Cafe), west across Seventh Avenue (the Feenjon, the Fat Black

Pussycat, Phase Two), and back with stops at the Night Owl and the Cafe Bizarre. The bars, lunch counters, off-off-Broadway theaters, and artists' studios were a vibrant counterpoint to the local Italian social clubs and the genuine old-time espresso bars with ancient copper machines that went back to the prewar Greenwich Village of the American bohemians. You could buy a copy of *The Nation* or *The Daily Worker* from Maurice, a gray-bearded old-timer who had sold *The Masses* to the labor radicals from Union Square who walked through the Village on their way to the West Side docks to organize the Seaman's Union before World War II.

When I got to the Village, I was barely out of prep school and this was New York. I'd been there once before with my parents, but I was on my own and I was like a mouse in traffic. It was definitely the Big Time. One of the things that made me feel as if I might be able to make it was a cop, of all things. A regular New York City beat cop who worked the area around Bleecker and MacDougal, which I think is the Sixth Precinct. His name was Pops or at least that's what everybody called him. A humongous black guy, *big,* and I remember noticing him because I observed that the cops had a system of signaling without whistles—they'd whack a lightpost with their stick and it would go *booong!* If you heard that, you knew it was them, talking to each other. Pops sat down with me in Art Ford's one night. I was sitting there, eating my meal of the day. I had $4.38 from passing the hat at the Cafe Rafio and was having my french toast when he sat down and said, "What's your name?" I told him and he said, "Yeah? So where you living?" because he figured I was a little street kid and I was. I told him what I was and where I was and what was going on. Pops said, "Well, try and stay out of trouble and if you ever feel like you're in trouble, if there's anything real bad, come find me. I'll help you out." The guy was real nice, a nice, fatherly, big old black man, obviously real smart about kids. He knew exactly what to say to me. He was cool. That was one of the first cracks in the pavement, a little blade of grass coming up through the concrete. It gave me the confidence to face the street because I knew if the bad guys came after me, I could always yell for Pops. That was important because there was some hostility toward us new kids from the Italian community. They didn't like these new beatniks coming in and ruining their neighborhood.

That's how Von Emson got shot. He was the guy who owned the Cafe Rafio on Bleecker Street. The fight was over low-rent apartments. Von wanted the apartment that backed up to the Rafio from the other side so he could knock a door through and have his pad right there, which would enable him to take girls from his club back and ball them. Von Emson was a sleazeball. There was an old Italian guy, eighty years old, living in the apartment Von wanted, so he started pressuring the old guy, putting little threatening notes in the mailbox and stuff like that. One night, right in front of God and everybody, the old Italian gentleman walked up to Von Emson in front of the club and took out an old .38 with a six-inch barrel and went *wham!* Shot Emson right between the eyes and that was that. End of Von Emson. The old man was eighty; he didn't care. He was going and he just wouldn't take any shit. "You leave-a me alone-a! I'm-a live-a here all my fucking life-a. You don't-a touch-a my apartment." *Bam!* When I heard about that, I cheered.

> Students of urban sociology might find something worth investigating in the unique circumstances that characterize the bohemian quarters of both New York and San Francisco: Greenwich Village and North Beach are old-line Italian immigrant communities, both are bordered by Chinatown and the docks, both have been havens for nonconformists since World War I. One can only conclude that when you're living in your own urban ghetto, all your neighbors will look *different.* If you were Italian or Chinese, everyone else was totally foreign, so it didn't much matter who else was moving into the neighborhood: sailors jumping ship, bohemians, beatniks, hippies, or oddballs, it was probably all the same to the locals. If they could cope with each other, another group of crazies wouldn't create any significant environmental impact.
>
> Avoiding the hostility of the local old-timers and dodging the occasional gunshot were the folksingers and poets who would make up the new American musical renaissance. The

regulars included Bob Dylan; Doc Watson; Phil Ochs; Eric Andersen; Dave Van Ronk; Lisa Kindred; Fred Neil; Tom Paxton; Hoyt Axton; Tom Rush; Len Chandler; Dino Valenti; Vince Martin; Peter, Paul, and Mary; Bill Cosby; Tim Hardin; Richard Pryor; Lou Gossett; Hugh Romney; and Ramblin' Jack Elliott. Bob Gibson was there with his big twelve-string, showing David new chords, new changes, passing chords. The neophyte folkie was learning the mysteries of the twelve-string guitar. The Village was full of jazz, folk, poetry-to-jazz, off-off-Broadway cabaret theater. There were intimate cabarets like Jim Paul Eiler's Showplace and Jan Walman's Duplex, clubs where Barbra Streisand and Woody Allen were making their first tentative forays into performing. The audiences came from the Village mix of tourists, university and high school students, "bagel babies" (commuting weekend bohemians), old Italians, hustlers, drag queens, the first out-of-the-closet gays, a militant lesbian community, old lefties, working artists, longshoremen and sailors on liberty. It was an exciting place to be. Kevin Ryan was a well-read drifter who was recovering from a divorce by working three jobs and living behind a club called the Dragon's Den, where Dino Valenti was a regular performer. He found David on the streets:

KEVIN RYAN: *I had been working as a draftsman during the daytime and at night—this was during the folk move, when all the people who had been hobbyists in folk music suddenly became professionals and it became the hot music form. By about '58–'59, I was pretty well established in the MacDougal-Bleecker folk music action. I had a partner and we had a recording studio where we did demos and a couple of folk music shows—sustaining shows at WPIF. Bob Gibson had a talent management co-op thing and he met a lot of young people around the country that he liked and he said, "When you come to New York, come and see me." David came to the studio that we had on Cherry Lane and I asked him to tune up—sing a few things, play a few chords—just for levels and while I was getting levels we talked about his guitar playing. I said, "You sound like a guitar player I like named Travis Edmonson." Before that day was out we got well acquainted. I had a spare room in my apartment on Bleecker and Thompson streets. David moved in and slept on the couch. He was the first of the California Golden Boys I'd ever met—preaching a sort of doctrine of "lay back" and "let it flow" and he was very articulate, very quick to pick up on new ideas. He bought Robert Heinlein's* Stranger in a Strange Land *on one of his trips to California. In New York, once all the California and Colorado people like Judy Collins began to arrive, the old folk purists began to suffer a great deal. I mean, New York was pretty hard and academic in folk music; Boston was even worse.*

I don't think anyone who met Dylan when he first came to New York would have really believed that he was going to live more than a couple of years. He was intense, constantly in motion. He's like peddling a bicycle, standing still. And he was pushy. Him and Crosby were rank beginners at the same time. Dylan was one of the kids that you had to teach not to pop their p's, while Crosby was a guy who liked to sing "Summertime," which is a great song but not what you'd call folk music. David was appealing; his charisma was always there. He moved into the apartment I had and actually it ended up as a one-room apartment. It began as a two-room, but they'd had a fire just before I moved in and had never really gotten around to repairing the other room. It was painted but not furnished. Within a week or two of him moving in, another singer, a black friend of David's from Chicago named Terry Collier, joined us. Then some girls moved in. I wound up on the couch. Terry wound up with one of the girls in the double bed and David and someone named Renee were on the floor. By this time, I had given up all pretense of being respectable. I was smoking dope for the first time in my life, I was keeping it together but didn't really have any money and David had money from his folks and he flew back and forth. He was the only broke down-and-out musician I knew who flew jets.

Terry Collier was a talented black musician from Chicago who came to Greenwich Village to break out of the ghetto blues trap, to be an intellectual, to confront issues of race and music. Kevin remembers that Collier would carry his guitar case whenever he went out, whether he was going to play or not, just so people would know he was a musician and not some street black commuting from Harlem. Terry and David sang together as a team, the first professional dates David played as a duo (not counting his sibling partnership with Ethan).

After I moved in with Kevin, I dragged Terry Collier home. Then we both dragged girls home until there were five of us living there. Terry was a slightly rotund, extremely talented young singer-songwriter. We met at the Bitter End, a new club that just opened on Bleecker Street. It used to called the Cock 'N Bull. It was on one of the Monday night hoots. Terry and I liked each other's style, more modern than folkie. We were folkies, but we were writing our own songs as well and we knew about jazz. We weren't folkie purists and we didn't want to be slick and commercial. We were into it. Terry impressed the shit out of me and I went up to him and said, "Hey, man, you're really good." He felt the same way about me. We started learning each other's tunes and trying to sing with each other and it worked. We became an item at those Monday night sessions: David Crosby and Terry Collier, Terry Collier and David Crosby. The only problem was that there was some weird feeling from some people because one of us was white and one of us was black. That was still a novelty. We were generally well regarded and I like to think that if we had continued together we probably would have gotten a recording contract. We had a definite thing happening. He didn't come with us when we went south and the next time I saw him, years later, he was playing in a club on the South Side of Chicago, where he had obviously acquired a large following of devoted fans. They loved him. I don't know if he ever recorded because I lost track of him after that.

KEVIN RYAN: *David's a rebroadcaster—a modulator—takes the energy, modulates it, beams it back, all subconscious. I was exhausted from working a day job and a night job and years of fighting custody battles with my ex-wife and David wanted to leave New York. It had been a very cold winter and he wanted someone to travel with. We got along well and he didn't like to be alone; he never has. We had two directions to go: Boulder, Colorado, because we knew people there like Judy Collins, who could help us find gigs around Boulder and Denver, and Coconut Grove, Florida, where a lot of other friends [Vince Martin, Fred Neil, Lisa Kindred] had all gone. We were going to flip a coin, but Vince showed up; he and Fred and Lisa probably sold us on going south. We traveled by Greyhound. To this day I'll never again be on a Greyhound bus with David Crosby. He's the world's worst traveling companion. I've been on long bus trips since then, but that was the first long bus trip of my life. We were on the Jersey Turnpike and David was saying things like "God, aren't we there yet?"*

The bus ride south is recalled by David for other reasons. It was a time when public facilities like bus stations in the South were being desegregated. Once they were south of Washington, D.C., they could see the WHITE ONLY and COLORED TO THE REAR signs coming down, fresh paint over the old color bars. When David and Kevin arrived in Coconut Grove, it was a sleepy bohemian enclave, a suburb of Miami, with the classic preconditions for the new lifestyle: low rents and a tolerant and congenial local population. Like Provincetown, Aspen, Big Sur, Venice, Old Town in Chicago, Gaslight Square in St. Louis, Greenwich Village, and San Francisco's North Beach, it was a perfect place for folksingers, poets, ex-beatniks, coffeehouses, novice impresarios, sandal makers, and entrepreneurs. This was a climate in which marijuana and folk art could flourish. When David and Kevin arrived, they checked in with Vince Martin, who found them a place to live with a couple of friends of his, Bobby and Karen Ingram. David made the discovery that Bobby and Karen smoked weed:

KEVIN RYAN: *He came and woke me up in the middle of the night and whispered, "You know what? Bobby and Karen are heads!" I said, "What? You're kidding." Because it was like smoking dope was really illegal and everything. Well, this was just the beginning, since in the next several years dope became more and more what everyone did and that was the time of "Each one teach one" and we became kind of the Johnny Appleseeds of weed at this point because the more uptight people we met, the more people we turned on. It was a time when you wanted to turn everyone on.*

It wasn't until a decade later, when the demand outstripped the supply for the first time in history, that the old heads finally realized that the problem with turning everyone on to grass meant that sooner or later there wouldn't be enough to go around and, worse yet, the price would go higher and higher. When David started in 1960, it was the era of the nickel bag of weed (a quarter of an ounce, more or less, for five dollars) and the hundred-dollar kilo (2.2 pounds), reducible to fifty or sixty dollars if purchased in bulk.

Bobby Ingram was a New York kid from Brooklyn who had come out of the U.S. Navy, where he served on submarines. After his discharge, he worked as a merchant seaman on tankers to the South. His family moved to Miami and Bobby wandered into a club and met Vince Martin, who was singing and accompanying himself on guitar. Ingram's father had been a guitar player in the big band era and Bobby fancied the instrument and sang some himself. Ingram, Martin, and a partner named Al Mammot opened a place of their own for the new music.

BOBBY INGRAM: *We had put together the first coffeehouse in Miami and I was singing in a bar called the Gold Dust Lounge up across the street from the old Playboy Club up on 79th Street in Miami. We called our club the Coffee House and when it opened we all started playing in these joints and a scene developed. In Fort Lauderdale there was a place called the Cafe Catacombs. I was working there and met Lisa Kindred. She was playing the first twelve-string guitar I'd ever seen and she was the first one that ever mentioned David's name. She had just come down from the Village and she got it into her head that Crosby and I were supposed to meet and do some singing. Then this guy came to town, wearing one of these Harry Belafonte shirts, with a wide black belt and jeans and everything, a cocky little kid, eyeballing all the girls, including mine—ogling my old lady. But we got on anyway because we were both playing nylon string guitars and somehow we got into jamming that night. We had a real easy vocal thing, a harmony we later described as "formation flying," it was that close.*

We had the Coffee House and a place opened around the corner called the Cafe Trivia. Some of us used to work double gigs. We were making ten bucks a night, so to double our income we'd work another club. If you could time it right, you could play two clubs at once. That was all patterned after what was going on in the Village at the time. Tommy Rush was coming down from Boston, Lisa from New York. The following year Buffy Sainte-Marie showed up. Fred Neil played there all the time, Vince Martin was a local boy and a regular, and Cass Elliot came through. Crosby would be onstage with his nylon string guitar, saying, "I'm really not a folksinger, I really want to be a rock 'n' roll singer," and going into some Ray Charles song. And singing songs like "Summertime" and writing—he was beginning to write songs. David was a hyper young kid and he knew Bud and Travis. That was heavy, knowing someone who had a record. He also knew Bob Gibson and that was heavy 'cause Gibson had made records. There was a string of girls that would pass through our lives on David's side of the fence, lots of them. He rented a little garret on 17th Avenue where there was no air and within a couple of nights after we met him we were hanging out like we knew each other for years. We used to go to a place called Dean's Waffle Shop late at night on Coral Way. We always had so much energy—play a gig, keep the joint open until 4 A.M., jam and entertain ourselves, no one else in the clubs but a few of us. Then go to Dean's or the Trio Diner and one night David made a gesture and I made a gesture and we both flashed on the fact that we smoked reefer. He had this bag of incredibly bad pot he brought down from the Village. It was the worst reefer ever. We sat around for days, trying to get high on this stuff, positive that the next joint was going to do it, but it never happened. I think it was the first and last time David ever had any bad pot. That was 1962.

That winter and the following spring David played and sang all over south Florida: solo, with Bob Ingram, another singer named Mike Clough, and with Ethan, who came down from

California when he heard about the folk scene in Coconut Grove. Miami was the southern corner of the established folk circuit, which now included clubs and coffeehouses all over the country. In every city and in most college communities there was a place where folkies could play, usually for ten dollars a night. The places were all the same, whether they were in Ann Arbor, Madison, Austin, Berkeley, St. Louis, or Colorado Springs. They all had quaint and whimsical names, inspired by J. R. R. Tolkien, Chaucer, Kerouac, Sartre, or Camus. All decorated and staffed with an air of beatnik nihilism: Tiffany lamps, round oak tables, mismatched chairs, beautiful contemptuous waitresses with long hair and black tights, a small raised stage with an underpowered spotlight and sound system, and minimalist dressing rooms off the kitchen and toilets. The musicians carried their own instruments (guitar, bass, banjo, zither, or autoharp), provided their own transportation, and made their own living arrangements. The booking and audition process was simple word of mouth. If the club owner hadn't heard of you, you could always do a twenty-minute "guest set" of your best material and hope. Performers had their own grapevine, providing constant updates on what clubs treated you right, which owners were scumbags, whose check you had to cash right away, where you should insist on being paid in cash, and the name of the local connection (if any) for grass and pills. In all, a happy time for rootless vagabond folkies. David's obsession with sex earned him the nickname Old Tripod.

I don't remember it quite that way. I liked women. What else can I say? It was incredibly easy to open joints in those days. I'll explain about coffeehouses. Bobby Ingram had a jar of Dexedrine and he and I used to pop one of those little suckers and ride it until it was time to pop another one. We could invent a coffeehouse right there. We didn't have business permits and licenses and all that. It was fabulously simple because we could open clubs overnight.

BOBBY INGRAM: *We opened the Coffee House, then the Trivia opened around the corner, then Larry Marks opened the Catacombs in Lauderdale, then the other guy opened up the Cafe Pegasus. I played at the Pegasus with George Carlin. David and Ethan played at the Catacombs a lot. I remember Carlin getting up onstage one night with an ampoule of amyl nitrate and explaining to the audience what it was. [A vasodilator whose medical purpose is treatment of angina; known as "poppers," amyl nitrate was used for the sensation of a suddenly increased blood supply to the brain—the "rush." Used as an adjunct to orgasm or any other high.] Carlin cracked the thing and then squeezed it, took a hit, and offered it to anyone in the audience. Some guy came out of the back of the room and took a big ol' whiff, walked back into the audience, and said, "This ain't shit . . . Whooooooaaaahhhhhhh!" and he lets out this howl. Carlin would get up there with a book and he'd flip through it—it was a book of his stuff—and say, "Nah. I did that one last night." Then he'd do his raps. That was an amazing year—1962—because about three years of life were squeezed into it.*

That's because we didn't go to sleep the whole year. We were just awake a lot more. Kevin was working at his trip, we were singing, and Kevin got some of my early sets on tape and made some demos that are still around somewhere. When we got there, it was heaven. This was Coconut Grove before anybody but the gay people discovered it. We were the prototype hippies before anybody even knew there were hippies. On a typical day we would get up late, goof off, amble or ride our bikes down to the Grove Pharmacy, which had a little restaurant in it. We would all hang out there, drinking iced coffee, making interesting patterns in the coffee with milk. I came down there with some weed that I had scored in the Village, so I could be the big man around town, and it was no more weed than I'm the London Bridge. It was just green vegetable matter, bearing no resemblance to anything that would get you high. At first there was only one little coffeehouse down there and another one up in Fort Lauderdale. Every night the bill would be all of us. In the afternoons we'd play guitar and chase each other around. After work we could get the sailboats from the sailboat rental concession and take some joints and go out and cruise around Biscayne Bay, higher than kites, singing, baying at the moon, and sailing. We'd go to a place called Fair Isle and go skinny-dipping at night. It's all commercial now: T-shirt shops and boutiques and bars, but back then, it was us on bikes, whizzing through this beautiful jasmine-scented night in love with life, smoking pot, happier than clams. Sailing boats and writing songs and feeling like we were just on top of the world because it was still a real town. There were hardware stores on the main drag. No cookie stores. You could get your shoes fixed. You could buy a hammer and nails. The Laundromat was where a hotel is now and you could do all your clothes for fifty cents. It was a great, great time in my life.

ETHAN CROSBY: *David took off with Bud and Travis and ended up in Miami in 1962. I don't know how he got there, but he sent me a record, a pressing of some of his songs, and it blew my mind. I called and said, "Hey, do you want a bass player?" My brother said, "Sure," so I packed up my whole scene and moved into my Volkswagen bus with my dog and my bass and went to Miami in January and joined forces with him and we played all around Coconut Grove, Miami, Fort Lauderdale. It was a magic time in the area. There was a real energy rush at that point. Mike Clough and Bob Ingram were playing with us and Cass Elliot turned us on to a club in Omaha called the Third Man and we called up and got the gig. David and me and Mike Clough took off in my Volks bus and Mike Clough's little TR3 and got there and there was a trip that went down with the ladies.*

As was customary when moving to a new location with no guarantee of friends or companions, the group encouraged a few lady friends to follow; in this case, the girls were hovering around the age of consent and their parents were not pleased to see their newly emancipated daughters following a quartet of scruffy folksingers into the American heartland. This wasn't common behavior yet, although in later years the institution of groupies would become a well-chronicled sidebar to the rock 'n' roll lifestyle. In Omaha, Nebraska,

David wasn't particularly happy to see the ladies show up at the gig.

ETHAN CROSBY: *These two ladies jumped in a hot little Corvette and followed us from Florida up to Omaha. One of the girls had wealthy parents and they were not cool about their little girl running away a few thousand miles. So when she made the sad mistake of calling them to let them know that she was okay, they snookered her and said, "We'll send you some money. Where are you?" She told them where she was, which was where we were too. A few hours later, the heat walked into the hotel room and busted us. Her parents were waiting at the plane at the Omaha airport when the cops delivered her.*

The misadventure with the police led to an angry father threatening to prosecute the itinerant musicians for violating the Mann White Slave Traffic Act (which prohibits the transportation of women across state lines for immoral purposes). It wasn't the only drawback to the Omaha date. What happened was enough to make a young folksinger start to hate the cops.

ETHAN CROSBY: *In fact, the cops stole David's guitar. Flat-out stole it, which I know because I filed an insurance claim on it, since after they rousted us and everything, it turned up missing. The insurance company traced it to the police department, only they didn't have any knowledge of it. Then, a year or so later, I think, it even turned up at a pawn shop. I finally got the insurance company to pay off on it. We stayed in Omaha and worked in various configurations and while we were doing that we ran into other people: Chicago John Brown, Buffy Sainte-Marie, folks like that. But the end of Omaha was when David and I had a major hassle and we all split up and I came west with Mike Clough.*

The Denver heat were a lot different from the New York cops I had gotten to know. They certainly were a lot different from Pops. New York cops know how to get along with you. They have to—they live out on the street right alongside of you. They have to work it out, on foot, face-to-face. Denver, L.A., places like that, the cops drive around in their cars all the time, hardly ever get out except to settle a beef or write a ticket. So when they're out there, separated from their radios and shotguns and paperwork, they're a little nervous and that's scary for the rest of us. New York, they walk around, they got all this crap hanging from their belts, everyone can see they're not supermen or storm troopers, just guys trying to do a shitty job. Anyway, after Denver, Ethan went west and I went up to Chicago.

In Chicago, David stayed on Wells Street with John Brown and played at folk clubs in the nearby Old Town section. Brown, in addition to folksinging, would eventually own a leather shop in Piper's Alley called Ecclesiastical Footwear, so named because the major new fashion footwear for folkies was the leather sandal, similar to those worn by monastic monks. Without possessing the skill or training for bootmaking and shoemaking, any competent craftsperson in the sixties could open a leather sandal shop. In fact, most of them did. Chicago was a great place to hear music of all kinds, especially black music. It filled such places as the Club De-Liza, where Willie Dixon and the Chicago Blues All Stars played, and the Sutherland Lounge, where Miles Davis was working regularly. Buddy Guy and Junior Wells were playing Chicago blues, along with such legends as Howlin' Wolf and Muddy Waters. The folk scene was represented by clubs like the Fickle Pickle, the Gate of Horn, Old Town North, Mother Blues, and the Quiet Knight. White musicians like Paul Butterfield and Michael Bloomfield were already hanging around Maxwell Street on Sunday mornings, swallowing great chunks of street music, gorging on the feast of blues. It was a time before racial tensions escalated and well-dressed whites could go to black clubs without provoking confrontations over "slumming" and "ripping off the culture." Dressing well was interpreted as showing respect for the clubs and cafes and suitably attired whites might even be seated down front, where they could soak up the jazz that poured off the cramped stages into the appreciative rooms. On the predominantly black South Side, the Tivoli and the Regal theaters had live stage shows featuring the likes of Count Basie and

Lambert, Hendricks, and Ross. And, to top it all off, on Ontario and Wabash, Bob Dylan was sitting in at a hip club called the Bear.

A skinny Englishman with a big nose and a taste for Chicago-style folk and blues found his way into David's company; it was Clem Floyd, another singer and a fellow doper. Together they bopped around the city, cruising the bars and lounges between their jobs, two more in the happy audiences who heard the jazz greats. It's not reported what he wore at night, but a few years later David would get John Brown to make him a leather cape, the first of a long line of exotic clothing and accessories. Clem would go to Los Angeles, marry one of the Babitz sisters (Mirandi), and open a leather shop of his own on the Sunset Strip. Clem and David played for a while as a duo, then linked with Lydia Wood, a talented singer-songwriter who wrote "Anathea," one of the prettiest tunes in David's solo repertoire.

I was particularly influenced by the likes of John Coltrane, Elvin Jones, and McCoy Tyner, all of whom were playing in and around Chicago. I knew that Coltrane was a heavy because someone had turned me onto "My Favorite Things" and my mind was boggled. Clem and I learned that Coltrane was playing in Chicago, so we went to see him: Me, Clem, and this tiny German hooker who was called the Duchess. That was her name. She was knee-high to a grasshopper with giant tits. She was blonde and German and the blacks loved her, especially the dealer-pimp guys on the South Side of Chicago. She was the one who took us down there, to a club called McKey's, which was at 163rd and Cottage Grove, which I can say is very far down. Very far. We were absolutely, I swear to you on my word of honor, the only three white people in there. Duchess just snapped her fingers and we had a table. We had taken every drug we could get our hands on, smoked our brains out, so I was very high and a little bit drunk when they started to play. John Coltrane's band at that time was Coltrane on saxaphone, McCoy Tyner on piano, Elvin Jones on drums—a drummer of monumental power—and Jimmy Garrison and Reggie Workman, both playing bass. This was the ultimate acoustic jazz band. They took jazz as far as you can take it acoustically. The only place left to go when these guys got through was to electrify the band. They wrung, wrang, forced, demanded out of their instruments every single thing that acoustic instruments could deliver under any circumstances known to the human mind. They were the best. Unquestionably, absolutely, totally miles ahead of Horace Silver and Cannonball Adderley and everybody else in the world at that time. In my humble opinion. Bad.

The way they'd play a song was they would start out all together, very unified, playing a jazz tune. One song was a set, and a set was one song. After a while, they'd take it and start to fuck with it, individually expressing themselves, Coltrane first. Coltrane would rip your head to shreds and then go off the stage. When he walked off the stage this particular night, on this particular song, he didn't stop playing. He just walked off into the distance. Then it was McCoy Tyner's turn. McCoy Tyner would rip your head to shreds for a while. One of the best keyboard players ever, from whom I learned a great deal about chord structure. An enormous influence on me because he had to play an open-ended kind of ninth, seventh, thirteenth kind of chords, just to make enough room for Coltrane, who wouldn't stick to a normal mode. Coltrane was going to take that melody wherever he wanted to take it and you had to play open-ended kind of chords to be able to create a frame of reference that would be right for Coltrane. So McCoy Tyner finished. Then it was Elvin's turn. Now, Elvin Jones was probably one of the most powerful drummers I ever heard. He played with an intensity and a force and a sureness that was physical, palpable. When he started to get into it, he made me stand up out of my chair and back up. He drove me back from that table, into the aisle, and all the way to the back of the room by the sheer force of what he was playing. I realized I was at the back of the room when my spine bumped into the back wall. I went into the men's room because I couldn't handle the intensity. I was leaning my head against the cool vomit-green tile and drawing deep breaths, trying to calm down, when the door went *wham!* and in walks John Coltrane, still playing at top intensity and volume, totally into it. He blew me out so bad I slid down the wall. The guy was still playing his solo. He hadn't stopped. I don't think he ever knew that I was in that room. He never saw that little ofay kid in the corner, you know, but he totally turned my mind to Jell-O at that point and that was my John Coltrane experience.

Clem and David and Lydia Wood started south for the winter, driving in a 1958 Chevrolet Impala. Clem had scored some Acapulco Gold, the first of the premium imported varietals of grass, and it was the first time David ever smoked the Good Stuff. The Duchess stayed in Chicago to make her fortune. In Florida, they played some more around Coconut Grove and David demonstrated surprising generosity to Bobby Ingram. Ingram and Karen had gotten truly married with prototypical post-beatnik and pre-hippie casualness.

BOBBY INGRAM: *Karen woke me up one morning and said, "We're getting married." I said, "Okay, we'll get married." David, Kevin Ryan, and Lisa Kindred were at the wedding and we went back to the Coffee House that night to work. People asked, "What'd you do today?" and I said, "We got married." My father gave us some little piece of property up in Lake George, New York, for our wedding and suggested that we check it out. We didn't think we could, since we didn't have much of anything, but Dave came up and he says, "I got an old bank account in some bank in the Village and here's a check for a hundred bucks." We never did get up to Lake George. We got as far as the Village and never got out of the Village until we ran out of money. Karen and I got back to Miami on the hundred dollars that Crosby gave me.*

In the summer, Miami was a sinkhole of sweat and inactivity. David migrated west and north, back to San Francisco. As usual, there were some familiar faces on the scene, which was then on Upper Grant Avenue in North Beach. Howard Hesseman worked as a bartender, manager, and booker at a local club, the Coffee Gallery. Now a well-known film and television actor, he was then one of the few pacifist barkeeps in North Beach. Most bartenders keep a sawed-off pool cue or a baseball bat under the bar to regain control if things get out of hand. Hesseman, at the beginning of every shift, would place a shotglass full of strong pepper every two feet under the bar. If a rowdy drunk or heckler would threaten the peace, a shotglass full of cayenne would make them manageable enough to move out the door onto the street without resorting to heavy bouncing. As a favor to performers passing through, Hesseman could find grass for wandering troubadours like Crosby and Dino Valenti, who was playing the Bay Area folk circuit at the same time. Twenty-five years later, both Hesseman and Crosby would be celebrating each other's sobriety. Hugh Romney was living in San Francisco, first experimenting with the psychedelics that would eventually cause him to change his name to Wavy Gravy and become the leading clown-philosopher-philanthropist of the counterculture. He produced *The Phantom Cabaret,* an evening of avant-garde theater that began in New York with the first presentation of Tiny Tim at the Living Theater. In San Francisco, Romney presented an evening with Sandy Bull at the Coffee Gallery and again at the Committee—an evening concert distinguished by Romney's appearance in his "meat suit." The "meat suit" was actually an old sport coat covered with cold cuts: salami, bologna, pastrami, and the like, all laboriously pinned and sewn in place by this author, who was a stage manager at the famed North Beach improvisational cabaret theater. It was there that David found the concept of "meat suit" an apt metaphor for the physical self outside the mind.

Dino Valenti offered David a place to stay in Marin County, just across the Golden Gate Bridge in Sausalito. There, along the waterfront, was a long-scuttled Oakland ferryboat called the *Charles Van Dam.* Big enough to hold crowds of commuters and their cars, it was beached and became home to Valenti, Crosby, and a horde of assorted runaways, waitresses, folkies, and local schoolgirls fascinated by the new music and the bizarre folk who made it. Valenti affected black capes and a speed freak's machismo and deserves a story of his own: raised as a carny's kid on the midway, his parents ran girlie shows. His childhood was spent in tent shows, fleecing rubes who wanted to see naked flesh; his tutors were the carny strippers. He learned guitar from his father, served in the Air Force, and hit Greenwich Village in 1960. His guitar style was overpoweringly aggres-

sive and in his Village days he would never walk anywhere;
he would stride. In those innocent years, he would carry
ampoules of injectable methamphetamine in the broad
leather wristband of his watch in plain sight.

Dino was also responsible for writing a gentle and beautiful anthem, the song "Get Together," which became an
enormous hit for other artists, for which he was paid next to
nothing. He recalls David's voice as "angelic" and spent
many nights trading chords and writing songs with Crosby
when they should both have been asleep. Dino's other name
is Chester Powers, but to anyone who ever saw his performances, Dino Valenti is his real name. Recent brain surgery
removed a fistula of knotted veins that his surgeons told him
were normally found only in autopsies of serial killers or the
institutionalized insane. Living more or less quietly in Marin
(he still drives a characteristic black Harley-Davidson), Dino
is still writing and performing music and assures us he's no
longer a sociopath.

Staying one jump ahead of bad weather, David left
Northern California in the fall and headed for Los Angeles
to Venice, where he would share a house near Venice Beach
with David Freiberg, Ginger Jackson, Paul Kantner, Sherry
Snow, and Steven Shuster. Living communally, they kept
money in a jar on the mantelpiece. Each put in what he or
she earned and each took out what he or she needed. They
were contemporary communards and in that time it worked.
The intense closeness and interdependency of the lifestyle
would later be labeled "hippie," but at the time it was uncat-
egorized. Heinlein's *Stranger in a Strange Land* had a lot to
do with it—everyone was reading the book, many took it as
a blueprint for a new age, and the concept of bonding with
unrelated like-minded people as "water brothers" was not
only intriguing, it gave people a mutual trust in each other.
You had to be there.

After the time I lived with Dino in Sausalito, David Freiberg
and I hitchhiked down the coast to Venice and when we did that, I
wound up alone at some kind of lodge, tourist cabins, something
like that. The guy hired me to sing there that weekend, but it was
still only Tuesday. Still, he was going to pay me seventy-five
bucks, which would've paid for my bus fare to L.A., and he gave
me one of his little empty cabins to sleep in. So I started sitting

on the front porch of the cabin playing my guitar. Well, a couple of hippies pulled into the parking lot, wandered over, and a couple more, and a couple more. Pretty soon there was a crowd of hippies. The guy says, "No no no—you're scaring off the tourists!" He paid me twenty-five bucks just to go away. It was the only time anybody ever paid me not to sing. But he did, so I didn't, and the people who gave me a ride up to Monterey with my twenty-five easily earned dollars—with which I bought my bus ticket to L.A.—were some hippies in an old mail van and one of them was Michael Clarke and he had a conga drum. Standard hippie gear, only this was before anybody was calling them hippies. They were still beatniks. Jack Kerouac stuff. And that's how I met Michael Clarke.

Paul Kantner is a little younger than David, but he was hanging out in California at the same time, with many of the same interests. It's no wonder they eventually spent time side by side and was probably inevitable that they would later become good friends and write music together. Kantner went on to become a founding member (with Marty Balin) of the San Francisco-based group Jefferson Airplane. Grace Slick was lead vocalist.

PAUL KANTNER: *We used to run a coffeehouse down in San Jose when I was in college and David came through there. God knows how he found out about it. Him and Dino Valenti and people like that would come up from L.A. and locally we would get Malvina Reynolds and Jesse Fuller and the New Lost City Ramblers, a whole range of sort-of-folk acts. This was in a small coffeehouse, with a music store in the place, selling strings and dope under the counter. Marijuana. Nothing else. I still have David's guitar strap. It has BIG FOLK GUITAR STRAP written on it. He might be interested in getting that back someday. David, Dino, Travis Edmonson, Hoyt Axton. Original rock 'n' roll demons before rock 'n' roll even existed. I didn't know that crowd other than as an observer. I wasn't a fan, just somebody who went and saw music. We went to Los Angeles and moved down to Venice Beach with the idea of becoming stars in the folk world at the*

Troubadour or something like that. But we spent all our time on the beach, smoking dope.

GRACE SLICK: *I don't know exactly where it was, but my first impression of David was I had never seen anybody who had that much interest and joy and spontaneous reaction. He was like a child in his willingness to put his feet into it, into everything. He would react to a carving of a boat or a whale or a girl's body or something that somebody had made or music or carpentry or whatever with this joy. You didn't even have to look at what the object was, you could just look at his face and be delighted because there was a human being getting that childlike excitement out of stuff. He did that continuously!*

In the meanwhile, Ethan and Mike Clough had stuck it out together and had landed a job in a slicker, more commercial folk group than David or any of the other purists ever envisioned. It was called the Les Baxter Balladeers and it was a natural outgrowth of what was happening in folk music. If the Kingston Trio was bigger than Bud and Travis and Bud and Travis sold more than Hoyt Axton, then what about four singers in one group? Or five? Or ten? Thus were the New Christy Minstrels and the Back Porch Majority and the New Lost City Ramblers born. (In all fairness, it should be noted that acoustic groups are as old as country music; the Carter Family and Bill Monroe and the Bluegrass Boys proved that very early on.)

BOBBY INGRAM: *The lines were drawn between commercial and ethnic folk. I remember we recorded a track one time and Les Baxter dubbed drums on it. I was furious. One didn't use drums. And he had—he was an ethno-musicologist. He knew everything there was to know. We used to go see Olatunji at the Troubadour and Les could tell you, "That's West African. That's Nairobian. That's from Uganda." He knew that stuff. My mother, who was a dancer and a friend of Sally Rand [a legendary stripper of the thirties], brought Sally to hear us one night at the Ice House in Pasadena. Sally came back to the dressing room, a flashy old broad, and she says, "You aren't folk-*

singers." *She told us straight away.* *"You guys aren't folksingers."* *We said, "What the hell do you know?"* *Turns out she was raised in Appalachia someplace. She said, "You didn't do any play party songs. You didn't do any quilting songs. You didn't do any reels." And she gave this whole litany of all the stuff that we didn't do. We weren't folksingers. Well, shit, we knew we weren't folksingers.*

ETHAN CROSBY: *Doug Weston of the Troubadour introduced us to Les Baxter. He auditioned us and hired us on the spot and less than two weeks later we opened with this terrible group at the Desert Inn in Las Vegas! We were wearing scarlet bellboy jackets and faggot boots and doing the whole number and Vegas is the sleaziest place I have ever been. We played that gig for what seemed like a month and came back to L.A., played a few gigs, and did a TV show called "The Lively Ones." Finally I went to Les and said, "Look, man, this really sucks. I have a suggestion. Fire everybody but me and Mike and hire my scuzzbutt kid brother who sings good and this guy from Miami named Bob Ingram and we'll have a real group."*

BOBBY INGRAM: *So I went out to L.A. I had never been west in my life and David met me at the airport and took me around to give me the grand tour, the reverse of what I did in Miami with him, when I gave him the Miami tour. I got out to L.A. and he gave me the L.A. tour, showing me the Capitol Records building. He had a place with Dino Valenti up in Laurel Canyon. And Dino would go and throw up every half hour or something and I couldn't understand what was going on, but as soon as I got to town we started rehearsing intensely and were supposed to go on "The Andy Williams Show." Immediately! I thought that was the way L.A. worked—you're in a band, go out there, go on television. They made us wear these red jackets with no collars, until I discovered that the bellhop at the Beverly Wilshire Hotel was wearing the same jacket. So I went into the William Morris Agency and raised hell. So we had two jackets: red ones and gold ones. And we hated them. But Les somehow got us a gig at the Ice*

House, where Glen Campbell was doing Wednesday nights. We were given a record deal with Reprise. I have the only copy.

ETHAN CROSBY: *It was a hot little group and we got hired by Jack Linkletter to go out on tour. Jack was doing the "Hootenanny" show on television and he took advantage of his exposure and took this tour out. Jack and I had gone to Emerson Junior High School together years before. We were the Jack Linkletter Folk Caravan, with Joe and Eddie and their guitar player; the Big Three, which was Cass Elliot; Tim Rose; and Jim Hendricks, also known as Not the Black Guitar Player. Same name, totally different guy. White. Then there was a single lady singer named Rawn McKinnon and us New Balladeers. We did thirty one-nighters on a lousy bus; it was a grim trip. And it wasn't a custom bus or anything like that, just a lot of seats and our instruments and some stage equipment and stuff. What everyone wanted was the bench seat in the back where you could lie down and get some sleep. You'd kill for that. Cass was flaked out back there once and the bus hit a big bump and it literally picked her up and dropped her on the floor. Boom! We thought someone had shot the bus. It was a crazy tour.*

BOBBY INGRAM: *We played in Sacramento at the State Fair with Peg-Leg Bates [a one-legged tap dancer]. We started the tour in Sioux Falls, South Dakota. We'd do things like play Minneapolis-St. Paul, get on the bus, drive all night and the next day, and perform the next night in St. Louis, Missouri. I remember we were doing Fred Neil's songs, so we were always talking about Freddy. Joe and Eddie, being black, were fascinated with some of these songs, which they figured were written by a black man, only we never let on that Freddy was white. We wound up in Baltimore and our next date was in Trenton and then New York, where we were scheduled to do "The Tonight Show" with Johnny Carson. Only it didn't work out that way at all.*

ETHAN CROSBY: *David and I were having breakfast when Eddie [of Joe and Eddie] came into the restaurant. That black man was so pale he was white when he said, "They just shot Kennedy." On the ride up to Trenton on the bus everybody was listening to the radio, wondering what's happening, and Trenton was canceled, thank God, but the next night we were supposed to play the RKO Keith in Flushing, New York, and we couldn't get out of it.*

BOBBY INGRAM: *President Kennedy was assassinated in Dallas and all I can remember thinking was "Boy, there goes the Carson show."*

I was in a restaurant when somebody ran in and blurted out the news that someone had shot the President. The rest of the day, everywhere you went people were grief-stricken, standing around listening to radios and looking at each other with this lost "What are we going to do now?" look. It hadn't really occurred to anyone that this could happen. The country wasn't ready for it. We all had a guy in whom we believed—right, wrong, or different. That was the real magic of John Kennedy, that we believed in him. We found out later he was no saint in his soul, but neither is anyone else. I felt he was more sincere and more equipped with values and brighter—much brighter—than the average politician. He had his own money, so he didn't have to make as many compromises as most guys in that seat have to and want to. It's a power broker's seat and most guys who sit in it are there to broker power and money. They look on the presidency as a figurehead spot, the hood ornament of the country. When Kennedy got shot, the country was less sophisticated and more naïve than it is now. We hadn't gone through the introspection and divisiveness and pain that Vietnam cost us. We hadn't been disillusioned the way we are now, so the people, from top to bottom, were in shock. When we got on the bus and went to try and play someplace, we didn't want to play and they didn't want to hear it.

ETHAN CROSBY: *Cass Elliot cried all the way to New York City. It was truly the end of the line. The day after the President was assassinated, we played four shows: two matinees and two evening perfor-*

mances with Walt Disney's Incredible Journey *at the RKO Keith in Flushing and for all four shows maybe sixty people turned up. Just our friends. Fred Neil and a bunch of the local crazies.*

BOBBY INGRAM: *We introduced Joe and Eddie to Fred Neil and they were quite astounded to see that the guy that wrote all these great blues tunes had freckles. They never knew he was white. Fred and Vince Martin were playing at the old Provincetown Playhouse, but that was it. The tour was over. It really ended with a whimper.*

FOUR

· · · · · · · · · · · · · · · · · · ·

Back in Los Angeles, David rejoined the California folk circuit. As 1963 turned into 1964, the country got used to having Lyndon Johnson in the White House and the top chart hits were things like "There I've Said It Again" by Bobby Vinton, "You Don't Own Me" by Lesley Gore, "Louie Louie" by the Kingsmen, and "Surfin' Bird" by the Trashmen. Spring changed all that; the *Billboard* number one hits that followed Bobby Vinton were all by the Beatles. For fourteen weeks, "I Want to Hold Your Hand," "She Loves You," and "Can't Buy Me Love" stayed on top. (In May, Louis Armstrong's version of "Hello Dolly" took over.) The new music clubs in Los Angeles stuck together in the same neighborhood, the same as in New York and San Francisco and Chicago. Folkies, beats, and jazz heads found themselves cruising an unincorporated patch of Los Angeles County that sat squarely in the middle of the upwardly mobile West Side. Known then as "the Strip" and "Boys' Town," in the eighties the area became incorporated as the city of West Hollywood. It's bounded on the east by old Hollywood, on the north by the Hollywood Hills, on the south by the Wilshire District, and on the west by Beverly Hills. The Strip itself is Sunset Boulevard, which runs west through Beverly Hills on its way to the ocean.

The original rumor was that the wise guys who ran the

"victimless crimes" business in the twenties and thirties per-suaded civic and political interests that L.A. ought to have a well-situated zone of economic opportunity, free of bother-some zoning and loosely policed. The Strip was it. Within its boundaries were Schwab's Drug Store, the Garden of Allah Apartments, nightclubs like Ciro's and the Mocambo, and Preston Sturges's Players Club (now a Japanese restaurant and sushi bar). Clinging to the fringes are the Chateau Marmont Hotel and the steep wooded side streets that were once lined with the parked expensive cars of studio playboys and downtown businessmen. They were visiting the discreet brothels and gambling dens that studded the Hollywood Hills in Raymond Chandler's and Nathaniel West's film noir Los Angeles. In the early sixties, a lot of glamour left the Strip while smaller, more intimate clubs started to open. The area was lightly patrolled from a small brick substation of the Los Angeles County Sheriff's Office, while L.A.P.D. and Beverly Hills black-and-whites prowled the boundaries. A couple of adventurous brothers from the Bronx, Mutt and Herbie Cohen, opened the Unicorn. Mutt was a lawyer who eventually specialized in entertainment law, while Herb was a former merchant seaman with an entrepreneurial flair who went into personal management. Together they enjoyed suc-cess and practiced a kind of hard-nosed hipster aesthetic. Herb began with a club in the depraved heart of Hollywood called Cosmo's Alley and moved west to the Strip to capital-ize on the growing music scene there. Doug Weston was run-ning the Troubadour. Jim Dickson was a local jazz buff and recording engineer. Eddie Tickner was an accountant who did the books for the fledgling enterprises. Benny Shapiro was a rootless New Yorker who came west to get in on the action and wound up managing the Cafe Renaissance.

JIM DICKSON: *I met maybe two hundred people in Hollywood, proba-bly all two hundred smoked dope in those days, including Lord Buckley. Everybody who got high knew each other then. When Herbie Cohen opened Cosmo's Alley, they decided they were in over their heads and they were going to get this slick guy from New York who knew it all, so they hired Benny Shapiro. He made a deal. Waitresses could only steal twenty dollars a night and the cashier could steal twenty-five. Benny took a hundred and people were stand-*

ing in line to see singers like Odetta and that's when I got interested in folk music.

Dickson had recorded the underground cult comedian Lord Buckley and had a solid jazz background; he worked on and off at World-Pacific Studios, a small progressive label that included artists like Miles Davis and Hampton Hawes. Dickson had recorded some of their folk artists and he was cruising the local clubs when he met David Crosby at the Unicorn between sets. There was still money to be made discovering new talent—a few years earlier, a couple of agents named Albert Grossman and Roy Silver had quit the agency business to become personal managers, signing a few new acts they found in Greenwich Village; together they signed an odd folksinger and a black comedian. When they split up their business shortly after, Roy says they flipped a coin and Albert got Bob Dylan while Roy got Bill Cosby.

JIM DICKSON: *I did an album with the Greenbriar Boys, which was sort of half-folk, half-country, a lot of it based on Rose Maddox, a little bit too hillbilly for the folk world, and then from that I went with the Dillards and somewhere in there I went into the Unicorn. They didn't have a stage because they didn't have an entertainment license, so you just sat at a table and played and David was sitting there, playing at a table. There was this young guy with this nice clear pretty voice and not a soul in the place paying any attention to him at all, just singing his heart out, being totally ignored by a crowd that was too hip. It was David Crosby. He showed a minor jazz influence, but in a crowd that was into Ornette Coleman it wasn't enough. I thought, "Gee, this guy would be great in a group. He's got the kind of voice that would really harmonize." So I went over and introduced myself to David.*

David knew me because I had recorded Dino Valenti and paid a hundred-dollar advance for a song called "Get Together." That was me and Eddie Tickner. It was our first song for the new publishing company we were starting because I was having trouble with folk music records. There'd be an original song or two and nobody wanted to publish them, since all they could do would be maybe a couple of thousand units and who gave a damn? The record company would say, "You can't put that song on unless it's published because we can't release it," so we just started the publishing company in the blind in order to do that. Dino needed the money for a car payment. He was about to lose it that day, so we gave him a hundred bucks for his song and that's how we started the publishing company.

"Get Together" became a monster hit when it was recorded by We Five in 1965 and twice again, in versions by Jesse Colin Young and the Youngbloods, in 1967 and 1969; it was popularized as the theme song for the National Council of Christians and Jews! Dino never got much more money, but Tickson Music made a bundle. Albert Grossman had already persuaded Bob Dylan to publish his own songs. Dylan was the frontrunner of the Age of the Singer-Songwriter. Even the Beatles didn't own their own publishing when they started, but the handwriting was on the wall as well as on the new recording contracts; the poets who created the songs got to own their own copyrights and profit from their creations. It would make a difference measurable in many millions of dollars, most of them flowing back to the people who made the music in the first place.

JIM DICKSON: *David used to sing at the Troubadour hoots on Monday nights; whoever was running the hoot would always move David down the list until it would be almost closing time and there was no one in the place; that's when he'd go on. I was recording almost every folksinger at the Troubadour. I'd go over when the club closed and people would be looking for something to do. I had the key to the studio at World-Pacific and I could record anyone I liked. I took David into the studio. We had to use a stock of used tapes that they were too cheap to throw out and too nervous to use again. If you look at the Preflyte reels, you'll see green tape and brown tape and red tape with splices in the middle of it, every damn thing. Pretty soon David was storing his suitcase in my garage. He didn't live any-where. He could find people who would let him stay on the couch, but they wouldn't let him unpack his clothes. I had a house in Laurel Canyon and he'd come over and leave his suitcase; at that time I had better dope than he had. I'd get him high and we'd talk and he was convinced I was a genius. It was the dope.*

At the same time as David was couch-camping in and around Laurel Canyon, Roger McGuinn and Gene Clark were similarly hanging around on the Strip, playing hoots at the Troubadour, jamming together, trying to find a sound that they liked. McGuinn was fresh off the road playing behind the Limeliters and the Chad Mitchell Trio, Clark had just finished a Canadian tour with the New Christy Minstrels. Roger's first name was then Jim. (He changed it when he joined a small Moslem-oriented subsect called Subud, an affiliation that usually results in a name change.) Bob Gibson's partner Bobby Camp had become Hamilton Camp a year earlier. Hereafter, both McGuinn and Camp will be called by their current names. Gene Clark was one of twelve children from a farm in the Midwest who traveled west with his guitar, writing songs and playing where he could.

GENE CLARK: *One of the reasons that I hooked up with McGuinn, before David even came on the scene, was that Roger was singing Beatle songs and I was into that. The Beatles had broken in Canada and there was some stuff about them in magazines here and there, but it hadn't happened big in the States yet. Me and McGuinn both had acoustic twelve-string guitars and when I spotted him sitting over in the corner in the Troubadour, singing a Beatles song, I thought, "Man, this is the only guy I know out of this whole folk thing that's into the Beatles." Maybe Hoyt Axton, maybe Joe and Eddie and a couple of other people on the scene thought we had the right idea, but most people thought it was bullshit English rock stuff. Roger and I got together and started making up songs, singing as much harmony as the two of us could get in double leads. Roger says, "Let's be a duo. Let's do a Peter and Gordon or Chad and Jeremy kind of thing." I don't know if Chad and Jeremy were even out yet then, but Peter and Gordon were, so I said, "Great idea." We tried for a while and decided that our voices were in the same range; we needed another voice to make the thing really work. We had always liked the Limeliters and the Chad Mitchell Trio harmonies, so we went looking for another guy, wondering where we could find someone. One night we're sitting at a hootenanny at the Troubadour and this guy is onstage who comes on very arrogant and kind of like puts the audience down. I said, "Who is this guy?" Roger said, "I know him." He didn't want to talk about it. Then the guy sang and I was just blown away. I just said, "Man, is he good! That's it. You can't ask for any better than that." McGuinn said, "No, man. I know David. We tried to work together. It's impossible. It'll never work." They knew each other in Santa Barbara or something like that. I don't know whether someone went to David and told him, "Look, these guys are interested in talking to you," but we were singing one night and David just walked up and sat down beside us and started singing with us, kind of uninvited, certainly unannounced. It sounded great. Him and Roger went somewhere and talked for a while and within a day or two David was saying, "Hey, I'd really like to sing with you guys. I'd really like to be in your group," and Roger's saying, "Oh, man. I don't know." Eventually, David came to us with the proposition: he knew a guy named Dickson who had a studio. He would take us there and get something accomplished. We agreed it would be a good approach.*

JIM DICKSON: *David comes in and says, "I've found these two guys I want to sing with and if you get involved I can do it." He was putting the pieces together. He brought them into World-Pacific and made the very first audition tape I ever made of the three of them singing together. Because of the British Invasion thing that was happening, they're singing with these English accents. It's marvelous, really, and funny. But they had a sound. There's no question about it. The Byrds. Gene Clark and Roger McGuinn and David Crosby. All I knew was that I wanted a group because in folk music there never emerged a male lead vocalist who won. Dylan was out on the edges with a different kind of thing. Bob Gibson had just a little too much Chicago Dixieland bounce. There was no winner. There wasn't going to be one. Nobody in folk music could sing with the authority that winning pop singers had, so it had to be a group.*

Let me say this for the record: Roger McGuinn is a genius. Even when he was Jim McGuinn. Any McGuinn. Any McGuinn he wants to be. The man is an absolute heavyweight. I first met him when we were folkies. He was playing guitar behind the Limeliters, who had recruited him out of the Chicago Folk Institute, which was a folkie guitar player thing. I was impressed; he was hanging out with the heavies! Then time went by. We went our separate ways, played the circuits, and by the time we were back in Los Angeles, I was no accomplished musician or anything, but I knew a lot more than when I started. We met again in the little bar in the front of the Troubadour. This time he's with this guy from the New Christy Minstrels and the Christy Minstrels actually had a hit record.

Now here's a story of success gone wrong because as soon as the Minstrels had a hit, their management and their founding guy, Randy Sparks, trademarked or registered the name of the group and started cloning it. As many bookings as they had that overlapped, that's how many editions of the New Christy Minstrels there were. They'd hire folkies off the street, put them in the wardrobe, teach them the standard changes and arrangements, and send them out to wherever the act was booked. There were probably three or four sets of Christy Minstrels playing simultaneously and each audience was sure they were seeing the one, the only, the Original, blah-blah-blah. It was the grossest kind of abuse of the system and Gene Clark somehow had wound up in one of those units. But the important thing, the real deal, was that he was one of the few who had obviously listened to that first Beatle record, the same as me and Roger, and he had just as obviously said, "Hmmm, what is this?" And what the Fab Four did was just what I said, they took rock 'n' roll beats and instead of having the usual three-chord change, you know, they had put folk music kind of changes in them. They had relative minors and real music. Sure, they did "Twist and Shout" and that other stuff, but in the songs they wrote there were infinitely better chord changes and melodic content and, to top it all off, you could hear the influence of the incredible Everly Brothers.

At first the Beatles' lyrics were pretty much the same as any pop stuff. They weren't trying to get heavy. The noticeable difference was in the chord changes and progressions and I said, "Aha! I know where that is. I know how to do that." Gene and Roger were starting to do it already, singing these songs of Clark's. Roger was playing them and he could play that Beatle feel. Roger could cop anything from anyplace, except that he didn't do it like a copyist. He would take a thing and make it his own. That was the genius of it. He didn't just copy somebody; he'd take the essence of their idea and turn it into his idea. Synthesize something with something else and come out with something new. And he did it repeatedly. Y'see, I think that's the essence of creating new music because new music doesn't just appear out of thin air. People who say, "I created . . ." are bullshit. Everything has roots and new music comes from synthesis, from taking other elements, usually widely dissimilar elements, and pulling them together in relationship that maybe didn't exist before. Or at least not recently. I loved it. We started singing. Roger was playing and I started singing with them. Harmony. Which was something I could do, while neither of them was real good at it. We knew we had some stuff.

GENE CLARK: *It began where we were going to parties. I remember Ian and Sylvia being around at that time [Canadian folksingers Ian Tyson and Sylvia Fricker, also clients of Albert Grossman], the Modern Folk Quartet, people like that. They were hanging around and it had the vibe that "This is a cool thing." We went to a party one night somewhere in Laurel Canyon. We got there with our guitars and decided to sing for everybody and it was a monster success. Everyone loved it and it was like a folk in-crowd, all going crazy. After that we were a little bit of the center of focus among a certain crowd of people, like, "This is a happening little trip going on over here."*

We didn't have a formal agreement at first and Jim Dickson knew a lot more about show business than we did and an infinite amount more about the recording business because we knew nothing. Zip. Zero. Nada. Dickson was smart and besides that he had good weed. Dickson was a bright man and a controversial one and he knew an awful lot of people: Albert Grossman and Bob Dylan. Lenny Bruce. Lots of people in Hollywood. We were impressed because he had a demo of a couple of tunes of Dylan's that Dylan hadn't put on an album yet, one of which was "Tambourine Man." We were singing Gene Clark's songs and saying, "Hey, let's put a band together." Then one night we went to see *A Hard Day's Night* and I can remember coming out of that movie so jazzed that I was swinging around stop sign poles at arm's length. I knew right then what my life was going to be. I wanted to do that. That was It. I loved the attitude and the fun of it; there was sex, there was joy, there was everything I wanted out of life, right there. They were cool and we said, "Yeah, that's it. We have to be a band. Who can we get to play drums?"

I thought I could play bass, but we found out very quickly that I couldn't do that. Playing bass and singing at the same time is like being able to dial two telephones at once with both hands. All credit to Paul McCartney, I can't do it. I could, however, play rhythm guitar pretty well and sing. Dickson knew Chris Hillman, who was a mandolin player when we found him with his own bluegrass band called the Hillmen, and he was looking to find some way to grow. He wanted to expand and get farther along. I knew Michael Clarke from Big Sur, when I had hitchhiked and gotten paid for not playing. That was the band. For the next few months we worked almost every night with Dickson, who bribed us with cheeseburgers at the end of the session—never before. For most of us, the free food was a major enticement; we were all living on minimal budgets, hustling free places to sleep, finding low-rent pads, bumming meals from clubs that served food, where the waitresses liked us.

Most of the liaisons with waitresses were born out of man's two major drives, food and sex. A waitress who liked you might come home with you and if you didn't have a home she might have a place of her own that you could call home for a night. These same charitable goddesses of the night might even be persuaded to sneak a club sandwich out of the kitchen or make a "mistake" on an order to a straight customer—that way there'd be a leftover sandwich or fruit-and-cheese plate to ease the pangs of hunger of the ravenous, skinny folksinger in the small dressing room upstairs. Crosby was as thin then as he ever was, living on cold cereal in the morning and cheeseburgers at night; pictures taken during the early sixties show him with cheekbones that haven't been seen much since.

The band was: Roger McGuinn on lead guitar; Gene Clark, David Crosby, and McGuinn on vocals; David Crosby, rhythm guitar; Michael Clarke on drums; and former mandolin player Chris Hillman on bass. Despite their experience kicking around the folk circuit, they were far from a polished ensemble. Only Crosby, Clark, and McGuinn were playing their normal instruments. Clarke had played beatnik bongos and conga drum, but had no experience with conventional drumming. During the early rehearsals, he played with wire brushes on a cardboard box, since there was no money for new instruments. The experience of working with Dickson in a professional studio was invaluable to the early Byrds, however ill-equipped and inexperienced they were. In the compressed space of months in the summer of 1964, they were learning lessons that other bands would have to learn after the fact, on their own time and money. Working with Dickson, the Byrds learned without a contract, without experience, and without outside professional management and record company "advice."

The deal was that after they would get through doing their legitimate big-time jazz three-track recording, we could go in to World-Pacific. Sometimes it'd be in the middle of the afternoon, sometimes in the middle of the night. Whenever it was, we could go in as long as we cleaned up after ourselves. Under Dickson's wise and firm tutelage, we shaped ourselves into a band in a fifth of the time it took everybody else to do it. All the other bands had played together for years. We did years of work in that studio in only months, by playing and having to listen to it back. At first that was an awesomely painful experience. "No, we don't sound that bad, do we?" and "Oh God, no! Michael, you got to learn to play those things." It was truly terrible. Michael Clarke, when he started out, was the only drummer who could, without any awareness of it at all, turn the beat around, back to front, three times in one song. No kidding, actually put the front beat on the back beat. Play five-note four-bar four times. And none of the rest of us were that much better. Roger was the only one who could really play. Christopher picked up bass very quickly.

I can remember standing in front of a mirror with my new Gretch guitar. I was so happy. I was standing there, trying to figure out how to stand up and play. Folkies didn't do that. We were used to sitting on high stools or something. There I was, alone in front of the mirror, muttering to myself: "Let's see . . . How do you . . . like this? Or: No, maybe I need to lengthen the strap a little bit . . . Let's see . . . How does this look?" Dickson said I was trying to wiggle like a rock 'n' roller and I just couldn't. I'd try to get a look going. It was hysterical. If only someone had been hidden in the closet with a video camera. It would have you on the floor, rolling, holding your stomach to see me trying to practice learning how to play guitar standing up. God, it was funny.

Los Angeles was becoming the locus of the new music industry as the sixties began their erosion of the East Coast's monopoly on cultural standards. For the first time, social and cultural trends began on the Pacific side of the continent (what Dan Jenkins calls "the Left Coast") and drifted east to New York, Boston, and Philadelphia. "American Bandstand" was supplanted by "Shindig" and "Hullabaloo," with sun-streaked dudes and surfer chicks dancing in miniskirts and go-go boots; California culture was becoming a national standard. For a band to succeed, it had to have Top 40 AM radio airplay and exposure on a nationally televised dance show. It also had to have a record. At World-Pacific, Dickson and Tickner recorded enough material to eventually release an album, years later, called *Preflyte*, a collection of seminal Byrds material. At the time, however, only a couple of songs made it to the commercial demo stage: "Please Let Me Love You" and "Don't Be Long." Both songs are forgettable and comprise just the trio of McGuinn, Crosby, and Clark. The band, not yet the Byrds, was called the Jet Set (by McGuinn) and Elektra, the company that released the record, identified the band as the Beefeaters in an attempt to cash in on the fascination for all things British.

Jim Dickson was trying desperately to get the group an audition, a contract to record a demo tape, anything to move them out of the cornflakes-and-cheeseburger league. The first priority was to get them a decent set of instruments. Luckily for the boys, Dickson and his partner, Eddie Tickner, had a few friends with money. Tickner, the accountant, handled some bookkeeping for Naomi Hirschorn, a wealthy woman whose family was used to subsidizing the arts, although usually on a grander scale (the Hirschorn Museum in Washington, D.C., was endowed by the same family). Dickson and Tickner approached Naomi and offered her a deal: 5 percent of the band's gross for an initial investment of five thousand dollars. In retrospect, it was a good deal. At the time, it must've seemed a risky flier, a crapshoot on a band with no name, little experience, dim prospects, and no recording contract. To Naomi Hirschorn's credit, she went for it.

When Naomi agreed to finance our instruments, it was probably the best five-thousand-dollar investment anybody ever made. I'm sure she made it back twenty times over. We went out and got a new set of Ludwig drums, a new Rickenbacker twelve-string, and a new Gretch six-string. Guess where we got all those ideas from? The Beatles. We were Beatle-struck. Who could not be struck by the Beatles?

JIM DICKSON: *Eddie Tickner called them "the lads" and concerned himself with "Did they have enough to eat?" and stuff like that. He couldn't relate to the toys they wanted and all that bullshit. To him, that was just stupidity, but he wanted to make sure that they got enough and that motivated him to get us a job at Ciro's. He was worried about Naomi Hirschorn ever getting her money back. The*

Byrds' first public gig was booked by Lenny Bruce's mother, Sally Marr. She got them a job at Los Angeles City College, noon assembly, for a half hour, in the yard with nothing but their own equipment, so for a sound system they had to sing through their new guitar amplifiers. It was their first paid job, fifty bucks for all five of them, and happy to get it. Ten bucks apiece, boy! That's a week of cheeseburgers.

The Byrds were in business as a group, with pictures of ourselves holding our new instruments, choices dictated by publicity photos of the Beatles, who posed in front of Ludwig drums, holding Gretsch and Rickenbacker instruments. McGuinn, Clark, Hillman, Clarke, and I were all letting our hair grow longer, just like the Fab Four moptops from Liverpool. It was all new to us—the first time Michael played on real drums, the sticks flew out of his hands. The resiliency and bounce of the stretched drumheads was something he had never experienced in months of whacking cardboard boxes. Michael also had the longest hair of anyone in the group. Of all the Byrds he looked most like the prototypical British Invasion rocker. So much so that when the Rolling Stones played in Los Angeles, we got to sneak in backstage by sending Michael out as bait, walking him by the first group of hyperventilating teenyboppers we could find. When the girls saw Michael, they squealed and pursued him en masse. We swooped down around Michael and made a dash for the stage door, where a confused union stagehand saw long hair, young men, screeching groupies, and assumed we were part of the show. We dived through the open door and melted into the backstage clutter, riding the image safely past security. All the Byrds were affecting English accents for the occasion. It was a more innocent time and backstage security was a lot easier. "I'm with the band" was a password that still worked.

JIM DICKSON: *I was going around to all these shows that were popping up, trying to get the Byrds on them. We went to Benny Shapiro's house, where David and McGuinn and Gene took this home tape machine in his living room and played it while they sang live to the tape. Benny had this big cathedral-ceiling living room and didn't know what to make of it. He never knew unless somebody told him anyway. He used to ask us, "Do you think Horace Silver's okay?" But Michelle, his daughter, who was about eleven at the time, was upstairs. She heard these voices coming up, they sounded like the Beatles to her, so she came running downstairs, all excited. The next morning Miles Davis was over for breakfast and Benny told him, "I don't know what to do. Dickson's got these kids and my daughter thinks they're hot stuff." Now, I'd done fifteen shows for Miles, live shows with Oscar Brown, Jr., so I guess he remembered me. Miles called Irving Townsend at CBS Records. Irving had been kicked upstairs and out to the West Coast and all he was recording was the Air Force Band and stuff like that in CBS's one big studio. He calls the head of A&R for CBS/Columbia and says, "Give these kids a chance," so they arranged an audition. So indirectly you can say it was Miles Davis who got the Byrds started.*

By the time they went into the CBS/Columbia studio, the Byrds had come up with material that was special to them. Dickson got Albert Grossman to let the Byrds sing "Mr. Tambourine Man," not yet released. The demo was sung by Bob Dylan and Ramblin' Jack Elliott. It was something the Byrds felt sure they could do. On the demo session (a kind of low-budget warm-up for the real thing), the Byrds did the singing, but the musicians who played the instrumental tracks were experienced studio session players: the ubiquitous Glen Campbell on guitar, Leon Russell on keyboards, Larry Knechtel on bass, and Hal Blaine on drums. By the time their first album was recorded, the Byrds would all play on it, but on that first single the studio didn't trust them to play to "professional" standards, Dickson apparently concurring. Terry Melcher (Doris Day's son) was brought in to produce the album, despite Dickson's history with the band.

JIM DICKSON: *Terry had pull because his mother owned a lot of stock in CBS. Hell, she practically owned the company. During the days of 90 percent income tax on salaries during World War II, one way to defer taxes was to take stock instead of wages. So Doris took a lot of stock and whatever Terry wanted to do at Columbia Records he got to do. Luckily, he wanted to do the Byrds. McGuinn became the leader because he had played on some sessions before and he knew the leader got double and that was all he really cared about, getting paid double-scale. Gene was more like the coach, saying things like "Come on, guys. Let's do it." He had that kind of an attitude. David, of course, had the answer to everything after it got to a certain stage. At first, he was very humble. That didn't last long. Maybe a couple of days. It just wasn't David. Michael and Chris came to me and they were even more resentful because they weren't under contract. They signed as singers because that's the way that CBS saw them—just singers. The company could hear that they weren't musicians from the audition tapes we made at World-Pacific. It was some job to get Terry to go along with McGuinn. I said, "We gotta have McGuinn because otherwise there's no flavor of what they're going to sound like."*

Chris and Michael were very resentful and they came to me outside of the first Ciro's gig to say, "Oh man, this music sucks!" This was before the record broke, of course. But these boys are saying, "We have to be a blues band now!" Can you imagine the Byrds playing blues? "Chimes of Freedom" was the last thing to finish the first album and by that time you could have touched me in the middle and I'd have fallen apart in a hundred pieces. I'd had it. I was desperate. And when David balks at playing something he'd just invented, we get into a huge fight, with him ready to walk out and me wrestling him to floor and getting on top of him. I did everything I could to scare him. I told him, "You're going to have to go through me. I'll fight you to the fucking death. You're going to finish this fucking tune. Blah-blah-blah." That's how the album got done.

Dickson, all through the winter of 1964 and into the spring of 1965, worked to make the Byrds "happen." In later years, the process would be known as "building heat" under the band. At the time, it was a genuine grass-roots effort by

Dickson to establish some kind of reputation for the Byrds, even if only at the local Los Angeles level. Television, the movies, radio, and recording companies had the power to focus national attention on the right band. The trick was to get the band on radio, television, records, and into the movies.

There were other forces working: an explosion of "youth culture," a big bulge in the population curve as World War II baby boomers became old enough to drive and drink, and the discovery of recreational drugs by the children of the middle class. In L.A., new music clubs kept opening on the Strip. Not just folk clubs, but clubs that played rock 'n' roll. Gazzari's, the Whisky a Go Go, the Trip, and It's Boss all joined or replaced the Crescendo, the Unicorn, the Ash Grove, and the Troubadour. Kids with cars or with their parents' cars cruised up and down Sunset Boulevard. On a weekend night, it could take four hours to navigate the mile and a half from the Beverly Hills city line to Schwab's Drug Store. One of the grand old nightclubs, a multi-tiered showroom called Ciro's, had reopened. It had closed when Hollywood types stopped putting on formal wear to go out at night and get into trouble—or at least into Hedda Hopper's or Louella Parsons's columns. Once Ciro's was a formal supper club where studio-groomed stars went on dates arranged by the studio's publicity department. It was reborn in the sixties as a raucous music club. Today, in yet another incarnation, it's the main showroom of Mitzi Shore's Comedy Store. As the Troubadour proved when it switched to punk and heavy metal music, a good and lucky venue will survive.

In a city of hope and hoopla, where eardrums were callused by years of exposure to press agent chatter, Dickson's job was to build heat in the club, light a fire under the Byrds, and have the whole world hear the sound, not just the sizzle.

JIM DICKSON: *You could say that it was Miles Davis and Benny Shapiro who helped get the Byrds going. Them and a whole gang of my contemporaries who got on the bandwagon real fast and were wonderfully supportive. Even Lenny Bruce came down to the studio and to Ciro's. There were people we didn't know who helped out, once they saw what was happening. They didn't have to be told. The people at* Time *magazine saw the scene and the Byrds, for that first period, became like champions to them.*

What Jim did was tell everybody in Los Angeles that he knew was hip, "Listen, I've got this band playing down there and we have to create a scene." This is Ciro's we're talking about. Whenever we played there, Dickson made it a happening. He said, "You've got to come and you've got to bring everybody you know who's hip and groovy and you've got to bring whatever foxes you know because we're going to make it happen."

JIM DICKSON: *We had them all. We had Jack Nicholson dancing, we had Peter Fonda dancing with Odetta, we had Vito and his Freakers. David would come in and start out and the band had to do five sets a night. The first set they'd be like they didn't even remember each other's names, they were so bad. Then they'd get a little warmed up by the second set, but the crowd was with them because everyone would remember they'd been great the night before. About the middle of the third set, there was a Beatles song and then David would say, "What a lucky guy I am." It made you smile and that was always the kickoff. It was always in the third set that it would start to get good and by the fourth set David would be out there, grinning like a kid, as if to say, "Boy, this is such a great party," and there'd be all these freaks jumping up and down, Vito with his wife nursing her kid on an exposed breast . . . We made lines in front of Ciro's that hadn't been seen since Peggy Lee played there.*

Vito and his Freakers were an acid-drenched extended family of brain-damaged cohabitants. Dickson had started the hype at Ciro's at exactly the right time. The bland stretch of boulevard drew roving teenagers from all over the Los Angeles basin, from the far reaches of the San Fernando Valley, and from the beach communities to the south. In the favorable Southern California climate, a new scene could start at any time, without waiting for a spring thaw or midsummer madness. Abundant supplies of grass were coming up from Mexico at prices that sound like Depression era fantasies: an ounce of marijuana cost twenty dollars, a single kilo went for under a hundred, and for entrepreneurs who wanted to deal weight, multiple kilos would be delivered in a rent-a-car to the residential garage of your choice for fifty-five or sixty bucks per 2.2-pound brick, each kilo wrapped in colored cellophane and Mexican newspapers after compacting.

Bob Neuwirth was an art student from Ohio who found himself playing guitar and harmonica around the Boston-Cambridge campus area; he was there when Joan Baez, her sister Mimi, and Mimi's husband Richard Fariña ignited the local folk music scene, along with Jim Kweskin and Maria Muldaur and the Kweskin Jug Band. In Greenwich Village, the only other folksinger with a wire harmonica rack around his neck was the skinny kid from Hibbing, Minnesota, the soon-to-be-legendary Bob Dylan. The Two Bobs gravitated toward each other and Neuwirth eventually replaced Victor Maimudes as Dylan's road manager and constant companion. The peripatetic Neuwirth survived twenty-eight years of folk, rock, folk rock, blues, and art rock, working closely with Dylan, Jim Morrison and the Doors, Janice Joplin, Kris Kristofferson, the Band, and every major act that passed through the Albert Grossman office. In his time he has played and dealt with every kind of artist, manager, engineer, roadie, groupie, junkie, dealer, drunk, user, painter, poet, filmmaker, fashion model, art dealer, and ordinary citizen from Venice, California, through every concert venue in North America, past New York and on to London, Paris, Rome, and Zagreb. Well, maybe not Zagreb. Completing his ninth year of sobriety, he is a frequent speaker at meetings of recovering substance abusers and has returned to his first love, painting. In his Venice studio, he recalls those times and Bob Dylan's meetings with the fledgling Byrds:

BOB NEUWIRTH: *Certain of us were very taken by the Beatles—from a musical point of view, as opposed to "Let's go out and cut our hair like that." It was sort of like these Beatle guys are onto something, moving European harmonies into an Everly Brothers sack, shaking them up with rock 'n' roll, rockabilly beat and throwing them back across the Atlantic. From left field comes this English rock 'n' roll sound which nobody anticipated, which had the beat—put the drums back into the deal—and then suddenly all the folkies were caught with their picks out, saying, "What is this?" and "How can we get some?" That's when it reached critical mass. It just kind of happened and the people that were on top of it, like the Byrds, had a headstart. Now we take it for granted that everybody writes his or her own songs or that people suddenly have a Top 40 hit. It just didn't happen in those days. It didn't happen at all, much less for a sort of electric folk band to do it. It was a whole new radio sound and it wasn't like the Beatles, either. The Beatles were still on the bubble-gum end of the dial. They weren't into their* Rubber Soul-Sgt. Pepper *stuff. They were not complicated. They were just dumb. They were dumb enough that all the little kids liked it and because the little kids liked it, we all got to hear it. And as soon as we got to hear it, we started wanting to be little. So we figured out ways to like become kids again. It was actually the second part of the music revolution. Later there was a third part, when acid got stirred into the mix and it went zooming to the real psychedelic level of pop festivals and all that shit.*

I distinctly remember hearing "Mr. Tambourine Man" in Albert Grossman's office in New York City. Bob Dylan's version was a couple of years old by then. Bob and I went to the office, cynical as usual, looking forward to reading the fan mail and having great cheeseburgers downstairs on East 55th Street. Somebody said, "Well, there's this 'Mr. Tambourine Man' record," and I said, "Put it on." It was great because no one could figure out how anyone except Peter, Paul, and Mary could ever cover any of Bob's songs. They were so unique and forceful that no one could imagine anyone else singing them; they were so dependent on phrasing and inflection. There was this high mountain edge—no one with a commercial sound could get ahold of any of those songs. We heard the record and cracked up and Bob loved it. Albert wasn't quite that quick to commit, but the upshot was that we thought this was a good idea. We didn't get particularly head-bangingly ecstatic with it because nobody knew if it had a chance to get on the radio or anything like that, but we were thinking, "Hey, well, those guys didn't miss the point entirely." Soon after, in L.A., I met David, who sang so well. Such a clean clear voice—he was a really great singer.

We drove up to San Francisco to play the Peppermint Tree. We had a black 1956 Ford station wagon that we had bought from

Odetta for a reasonable sum like six hundred bucks or something and we took that with all our equipment and all five of us in it and drove to San Francisco. We stayed in some dive, some set of rooms up above the club, which was on Broadway in North Beach, just west of the Committee, and awesomely bad. When we got there, they told us that we were expected to play five sets a night, seven sets on a weekend. We said, "What?" We had never played that many sets for that many nights. Gene Clark was so overcome he got sick and just copped out. Not only was it that bad, but when we started there were two go-go dancers, girls in fringed bikinis, one on either side of us, trying to dance, smacking their gum. They'd say things like "Don't you guys know anything with a beat?"

We're doing our set, with things like Dylan's "Chimes of Freedom." It was a total mismatch. I wish to God I could re-create it. Anybody who saw it now would be in hysterics. It was just funnier than shit and we loved it. San Francisco was a wonderful place and after we started packing the place, which was only a couple of nights into the gig, the manager said, "Oh, wait a minute, hey . . ." and we renegotiated. Then we did three sets a night and the go-go dancers went elsewhere and we filled the joint. To the rafters. Everybody in San Francisco came. All they'd ever seen up there that was anything like us was the Beau Brummels. It was the Byrds all the way after that. And while we were playing this North Beach go-go palace, "Mr. Tambourine Man" started to get airplay. Big Daddy Tom Donahue broke us on KYA.

An urbane and privately mad Englishman named Derek Taylor, who had been a critic for the *Daily Express* in Manchester and the press officer for the Beatles, set up shop in Los Angeles as an independent music industry press agent. Representing Byrds archrivals Paul Revere and the Raiders as well, Taylor found himself in the Byrds-Tickner-Dickson offices in a newly erected office tower, an incongruous highrise at 9000 Sunset Boulevard. There Derek christened the Byrds "America's Best Group" and wrote endless reams of copy for magazines like *Tiger Beat* and *Teen,* extolling their magic, comparing their inventiveness and originality with the Beatles, and pointing out to the trade press their surprising success. ("Mr. Tambourine Man" was the biggest hit for Columbia Records in two and a half years, Taylor wrote in his memoirs, the first number one act on that label since Steve and Eydie.)

JIM DICKSON: *I went and saw Derek Taylor and said, "I'll give you two and a half percent and you do what you think it's worth. We won't demand anything from you, but what we want the most is help breaking the record in England." I'd figured out that everybody was looking at what was happening in England and there were no American groups getting on the charts. If we could break the record in England, then everybody would notice. Through his KRLA connections, Derek got a half dozen disc jockeys on the West Coast to want to play the record, but none of them could get it by the program director and there was this guy in San Francisco, Tom Donahue. Big Daddy Tom Donahue. He saw this record sitting there, supposedly serviced by CBS and not promoted at all, and he noticed that it was written by Bob Dylan. Donahue knew his Dylan and he had never heard of "Mr. Tambourine Man." So he put it on and the following Tuesday, at Ciro's, there were about three hundred people from San Francisco who had been out that Sunday on acid and when they heard "Mr. Tambourine Man" instead of "Splish Splash" or whatever else they played, hey, they showed up smiling.*

We knew it was a hit when we were back in Los Angeles, riding down Sunset Boulevard in that funky old station wagon, and KRLA played our "Mr. Tambourine Man." We freaked! There is no feeling I'll ever have like that time, hearing our tune on the car radio, without warning, for the very first time ever. And then they played it again! It was such a hot hit that they played it two or three times in a row. By that time we were so excited we had to pull over. Couldn't drive anymore! I mean, we knew at that moment that our lives had changed. Literally. We were going to be able to make a living at playing music. We were going to be one of those fortunate few who were actually in show business. I had moved out of Dickson's basement up in Laurel Canyon and rented a little place of my own that was like a basement closet. It didn't even have a window. I didn't have any money. I never had any money. I didn't have any money from the time I left home in 1960 until a couple of months after "Tambourine Man" hit in 1965. That was when we started making money. Then I bought a new green Porsche. That's when I started realizing that the sixties were going to be interesting times.

The Byrds' success was sudden and pervasive. In 1965 three of the biggest singles on the charts were by the Rolling Stones ("Satisfaction"), the Beatles ("Yesterday"), and the Byrds ("Turn! Turn! Turn!"). Although their album sales never reached the stratospheric heights of the Beatles or the Rolling Stones (no Byrds album made it into the *Billboard*'s annual Top 10 album charts), the Byrds' influence was seminal. They were riding the crest of a wave that represented a sea change in popular American music. The single of "Mr. Tambourine Man" was number one in June 1965 and the album of the same name hit the charts in July. In November "Turn! Turn! Turn!" did the same thing as a single, shooting to the premier spot in *Billboard*, to be followed by the album in February 1966 and seven months later, in September 1966, by *Fifth Dimension*. Songs from *Fifth Dimension* released earlier as singles made Top 40 chart positions and more Byrds' singles kept appearing every few months through 1968. The albums floated into the *Billboard* lists and stayed there for six months at a time. Every time the band went into Columbia's studios, they came out with hits.

By contrast, working conditions for rock bands in live performance were in an early stage of evolution. Despite the presence of sex, drugs, and rock 'n' roll, the road was still a dismal place to earn bucks. Since the seventies, most concerts and tours feature an opening act, perhaps a "guest artist," and the headline act, which is expected to fill the majority of the evening. Today, when Bruce Springsteen or Crosby, Stills, Nash, and Young or Michael Jackson or U2 do a show, what you see advertised is more or less what you get. In the early sixties, rock 'n' roll shows had a different flavor. Promoters and audiences expected (and got) something very different from today's stadium and arena shows. It was believed that no single act could command the loyalty and audience required to fill even a modest hall; it was a throwback to the days of vaudeville, which was something cigar-chomping balding bookers understood. The only other parallel to sixties rock was the craze for big bands in the forties, when a Tommy Dorsey or Benny Goodman "orchestra" would criss-cross the country in a bus, playing a succession of dates in roadhouses, casinos, hotel ballrooms, and an occasional downtown movie palace.

The rock performance aesthetic hadn't emerged yet, although in San Francisco there were pioneering innovations in the works. By 1966, Bill Graham was beginning to present local bands "in dance/concert" at the Fillmore Auditorium and Chet Helms had an entrepreneurial commune called the Family Dog, who did the same at the old Avalon Ballroom. But nationally, live rock 'n' roll concerts consisted of "sock hops" and gymnasium shows and the standard performance featured six or more acts with current records on the charts, traveling by bus and playing one-nighters, in a depressing grind that combined the worst elements of touring and performance. Impresarios like Alan Freed and Dick Clark put together packages of hit record acts and sent them out in bunches, like musical bananas. Even the Beatles traveled with a group of acts. (Remember Bobby Hebb, singing "Sunny," and Cyrkle, the band with the big hit "Red Rubber Ball"? They were on the same bill as the Beatles and the Fab Four did less than fifty minutes a night on their last American tour.)

The Everly Brothers, acknowledged by most artists and critics as the most influential American group in the early history of rock 'n' roll, were victims of those historical booking practices. In 1970, after taping a comeback shot on a short-lived ABC-TV series called "Music Scene," Phil Everly would sit in a West Hollywood music business bar and restaurant called the Black Rabbit Inn and share a glum recollection. "The most money we ever made playing live was in 1958 after we had three singles in the Top 10: "Wake Up, Little Susie," "Bye Bye Love," and "All I Have to Do Is Dream." We did a Dick Clark bus tour through the Midwest, playing one-nighters six nights a week, and we got paid $3,500 per week. Not per show, per week. For the two of us." As Phil Everly was saying that, supergroups (including Crosby, Stills, and Nash) were filling sports arenas and stadiums, appearing for guarantees that would net each member millions for a successful thirty-city tour. In 1965 that wasn't the case. It was still a bus-and-truck world, although once the Byrds began touring, it didn't take them long to discover alternatives. Not only did they seek a different mode of transport, they began exploring and integrating distinctly different musical forms.

It worked like this. We were on a tour called the Dick Clark Caravan of Stars. The Byrds were out there doing "Tambourine Man" and "Turn! Turn! Turn!" Those were our hits, so that's all that we sang. Everybody sang just their hits, on and off, thank you very much, here's the next big act. There was us, a group called the We Five, who had a hit called "You Were On My Mind," and good old Bo Diddley. The lead act was Paul Revere and the Raiders, whom I insisted on calling Paul Revaid and the Rear Doors. They would wear these colonial outfits and stand on their amps, dancing on the equipment. Pure corn, but there they were. Later, they tried to follow the trends, only they didn't do that well at it, so they tried to deny the trends. They had a song called "Kicks," remember? It was their antidrug song. If the Byrds were going to do drug songs in 1966, Paul Revaid and the Rear Doors would do antidrug songs.

Anyway, in the summer of 1965, we were all out on the road and we wanted to smoke pot, which we liked to do. We also couldn't handle being locked in a bus with the We Five and Bo Diddley's band and the Raiders. It just wasn't happening. And when I say bus, I'm talking about a Greyhound here, not one of the air-conditioned custom coaches that we have today, with the big beds and the VCR and the staterooms and the advanced electronics. Just a big, dirty old bus. A first-class tour was one in which each person had two seats and the Dick Clark Caravan of Stars was not a first-class tour. So after a while, we broke new ground and started another rock 'n' roll trend. We rented an early motor home, some prototype RV, with beds. Roger rigged a Fender Showman amp in the back to play cassettes and me and

Hillman would do most of the driving 'cause Gene and Roger were not great drivers.

This was the time when I was trying to program my partners. I had a tape of John Coltrane's piece "Africa Brass" and I was trying to program it into McGuinn, along with Ravi Shankar. Those were the two main things I was trying to pour into McGuinn's head. I don't know why I should be so presumptuous as to think I knew how to influence McGuinn, but I was and I did. So we're driving along in this motor home and we come up to a railroad crossing, where we had to stop to let a train go by. This, by the way, is the time when we're writing "Eight Miles High." We come up to a railroad crossing and we have John Coltrane blasting on this huge Fender amp in this little motor home and we are groovin' on it heavily. I look up and I see the train that is passing us is full of coal. It is a "Coal Train." It was probably the dope and the time on the road and the song we were writing, but I remember thinking, "Boy, this is pretty fucking cosmic."

It got so that I bathed Roger regularly in Coltrane and Ravi Shankar. Jim Dickson turned me on to Shankar and blew my head out completely. I thought he was and probably still is one of the finest musicians on the planet. Because of the Coltrane influence, the guitar solo in "Eight Miles High" was shatteringly different and I have to take credit for that at the same time as I acknowledge that it was Roger who played it. Roger, you know, has brilliance. He synthesized something new on the electric guitar, playing that Indian-flavored stuff on "Eight Miles High." He blew the minds of everyone in the musical world at that time. Nobody had ever heard anything like that in their lives because they had only listened to guitar players. They hadn't listened to a horn player. They couldn't translate a horn player's feel onto a twelve-string guitar. Who's kidding? Nobody could do that, except that Roger McGuinn did it.

With Gene Clark writing prolifically, Roger exploring new musical directions, with the others all contributing, the Byrds were becoming the pre-eminent American rockers,

fusing folkie chords and sensibilities with the English beat, mixing in a little jazz and psychedelia, and pioneering a life-style that stressed good times, good sex, and good drugs. A botched tour of England was the only glitch in the program. The Byrds were victims of their press and the predictable British reaction to any band calling themselves "America's Answer to the Beatles." That wasn't Derek Taylor's idea. In his memoir, *As Time Goes By,* he recalls that the promoter who booked the band in England was Mervyn Conn, "whose idea of launching an American group lately translated from folk into rock was to put them in a West Indian blues club and later into an Irish ballroom for something like 11/6 [eleven shillings and sixpence] a head, less fines for swearing or pissing in the wash-basin." That was about a dollar and quarter in U.S. currency. It was Conn who relentlessly billed the Byrds as "America's Beatles" and booked them into a succession of toilets and dives. The British pop music critics were prepared to hate the group, despite their success in the charts. They were unkind to the Byrds, audiences were less than manic, and the tour's only saving grace was the oppor-tunity to Meet the Beatles.

By the time *Abbey Road* went down, I was friends with them. On the first British tour they just came around and were very kind to us. At one point we were playing in some shitty little club that was packed; I looked out and there were John Lennon, Paul Mc-Cartney, and Brian Jones. That was them out there and God, I was totally terrified. I couldn't believe it. We were bad that night: Chris Hillman broke a bass string and the stage was so small that McGuinn and I had to play on the same amp, which totally de-stroyed our guitars. It was a disaster happening, right in front of our heroes. But that's the kind of tour it was. When we played another place in Soho, things were worse. When we got there, the owner came out to meet us and welcome us to the club and he was covered with blood. Not his—the club was the kind of a place where they had two or three fights an hour and when we played, they didn't care for us. It was primarily a black audience and they didn't like us at all. Paul McCartney was there and he took me and McGuinn home in his Aston-Martin. Scared us to pieces because he was driving drunk, but he was very kind to us. I'm not a big fan of Paul's because I don't really like the attitude that he projects, but at that particular moment he was extremely gracious. I remember it and I thank him for the kindness. He was very generous. George Harrison was the most friendly to me and the nicest. He and I sort of became friends. I'm not sure if it was me that did it, but there are people that tell me I turned him on to Indian music. I know I was turning everybody I met on to Ravi Shankar because I thought that Ravi Shankar and John Coltrane were the two greatest melodic creators on the planet and I think I was probably right. George and I got along very well. He's a very nice, very genuine, not at all starstruck with himself. The Beatles, obviously, were not impressed with us, but they had a lot of respect for us. They felt that we were the most original and inno-vative American band. There wasn't any question about it. They made that very clear, said it over and over again, whenever they were talking about the Byrds. Safe to say they loved what we were doing, just as we loved what they had done and were doing then.

When they came over here and toured America, they called me and I went to see them at the place they were renting in Benedict Canyon and again up on Blue Jay Way [not only a Beatle lyric, but the name of a real street above Sunset Boulevard]. I'd visit them in whatever places they stayed when they were in Los Angeles. We'd meet and hang out, sometimes for days at a time. I was their connection for getting good weed and, in some cases, acid. We played guitar together. We talked together. We watched movies together. Basically, you could say we had a great time. I had an enormous amount of respect for John Lennon and I think he liked me—at least he told other people that he was my friend. I loved him and thought he was a totally fantastic man. He had the quickest mind that you could ever ask for, fast and funny and blessed with such a dry wit it was acerbic. Lennon's approach was dry, cutting, even bittersweet and he saw stuff in a way I just loved. He was a wonderful cynic and skeptic in the best sense of those words. I don't remember where I was when he was shot, but

I can easily recall being desperately unhappy about it, for several reasons. For one, we lost John Lennon, one of the nicest men you could ever meet, blissfully dedicated to human causes, someone to whom that should never have happened. Second, we lost him simply because there was some son of a bitch out there that was so fucking crazy that he wanted to be the guy who shot John Lennon. That's why he did it and that's beyond sanity and reason. Finally, the incident totally reinforced my worst paranoia about how we draw nut cases and why I should carry a gun. I used it as an excuse of why I carried a gun for years afterward—with some validity. Not much, but enough to get away with it.

Another popular band working in England at the time was called the Hollies. Formed as a "beat" group in 1962, they had singles hits on the charts in the United Kingdom a couple of times a year every year, which made them an important band. They started making inroads in the U.S. market as part of the British Invasion with their first *Billboard* Top 10 hit, "Bus Stop," in September 1966. Working-class lads from Manchester, England, they were doing all right when they came to America to tour. One of the two guitar players was a slender, poetic gentleman named Graham Nash. Eventually, his life and Crosby's would become inextricably intertwined, but first they had to meet. Graham remembers:

GRAHAM NASH: *My first experience with the Crosby vibe was in early '66 when I was in America with the Hollies, playing at the Paramount Theater in New York City in Times Square. I was always the one to go down to the jazz clubs, down to the Village Gate, down to the Vanguard, to see all the weird people: Mingus and Miles Davis and Gillespie and Gerry Mulligan. I was walking in the Village one afternoon when I saw the Byrds walking along Bleeker Street, all four of them, and there was Crosby in his leather stuff, with his hat and his cape. I'm basically shy, I didn't like to say hello, even though we were in the same business and we were both making hit records at the time. I just didn't feel that I could approach him because he was in a surly mood, an unapproachable mood. That was the first time I'd ever seen him. The second time Cass brought me by his place when the Hollies were playing L.A. This time he was more approachable, lying flat on his back on the settee in a blue and white striped T-shirt with a tray of dope on his chest, rolling deadly joints.*

David came to England with the Byrds when they were playing on that ill-fated English tour, when the promoter had billed them as America's answer to the Beatles. That was blasphemy! That was like saying America's answer to the Queen. At the time, there was nobody bigger or better or more loved in England than the Beatles. It was absurd to compare anyone with them, so the British media immediately absolutely trashed the Byrds, regardless of whether their shows were good or not, and I'm sure that some of them were and some of them weren't. I saw them down at a club called Blazes and I was astounded because I think I saw either Crosby or McGuinn pull out a joint and start smoking on stage. The next time Crosby was in England he was staying at a hotel called the White House, appropriate for David in that it was a good hotel but it was full of blue hair, suits, and tuxedos, so I said to him, "Listen. My wife and I have an apartment here in town. Why don't you come and stay with us?"

He came and stayed with us and this time I really got to know him. One day I said, "Listen. We're going on an interview scene with the Hollies. Do you want to come along, hang out, and have a laugh? So we got smashed and went over to Pie Records in London, where the Hollies were being interviewed. This one guy who's talking to me turns around and asks David, "Aren't you David Crosby from the Byrds?" David says, "Fuck off." I clutched my throat as David proceeded to tell this guy that he was not here as part of the Byrds, he was here as my guest and he didn't want to be asked any questions and the reporter should mind his own fucking business. This was a novel approach to doing interviews that I hadn't encountered, you see, because the Hollies would all stand on our heads here and do whatever we were asked. We were a good little singles hit-making band and we'd been brainwashed into thinking that was the thing to do. And here was this guy whom I totally respected who had an entirely different perspective. I decided that this Crosby guy who was sleeping on my floor was neat.

The British Invasion that propelled the Beatles, Rolling Stones, Animals, and Kinks into American pop music consciousness also marked the end of an era of primal rock 'n' roll, the outlaw music drawn from black rhythm and blues and rockabilly in Memphis. Elvis was out of favor and the fifties, Eisenhower, and the Mickey Mouse Club were over. In their place, yet another new age was dawning. Recalled now as the decade between 1960 and 1970, what most people think of as "the sixties" was actually the decade between 1965 and 1975, encompassing the Beach Boys and the Sunset Strip, the Monterey Pop Festival and the Summer of Love in San Francisco's Haight-Ashbury district, the long hot summer of riots in 1968 and the end of American military involvement in Vietnam, marked by the fall of Saigon in 1975.

Recall the images and icons of the period: flowers, peace symbols, rock concert posters, love beads, bell-bottomed pants, miniskirts, hippies, news film of the war, demonstrations protesting the war, and the faces of Lyndon Johnson, Richard Nixon, John Lennon, Archie Bunker, white supremacists, Black Panthers, gurus, and pop stars. The events of the time were campus riots, student unrest in Europe, the assassinations of Bobby Kennedy and Martin Luther King, Jr., and the slogans included "Turn on, tune in, and drop out," and "Don't trust anyone over thirty." What is now the youth culture was then the Woodstock Nation.

By the time everyone was being cued by the media to react, the baby boomers' youthful experimentation with sex, drugs, and rock 'n' roll was functional reality on the all three of the country's coasts: East, West, and Gulf. Driven by the inexorable pressure of television, the movies, and the new alternative press, the limits of permissable behavior stretched up and out as new goals and standards of conduct rolled in toward the heartland. The kids already resident in New York, L.A., Miami, Austin, San Francisco, or New Orleans were starting to do in private what everyone would be talking about doing in public as the decade turned. What everyone eventually accepted as the norm by the seventies would become outmoded and dangerous by the eighties. Southern California was becoming home to a new class of restless, unsupervised teenagers with time and affection to spare and as young Crosby's resources and situation improved the fans and friends attracted to him would grow in number and quality and more and more he would be required to do less and less to enjoy too much of everything.

FIVE

....

You want to know how it will be
Me and her or you and me
You both sit there with your long hair flowing
Your eyes are alive, your minds are still growing
Saying to me, what can we do
Now that we both love you
I love you too

But I don't really see, why can't we go on as three

Your mother's ghost stands at your shoulder
Got a face like ice, just a little colder
Saying to you
"You cannot do that it breaks all the rules
You learned in school"
I can't really see why can't we go on as three

We love each other it's plain to see
There's just one answer comes to me

Sister-lovers, Water-brothers
And in time maybe others
So you see what we can do
Is to try something new
That is if you're crazy too
I don't really see why can't we go on as three

"Triad,"
Words and Music by David Crosby

GENE CLARK: *Being a bunch of semi-rough guys, with a Stones-y kind of attitude that we all had, being on the street, we weren't the favorite of the chicks until we became a hit rock 'n' roll group and then, all at once, we were in seventh heaven. We're not talking about beatnik girls—we're talking about Beverly Hills! It was hip to be with a Byrd and each guy had his share of chicks with brand-new Corvettes and MGs and the whole thing. I got to say that, reflecting on it, it was one of the highest times in my life. Every age and size of beauty, late teens and early twenties, all these beautiful girls and none of the threat looming like today. You weren't going to die from getting*

106

laid. Crabs or the clap and maybe if you were really unlucky you got syphilis, but you could still knock that out. It wasn't anything that would cause you to fold permanently. You could go see Dr. Feelgood once a week and get your shots and hit the street again.

So it really was, I got to say, an incredible period of time. It was a new thing and no other groups were making that kind of money yet. We were one of the first American groups to really make money and God, everybody had new Porsches. I had a Ferrari. I know David and Roger and Chris and Michael all rushed out to get Porsches and that was it. We were kings in Hollywood for a good while. If you think about any teenage male's fantasy from the fifties on, what he would like to have happen to him in his prime, in his late teens and twenties—we got to do that. Think of it, man. "I'd like to be a rock 'n' roll star with all the beautiful women in L.A. and all the money I can spend . . ." It was like winning a big lottery.

Debbie Donovan was fifteen, living in the "flats" of Beverly Hills near the eastern border of the city, which abuts the Sunset Strip and West Hollywood. Her stepmother was actress and comedienne Imogene Coca, who had become one of television's first genuine comedy stars playing opposite Sid Caesar on "Your Show of Shows" in the fifties. Debbie's father was King Donovan, a less public figure who was a respected legitimate theater actor. In the afternoons, when she wasn't attending ballet class or going to the orthodontist, Debbie played with friends in a small grassy square on the northwest corner of Santa Monica Boulevard and Doheny Drive. Whenever a film wants to establish Beverly Hills as a locale, they usually use a small sign that's on that corner. It's the ornate logo that says CITY OF BEVERLY HILLS and it's the one you've seen in movies like "Beverly Hills Cop" and "Down and Out in Beverly Hills." The little park is just behind it and one afternoon in 1965 Debbie Donovan heard amplified music drifting out of the open doors of the Troubadour, located across the street in West Hollywood.

DEBBIE DONOVAN: *I lived a couple of blocks away from the Troubadour and my girlfriend and I used to go over and play in the park. It was when the Byrds were just starting because Doug Weston [the original owner and manager of the club] used to let them rehearse there in the afternoons. We heard this music and we just sort of went, "Oh! What's this?" and saw these weird-looking guys with long hair in Carl's Market, right across the street. We were twelve or thirteen years old and this was before they had made any records. All they had by way of publicity was an 8 × 11 sheet of paper with five little photographs down on the bottom. That was their whole press kit and David was still called Li'l David. He hasn't told you that, I bet. I saved that for a long time; I got their signatures and he signed it "L-i-apostrophe-l David." He was ten years older than me. We became little fans, almost a club, to look out after the Byrds. We'd do things like steal steaks out of the freezer and sneak over to where they lived and leave food in their kitchens. Not all the time, just every once in a while. They liked us because we were the audience they were going for, barely teenaged girls. They let us hang out around them and that was a big deal. It changed the social structure of my life because I no longer associated with my group of kids at school. The Byrds Fan Club was formed by Christine Hinton, who lived in Santa Monica, and they were all older than me. I stopped taking ballet because it was embarrassing. "What would everybody think if I took ballet?" My mother curses me to this day for not continuing. But that's the way it went and I stayed with these older girls—sixteen, eighteen years old—and as soon as they could, they moved out of their family homes and got their own apartments, right around the Strip and in Hollywood.*

The girls with whom Debbie started running were uniformly pretty, even beautiful, with a particular Southern California style that was deceptively artless in appearance: straight hair (ironed flat if it didn't naturally hang that way), sophisticated eye makeup with no other visible cosmetics (beyond what was required to cover teenage acne), and athletic bodies in hip-hugger jeans or miniskirts. Hollywood and the Strip were a delight for voyeurs of any age. A prominent cartoonist for a men's magazine was driving in circles around Hollywood High School at 3 P.M., lost in lustful contemplation of student bodies. He was stopped by police and questioned as a possible sex offender. Debbie's friends came from homes with divorced or separated parents, where fathers were generally absent or distant. The local lifestyle was permissive and the Pill minimized the procreative problems of premarital adventures. The postwar housing boom provided the rootless upscale population of Southern California with plenty of affordable transient housing, from tacky stucco "fifties moderne" apartment complexes with shag carpets and louvered glass windows to quaint wood cabins in the hills and canyons. Laurel Canyon became the area of choice for the growing population of musicians, songwriters, poets, screenwriters, actors, and dope dealers. L.A. was absolutely happening and the Byrds were not only helping make it that way, they were personally experimenting with lifestyles that put pop music at the point of forces marching toward a generational conflict. Some young women, in that time before conciousness-raising, became camp followers to an army of musicians. The affectionate diminutive "groupie" was probably preferable to the terminology of the big band era of the forties, when women who chased musicians were called "band rats." Reine and Tracy Stewart were sisters, born and raised on the East Coast. Their mother drove to California to live with her twin sister and took her teenage daughters with her. Christine Hinton was the daughter of a career army officer and had moved to Santa Monica with her mother after living with her father at the Presidio, a U.S. Army post in San Francisco. An archetypal beauty, her particular fascination was for David Crosby, on whom she fixated. Reine Stewart sets the stage:

REINE STEWART: *In 1964 we lived in Palos Verdes and we were going to a place called Reb Foster's in Redondo Beach, the local hangout for music and kids and beach and whatever. We met the house band there called the Crossfires, who eventually became the Turtles. After they changed their name, they started to play at a gig in Hollywood at a place called the Crescendo on Sunset Boulevard across the street from Ben Frank's. I was fifteen and my older sister, Tracy, was eighteen. We'd tell our parents we were going to Reb Foster's and instead we'd go into Hollywood to see the Turtles. Our parents had no idea that we had switched our territory. One weekend—it was Easter weekend, 1965—Tracy and I went up there and found out the club had changed names and ownership. It was now called the Trip.*

The Byrds were playing, so we met them and liked them. It was right after they played at Ciro's and we used to see David a lot. He'd come flying down Sunset Boulevard on his motorcycle with his cape flying out behind him. It was great. Michael Clarke was living in Terry Melcher's house up on King's Road. We used to go up there a lot. Stay all night, drive back to Redondo Beach, sneak in around daylight, climb into our little beds and wait for the alarm to go off, and get up and go to school. That summer the Byrds played our high school, Palos Verdes High. Tracy had a crush on Gene. I had a big crush on Chris Hillman and David was just somebody that was there, though we were all friends.

Christine invented the fan club. She was the fan club. At first it was a Byrds Fan Club, then it became a David Crosby Fan Club. I liked Chris, Tracy liked Gene, and Christine was totally mad for David. David was her life. She moved to an apartment across the street from the Whisky a Go Go to be near David and the band. Tracy and she used to sit up nights and talk about what she was going to do to get David. She was totally determined. Nothing deterred her, no matter what he said or did, no matter how he treated her. The apartment was behind the gas station at the Whisky, so we used to crash there. In fact, we ended up basically living there. Right on Clark Street just above the Strip. We used to look out the window and as soon as we saw one of the guys go into the club to rehearse or hang out or whatever, we'd go racing across the street.

DEBBIE DONOVAN: *Christine positioned all of that stuff. She was kind of the ringleader, she was the one who said, "We're making a fan club," and I was the only one that was still a virgin. I was the outcast. Everybody giggled at me and used to say, "I can do things you can't do." That was Christine and Reine and that was a big deal and it just wasn't what I was doing. I never went to any dances. During my entire high school career, I only had one date. I was scared to death of sex. I just didn't want to have anything to do with any of that. And because there was a lot of sex available, the guys in the band saw me more like a little sister than anything else. It was like a protective shell around me and my friends, with David saying, "No, you leave them alone. Take anyone else, but leave them alone." It was exciting and I was having a great time.*

GENE CLARK: *"Mr. Tambourine Man" was a hit in twenty-six countries or something like that. It was monstrous! It was the biggest-selling single and sold more records in that period of time than Columbia Records had since Johnny Mathis did "Wonderful Wonderful" or something like that. It really shocked everybody. The first time we got mobbed by girls screaming at a concert, which really didn't turn me on, it registered that we actually had pulled it off, that everybody loved us, we were bigger than any of us expected, and we were out with the Beatles, and security guys were escorting us through airports. How do you deal with it? I was barely nineteen years old and Michael and I were roommates at the time and there were fifty kids outside the house, waiting for us or a piece of something that belonged to us, trying to get an autograph. Your lifestyle immediately changes. Each guy has his little crowd of girls that thinks he's the best and Jim Dickson and Eddie Tickner, who are ten years older than us, they don't know how to handle it either because they're sitting on millions of dollars and they don't know what to do. They're saying, "Oh my God, what have we got here? We've created a monster. What do we do now?" We weren't really prepared as well as Jagger and the Stones and John and the Beatles. Those guys had already been on the road for five or six years, taking their hard lumps. That shit just split us up like an atom.*

Jim Dickson and Eddie Tickner, already displaced in the studio, were perceived by the band as being out of their depth and unprepared to manage a true superstar group. Fame and financial success started to erode the relationships within the band and between the band and its management. Gene Clark, who hated flying as much as David and Roger loved it, was beginning to wonder if touring was worth it. The songwriter with the most material on the best-selling albums, he was reaping the lion's share of the lucrative composer's, lyricist's, and publishing royalties. By 1967, his com-

bined performance and author's royalties were piling up at
the rate of a thousand dollars a day. (Adjusting for inflation,
that would be twenty-five thousand dollars a week in 1988.)
The others trailed Clark, but they were all making a lot of
dollars for young men just out of their teens who had not yet
voted in their first presidential election. Unfortunately, as
soon as the financial statements began to arrive, motivations
changed. Originally, the only test of material was that it be
something that the group and its management and record
company agreed would be the best song to record. After a
few albums, each member of the band pushed to get his
songs recorded, not for the good of the record but for the
individual royalty account of the particular writer or writers
involved. David was writing songs that incorporated new
musical ideas, tunes and chords that drew on jazz and Eastern music. His was the most progressive music and the easi-
est to reject. Things grew more bitter with each passing
month.

JIM DICKSON: *I had one great row with David at the "Hullabaloo"
show in New York. David had decided that his new image was to
wear a pea coat and we're back there, ready to do the show, and
they've got these birdhouses around because it's a corny set and a
tasteless show anyway. I tell David, "You look like a butterball with
fuzz in that coat." It made him look fat before he was fat and
everybody was supposed to look young and pretty in those days, so I
tried to get him to take off the coat. It was a struggle and it got down
to the point where he said, "If you say one more word, I'm walking
out the door." I let it go and David went on with the pea coat and
two weeks later he sees the show and I get a call from San Francisco:
"Why didn't you rip it off me? I look terrible in that!" That was the
end of the pea coat. Then he got the cape, which I didn't mind.
Somewhere there's a picture of David on a motorcycle with a crash
helmet and his cape. I still have that picture. I think it's what
prompted someone to call him Lawrence of Laurel Canyon.*

Peter Fonda was a young actor with a famous name and
sister. He had appeared in a biker film, *Wild Angels*, for
Roger Corman and was beginning to attract a cult following.
He loved the new music, enjoyed and identified with the

people who made it, and saw the political implications of the "youth revolution." There was no generation gap between Fonda and Crosby and David had credentials in the film community. After all, he had studied acting with Jeff Corey, his father had won an Oscar, and Floyd worked for Roger Corman, the same as Peter. While sister Jane was off in Europe making *Barbarella* with Roger Vadim, Peter was finding new friends on the Sunset Strip, among them the Byrds.

PETER FONDA: *David was the most outgoing and the most polite. His manners were always terrific. All of us, the entire band, became tight friends from the get-go, they all would drop by and visit my house because I was married to Susan, my first wife, and we had home-cooked meals. David came around the most. At first David didn't have a Porsche and, as a matter of fact, he wanted one of my motorcycles. This is what I did wrong for David in my career as his friend. I actually did give him the motorcycle. I'd be cruising up Laurel Canyon and David would go by, not recognizing my car, with a cape flying off his back, on my fucking Triumph, like a bat out of hell to his house. I thought, "What have I done to this guy? He has such a fabulous voice. He's going to die. Hit a telephone pole and that's the end of it." He didn't wear a helmet. I lent him some money once for something—not a lot—and he said, "I'll tell you what. I'll give you this guitar." I said, "You don't have to do that, David." He said, "No no." He said, "I'll feel better. You take this guitar. It's a good guitar." It was a super guitar. And he never bothered to reclaim it, even after he paid me back. I'd say, "David, I got your guitar." He'd say, "No no, that's all right, that's all right." Terrific. I pick up a nice new guitar. When he got the Porsche, he got rid of the motorcycle and I felt much better. I was worried about him and the Porsche, but at least it wasn't the motorcycle.*

It was time for David to have a house of his own. There was enough Byrds money to acquire one and instead of a Hollywood Palazzo or Laurel Canyon Laid-Back, David found a property in another canyon, farther west, separating the affluent enclaves of Beverly Hills and Bel Air. It was Beverly Glen Canyon, another self-sufficient community of artists, actors, and outlaws. Halfway up the hill is a little shopping center with a grocery store, a real estate office, and a cleaners (echoing the Country Store corner in Laurel Canyon). Crater Lane runs uphill to the west and at the top of Crater, Lisbon Lane continues uphill in a tight turn that discourages uninvited drivers from continuing. A couple of little wooden houses sat on Lisbon Lane; David bought one and then the other. Into his house he loaded crystals, stained glass, and enough custom carpentry and finishing work to create a unique environment. In addition to a king-sized sleeping alcove constructed for no-pajama parties, there were secret stashes behind cupboards and cabinets and lots of niches and shelves for an ever-growing collection of curios, artifacts, guitars, guns, and custom knives. Gold and platinum records were stacked with artful disregard on the floor, against the walls, and as a doorstop in the bathroom.

As 1966 turned into 1967, the youth revolution came to the Strip. The focus of the disturbance was a small coffeehouse, painted purple, called Pandora's Box. It sat on a triangular patch of dirt in the middle of the intersection of Crescent Heights and Sunset boulevards. On the east side of the street was the famous Schwab's Drug Store. Opposite was a bank and plaza, occupying the former site of the Garden of Allah Apartments, where Robert Benchley and Dorothy Parker and a host of other thirties literary lights had blinked erratically during and between studio screenwriting deals. Pandora's featured the usual menu of espresso, cider, poetry, folk music, beatniks, and teen runaways and was a mildly popular hangout. Unfortunately, it sat on ground that was to become part of a street-widening traffic-improvement project and would eventually be razed. Where it once stood is today nothing but a broad intersection. The club was probably surviving on a month-to-month lease while its owners awaited demolition. Because of its location, Pandora's Box was a highly visible reminder of what was happening to the Strip and an obvious target for local authorities looking to do something about the youth explosion in their midst.

JIM DICKSON: *As I was getting alienated from the group, I got involved in this thing called CAFF, Community Action for Fact and Freedom. We got people out on the street with bands and were monitoring them when the Sunset Strip thing exploded and I felt person-*

ally responsible. I brought all those people up to the Strip, all these kids, and the cops are out there, beating them up. Although I was probably the only Republican in that whole culture, it didn't seem inconsistent to me to be for civil rights. It seemed natural. I was always a Lincoln Republican anyway.

Eviction notices were posted and the whole local youth subculture of musicians, groupies, hangers-on and visiting Valley teens closed ranks in an eruption of protest. All of a sudden, there were signs, people marching and chanting, and a traffic-stopping curb-to-curb mob of beaded, fringed, costumed, painted protesters. The police characterized the milling teens as a "riot," issued a riot call, and began practicing their new crowd-control tactics, using Mace, batons, and tear gas. Stephen Stills was working up the street in the Buffalo Springfield and was moved to write a song about that confrontation that became the powerful anthem "For What It's Worth," written and released within a month of the event. It was one of the first instances where rock 'n' roll drew on contemporary political experience for material. The musicians began to speak for their own generation. Friends of musicians, actors with similar tastes in politics, religion, and recreational drugs, were drawn into the scene. Brandon DeWilde, a child star grown into a handsome young man, was immersed (with Fonda and Crosby) in the Canyon culture. A frequent houseguest at Crosby's Lisbon Lane house, Brandon eventually died in a single-car wreck, like Jimmy Dean before him. At the time, the riot on the Sunset Strip was such a media event in Hollywood that it eventually became a title for a quickie drive-in exploitation movie.

PETER FONDA: *When the riots happened, we went down to the Strip to check it out. Brandon DeWilde and David took movie cameras. I had a couple of Nikons. When the sheriff's department disembarked from a couple of buses and came charging at us all, David and Brandon got away by slipping down an alley behind Bullwinkle's, across from the Chateau Marmont. I was caught in the pincers: LAPD moving west from Hollywood, sheriff's department coming east down the Strip, pushing all the people who had started marching around the Whisky. Somebody fell through the window at the Liquor Locker by accident, the cops got all excited because they heard plate glass shattering, so they started busting everyone in sight. I was the first. Thank God John Denver and Maggie Denver were there and saw me go into the bus, all manacled. I hammered the window and I told John to call anybody. And he got ahold of somebody who bailed me out. I was ready to take these guys on. Most of the other kids were scared shitless. There were about a hundred and fifty of us in one tank at the West Hollywood sheriff station.*

JIM DICKSON: *I was too caught up in the whole thing. Politics, music, all of it. Even Terry Melcher, as shallow as he was, recognized that and was quoted as saying, "Jim Dickson's got great taste, but he was too emotionally involved." Well, when you get successful, each person has his own groupies who will reinforce anything he says because they want to please him, because they want to be liked by this artist. It's very hard to keep any kind of control over that, even though you may be fairly sure that you have a vision that you want to accomplish and a community that you want to please and to whom you want to be true. Melcher and all those front-office types never saw anything like me and Crosby fighting in the studio, with me on top of him on the floor, threatening his life. That was after we already had a hit and the control booth was full of people, including two or three CBS executives. We were not at all self-conscious about it. We were organically living out our differences. Which is all that really counts. After that fight, I never thought I could go on much farther with the band anyway.*

We had a couple of very good years together. Dickson had his own faults. I portray him the best I can, but he's also a guy with a heavy temper and a large ego and he was sometimes heavy-handed. And we had our own egos. Eventually, it had to lead to conflict. Jim once beat up one of the members of the band. The guy was caught flagrante delicto with a young lady that Dickson had an interest in. Dickson, at that time, always had an interest in young girls. This band member, who shall remain nameless, except that it wasn't me, was with a young girl and was beaten up for it. I think I'm the only one who ever punched Jim and the only reason I got away with that was because Barry Feinstein and Gene Clark grabbed Jim before he could get back at me. It took both of them. Me and Dickson were having a disagreement about how we should make a little bit of film that Barry was shooting of us out on the beach in L.A. Jim was trying to keep it organized and get it done and we were being sullen and punky. He just got mad and said, "You goddamn do it or else!" and I said, "Hey, fuck you." We already had lots of little disagreements and maybe even a fight or two before that, so I stood up on a little ice plant bank and punched him right in the mouth. Didn't even slow him down—he was so mad he was going to take me apart. It was no big deal. I love the guy. But it happened. A day at the beach.

The fact of the matter is that Jim shaped the band and it couldn't have happened without him. No question about it. Even if we had fallen together organically, it would have taken us five or six years of playing together to achieve what we did in less than a year at World-Pacific, listening to ourselves on playback. Other bands didn't get to do that. We just went straight up, and out, and eventually dumped Dickson. We took our whole scene elsewhere. We were finally tired of Eddie and Jim and our career was not advancing anymore. Gene had left the band and the guy we took it to, as it turned out, turned out to be a total sleazebag, a real rip-off artist. And, to be perfectly frank, I was largely responsible. If I had only known . . .

I wasn't real happy about my role in the group. I was starting to write good songs. I had written a couple of things that made me proud and nothing was happening with them. I almost had to include the other guys in it before I could get it on the record; it was that sort of thing. I had a large ego and Roger and I started having conflicts with each other over material, business, expenses . . . everything we did was a potential source of disagreement. In the end, Gene quit first. He said he couldn't ride the airplanes anymore. I don't really think that was the reason. I think it was tough for him to deal with me because I kept saying, "Gene, don't play. Let me play." Gene was not a good guitar player. He has a bad sense of time. He drags time and when he played it was a disaster. I was much better at it than him and I used to tell him that, which is not a good thing to do. Then they tossed me out. I was sitting in my house in Beverly Glen Canyon up on Lisbon Lane, when Roger and Christopher came over in two Porsches. *Vroom, vroom, screech!* Footsteps on the stairs, door opening, they enter and just start right in: "Hey man, basically we want to get you out of the band." "It's not working real well . . ." "We're disagreeing all the time . . ." "You're real difficult to work with . . ." "We don't dig your songs that much and we think we'll do better without you." To this day I *love* remembering that last particular phrase because it was certainly less than a year afterward that we put out *Crosby, Stills, and Nash*. I got some cheesy settlement, a total of maybe ten thousand dollars for my part of the name. By that time I was already doing drugs and the ten grand sort of went. I was snorting coke and I had already started doing heroin.

That's a confession that's surprisingly out of character; the David Crosby of the late sixties was seen by most of his peers (and certainly by the rock press and biographers) as someone passionately committed to a lifestyle that included light recreational drugs. Pot was great, acid and the organic psychedelics equally marvelous. Like many California dopers, David stood foursquare for the enlightened and responsible inclusion of marijuana as a daily dietary supplement, like vitamin C. LSD was for more serious occasions, like seeing God or experiencing the Oneness of the Universe. Mescaline, magic mushrooms, psilocybin, and peyote were for a less profound but equally illuminating experience. Speed was a trucker's drug, useful for the long haul and the occasional all-night writing or recording session, while cocaine was an expensive treat that put a finely honed edge to any pleasurable experience, like sex, performing, sex, concertgoing, or sex. Heroin was always the universal no-no, since the conventional wisdom was that it was a debilitating, addictive, expensive, and essentially numbing drug; smack was a

downer—heroin junkies were unreliable, liable to steal from
you, and couldn't enjoy sex. Men couldn't get it up; women
would nod out during the act. Alcohol was the straight
world's drug of choice and not generally included in the pop
pharmacopoeia. Janis Joplin and Jim Morrison aside, nobody publicly drank anything but beer, wine, or champagne
unless they were blues musicians. Hard booze and the blues
had enjoyed a special relationship from the start.

Conventional wisdom was wrong. Heroin was always a
constant presence and the stereotypical junkie musician
nodding on the stand was not the average rock 'n' roll
smackhead. For those who liked the drug, it was an un-
equaled and comforting buzz, a pleasant time-out from hassle. There was always a subculture of heroin users in the
business and a network of suppliers to feed them. Remember
that the average pop music star or recording artist doesn't
face the disabling side effects that are a constant problem to
the street junkie. First—and probably most important—the
working pop-star-user doesn't have to scuffle for money to
support the habit, which rules out a whole category of conduct unbecoming a human being, like lying, stealing, and
borrowing the kid's lunch money. Second, in manageable
doses, heroin is a soothing, enjoyable high for the hypersensi-
tive or emotionally burdened; they think it calms, relaxes,
and anesthetizes the emotions, that it somehow puts feelings
on hold. With reliable road managers and a supportive staff,
rock 'n' roll star heroin users can indulge themselves without
robbing anyone of anything but precious time. Later, in the
seventies, when pop stars in their twenties checked out before their thirties, the fatal potential of heroin, opiates, bar-
bituates, and alcohol would become apparent. In 1968 heroes could die young in a plane crash or a wrecked car, like
Buddy Holly or James Dean. Nobody thought we'd begin
finding rock 'n' roll's best and brightest all cold, stiff, and
blue, choked by their vomit on the floors of cheap hotels.

It was always the bad drug, always the worst. It got a little
more open around the time that Cass and I were doing it, but it
wasn't something you told people. It wasn't anything you bragged
about, you know. The first time for me was with a needle, although after that I snorted it for a long time without ever getting
truly hooked. The debut dose was some China White and it was at

my house in Lisbon Lane. I remember shooting it. It was like a big warm blanket. Someone cooked it and shot me with it because I asked for it. I couldn't do it to myself. I was terrified of needles, but I was willing to do anything that I thought would get me loaded. I loved getting loaded. Me and Cass Elliot were closet junk takers and used to get loaded with each other a lot. We loved London because there was pharmaceutical heroin available in drugstores.

> Great Britain took a different approach to heroin addiction and considered it a medical problem, not a police problem. Consequently, a registered addict could get heroin pre- scribed in pill form by a physician and fill the prescription at any pharmacy at minimal cost. This limited the criminal problems associated with addiction, since junkies didn't need to steal or sell their bodies to support their habits. Prudent or desperate British junkies could always sell their little pills on the open market to users who didn't want to go through the complications associated with registering as addicts.

You could get "jacks," which is what the English called the little pharmaceutical heroin pills. Government dope, in these in- jectable tablets that you crushed and dissolved in order to shoot them. Me and Cass used to just mash them up and snort the powder. In case anyone's wondering, that's what the Rolling Stones song "Jumping Jack Flash" is all about. Cass took lots of pills, usually from the opiate family: Dilaudid, Demerol, Perco- dan, downers of all sorts, and we did a lot of coke together. Nobody knew and I always did heroin with coke. Speedballs, just like John Belushi. I don't know how to explain it, except for the fact that there were things I didn't want to face. I wasn't strung out back then. I didn't get strung out on anything until I overdid sniffing cocaine and that really didn't happen until the mid-seven- ties. Until 1973 I could always stop if I wanted to—go sailing, leave hard drugs ashore, and just swim and dive and sail and eat good food and make love until it was time to go ashore and make music again. At that point, we thought that it really worked. Sex,

drugs, and rock 'n' roll. Getting strung out was a slow process and
I didn't get strung out on heroin until I got turned on to Persian
Brown. Then I was hooked, but as an adjunct to basing. I don't
think I was ever really a heroin addict until I was a base addict.

David was a closet case, sneaking hard drugs when he
wanted, keeping it a secret from everyone except carefully
screened suppliers and dope partners like Cass. Heroin was
not part of any regular regimen. Publicly and generally,
David was pro-grass. A connoisseur of grass, he was the first
man in anyone's experience who could hold forth on weed
the way oenophiles go on about wines. Crosby could handle,
then sniff, then taste an anonymous batch of marijuana and
name the growing area, the harvest time, and the probable
mode of transport that brought the dope across the border.
He could identify vintages and varietals and catalog the differences between cannabis indica and cannabis sativa. His
expertise attracted dealers who recognized a true aesthete,
willing to pay top dollar for top product. At his house in
Lisbon Lane you could find red Lebanese hashish in its original cotton wrapping with the government seal on it, as well
as tarry Nepalese temple fingers, gummy African bhang, and
the "southern tricolor": Panamanian Red, Acapulco Gold,
Mexican Green. In those days pharmaceutical cocaine appeared in its original brown glass bottles with the medical
labels and seals intact: COCANIUM HYDROCHLORIDE, SMALL
WHITE FLUFFY CRYSTALS, POISON. Other times the product
would be pearly white powder from Bolivia via Colombia or
the sought-after Peruvian flake, with its distinctive opales-
cent cast.

In the summer of 1967, Alan Pariser came up with an
idea for a pop musical festival. Alan had been dragooned by
Jim Dickson into producing the CAFF benefit concert. The
event had put the Byrds; Peter, Paul, and Mary; the Doors;
Hugh Masekela; and the Buffalo Springfield on the same bill.
They had wound up jamming together in a minifestival of
folk and rock. Pariser sought to repeat the experience, discussed the matter with photographer Barry Feinstien, who
suggested Benny Shapiro as a man who might help—Benny
had booked acts into the Monterey Jazz Festival and at least
knew the venue. Alan and Benny incorporated and Alan
went off to Monterey to book the fairgrounds and get the
necessary permits. When they went to Lou Adler and John

Phillips to discuss the participation of the Mamas and the Papas, Adler and Phillips manipulated their way into a full participation in the festival; Benny was bought out for eight thousand dollars and Alan stayed on as producer (they couldn't get rid of him; he had the paperwork and permits in his name). Derek Taylor was hired as press representative and off they went to San Francisco to engage the Northern California bands.

The San Francisco music scene had grown increasingly self-reliant and self-obsessed; Northern California bands like the Grateful Dead, the Jefferson Airplane, Big Brother and the Holding Company, Blue Cheer, Sons of Champlin, and the Charlatans already had a solid financial base performing in the Fillmore-Avalon ballroom venues, had made their first hit records, and mistrusted anything with beads and flowers that came north from Los Angeles. The hipper-than-thou ethic was based on a long history of carpetbagging management and record industry raiders "ripping off the culture." Jack Nicholson, not yet a paragon of the subculture, had to play a long-haired hippie musician in a youth culture exploitation movie called *Psych Out*. He had more hair then, but still had to wear a fall for a ponytail. (The progressive filmmaker Henry Jaglom shows up in this same film with sideburns obviously pasted on, playing another hipster, and Bruce Dern plays a mute called the Seeker. Lee Strasberg's daughter Susan plays the Girl. It's definitely worth renting the videocassette.) Scott McKenzie made his sappy hit recording of "San Francisco," which prompted thousands of kids to migrate to the Bay Area. Eventually, the important San Francisco bands came to Monterey. Janis Joplin, singing with Big Brother and the Holding Company, made the splash heard 'round the rock 'n' roll world and the entire event was recorded in a theatrical documentary called *Monterey Pop*, where David is seen to smile and say, "Great sound!"

Alan Pariser was one of the originators and backers of the Monterey International Pop Festival. I had heard about it all through its evolution as it grew from an idea into a real event. The Byrds were still working together as a band and we agreed to appear. Neil had left Buffalo Springfield and the band was wavering; Stephen asked me to work with them, which was fine with me because Stephen had great songs. I heard him writing "For What It's Worth" in my house, playing those guitar licks. I *knew* the man could write incredibly well and that had always been bait I had to take. I couldn't resist a good hook. I started hanging out with the Buffalo Springfield. Chris Hillman had taken me to hear them at the Whisky a Go Go on the Sunset Strip. Hillman was always good at spotting bands—he turned me on to the Doors, among others. The first time I heard Stephen Stills and Neil Young play guitar together, I heard a conversation, not a competition: the best kind of lead guitar I'd ever heard—outside of Jimi Hendrix—and I liked Stephen because he was the same kind of brash egotistical singer-songwriter and musical outlaw that I saw in myself. The Springfield had a short half-life, about a year [March '67–May '68]. Before they finally came apart, they asked me to be in the band. I went up to Monterey to play with them; I was a Springfield for a short while. When I got to Monterey, I found a whole other thing going on besides the music.

Me, Paul Kantner, and David Freiberg were sitting on the edge of the stage, watching Hendrix play. Nobody had seen anything like it in our lives, which seemed much longer at that moment, since Owsley Stanley was walking around the festival in a short leather jacket, which had two pockets, both of which were stuffed with tabs of acid in brightly colored purple tabs. I had met Owsley at the L.A. Airport; he walked up to me unannounced and without me knowing him. He said, "My name's Owsley," and handed me a little vial of small crude blue barrels—the original Blue Cheer. It was wonderful. The next batch he gave me were White Lightning, which marked his acquisition of a truly professional tabbing machine, that turned out hard little double-domed white tabs; Purple Haze was the next batch and it was that mind-bending medication that was nourishing the psyches of the crowds at Monterey. Purple Haze is what Hendrix had taken before his set and it's a safe bet that he was thoroughly psychedelicized when he played, but not to the point of being incapacitated. When he set his guitar on fire, it wasn't a totally spontaneous act—he did remember to bring that can of lighter fluid onstage with him.

I was never able to play while that stoned on psychedelics. If I was fully dosed and tried to play, I'd be in another room with a guitar three feet thick, while still onstage with the band with which I was supposed to be playing. In one case, that was the Byrds at Fillmore West. Guitar strings would turn to rubber, my hands would pass entirely through the instrument, and the audience (if I saw them at all), could be anything from a field of waving buttercups to a pack of howling demons.

> David had an adoring association of women following him everywhere. The little house on Lisbon Lane was a hotbed of sybaritic activity. Other houses and other friends provided a local party route. There was Cass's big house off Mulholland Drive, Peter Tork's house on Shady Oak in the Valley, Peter Fonda's place in Hidden Valley, and the hideaway cabins and estates of the rockers, folkies, dealers, and assorted industry types strung up and down the Hollywood Hills in Beachwood, Bronson, Laurel, and Beverly Glen Canyons and the drives and ways above the Sunset Strip. Someone's house on Bluejay Way provided the Beatles with inspiration for that song when they stayed there during an American tour. Days began at noon and ran in multiples of twelve hours. A Wednesday could last until the weekend, given enough conversation, music, dope, and sex. People slept wherever they passed out and there was always a mattress on the floor somewhere if you got too high.

The only time I can remember being bummed on acid was the night that Lenny Bruce died. I had dropped acid with a guy who had worked for the Byrds as our equipment tech. The two of us drove down to the Strip in his VW van because we thought it was a good idea to go see some live music at the Whisky. Jim Morrison was there and Morrison, as far as I could tell, had a masochistic bent; he sublimated it. He'd go out and get monumentally trashed—drunk, high, and really polluted—and pick a fight with someone who would beat him up. He did it repeatedly. As an example, I can remember a party that went on at John Davidson's house in Calabasas. John, who was definitely not identified with sex, drugs, or rock 'n' roll, never knew about this party because he was away on the road. His ladyfriend was seeing someone in the Committee and she invited all these Sunset Strip rockers to John's horse country ranch home. Jim Morrison and Janis Joplin are both there and Jim tells Janis Joplin she can't sing the blues, which does not make her happy. Her first reaction was to run out of the room, crying. Then, being the spunky bluesy bitch she was, Janis picked up a bottle of Jim Beam bourbon (the square one with the sharp corners) and, instead of taking a drink, took the bottle back into the room with Morrison, where she broke it on his forehead. Jim went down onto the rug, but not completely out of it. He had enough consciousness left to puke into the shag carpet around his face.

Returning to our narrative of me on acid, Jim Morrison was at the Whisky, when we walked in. I'm wearing sunglasses because I'm thoroughly dosed and the lights of the clubs on the Strip need deamplification before they hit my retina. Morrison comes over to where we're standing in the back. He attacks us, actually jumps at us, saying to me as he does, "You can't hide behind those shades." I wasn't hiding behind those shades, I was somewhere outside the orbit of Mars and simply teleported across the room, which is exactly how I remember it. Later, we heard that Lenny Bruce had died and that particular news hit hard and hurt. Jim Dickson had brought Bruce to see us during our earliest formative days at World-Pacific Records and the arrival of the foremost comic mind of our generation had truly awed us. Lenny came with an entourage and was gracious, kind, and enthusiastic about what he heard. To us scruffy singer types he was like a prince from another land. I remember then that we were thrilled and that I was well and truly moved. I was moved to a profound gloom when he died and it wasn't just the acid that put me on that classic bummer.

I generally didn't do psychedelics and go out on the town. I tried it a few times and remember frightening the salesgirl at Wil Wright's ice cream parlor on the Strip because my trip companion and I had "funny eyes," and looked at her in some way that she interpreted as threatening, weird, and discomforting. Therefore—and thereafter—my favorite place to be with a radically altered consciousness was on the beach, near some water. Once, with McGuinn, we had taken some acid and gone to the beach; as the first rushes came on, the police came down to talk to us. McGuinn got to talk to the heat while I *became* a sand crab and scuttled down into the sand, burying myself in the beach.

For less than maximum dosage, I learned a trick from Paul Kantner and Grace Slick. They taught me to put some Orange Sunshine in a small metal can, something like the little containers in which Tiger Balm came packaged. You could then shake the can, rattling the tabs and shaking dust off them. Then you'd open the can and sniff the lid, inhaling just enough dust from the tabs of acid to initiate a mild and controllable trip of manageable duration. It was the psychedelic version of James Bond's saying that his cocktail should be "shaken, not stirred."

Life in the hills and canyons was a free-form come-as-you-are party. Unless a band was recording or touring, there was lots of free time to enjoy a lifestyle formerly only available to dilettantes with independent incomes and inherited wealth. In the absence of hereditary titles and divine right monarchy, America always re-creates an aristocracy, usually drawing on sports, politics, the arts, and show business. The new princes and princesses of rock 'n' roll lost no time exploring a way of life that had led Old World nobility to ruin and revolution. The popsters looked to their courts and searched for faithful subjects, purging and discrediting the disloyal and disrespectful. Managers were not to be trusted, businessmen were suspect, and lawyers were not counselors; they were hired guns employed to improve a deal or get you out of jail, trouble, or an old contract.

JIM DICKSON: *When they got to be stars, led by David, I got pushed farther and farther out of the picture until eventually they took the band right out of our office. That ruined me in the business. When David Crosby was the last guy playing at a Troubadour hoot night, nobody would listen to him. When he became a big star and was hanging out with the Beatles, everybody thought he was an oracle, so everything he said was true. Including lines like "Jim Dickson doesn't know what he's doing." I was out of the business as a result of David and I was bitter about it. Very bitter. We didn't talk again until David got a boat and didn't quite know what to do with it.*

One of the bonds that eventually reunited Dickson and Crosby was their mutual love for sailing. When David had been ejected from the Byrds, the cash settlement didn't last long. As 1967 ended, David was basically an unemployed musician, albeit from a world-famous group. He had a wide network of friends, but most of all he wanted to make music. The Buffalo Springfield was collapsing; there wasn't a place for him in there. The San Francisco groups were sympathetic, but they were already formed. The ever-friendly Jefferson Airplane gave David a platform when they recorded songs like "Triad," a tune the Byrds had steadfastly rejected. David was including San Francisco as a regular alternative to the house on Lisbon Lane, staying at the Grateful Dead's ranch in Novato, in Marin County, or at one of the two quaintly pschedelicized Victorian mansions in the city owned by the Dead and the Airplane, respectively. By the fall of 1967, the Summer of Love had ended and winter was arriving. Florida seemed like a good idea and David took off for a long-overdue return to Coconut Grove to greet old friends and revisit the scenes of his folk days. He had left the Grove a broke folkie; he came back a broke star. The Byrds were continuing without him and the only income that David could expect would be royalties from past work that were substantial but sporadic and variable.

When I was down there as a folkie, I used to do all kinds of sailing. At least one of us was always working at a boat rental yard, so we'd get permission to take them out at night and sail around Biscayne Bay all night long, smoking joints and laughing like fools and having a great time. After the Byrds, I came down and hung around, looking for a boat. Wasn't quite sure how I would get it, but I knew something would turn up that would be right. Bill Bolling, a good sailor whose daughter Tiffany was a world-class beauty, was helping me, along with Ingram and my old pals from the Grove. One day in Fort Lauderdale, driving over one of the bridges, I saw her, right there at Port Everglades. A schooner with beautiful classic lines. In the car I said, "That one." We went and checked it out. They wanted sixty thousand for her and she wasn't worth it. So we let it be known around town that I was a dumb hippie from the coast who didn't know anything. Then Bolling started rumors through friends of his that she had rot. A lot more rot, structural rot, than she actually had. The rumors worked. The guys who owned her owned a boatyard in the marina. They had bought her on spec and didn't have any idea what was going on. They heard these rumors and panicked. A few weeks later, I showed up and said, "Gee, nice boat," and made a lowball offer. I got the *Mayan* for $22,500, which I borrowed from Peter Tork, who was flush with Monkees money. It's the best spent money I ever spent. The *Mayan* stands for the good things in my life: health, sanity, and freedom—all the positive values.

KEVIN RYAN: *All of a sudden he showed up at my house one day and said, "I've found the boat," as though we had been talking about it five minutes before. He found the boat that we'd been talking about all those years ago in Greenwich Village and during our first days in Coconut Grove. Another of David Crosby's discoveries. He went off to the boondocks and came back with talent again. I moved onto the boat in Fort Lauderdale for the next several months. We were going to refit the* Mayan. *There wasn't any real money to do it; it was all hook or crook, you know. There were great schemes in the night about how we were going to steal a generator, not buy it, but it never came to anything.*

When we got it, we sailed it around, across the Gulf Stream to the Bahamas and down to the Carribean. Paul Kantner and Stephen Stills flew down to join me one time and we wrote "Wooden Ships" on the boat while it was tied up right in front of Bill Bolling's house. Then, as if finding the *Mayan* wasn't reward enough, that same winter, I met Joni Mitchell.

Roberta Joan Anderson was a folksinger from Saskatoon, Saskatchewan, in Canada's prairie provinces. Married to a folksinger named Chuck Mitchell, the two sang together until their divorce in 1967. Joni kept the last name and her half of an evenly divided split of their furniture and fixtures and moved to New York on her own to continue singing her songs on the folk circuit, counting herself a lucky woman because she could work forty weeks a year, kept her rent paid through the end of the next month, and had four hundred dollars in the bank. She was planning a career in retail clothing sales and design and had already begun accumulating (at bargain prices) the art nouveau and Tiffany antiques that would come into vogue years later. Joni Mitchell's original material was complicated and jazz-tinged and fell into no currently popular category. If anyone labeled it at all, it was "art folk" and unique to Joni. Her audience was the hipsters and progressive folkies in little coffeehouses and clubs around the dying folk circuit; the Byrds and Dylan had gone electric and magicians like Jimi Hendrix and Eric Clapton were expanding the limits of electric guitar technique while the technology struggled to keep up, with more and bigger amplifiers of hitherto unimagined power. It was the dawning of an age when the only realistic limits to the total wattage onstage would be the electrical capacity of the power lines feeding the auditorium. A willowy blonde with big blue eyes and high cheekbones, singing art songs in a bell-like soprano with a Canadian accent and accompanying herself on acoustic guitar and dulcimer was not anyone's idea of the Next Big Thing, but her work was unmistakably different and she was attracting attention.

JONI MITCHELL: *I was folksinging in Coconut Grove, Florida, at the Gaslight South. I hadn't make a record yet, but Joe Boyd had taken me to England with the Incredible String Band and I'd done some work in little coffeehouses there. I'd come back all Carnaby Street, with false eyelashes, sequined belts, flashed out. David had just pur-*

chased the boat that he loved. I remember being introduced to him and thinking he reminded me of Yosemite Sam. I used to secretly call him Yosemite Sam in my mind. I don't think I ever called him that to his face, but I might have. He mistakenly thought I wrote a song called "Dawntreader" for him and was thinking of naming his boat Dawntreader. He ended up keeping the original name, Mayan, which was good because it had a history already. I guess people identify with songs that you write and think you wrote them just for them.

David was wonderful company and a great appreciator. When it comes to expressing infectious enthusiasm, he is probably the most capable person I know. His eyes were like star sapphires to me. When he laughed, they seemed to twinkle like no one else's and so I fell into his merry company and we rode bikes around Coconut Grove and the winds were warm and at night we'd go down and listen to the masts clinking down on the pier. It was a lovely period and soon we became romantically involved.

When it came time to make my record, David did me a solid favor for which I am eternally grateful, because the way you enter the game in this business is usually the way you stay. It takes a lot to break typecasting and the way you come into the game is crucial, which was something I didn't realize at the time. In retrospect, I realize the importance of it. David put me into the game at a certain level and helped me keep control of my work, which I do to this day. In those days I resembled a folksinger to the untrained ear and David knew that there was only one record company that was even interested in someone who resembled a folksinger. What David and Elliot did was make me look like the New Movement. The record company was going to "folk rock" me up and David thought that would be a tragedy, that my music should be recorded the way I wrote it. He appreciated it the way it was and since he had been in the premier folk rock group, he could go to the record company with some authority and say, "I'm going to produce her," and the trick was that he was not going to "produce" me at all! The way David put it, he'd produce me minimally. He said, "It's like you're sitting *on the patio of the Old World Restaurant and a girl goes by in blue jeans and after she goes by you think, 'Did she have a little lace down the seams of her blue jeans?' " Anything we added would be minimal; that's the way we proceeded.*

Elliot was Joni's manager, a young man who had quit his job at the William Morris office in New York after hearing her sing in a Greenwich Village folk club. He was Elliot Rabinowitz from the Bronx; he changed his name to Elliot Roberts for show business. He followed another bright young William Morris agent named David Geffen out of the mailroom. Their paths would all become intertwined later, but in the winter of 1967 David Geffen was head of the television packaging department at the William Morris Agency, David Crosby was an ex-Byrd shopping for a schooner in Florida, and Elliot Roberts was a manager with one client and a little office on West 57th Street in New York that he could easily leave to accompany his client to Coconut Grove, where the climate was a lot more pleasant.

ELLIOT ROBERTS: *David Crosby is responsible for my coming to California. When I first met him, he was going with Joni Mitchell; Joni was my only client. I had just met Joni at the Café au Go-Go in New York, and the day after I first saw her play, we left on tour. We did a month of clubs, Joni went to Coconut Grove and met David Crosby, and in the meantime I went to California alone to meet with Mo Ostin at Warner Bros. to get Joni a record deal. She called up to say she was coming back with David Crosby and David was going to produce her first album. They showed up at my office in New York and David looked as he looks now: he had long hair flowing to his shoulder, he had the trademark mustache. He looked just like he did on his Byrds album covers. He was the first hippie that I met in that era. He didn't talk very much. He seemed slightly paranoid. He had gotten a bad rep. He was constantly being written about in the music papers as the Bad Byrd, you know, the Byrd That Got Away. The three of us went to California to start on Joni's album and stayed at B. Mitchell Reid's house; I slept on the floor in the basement on a mattress and David slept in the big bed with the little woman.*

KEVIN RYAN: *The Byrds never played Miami much, so we didn't see David for a long time. At one time, he and Chris Hillman showed up down there with the leather capes and leather hats and we went to a new coffeehouse called the Flick. Hillman didn't like it. He was a little bored, so he just walked out on the street corner in this black part of Coral Gables. He just went out to get a cab in a part of town where you don't see a cab go by for four or five years at a time. Later, when Simon and Garfunkel played the Gaslight, I asked Garfunkel, "Listen, you know McGuinn and Crosby. What are they into?" And he said, "Man, you wouldn't believe it. They are Galactic Overlords." I knew what he meant.*

ELLIOT ROBERTS: *Everyone knew David and David knew everyone. He was a sort of a guru to me, in that he brought me to California and showed me everything. Just the fact that I was with David gave me a seal of approval. "Hi, David Crosby said to give you a call" would get me in to see people or into clubs and David would come with me a lot of the time. David was the focal point; he was the scene. When David went anywhere, that place became the scene. When we went to the Whisky, our table was where everyone else wanted to stop and say hello. If we went to the Trip, the seas would part for David and people would get up from tables that already had drinks on them and David would sit down somewhere and that table would become the royal court. People would come by and pay their respects to David. Homage, actually. To me this was all incredibly bizarre because he had just been fired; he was an unemployed musician. But he knew just where to go when we started recording Joni's first album. The very first day in the studio at Sunset Sound, about an hour into the session, an engineer comes in and tells David that the Buffalo Springfield were in the room next door. Joni says, "You've got to meet Neil Young. I know him from Canada. He's in the Springfield. He's so funny. You're going to love this guy."*

The recording went well; Joni and David lived together as they worked on the album and he took pride in her and their work together in the studio. Elliot, in the meanwhile, was offered a bed at Stephen Stills's house, where the other houseguest was drummer Buddy Miles. It lasted a few days until Elliot couldn't stand it anymore. The neophyte manager next stayed with Neil Young, another generous man with a couch. That led to a management contract with the brilliant young Canadian lead guitarist, already preparing to depart the rapidly dissolving Buffalo Springfield. Within a couple of months, Elliot Roberts had rented a house in Laurel Canyon, up the road from Joni Mitchell's little wooden California bungalow, and was managing Joni, David Crosby, and Neil Young. David was a difficult client for many reasons, but nothing tops a manager's nightmare list like getting arrested with a client.

ELLIOT ROBERTS: *I took Joni to the airport on a Thursday because she was opening in Toronto on Friday. I was going to meet her the next day; I was taking the 10 A.M. flight, which got me there at 6 P.M. for the sound check. After I took her to the airport, David came by in his van and picked me up. He was moving some stuff from his house to Cass's house, where he was going to stay for a while. We come up San Vicente and make a left at the Whisky. David has a pipe and he's smoking grass and we're passing the pipe in the front seat. A cop pulled us over right in front of the Whisky. We get out of the car and they open up the back and they take out a kilo of grass and a loaded gun. I had no idea what was in the car, I really didn't. Didn't matter, they arrested both of us. Now it's Thursday night and we're being interrogated until around five in the morning. David and I are interviewed separately, but we're kept in one holding cell, where I tell David, "I don't know what to say about this." David says, "Just say the truth. You know, you were riding in the car. You didn't know anything. That's it." I go, "Okay." So I tell the investigator it's not mine, David's my client, I'm his manager, we were just driving to a friend's house to drop off some of his clothes. When I get back to our cell, I tell David, "I didn't tell them it was yours, but I didn't tell them it was mine either." And David says, "Okay. That's what I said. I told them it wasn't yours." I go, "Bless you, David. That's incredibly sweet." By now it's morning, we've been there overnight, and around 9 A.M. David's attorney arrives.*

*He says, "I'm bailing David out and I could bail you out,
Elliot. It's $1,500. But since David has told the investigators that
you knew nothing about any of this stuff, you'll probably be released
in an hour or so. Besides, I just came from the corner where they say
they saw the pipe and I had a van drive by and there's no way in the
world that cop could have seen a pipe being passed, David will
definitely get off. It's an illegal search and seizure." My response is
"Okay, great. I'll save the $1,500 if you tell me I'm going to be
released in an hour or two." The lawyer confirms it. "You are going
to be released in an hour or two." I say, "Well, thank you. I appreciate the advice." And I stay. David, as soon as his paperwork is
processed, is released on bail. They take him out of the cell while I
wait—and I wait—until three in the morning, when they take me
out of the cell, chain me to eight other guys, put us in a bus with bars
on it, and take me to L.A. County Jail, downtown. Meanwhile, Joni
is in Toronto, calling the house because it's her opening night and
I'm not there. The girl I'm staying with is saying, "He went with
Crosby yesterday and then he was going on the plane. So he's probably on his way up there." Because there were times that I would just
stay with David and then hang out and crash at his house because
the dope he had, called Ice Bag, made you fall out wherever you
were. David, meantime, had assumed that I was going to be released
in two hours and he was gone; he was at Cass's house. I had made my
call, I wasn't getting any more calls; I was being hosed down in
County and put in a cell and given a uniform and a mattress. I was
there for four days with three of the largest, baddest guys you've ever
seen in your life and I was having crying fits constantly. Finally,
they managed to drop the charges and I was let go. But David did
the right thing, he actually did tell the guy that I had nothing to do
with it and they had nothing to hold me on and they subsequently
dropped the charges on me. Thanks to David, I had my first prison
experience. As for him, the lawyer was right. It was an illegal search,
the evidence was suppressed, he got off.*

Me and Elliot are driving along the Sunset Strip in my VW
van with everything I own in it. We're coming back from some-

place and Elliot is lighting a pipeful of weed. There's a sheriff's car going in the opposite direction and they said they saw him do it. They just pulled us right over and I had a whole kilo. I remember the sheriffs jumping up and down and saying, "Wow, the mother lode of gold. Look at that. Wow!" Then they found the gun and that got them even more excited, but in the end the lawyer got me off. Illegal search and seizure. Seize and suture I used to call it. Illegal seize and suture. I went right on working on Joan's album.

David took special pleasure in revealing Joni to his friends as if she were a precious, rare, and undiscovered jewel. One occasion is typical: on a quiet weekday night David dropped by the Tiffany Theater on the Sunset Strip to visit actor friends in the Committee, a satirical improvisational revue that had sent a troupe to Los Angeles after running five years in San Francisco. The Los Angeles company opened to enthusiastic notices across the cultural spectrum: the movie industry trade papers, the underground press, and the mainstream *L.A. Times* and *Herald-Examiner* all praised the irreverent actors. Their material, like the best music of the day, made references to the news, politics, and pop culture and commented shrewdly and with wit on the times. David, still the actor, had joined them onstage a couple of times (the improvisational form permitted this kind of freewheeling addition to the company) and loved appearing with them. After the second show, still wired from performing, some members of the company were looking for something to do when David suggested they come with him. Howard Hesseman, presently playing the title role in the TV series "Head of the Class" and known for his portrayal of Dr. Johnny Fever on another long-run show, "WKRP in Cincinnati," was one of the company, along with poet-actor Garry Goodrow, director Alan Myerson, and this author.

Instead of cruising Ben Frank's or getting a bowl of chili at Barney's Beanery, the Committee people followed David's van (a plain beige VW hippie camper with a Porsche engine) to a rented house somewhere in Laurel Canyon. It was the kind of rent-a-pad that will live as long as musicians have to come to L.A. to record and can't afford to stay in a hotel. The construction is fifties utilitarian stucco, with landlord's shag carpets, off-white drapes, louvered glass windows, and no furniture except for the musician's staples: a mattress on the floor, a clock radio, a phone with an extra-long cord, a couple of thousand dollars' worth of stereo equipment, and a row of hard road cases full of guitars. It was a model environment in which to smoke six joints and unwind after a show. At 4 A.M., when everyone was thoroughly blasted on the Cros's usual "collector's-only" weed, David said, "I want you to hear someone." Leaving the little group of comics and actors wrecked on the floor, he disappeared and returned with an ethereal blonde holding a guitar. There, in a hillside house in Laurel Canyon, a half-dozen stoned and lucky actors heard a never-before-recorded Joni Mitchell sing half her new album in the predawn light. The company was stunned. "We thought we hallucinated her." Joni nodded, said little, and retired upstairs while Crosby just grinned. He repeated the exercise with Peter Fonda and with others.

PETER FONDA: *She was brand-new, hadn't been heard by any of us. David came strolling in one day, having dropped by with Joni in the afternoon. Wonderful day. He said, "Fondle . . ." That was his nickname for me. He knew I liked to fondle the women, so he called me Fondle. At any rate, he says, "Fondle, I've got one for you." I thought he had some groupie or something, you know, so I said, "This is my house, David. My wife . . ." He says, "No no. Come on. Serious, man. Listen to this." And Joni, kind of shy, appears. Staring at the ground for something to do, she sees my twelve-string guitar leaning against the wall and asks, "Can I use that?" She grabs hold of my guitar and detunes the fucker and then plays thirteen or fourteen songs, warbling like the best thing I'd ever heard in my life. David's so proud and he says, "That song's about me and that song's about so-and-so and isn't this great?" Joni was fabulous. I was just bowled over by this fabulous person with a wonderful voice and a great style. Lovely.*

ELLIOT ROBERTS: *Sure, they played B. Mitchell Reed's house too. David invited some people over one day. I remember Cass was there, John Sebastian, Michelle Phillips, about seven or eight people, all heavy players. David says, "Joan," and called Joni out. She was upstairs and came down with her guitar and she played eight or nine of the best songs ever written. The next day B. Mitchell Reed talked about it on the radio, how there was this girl in town named Joni Mitchell that's recording an album and there's nothing he can play now, but whenever this album comes out, it's going to be one of the great albums of all time. David set it up so that when the album finally came out, everyone in L.A. was aware of Joni Mitchell. The first club date we played, at the Troubadour, was standing room only for four nights, two shows a night.*

B. Mitchell Reed was one of the legendary rock 'n' roll DJs of the period. Originally a fast-talking AM Top 40 jock, Reed eventually quit his job as one of the prime movers in the lucrative and influential Los Angeles market, where he anchored the late-afternoon and drive-time slots on KRLA and KMPC, the most influential rock radio stations west of the Mississippi. Eventually, B. Mitchell (the Beemer, as he was the first to be called) went into partnership with Tom Donahue, who was pioneering free-form FM radio, first over KMPX, and later on KSAN in San Francisco. Reid became the mainstay at KMET, "the Mighty Met," in Los Angeles. By the time Joni's record came out, she was an industry legend, properly positioned for breakout success. It followed, as did romantic complications between Joan, David, and Graham. If this were an opera, the next remarks would be sung simultaneously, as a trio. Since reading is a linear, sequential experience, top to bottom, left to right, one page after another, the reader will have to arrange the chords or triads. Three people's lives were braided together and others would join a tangled skein that would finally drive every one of the artists involved to write a song about the experience: Graham Nash's "Our House," Joni Mitchell's "Willy," and David Crosby's "Guinnevere," a song that's generally identified with Christine Hinton. In fact, the third verse of "Guinnevere" was inspired by Joni Mitchell. David believes that "Dawntreader" is at least in part about him and he's willing to concede now that at least a part of "Guinnevere" was for Joni.

JONI MITCHELL: *I was living with David. Graham and I had had a kind of an ill-fated beginning of a romance because we had met in*

Ontario, when I was playing one club in Ottawa and the Hollies were playing another. We finally got together in Winnipeg. He ended up at David's place and I was staying with David until my house was ready. Graham came down sick in David's house and I took him home to my new house to play Florence Nightingale. At first it wasn't really for romance's sake; he was sick and I still had some domestic chops because I hadn't been trained to be a celebrity. I had been trained to be a regular Frau. I took him home and was looking after him and I got attached—here was a mess. What was I going to say? I'm kind of going with David and we sort of staked claims, but I'd written all these independent songs, trying to explain my position to him: that I'm still in an independent mode. But I got really attached to Graham and I guess that's the first time I harbored the illusion of forever. I really felt for the first time in my life that I could pair bond.

GRAHAM NASH: *I camped out with Crosby and then I rekindled my relationship with Joan, whom I'd met a couple of years earlier in Canada. There was a party at David's house and Joni was there. I was already totally intrigued and in love with this woman and she invited me home. I went with her and I didn't leave for a couple of years. It was a cute little house. That was an incredible time for me, probably the most intensely creative, free, and special time I've ever experienced. Not only was I in love with Joni but I was in love with David and Stephen and I was in love with the music and I'd taken a giant chance.*

David had Christine, while Graham and Joni lived together in a little house at the foot of Lookout Mountain Avenue in Laurel Canyon. It's the setting of Graham's hauntingly lyrical song "Our House" and although that romance is long over and Joni has been married for years to Larry Klein, there's a little niche high on the wall in Mr. and Mrs. Klein's kitchen that holds a charming art glass vase—the very same one that's celebrated in Graham's lyric, written twenty years ago.

At that time, in particular, I subscribed to the hippie ethic of nonownership. I didn't feel that anybody owned anybody and I tried my level best not to be jealous or territorial about that kind of thing because I didn't want it done to me. I used to tell girls, "Look, you don't own me. I'm going to make love to whomever I feel like. This is just how it is. I love you and I'll give you all the love I can, but I'm not going to be possessed. It's not happening and if that doesn't suit you, leave now." Christine, because she was really in love with me, was willing to live with that and maybe she actually felt to some degree the same way I did. At least she accepted it for the large part and I didn't hit her in the face with it.

The thing with Joni and Graham was that I felt great about it. I wanted to be with Christine. I know I was happy with her and Joan was a very turbulent girl and not an easy person to be in a relationship with, particularly then. I was very happy for them. They were in love and it was cool. Graham was then—and is now—my best friend and I didn't feel any jealousy about it. I loved him and I loved her and I couldn't see being angry at two people I loved for loving each other. That just didn't make a lot of sense to me.

Joni was with Graham, David had started singing with Graham and Stephen Stills, and Christine Hinton's devotion to David was unwavering, self-sacrificing, and understanding. She moved into the house on Lisbon Lane as David, Stephen, and Graham began to sing together seriously. Each one came from a group where they had problems; old relationships were collapsing and new alliances were being forged. B. Mitchell Reed had played some of the early demos of Crosby and Stills singing together. He couldn't credit them because the music was not ready for commercial release and there was no Crosby, Stills, and Nash album deal yet. Reed coined the name Frozen Noses for the new group; the unique harmony blends were identifiable to knowledgeable listeners in the Los Angeles music scene and the whimsical name had enough of a drug reference to make it almost insufferably hip. (Cocaine, ingested nasally, affects the small blood vessels in the nose and produces a numbing effect that frequently results in a lowered skin temperature.)

We had fooled around. Nash was still in the Hollies. We actively courted him and stole him. I'm sorry, Hollies. They didn't want to do his stuff and I thought his songs were great. Stephen thought his songs were great and we loved singing with him. We fooled around together in Los Angeles, in New York, and in London. Stephen was able, on the basis of our demos, to get some money from Ahmet Ertegun, the president of Atlantic Records. We wanted to go to London to record and I remember Stephen coming back from New York or someplace with five thousand dollars in cash and throwing it up in the air, saying, "Yahoo, we're in business! There should be enough for some airfare here." This was with the understanding that we would sign with Atlantic, which was a good thing to do anyway, since Stephen was already on the label. I got Columbia to drop me, free of charge. Clive Davis did it and traded Nash for Poco. Stephen and I had made demos of "Long Time Gone" and "49 Bye-Byes" that were pretty good. They were actually fairly impressive things, although a little self-indulgent—I had six of Stephen's guitars on at one point in "Long Time Gone," but we kept the demos interesting enough to where people kept being willing to spot us some more studio time or buy us the odd plane ticket. We finally decided that we wanted to win big and that meant we were going to operate in the pool with the sharks and we knew we'd have to get our own shark, so we went looking for a shark and found David Geffen. We said, "Ah, here's one now." I insisted that we involve Elliot. That was my personal doing. We were going to sign with David Geffen and I insisted that Elliot fly out from California and be involved. I thought Elliot was more of a mensch and more trustworthy and I guess it was his sense of humor or something made me trust him a lot more. I knew that Geffen was competent to duke it out with people; there wasn't any question about that. As it turned out, so was Elliot.

David Geffen is one of the legendary hero-villains in Hollywood, a curly haired slender man who rose steadily and regularly from his first job to the present time, increasing his net worth and influence in geometric increments with every new success. He rose through the agency ranks, starting at William Morris and passing through IFA on his way to CMA, the predecessor of ICM. That alphabet soup of employers taught the brash newcomer everything he needed to know about contracts, contacts, and deals. Before he was thirty, he was managing Laura Nyro, a gifted songwriter with a modest series of hits and a fabulous catalog that made both her and Geffen rich. He began polishing the techniques that would see him rise to executive authority and ownership positions in powerful personal management firms (representing, all at the same time, Crosby, Stills, Nash, and Young; Joni Mitchell; the Eagles; Linda Ronstadt; Jackson Browne; Joe Walsh; America; and more), major independent record companies (Asylum Records), Warner Bros. Studios, and eventually his own impressive entity, the Geffen Company. A monumentally aggressive deal-maker, he's mellowed without softening and can be painfully candid when he shares recollections from his perspective.

DAVID GEFFEN: *It was after the Byrds. David was hanging out with Stephen and Graham and Elliot Roberts, who was my friend. They all had fucked-up contracts and everything and I was the guy who was supposed to be able to get them all free and clear of their other commitments. There was something real interesting going on, but John Sebastian, who they invited to join the group, didn't think it was worth shit and didn't join and I remember Ahmet Ertegun saying, "Well, they're no Association." [The Association was a soft-rock group that had huge hits with such tunes as "Along Comes Mary," "Cherish," "Windy," and "Never My Love."] When I went to Jerry Wexler to get him to give me a release for Stephen Stills, he threw me physically out of his office. I don't think anybody really was that excited about them. They thought it had a lot of potential. Elliot and I thought it had a lot of potential. But it wasn't like the world was jumping up and down at the idea of these three guys. Don't forget, the Buffalo Springfield never made it. David Crosby was no longer in the Byrds and was not that highly thought of. And Graham Nash* *was in a pop group called the Hollies and they were never very important in America anyway. It wasn't earth-shatter time. After a lot of* Sturm und Drang, *I made a deal with Ahmet for the band. A good deal.*

ELLIOT ROBERTS: *David Geffen and I became good friends when I was working in the mailroom at William Morris. David went from the mailroom to head of TV packaging in eight months, literally, and the way he did that was to sign Danny Thomas and Witt-Thomas Productions. Y'know how that happened? David Geffen would go into the mailroom extra early. He taught me all this. He'd say, "When are you coming in?" and I'd say, "Well, I usually get in at nine," and he'd go, "Well, get in a six-thirty. That gives us a good two and a half hours to read everybody's memos." And we would. He'd come in with me and even though he was now a full agent and in TV packaging, we'd still would get into the mailroom extra early to read everyone's memos. David showed me how the game was played. He saw that Danny Thomas was available and that all the big-shot agents were all saying that they were meeting with him and no one really was, so Geffen went and met with him and signed him! At the time, Danny Thomas had a few series on the air. He was a big production house with deals at all the networks, supplying them with shows.*

I was just out of the mailroom at William Morris and David Geffen was still my guru because I really didn't know what the fuck I was doing, so I still asked David what to do and how to handle myself. I was twenty-one and I had absolutely no experience except that on my first week on the job, I ran into Joni Mitchell at the Café au Go-Go, so I quit and just started managing Joni and David Geffen became Joni's agent. Then, when I signed Neil and started managing Neil, David Geffen became Neil's agent. Everyone that I worked with, Geffen was the agent involved. So when Crosby, Stills, and Nash formed and asked me to manage them, this problem came up and it was something I couldn't handle, given my lack of experience at the time. I didn't know the players and David Geffen knew them all. He was already a wunderkind in both the record business and in TV packaging. I'd call David and explain the problem and he'd help settle it. He actually arranged the trade of Richie Furay and Poco to Columbia for Graham Nash's release from Columbia and the Hollies. We got Crosby's release for nothing, since Columbia didn't want him. All it took was one phone call to Clive Davis. I said, "We'd like David Crosby to be released," and he said, "You got it. We don't want any part of him." At that point, the Byrds were still happening and everyone was convinced that Crosby was a bad influence in the Byrds and a bad influence overall and had no future. The Byrds were really going to take off because McGuinn finally had control and the Byrds were going to live up to their potential. Which, obviously, was not what happened. Crosby was, in fact, the heart and soul of the Byrds and what he wrote was considered important.

Ahmet Ertegun was the self-made president of Atlantic Records. Ahmet and his brother, Nesuhi, came to America in the forties with their father, a Turkish diplomat. As Turks, they weren't immediately integrated into white society, which left them free to explore the ghettos of Chicago and Washington, D.C., discovering a golden age of jazz and blues clubs. True jazz buffs and enthusiastic fans, they had a little money and a lot of appreciation for the music they were hearing. They decided to start a small record label, Impulse!, to popularize and capitalize on the music they loved: jazz and rhythm and blues. In the early days, it was the kind of catalog that was considered either esoteric or "race" music, featuring such performers as John Coltrane, Chico Hamilton, Coleman Hawkins, and Sonny Rollins. By the sixties, in partnership with Jerry Wexler, the Erteguns had pioneered releases on Atlantic by the giants of jazz and soul, artists like Aretha Franklin, Ray Charles, the Drifters, and Wilson Pickett, people breaking out of segregated distribution and into the history of American rock 'n' roll. A wry, sophisticated, and deliberately elegant man with an urbane air that manages to combine the quiet authority of the Godfather with the excited enthusiasms of the most dedicated fan, Ahmet Ertegun is one of the prime movers and elemental forces in popular American recorded music.

AHMET ERTEGUN: *I didn't know the Byrds, although I was aware of their music. The way I got to know David was through signing the Buffalo Springfield, who were a really innovative avant-garde American rock 'n' roll group, very distinct from their British counterparts and very distinct from the other American West Coast groups like Jefferson Airplane. One of the saddest days in my life was when they broke up because they never really achieved the kind of popular recognition they deserved. When they broke up, it became clear that I couldn't keep them all and the person I felt strongest about was Stephen Stills. I released the others and kept only Stills. At which point, into my life came David Geffen, who was an agent and who had been speaking to Stephen Stills, David Crosby, and Willy Nash.*

From the first demos they made I could hear that the harmony sound of this group was better than anything I had heard since the Everly Brothers. It was really very special. Stephen Stills had talked to me at length about how much he admired David and that Crosby was somebody who had a different understanding of life and a different approach to things than other people, he came from a motion picture family and had an understanding of art, was a jazz fan and a great composer, a great singer, and would I make some records with him. I remember meeting with David and hearing some of the songs. They didn't sound commercial to me. I don't remember the titles, but I can tell you this about the songs he played for me—I didn't quite understand them. But I was quite taken by him and I was quite impressed with the melodic approach. In my mind, I couldn't translate that into what would make a commercial record because at this point I was really interested in getting into what I believed would be an avalanche of rock 'n' roll music. David's material seemed to be out of the mainstream, so I said, "Well, this is very good, but let me think about it." I put it off, trying to figure out what it could be, and I thought, "Gee, this guy's a little crazy. They're going off on a tangent." When I heard the music a few months later, after they'd holed up on Long Island rehearsing together, I said, "My God, this is really something very, very special."

David Geffen and Elliot Roberts eventually formed a management company, the Geffen-Roberts Company. It became the successor to Elliot's original Lookout Management, the company that was handling Joni Mitchell, Neil Young, and now Crosby, Stills, and Nash, the group with a name like a law firm. The association was as complex as anything in the music business. By California law, Elliot Roberts couldn't directly negotiate for the services of his clients while acting as their personal manager. As an agent, David Geffen couldn't properly take a management commission on clients he was managing in fact, if not in name. For a while, Geffen supervised the bookings handled by the variety department at CMA, a major talent agency, while Roberts worked in a cozy little office with tie-dyed curtains, secondhand overstuffed velvet sofas, and antique American oak roll-top desks and tables. When the band became huge, the Geffen-Roberts Company was born. The deal between the two men was made on a handshake on the streets outside this author's house in Hollywood, late at night after a party for the Cros.

ELLIOT ROBERTS: *As we were going across the street, David [Geffen] said to me, "Listen. This is getting to be too much and I'm not crazy about being an agent." He had Laura Nyro then and he said, "Well, you got Crosby, Stills, Nash, and Young and Joni" and Jackson Browne was in the picture too, since we had just started working with Jackson. David said, "Listen. I'll leave the agency and we'll do Geffen-Roberts," and I said, "Gee, I don't know if I want to give up my whole management company and take it apart," and he said, "Don't be stupid, I'll make you more money than you've made alone," and I said, "Yes, David."*

DAVID GEFFEN: *The first Crosby, Stills, and Nash record [Crosby, Stills, and Nash] came out and "Marrakesh Express" was the most pop thing on the album, since Graham had written it. It came out as a single and did okay. Not great. I prevailed upon Ahmet to release "Suite: Judy Blue Eyes," which, in everyone at Atlantic's mind, clearly wasn't a single; Stephen cut it down and it turned out to be a big hit. I was their manager originally. Elliot and I were not partners at that time. [David's recollection is different: "If we had Gef-*

*fen, we had Roberts; when we got one, we got the other."] Elliot took
over their management when I went to CMA and became an agent.
This was the second act I managed and I've never had as unpleasant
an experience as managing Crosby, Stills, and Nash and then
Crosby, Stills, Nash, and Young because you had drugs, which I was
completely unaccustomed to. And you had tremendous egos. In my
experience, there was never anything quite like the egos in Crosby,
Stills, Nash, and Young. It was not easy. David was obnoxious, loud,
demanding, thoughtless, full of himself—of the four of them, the
least talented. And I think that he felt the least talented.*

ARTHUR GARFUNKEL: *I remember when they first formed. They were
one month old, a new group, and proud of their harmonies. They
came by New York and dropped in on me and Paul [Simon] to show
us their blend and they were magnificently tight. They were doing
"In the Morning When You Rise" and we joined the group that
night. It was a five-man group [Crosby, Stills, Nash, Simon, and
Garfunkel]. It was just too much. They were so up, their lights were
high-wattage over the fun of it all. "Listen to what we've just polished off." You could see they were sitting on a lot of fun to be had in
the studio because you have the brilliant Graham, who's so adapt-
able in that upper range and has such a perfect cutting edge and is
ideally suited to combination, from his Hollies experience. You have
Stephen, who has a real personality of a voice, and you have David,
the velvety sort of cement in their sound. It's what used to be in the
Hi-Lo's or in those old Four Freshman groups: the middle man does
the stuff that makes the chord work, but you never notice it. David
can be right in front of your eyes in a sort of velvety way and you'll
never notice him. David sings beautifully. You can't leave that out of
anything that has to do with a David Crosby story. I'm a singer.
There's a Zen-smooth kind of exhale in David's delivery. He has
great come-from-the-heart feel in his singing and he loves rock 'n'
roll. You can hear it.*

One way or another, in New York, London, and in Los Angeles, the tracks for the first album were being cut, first as

demos for Ahmet and the record company, then as finished productions for the record, once "the deal" was set. The process was still home-grown and collaborative and involved, by extension, many of the work patterns that had served David creatively during both his folksinging and rock 'n' roll days with Jim Dickson and the Byrds. The studio, wherever it was located, was not only a technological tool to record; it was an atelier, a salon, a place to bring friends, to get feedback and input (two recording terms appropriated by the personal growth movement), and, above all, a place to show off new work. In New York, demos were made with producer Paul Rothschild: "In the Morning When You Rise" and "Helplessly Hoping," both just exercises. Finally, the group decided they already knew how to make records, since they'd had considerable experience for young men in their twenties. Graham had the most, although he'd been limited by recording in England, where the technology lagged behind what was happening in American studios. In the aggregate, the trio believed they could find their way through the process with the help of a good engineer. The man they got was Bill Halverson and the studio in which they worked was Wally Heider's Studio #3, which used to be at the corner of Cahuenga and Selma in downtown Hollywood.

Heider was an engineer turned entrepreneur, one of the pioneers of the new science of recording popular music. Until the sixties, recording technique hadn't changed much since the invention of tube amplifiers. Songs were recorded in single takes, with a minimum of microphones, and a three-hour recording session could produce as many as four complete songs. It was a time when you could make a hit record on a quarter-inch tape recorder in one pass; most of the hits of the fifties were done in just that way. Even the Beatles recorded their first albums on the early primitive machines, where ten microphones feeding into four tracks was considered state-of-the-art. Wally Heider had the only working remote system (a portable studio that could make commercial, broadcast-quality recordings in the field). He had begun by following the big bands around, recording them with equipment carried in the trunk of his car. Eventually, he went into business for himself, buying raw space and turning it into quality recording studios. His enterprise coincided nicely with another revolution in recording, the abandonment of the major company studios.

The record industry had become increasingly impersonal

and institutionalized, with major players like RCA, Decca, and CBS/Columbia keeping in-house studios where they would record their contract artists. As newer, more compact technology became available, the cavernous old rooms built for orchestras and big dance bands became superfluous. The new music, the radio hits that grew out of rhythm and blues and rock 'n' roll, didn't need that kind of physical production space. The technolgically limited recording style of early rock 'n' roll contributed to the sound of the music. A methodology built around live performances by massed strings and horns was irrelevant to a musical form built around the electric guitar and organ, small instrumental groups, pronounced rhythm sections with a heavy backbeat, and singers of unique power and expression: people like Elvis, Chuck Berry, the Platters, the Coasters, the Drifters, and the Everly Brothers. The big studio engineers—men who had grown up with crystal radio sets and who had learned their business in radio and on massive, quirky tube amplifiers—had little patience or understanding for the changing breed of musicians showing up in their studios. Union work rules were followed and a developing take or an experimental session would be ruined by some senior engineer looking at the clock, declaring, "Break time," and shutting down the machines in the middle of a take. That had happened to the Byrds on their first CBS/Columbia date and it rankled. After the loose, jazzy, "Let's play it back and try it again" approach of Dickson in their World-Pacific studio days, the big-business union-label systems at the major studios were not only annoying, they interfered with the creative process. The old guys didn't know it yet, but the studio was no longer a passive space in which to record sounds; it was becoming a tool, part of the method, another color on the palette. The new recording artists weren't just reproducing live sounds, they were using new tools to make new sounds. By 1968, thanks to advances in electronic amplification, a trio like Cream (Eric Clapton, Ginger Baker, Jack Bruce) could produce a greater volume of sheer sound than any other accumulation of instruments, brass band or symphonic, in history. Heider had recorded Cream and Halverson had been their engineer.

BILL HALVERSON: *I had a relationship with Ahmet and Atlantic and I was doing a lot of live recording for Heider, so when they called to inquire about the studio for this new band, I was managing things and put my name on it. Didn't know what it was going to be, but it was something I wanted. I got in on the ground floor of the new music business and had the opportunity to be in at the tail end of the old era, the days of big band sessions at Capitol and United and live remote recordings in clubs and hotels. I got to watch Heider do some large dates and I learned how to do strings, learned how to do horns, which is sort of a dying art at this point when it's all done with synthesizers. Learned how to record more than one thing without a lot of mikes and tracks. I learned not to say no and I learned to try anything and I think that kept me the job with them. I was willing to try and I really encouraged them to try. We rarely said no and I think we broke a lot of new ground.*

They had the power, that whole vocal blend, and a lot of the acoustic stuff was real bright. A lot of the organ stuff was pretty new. All the guitar sounds were real new. That full bass sound was original. Some of my mistakes kept me the job for a long time. On the first night, I was overlimiting and put too much top end on the acoustic guitar. I thought I was in trouble, but Stephen loved it. We tried to duplicate that for years. They're amazingly talented and they taught me a lot. The first night the first thing we did was the basic track of "Suite: Judy Blue Eyes" and then they put on the vocals. Ahmet Ertegun and Phil Spector came in the next night and we played it for them and just put them away.

Heider's was a dinky little studio but it was technologically okay, with a sixteen-track machine. I think some of the main credit that needs to be given is to Stills. We felt like he was a wizard on instruments. He could play guitar and keyboard better than we could even think about. Nash and I could bash away on a guitar, I could do some interesting things in tunings, but Stills could play lead and play recordable keyboard and that was way ahead of us. For example, when we were trying to cut these tunes, Stills said, "Look, let me try to cut 'Long Time Gone' for you. Let me try to build the track. I know what you need." I said I wanted to play rhythm guitar on it. He said, "Give me a break. Let me try it. Just go away for an hour." He and Dallas Taylor, the drummer, cut that track by themselves. Stills played the bass, the organ, the guitar. Dallas played the drums. And it's excellent! It has a wonderful feel to it. When we came back and heard the playback, I just sat there, stunned. I didn't know how he did that. It was *my* song; I had written it. Fine, I'll take credit for that, but Stephen cut the track and did a great job on it. That ability of Stephen's gave us a lot of impetus. What really put us over the top was the vocals. When we sang, people had to sit down. They just couldn't handle it.

After that, it happened fast. Their old friend, disc jockey B. Mitchell Reed, was now working in progressive radio. Reed was on KMET-FM, where he could play anything he wanted. Here was another revolution that was changing the face of popular music. Begun by Tom Donahue in San Francisco, on KMPX, the new form did away with the limitations of Top 40 AM radio. It shunned "playlists" and was built on the extremist, even heretical view that DJs should be able to program "sets," play groups of songs back to back without commercial interruption, program material for their listeners the way knowledgeable people played music for their friends at home, alternating album cuts and singles, laying out tasty combinations of songs, using the radio as something more than sound fill between commercials. What Donahue did for radio is immeasurable; it's hard to believe that prior to KMPX (which switched to its new format in 1966) there was, in effect, *no* FM radio! FM existed in large cities and played mostly classical and ethnic music for a minority of listeners who had receivers that could receive the FM band. Once again it was a new technology that made the new music: FM could carry a stereo signal of vastly improved quality. By 1967, what was being done in the independent studios by adventurous individuals was now being broadcast in a way that could be received at home with something approaching full fidelity to the recording artists' intentions. Once stereo and "hi-fidelity" recording were the norm, people wanted, *needed* their radios to sound as good as their phonographs. By 1969, FM was booming nationally. Every major market had competing FM stations broadcasting pop music and even Top 40 AM radio was starting to play the longer album-style cuts. In that climate, *Crosby, Stills, and Nash* was released. By July, it was a Top 10 *Billboard* hit and would stay on the charts for the next hundred and seven weeks—more than two years! By September, "Marrakesh Express" was on the singles charts, followed by "Suite: Judy Blue Eyes." For Stephen, Graham, and David, it meant their lives had changed in a major way—again.

SIX

....

Look around again
It's the same old circle
You see it's got to be
It says right here on page 43
That you should grab a hold of it
Else you'll find
It's passed you by

Rainbows all around
Can you find the silver
And gold
It'll make you old

The river can be hot or cold
And you should dive right into it
Else you'll find
It's passed you by

Pass it around one more time
I think I'll have a swallow of wine
Life is fine

Even with the ups and downs
And you should have a sip of it
Else you'll find
It's passed you by.

"Page 43,"
Words and Music by David Crosby

We were inventing the music. We tried to be as fearless as we could. We tried to have a rule that we would try almost anything. I'll give you an example: when the record was done, we listened to it and said, "You know, the 'Suite' ["Suite: Judy Blue Eyes"] feels great, but it's got a lot of little rough edges in it and it's seven minutes and twenty-two seconds of music." So we recut it. That took forty-eight straight hours in the studio, with, I'm ashamed to admit, the aid of chemical stimulants. When we were done we said, "Wow, that's good!" Then we played the original, listened to that, and the original was still better. The feel was better. The second one, which you will never hear, was much glossier, more polished, despite the fact that we did it in one forty-eight-hour session—by that time we knew exactly what to do. The truth of the matter is that the first one had "the feel." We learned early on in the process that feel is everything. If music has any overriding criterion, it's feel, that's what it is. For whatever reason, we all understood that very clearly and that was one of the things that made the record as startling as it was.

The other advantage that we had all along is that the three (or four) of us all write wildly divergent material. We are such different people and we write so differently that it gives us what I like to call a much wider palette out of which to paint the album, much more than most people have. Most groups have one person who can write and he writes a ballad and he writes a rocker and that's it. We write an incredible spread of stuff—it's really soup to nuts—and that gave us an incredible advantage. "Carry On" is a strong song on anybody's record. When you put it next to "Teach Your Children" and put that next to "Déjà Vu," when you've got those three in a row and follow them with "Country Girl," you have an unfair advantage. And that's what we had on that first album; that's what we've had since then: songs. We've always tried to do only the best songs we had.

I'll make a little side trip here: a lot of groups, when they have several writers, try to apportion the tunes so that everyone has a fair shot at making the publishing and copyright money off the record. It's called "pie slicing." It was a bit of a problem in the Byrds because we all saw Gene was doing great, while we were all starting to come along as songwriters. When I left the group, I felt I was not being given my due as a songwriter. I was writing songs like "Triad," I was starting to write "Guinnivere," I was starting to write "Déjà Vu," I was starting to write "Wooden Ships," and I couldn't get my tunes across. I'd get maybe one song on an album. I felt stifled, same as Nash in his group and Stills in his, although I don't think Stephen had that problem as much in the Springfield. With all respect to my very talented partner, I think that on a record where there was nothing but Stephen's tunes he would feel that he needed to have more of his songs on the album.

The best part about cutting the first Crosby, Stills, and Nash album was the fun that we had. We were buddies. We hung out together. We were very different even then, but we were friends and we used to love, more than anything else, blowing people's minds. We would invite friends over to the studio and say, "Sit down, listen to this," and then we would play them "Wooden Ships" and they would go, "Aurghhh. How he do dat?" We would blow their minds! They would sit there and their brains would dribble right out their nose. They could not believe it and this was our greatest joy because we were all egotistical little show-offs and it was our biggest chuckle.

When we played it for Ahmet, he died and went to heaven. He came to California, came to the studio, and heard about half of the album, all that we had done at the time. He just listened to it and looked at us. Any other record exec in this business would have had dollar signs in his eyes. You would've been able to hear the cash register going off for twenty blocks away. Ahmet, to his credit, was truly moved. Sweet man that he is and gentleman that he is and cultured man that he is, Ahmet loves music. Truly, with his heart, loves music. Which is something that is rare in the record industry. There are exceptions, like the late John Hammond, who's a perfect example of a record company executive who put the music first. Hammond recorded Billie Holiday *and* Bob Dylan, for Chrissake. And Herb Alpert of A&M Records likes music. He *plays* it. But most of the guys are sensitive to sales and not quality; I think that's fair to say. Ahmet was moved, deeply moved. I won't go so far as to say he cried, but his response was at that kind of emotional level. He knew we had made some really incredible music and he was very proud of us. We were his boys. He took a parental stance with us from the very start. We were his band. He brought us to the company. He signed us and all our contact with the company went through him, alone. We were Ahmet's band and it was great. The amazing thing was that 1969 was the Year of the Guitar Player. This was the year that everybody wanted to be Clapton and Hendrix; that was the way everything was going. Jeff Beck was starting to be the guy in England and Clapton and Hendrix were heavy; they were monsters. The Who were kicking over their amps. There were smoke bombs onstage for the first time. And yet, all of a sudden, here comes this acoustic music, this incredible three-part harmony.

Let me digress again, about harmony. In two-part harmony, you have a lot of room to move around. You can go in relationship from the root, which is the melody, to another note, which can be a fourth, a fifth, a seventh, a sixth, a ninth, even a second and it can move around. And all of those different intervals have an emotional thing to them. For example, a minor third above the root gives one feeling. An open fifth is another kind of feel. With three people, the tendency is to sing what're called "triads," which is the normal three-part chord. Three out of the four notes of the arpeggio, the fourth being the octave. What we did, which made me extremely proud, was sing a lot of nonparallel stuff. I did some of my very best work being subtle, moving the middle part around in internal shifts that kept it happening. That's what made me proud. Those harmonies came out of the Everly Brothers, late-fifties and early-sixties jazz, and classical music. A lot of classical music. A ton of classical music. Thanks, Mom.

As I remember it, we put out the album and I took off and went sailing. I went down to the boat. We went to the Bahamas and I wasn't around when the thing got big. But I heard—it filtered down to Florida, which was way behind the times in those days. All of a sudden it was all over the radio. I missed the excitement of sitting in L.A., in the biz, getting saturated with winning. It's probably a good thing, given my ego.

In Florida, as *Crosby, Stills, and Nash* climbed the charts, the schooner *Mayan* was made seaworthy. With the first rock 'n' roll dollars that came in, David fitted her with new sails and rigging. He provisioned her, began sailing short runs from Florida, across the Gulf Stream, to the Bahamas, and south to the nearby Caribbean islands. A pickup crew was aboard and the Plan was to eventually bring the *Mayan* to California. But first, there was this nagging problem of superstardom: the band had hit and hit big.

Then as now, the test of a band's success was its ability to deliver a live concert performance. Concerts are also the way to make enormous amounts of money in a relatively short amount of time. By 1969, there was a new problem that faced recording groups when they performed live; ironically, it was a result of the freedom of expression afforded them by the new technology they found in the recording studios. Albums were no longer simple recordings of a performance as it might've occurred in a studio or a live location. Thanks to multiple tracking and signal manipulation, records were becoming complex creative combinations of different performances: layered, combined, overdubbed, echoed, equalized, panned, spread, sped up, slowed down, even played backward. (Techniques pioneered years earlier by jazz guitarist Les Paul, who literally invented the marriage of electricity and music, first by creating the pickup microphone for "electric" guitar and later by inventing multitrack and overdub recording.) Crosby, Stills, and Nash prided themselves on making their basic tracks as much of a performance as possible, but they were into the new technology as much as anyone—and ahead of most.

It made for fascinating listening, but it also made it difficult to re-create the recording in live performance, short of sneaking a tape onstage the way the Hollies did. Some of the problems would be solved years later, when sophisticated digital electronics could bring studio effects to performance public address speaker systems, but at the time it made artists and engineers crazy. Crosby, Stills, and Nash didn't go crazy, but there was stress as the group prepared to go out and perform live for the people. All the togetherness and good-buddy feelings in the world couldn't calm the anxieties of three disparate rock 'n' rollers from uniquely different bands, each one with his own history of public performance: David, the folkie soloist and group harmony singer and rhythm guitarist; Stephen, the guitar virtuoso and songwriter, the musician; and Graham, only mildly accomplished on guitar and steeped in a chart-oriented British Top 40 tradition that went back to beat and skiffle groups. They needed a place to rehearse.

Peter Tork had bought a big secluded house with a swimming pool on the Valley side of the Hollywood Hills. The house had a show-biz pedigree, like all the houses that celebrities buy in Los Angeles. The house on Shady Oak had been built by popular bandleader Carmen Dragon (father of Toni Tennille's partner, Daryl Dragon, a.k.a. the Captain), sold to Wally Cox, then acquired by Monkee Peter, who ran into financial problems and rented it to Stephen Stills. Reine Stewart had abandoned triads with Christine and David and was pregnant by Peter Tork, with whom she was living in a full-time relationship. (David had introduced her to Peter during the time he was borrowing the money from Tork to buy the *Mayan.*) Shady Oak was where Crosby, Stills, and Nash would rehearse for their imminent first tour. Among the women who frequented the premises was an actress named Salli Sachsi, a woman who had costarred in a few *Beach Blanket Bingo* films and had been widowed in her twenties when her husband crashed his private plane into the ocean off a Southern California Beach. She had drifted up into the scene on the Sunset Strip and fell in with the musicians she had known peripherally through her movies. She was one of the beautiful, long-legged, straight-haired women who found themselves caught up in the scene.

SALLI SACHSI: *Shady Oak was in Studio City on the side of a mountain. There were about eight people living there at the time. They had this film business going and Peter was just leaving the Monkees. There were Moviolas and editing gear and sound equipment and they were rolling film and editing and making music. Crosby, Stills, and Nash would come over to the house after being in the recording studio all night and have saunas and go swimming and just cool out before they went home and went to bed. They would have big feasts up there —big, long dinners, maybe thirty people: Reine, Christine, Reine's brother James, Riley Wildflower, Bobby Hammer, Barry McGuire— Owsley once brought a trunkload of steaks because we were mostly vegetarians and he thought everybody was pretty sickly and needed some meat! Jimi Hendrix would stop by there when he was in town. There was a music room, the walls were covered with oriental carpets, and Stephen would shut himself up in those rooms for days, eating Hershey bars and drinking Coca-Colas. There was no time zone; it was all music.*

ELLIOT ROBERTS: *David's influence as a creative force made other people creative. He was like certain athletes, ballplayers like Larry Byrd and Magic Johnson, who make other players better. David made other players better, made them play and sing above their capabilities, freed them up a lot. There was never anything like, "Well, that's all you can do and you can't go any farther," and "Well, this is all I really do and that's all I'm capable of." That didn't exist with David. He was such a character that he believed everything he told you; everything was a story to David. There were no yes-or-no answers, there were just analogies and metaphors. We were driving above Mulholland when Crosby, Stills, and Nash was just formed. David was telling me this whole scenario of what he was going to do and how he was putting this band together. Now, all of them take credit for putting the band together, but before it was really a band, David had it all figured out. We were driving in his van to Cass's house and he spelled out how Crosby, Stills, and Nash were going to happen and how these problems hadn't been solved yet but they were all going to be worked out and we were going to go to Atlantic and it was going to be the biggest American supergroup that ever was, that people just didn't know the talent involved, the caliber of the writers and the singers. Everything he told me on that ride came to pass. Every single thing.*

David hadn't predicted the fights and flare-ups in the group. Stephen had a mercurial temper and a sense of machismo that stemmed from his Southern upbringing and a background in military academies. Graham had a slow fuse that burned for a while before he exploded; he had equally strong ideas about how things should be done. David was a mediator and an instigator by turns, opinionated as either of the other two and combining their most provocative traits: Crosby was as quick to anger as Stills and as logical and methodical in his arguments as Nash. It was a volatile mix of personalities. A former gallery owner turned photgrapher named Bobby Hammer was immersed in the scene and recalls how it went:

BOBBY HAMMER: *In the studio they got along okay. There'd be little flare-ups here and there. The tour anxiety came from the fact that suddenly they'd have to be in front of fifty thousand people. If there was any kind of sound rehearsal or sound check on the day before the performance, there would definitely be a fight. And the bigger the fight, the better the performance. And if they got along real well in rehearsal, I knew it would be kind of a lah-de-dah walk-through show because they weren't nervous enough. But if they had a big blowout, if Stephen would freak out and scream about something and stalk off, saying something like "That's it and I'm not even gonna be here tonight," I'd think to myself, "Ohhhh boy, tonight's gonna be great." I've got some film I shot just before the Greek Theater that's a good example. The Greek Theater shows were some of the best and opening night was one of the best performances they ever gave. It was their West Coast debut and just prior to that they had two fights. I have both of them on film. Stephen ranted and raved and Graham said, "It isn't what he says, it's how he says it." It was incomprehensible—if you're an outsider trying to follow their fights, forget it. They'd insult each other, refer to each other's songs, compare real behavior to lyrics, call each other cop-outs for not behaving in the ways they wrote about in their music.*

Peter and David had both warned them not to set up outside the house because Shady Oak was in a canyon and they'd blow it. One Sunday morning Stephen moves all his amps outside, gets them stacked about eighteen feet tall, and starts to play solos early in the morning, freaking out the neighbors. David said that was a wrong thing to do and Stephen says, "You're a cop-out. You talk about letting your freak flag fly and you're giving me a lecture about where I'm supposed to play the music." It took me weeks to figure out what the hell these guys were talking about. And that's how they attacked, saying, "Well, you said this in the song and, therefore, this must be the way you live. If you don't do it that way, I disown you." Every-

one yells at each other and then three seconds later they're singing. That's what I always felt about their fights—big explosions followed seconds later by incredible harmonies.

True to the warnings, the police came to investigate the noise in the canyon and left without further incident. Salli Sachsi and Bobby Hammer would move into a small cabin next door to David's house on property that David annexed to his own. David started spending more and more time commuting in a triangle whose points included Los Angeles; Marin County, north of San Francisco; and Florida, where the *Mayan* was becoming increasingly seaworthy. Christine shuttled back and forth, often traveling in advance of David, getting Marin together if he was going there, hurrying back to tidy up Lisbon Lane for his return. And then there was the tour. The first public performance of Crosby, Stills, and Nash was in Chicago, their second concert was at what was billed as an "Aquarian Festival of Peace and Love and Music" scheduled outdoors on a farm in upstate New York, an event that came to be known as Woodstock.

I groan at the mention of the name; everybody always asks us about Woodstock. The two most frequently asked questions in my professional life are "Do you remember Woodstock?" and "How did you guys meet?" Woodstock was an amazing circumstance. My feelings about Woodstock aren't particularly strong, but it's significant to remember the amazing feeling that prevailed, a very encouraging thing about human beings. We haven't managed to do it before or since, but for that one moment we did something that tells you what's possible with human beings. For three days there was a very good feeling among half a million people. There were no serious fights. There wasn't a single reported rape. There was no real violence. There was no murder. There was no armed robbery. There was no racial violence. There was no mob violence. There was not one sign of the normal bad behavior that goes along with large groups of people.

Every other time you get that many people together for anything, including religious festivals, there are fights, murders, rapes, and robberies. Woodstock was a time when there was a prevailing feeling of harmony. If you had a sandwich and somebody else was hungry, you would give them half your sandwich. I saw hippies pushing a police car out of the mud because the policeman had just picked up a hippie girl who'd cut her foot on some glass; he carefully put her in the backseat and was trying to take her to the medical tent. I saw twenty hippies help that cop and I saw the cops help the hippies. I saw that wonderful guy in the movie, the Port-O-San man, with the outhouses—my favorite guy in the whole movie. "I got one son in Vietnam and another one out there in the crowd and I think we ought to help them out," he said. A lot of human beings managed to call up the best in themselves. The Hog Farmers [Wavy Gravy's extended family of bus-riding nomads] were exemplary. They gave unstintingly, without question, to everybody, didn't matter who you were. If you needed some help, they wanted to help you. The people in medical services did tremendous work. We were there for a couple of days. I slept in a tent one night, in a motel another night. Was it really an "Aquarian Festival of Peace and Love and Music"? Hard to answer because I didn't give a damn about Aquarian this or Aquarian that. I think astrology is complete bullshit, especially since I found out that the Reagans like it.

The other notable thing about Woodstock was that we were scared, as Stephen said in the film. What wasn't said in the movie is why we were so nervous: everyone we respected in the whole goddamn music business was standing in a circle behind us when we went on. Everybody was curious about us. We were the new kid on the block, it was our second public gig, nobody had ever seen us, everybody had heard the record, everybody wondered, "What in the hell are they about?" So when it was rumored that we were about to go on, everybody came. Every band that played there, including all the ones that aren't in the movie, were all standing in an arc behind us and that was intimidating, to say the least. I'm looking back at Hendrix and Robbie Robertson and Levon Helm and the Who and Janis and Sly and Grace and Paul, everybody that I knew and everybody I didn't know. We were so happy that it went down well that we could barely handle it; I was also toasted because we had some of that Pullover pot, that incredible Colombian gold that a friend of mine named Rocky had brought to the festival.

Woodstock was a classic case of being in the right place, at the right time, with the right management, and with the right stuff. That weekend has acquired a mythic stature and in pop iconography it's assumed that it was the media event of the year, probably getting more coverage than the inauguration of Richard Nixon as the thirty-seventh President of the United States or the box office success of Peter Fonda's low-budget outlaw-hippie-biker epic, *Easy Rider*. That may be, but it was also a time when we began bombing Cambodia, Neil Armstrong walked on the moon, and Ted Kennedy went off the Chappaquiddick Bridge with Mary Jo Kopechne. Other news? Crosby, Stills, and Nash won a Grammy for being Best New Artists and David made the cover of *Rolling Stone*. And then this:

DAVID GEFFEN: *The album came out. It was a giant hit. They proceeded to go on to Woodstock. I had booked their second concert together to be Woodstock. I was with them. I flew into La Guardia Airport. The headline of the* New York Times *said* 400,000 PEOPLE SITTING IN MUD. *So I said to Elliot, "You go. I'm staying here." Joni Mitchell and I stayed at my apartment in New York, where she wrote the song "Woodstock," having never been to Woodstock. She was with me. Then they heard the song, they recorded it, and it became the anthem for Woodstock. As for the movie, I would not allow them to use the footage of Crosby, Stills, Nash, and Young in the movie unless they used Joni's song with Crosby, Stills, Nash, and Young singing it as the theme of the movie. That's how that happened. The producers were either going to give me what I wanted or that was it. And since I represented a lot of important artists on Warner Bros. and Atlantic and Elektra Records, they just weren't going to fuck with me. So, they pretty much did what I wanted. Let's not kid ourselves. I was a formidable figure always. And was then. That's why the group came to me in the first place.*

David Geffen's brief account collapses a year of history into a paragraph; Woodstock, the event, took place in August of 1969. *Woodstock,* the movie, came out more than a year later, in 1970, with the CSNY version of Joni Mitchell's song as the title or theme track, just as Geffen had negotiated. In the intervening time a lot happened and everyone's life continued to change in radical and unforeseen ways. First off, Neil Young joined the group and played with them at both Woodstock and the Big Sur Folk Festival, which took place two weeks later. Big Sur was as small as Woodstock was big. It was held on the grounds of the Esalen Institute on the cliffs over looking the Pacific halfway between Monterey and Hearst's San Simeon on California's unbelievably scenic Coast Route 1. A film was made of that festival as well, produced by this author, who can be seen nude in a hot tub with Crosby and others. In it is a rare filmed performance of Joni Mitchell singing the earliest version of "Woodstock," the song, accompanying herself solo on the piano. There's also footage of a scuffle between Stephen Stills and a stoned heckler in the audience. A few weeks later, in Los Angeles, still wearing the same performance wardrobe, Crosby, Stills, Nash, and Young performed on ABC-TV's "The Music Scene." It was definitely their time. Who brought Neil Young into the band and when did Neil know it? There are several points of view:

AHMET ERTEGUN: *One evening after we had our first big success with CSN, David came up with Elliot to my house for dinner and after dinner I started to play these Neil Young records and I told them that as happy as I was to see Stephen Stills with Graham and with David, I was very sad that Neil Young was no longer with Stephen. There was a certain magic between them when they were with the Buffalo Springfield and that evening they said, "You know, we ought to talk to Neil," and I think the whole idea of adding Neil Young to the group came about then and it works with him as well. He is kind of part of them even when he's not there; they feel like he's the only person who could be with them. You can't really take any other person and add to that group.*

ELLIOT ROBERTS: *When David was telling me about the Springfield breaking up, he said I should definitely get Neil: he was the one. Even though David replaced Neil in the Springfield for about ten minutes at Monterey, Neil was irreplaceable. He brought intensity to the party that no one else could muster because he was so much more serious than anyone else. It was all life and death to Neil. For example: before CSNY, on this lousy bus tour with the Byrds, the Turtles, and Buffalo Springfield, the last gig the Springfield did together, we checked into a hotel next to a Pitch 'n' Putt golf course. Neil had a fever on the ride down on the bus and I love golf, so after we checked in the guys all went up to their rooms and I went to the golf course to drive a few. When I got back, Neil fired me. I said, "What for?" and he said, "This is serious, man. This ain't no golf match. This ain't no tourney. This ain't no party. This is serious shit. You should have been in your room waiting for us to call, figuring out something, plotting, planning, figuring out my life, figuring out my career, not playing golf." He hired me the next day and then he fired me again later and rehired me; it was that intense. David was the first guy to hip me to that. He told me to stick to Neil. "I got Stephen, you take Neil, and it's going to be a happening thing 'cause Neil's the one. Neil really is the talent."*

Chris Hillman took me down to hear Neil with the Buffalo Springfield and when I saw him I said, "Oh oh, there's the stuff." They had songs . . . Neil wrote great songs; he still writes great songs. Songs are the real dividing line between the people who've got it and the people who don't. You can hire all the hotshot guitars in the world. You can tie everything in the world to everything else and process this and keyboard that and electronicize the other thing, but if you don't have the song, you don't have the story. I don't care how much production you put on it. It's still a piece of junk if it's a piece of junk. Michael Jackson's "Bad" is just a piece of junk. It doesn't even matter if you get Quincy Jones to do it and Quincy's one of the best musicians in Hollywood. He's a goddamned genius and it still doesn't matter; it's a junk song. Neil's got the songs. That's what knocked me out; that's what made me go on about him. Then, when I got to know him, I realized he was really one of the funniest human beings alive. He's a hysterically funny person if he knows you and he likes you. He's very reserved and weird if you don't know him. But if he knows you and he feels comfortable with you, he will have you in total goddamn hysterics.

Crosby, Stills, Nash, and Young and Taylor and Reeves. That's what they were calling themselves. That's how comedian David Steinberg introduced them on network television on "Music Scene." It was more like a big law firm every day, with the first four being the senior partners and the last two, drummer Dallas Taylor and bass player Greg Reeves, salaried junior partners with a minor participation. Management was taking a commission from each of the individuals and making a good living. During the taping of their segment, lots of tension ruled the set. The band mistrusted television; it was monophonic, the sound technicians were using pretty much the same recording techniques that had served radio for forty years, and nobody spent a lot of time on getting the sound mixed right, since it all came out of a tinny three-inch speaker on a home television set that had a fifty-fifty chance of being black-and-white. The show had pretensions to hipness and this author was once again involved, this time as head writer (following a year with "The Smothers Brothers Show" on CBS).

"Music Scene" is a little-remembered anomaly. It was a forty-five-minute network television variety show, based loosely on the old "Your Hit Parade" format, in which each week's show would feature *Billboard*'s top chart songs, performed by the original artists. ("Your Hit Parade" featured hit songs performed by the show's regulars: Snooky Lanson, Dorothy Collins, Gisele MacKenzie, Russell Arms, and others. That's right, a pop singer named Snooky.) "Music Scene" lasted seventeen weeks and one can judge the producers' show-business savvy by recalling that they hired a director with two hearing aids and made him a producer too and fired Lily Tomlin, who was a regular on the show before her debut on "Laugh-In." In this environment, David, Elliot, and Stephen went up to the sound booth to listen to a playback. The engineer had long hair and was under forty, which was the network's concession to modern music. He was proud of his mix. "What do you think?" he asked, leaning back grandly in his chair. "It's shit." "It sucks." David: "If you think that sounds like anything better than dogshit, you have tin ears." They almost came to blows and only massive intervention prevented massive damage. David was growing to hate the Los Angeles music business and there was an alternative up north, around San Francisco and Marin County, where old friends were making good money playing under different circumstances and enjoying different lifestyles. In addition, there was the siren call of the sea from the *Mayan* in Florida. On occasion, all the lines would meet. Paul Kantner and Grace Slick of the Jefferson Airplane arranged such a convergence.

PAUL KANTNER: *Grace and I were playing down in Miami somewhere and had a little break, so we took some funky seaplane out to the middle of some atoll out in the midst of God knows where, landed in the lagoon where David was anchored, and stayed for a weekend or a week or whatever it was. He got some of our cookies, the ones with the little red dots, LSD. We were in the habit of fucking with each other all the time in those days. It was innocent and you didn't do it to strangers, but to each other it was sort of a prank, fun, ha-ha. David spent the whole day facedown in the sand, studying mollusks or something. Big sunburn on his back. We dove down to the bottom of this lagoon out in the middle of the total Atlantic, nothing around anywhere, and there was a whole bunch of garbage and deck chairs and stuff all down at the bottom of the lagoon. Fortunately, I didn't take too much acid that day. "Wooden Ships" was written for David's sailing thing. David stole the first verse of it off a church, where they had a little neon sign where they'd put a little saying:* IF YOU SMILE AT ME, *et cetera. We just ripped it right off there. Part of the artistic process. What we used to call "the folk process."*

GRACE SLICK: *What I saw—and maybe I'm looking through rose-colored glasses—was an amazing situation where he was able to have a couple of girls who were living with him in a sporadic chronic permanent way. They'd be with each other in the same room and one would be cooking and one would be sewing or rubbing his head and he was kind of like a little Sultan. They seemed to be enjoying it immensely and it seemed to be working. It was a sort of Hollywood Hippie thing, having these long blonde-haired lovely young human beings running around, sometimes with no clothes. I never really saw what might have been disturbing to other people. I thought everybody was happy with the arrangement. The bacchanalian thing was pure David. The Airplane was playing in Miami and we had several days off; we took a seaplane to get to wherever the hell he was. David was there with several girls, people all running around with no clothes on. Beautiful rosewood boat or whatever the hell it was [David: Honduran mahogany, yellow pine planking, and teak decks.] People were making food and pouring wine and singing songs with an acoustic guitar in the back of this boat with the sun going down and absolutely dead-clear water and it was one of those amazing periods of time. David was always pretty good at keeping those balls in the air—or wherever balls belong, so to speak. I was embarrassed because these women all had perfect figures, no tan lines, and long blonde hair. I had kinky brown hair, I was skinny at that point, with no boobs—one of them's bigger than the other—and knobby knees. "No, I'm not taking my clothes off." Not for moral reasons, but because there would be no comparison here, thank you very much. He called me the Chrome Nun. Call me Chrome Nun if you want, but I'm not taking my clothes off. Female singers, with the possible exception of Stevie Nicks, were not the best-looking of the lot. The groupies were generally better looking than any of the singers. Christine was with David and there were about eight other people aboard and it was very pleasant and unreal and you can't keep that way of life going forever. We were naïve enough to think we could.*

David had been spending more and more time in San Francisco; the lure of Northern California was already seducing almost everyone in the band and their success made it easy to buy into the temptation. Neil Young bought an eight-hundred-acre ranch south of San Francisco, Elliot Roberts bought property nearby, and Graham Nash, ever the urbanite, purchased a handsome Victorian mansion on the fringes of the Haight-Ashbury district in the city of San Francisco. Graham's house underwent a stunning renovation, all redwood and glass and fine joinery, with a recording studio in the basement. (It's presently a very elegant annex to a tasteful bed-and-breakfast hotel next door.) David was hanging out with Phil Lesh, bassist with the Grateful Dead, as well as Jerry Garcia and the rest of the band. The Dead had a ranch of their own, north of the city in Novato, a rural suburb in Marin County. It was a scene of prototypical psychedelicized and successful rock 'n' roll consciousness. Christine Hinton was happily assuming primacy among the women in David's life, with his gradual acceptance of her in the role of number one. Debbie Donovan joined them in a new house that David rented in Novato, close to the Dead's fun ranch.

ELLIOT ROBERTS: *I was living up north and Neil had already bought his ranch and I was going with David to Novato a lot at that time. We'd spend time at the Marin house because with Crosby, Stills, and Nash, you pretty much dealt with David when planning tours. I would run it down to David first, everything that I had planned, the problems we had with Ahmet, whatever was going on. David had just moved to that house with Christine. He had harems in L.A. and up north, but Christine was the thoroughbred of it all. She was his main woman and she'd come down to L.A. and run his L.A. trip and when he'd go up north she'd go up a day early and make sure his Marin trip was together; she was the captain of all his scenes. And there was no question that he loved her a great, great deal. The others? They were women, but she was his love.*

DEBBIE DONOVAN: *I graduated from Hollywood High in the Hollywood Bowl and as a graduation present I got tickets to Hawaii. So I took a girlfriend and we went over to Kauai and camped out and at the end of the summer, when I came back, Christine said, "Why don't you move up here?" So I moved to Novato, started going to school up there, and Christine had a lot of stuff organized. She knew what she was planning and she knew that David liked threesomes and all of that. So she figured, "Well, okay, if that's the way it's gonna be, then it's gonna be with somebody of my choosing." I'm assuming that they discussed it because back then things weren't not discussed.*

KEVIN RYAN: *The move out of Beverly Glen to Novato was one of the most colorful moves I've ever encountered. The Grateful Dead sent their road crew and they showed up on Lisbon Lane with a forty-foot flatbed truck, which couldn't make it up the last hundred feet of road, so Bobby Hammer strung all his lights out and there were people carrying boxes and furniture and anybody that dropped by would wind up with a box. Christine ran the whole thing. It was stunning to watch her be top sergeant. You'd say, "How ya' doing, Christine?" And she'd say, "Oh yes . . . this," and hand you a box. People would stop by to talk and wind up carrying something. At one point she and I stopped and for one hour we rolled joints for the trip back. The crew didn't want any money; they just wanted to be able to stay high all the way. We must have rolled forty joints, which just barely got them home. Christine was cool and in control of the whole number. She knew where everything went.*

David, Christine, and Debbie Donovan started to set up housekeeping in the country house in Novato. They had only been there a few weeks, the fall equinox had occurred, and the days were getting shorter. It was the end of September when Christine took the VW van and set out with Barbara Langer, who was married to Barry Melton of Country Joe and the Fish. They were on their way to the veterinarian with some of the house cats. Barbara later told the police that the kitties were rambunctious and hard to control; one of them got away and was climbing loose in the front seat. Christine's attention was diverted as she struggled to recover the cat and the van swerved across the center line into the path of a schoolbus coming the opposite direction. There was a head-on crash that killed Christine. Barbara was badly injured, but she survived.

A local sheriff's deputy came for David and took him to a local hospital to identify her. Christine, until that morning radiantly beautiful and memorably full of life and loving energy, was a dead body on a stainless-steel table. David returned to the house, stunned and shocked. The others, Graham Nash among them, were confronted with mortality, grief, and the irrevocable finality of sudden and surprising death. It would affect them all for years.

It was a very pretty day. Mickey Hart had sent over a horse for her to take care of and have and use. She was excited about it. She and Barbara took off in my little green Volkswagen van. A little later, I got a phone call later from one of the ladies at Mickey's ranch. She said, "I think Christine's been hurt. I think she's been in a bad accident. I think you better get to the hospital." We couldn't get Bobby Hammer's car started, so a guy named Slade took us to Novato Hospital. We had to drive past the wreck to get there and the bus was demolished. I remember saying to Slade at the time, "Jesus, I hope she's still alive." At the hospital, there was an ambulance pulled up to the back and the inside was covered with blood. An attendant was mopping it up with a sheet and I asked him, "Is she still alive?" He looked at me kind of strangely and didn't answer, so I turned around and started inside. A doctor asked me if I was related to the victim and I said, "Yeah, she's my girlfriend." He said, "We're sorry to tell you. She's dead."

I had no way to deal with that, nothing in my life had prepared me for that. I just said, "No no no no no." I think I screamed it, really. The doctor asked me if I wanted to see her and I don't know whether I should have said yes or should have said no because now I'm stuck with this picture of her dead that I can't get rid of. I'd much rather remember her alive. Yet, if you have to deal with the death of a loved one, if you have to learn to accept the fact they're gone, it helps if you see them dead. I did. She was. They loaded me in the car and took me back to the house and after that a highway patrolman came around. His name was Officer Walkup. The local paper ran about a two-inch squib about it on the fourth page or something: GIRL IN HIPPIE COMMUNE ON INDIAN ROAD DIES IN AUTO WRECK.

Afterward I remember Graham and Mitchell coming. I remember crying a lot. I remember one friend of mine who isn't around anymore, a guy I loved dearly, giving me some heroin. That was the only thing I found that caused a cessation of the pain. It was a bad choice for him to bring it, a worse choice for me to take it. The fact is that it doesn't work as an anesthetic. I prolonged and protracted my suffering immensely by trying to medicate it that way. If I had known how to deal with it right up front, it would have been much better, but I didn't know how to deal with it. I had no mechanism, no way to deal with it, nothing. I was completely at a loss, I made a bad mistake, and that's how it went.

DEBBIE DONOVAN: *I came back from school and one of the Grateful Dead's people stopped me in the driveway. David couldn't tell me. He had said, "Oh God, how am I going to tell Donnie?" That was my nickname. The guy came out from underneath the garage and said, "Christine's been killed." I said, "That's not very funny." I said, "That's not a joke." He said, "No, it's not." It was just a devastating, devastating time. Everyone gathered. There was a lot of support, there was a lot of confusion. I stayed at the house and took care of the cats and David fell apart. I fell apart too, but I was in the position of having to take care of some things that no one else did. I had to go and find the cats because they were in the car and the ones that weren't dead were still alive and had to be taken care of. Then there was her family to notify and arrangements had to be made for a cremation.*

KEVIN RYAN: *It was one of the strongest moments of my life. I walk in the house and there are already a dozen people there. Graham and a lot of Grateful Dead people and David, who's sitting on the edge of his bed crying. He'd been crying for an hour by then and he cried for three more hours. He'd stop, he'd kind of catch himself, and then somebody else would arrive and there'd be a big hug and it would set him off again.*

DEBBIE DONOVAN: *We had just gotten Christine's horse that day. Somebody from the Dead gave her a horse because she had always wanted one and the Novato house had a little stable. Oh God, we had to deal with getting the horse back and doing all that sort of stuff. I just unpacked one of the shirts the other day that John Sebastian had made for her, one of those tie-dyed shirts that he did. Why I keep it I don't know.*

SALLI SACHSI: *I was driving up Beverly Glen Canyon and I heard the DJ say, "This song is dedicated to Christine Hinton, who died today in a car accident." Bobby and I went up to help keep the place together and it was a difficult time for David and for everybody. In fact, it involved a whole group of people. David couldn't live alone in the house without Debbie, so he'd bring someone back from the tour, so there was always somebody else staying there. Leo Makota, their road manager, and Dallas Taylor, I think. They'd go out on the road and come back to recover. Bobby and I would help put them back together, cook lots and lots of meals. We fed them vitamins and the Grateful Dead would come over after dinner and eat chocolate chip cookies and there'd be about fifteen or twenty people in the living room, sitting around in a circle, and we'd pass around cookies and joints and someone would pull out a pharmaceutical bottle with cocaine and that would go around the room too. We all didn't know how to communicate so well, but there was a feeling of unity and it was an extended family; we were a support system. Theodore Sturgeon, the science fiction writer, would come up there for a while with his pet squirrel. Everyone was practicing nudism in this big house. So we would have big dinners, sitting around this redwood table, and Mama Cass would come for the weekend, only not nude. She'd go to the supermarket and come back with things like peanut butter that* *had jelly swirls in it and all these trippy sugar junk foods. I was frying bacon one morning, nude, with an apron around my waist, and who should come to the door but David and Clem Floyd and Mirandi Babitz, who had a boutique on the Sunset Strip. Mirandi and I became friends after that, but she said later that she thought I was about the dumbest chick she had ever seen, frying bacon with nothing on but an apron.*

An impending San Francisco concert for promoter Bill Graham was canceled, although they made it up later. Graham and David went to England and drank many brandies together; it was the only time that David's been a drinker. When it got too cold and gray in the U.K., they made their way to Florida, to the *Mayan*, then back to California, to start a follow-up album to *Crosby, Stills, and Nash*. This was to be *Déjà Vu*, with Crosby, Stills, Nash, and Neil Young. Recording proceeded in fits and starts: someone would throw a fit, the band would start recording. First of all, David felt he had to recover from the absolute shock of losing Christine, to whom he had made the first real commitment of his life. Regardless of how David had treated or related to Christine before, he had agreed to set up housekeeping with her in Novato, to move away from the L.A. groupie scene, and to devote at least some major portion of his life to that relationship. Before the invisible ink could dry on that intangible contract, Christine was gone and there was no recourse or remedy.

When I came out of the initial shock, Graham and I had flown to Florida for a bit, then gone to London. Then we went back to the West Coast and then I decided I wanted to bring the *Mayan* around. I also had some romantic notion about how I wanted to bury Christine's ashes at sea from my boat. Off of San Francisco Bay, outside the Gate. I went to get the boat and said to Nash, him being my best friend, "Hey, you want to come along?" He had been sticking with me because he and a number of other people were afraid I was going to commit suicide, I was so depressed. We got on the boat with one much more knowledgeable sailor named Barry Hupletz. A nice guy, unfortunately no longer

with us. Another one claimed by drugs, although back then he
was not into them.

The only real sailor in the group, Barry (affectionately nick-
named Barry Cuda and called Cuda for short) attended to
the serious navigation, while other hands were engaged for
the donkeywork of sailing: from the CSN road crew came
Leo Makota and Steve Cohen. There was a man named John
Haberlin and his girlfriend, singer-songwriter Ronee Blakley.
Joni Mitchell came down to join Graham and when the
roadies proved unequal to the task, Bobby Ingram and his
second wife, Gay, from Coconut Grove, replaced them. The
Ingrams had some experience in sailing, so the crew was
becoming salty enough to attempt the long run from Florida
to California. Along the way, there were splendid distrac-
tions and enough adventures to make the sail a memorable
trip. There was a woman in the crew named Anita Treash,
from Big Sur, a friend of David's best Big Sur friend, Don
Lewis, who came aboard to keep the numbers even.

We sailed off down through the Bahamas and then the Windward Passage. Anita was a sweetheart, very kind to me, even
though she knew that she was only being a nurse. I wasn't in love
with her or anything even resembling love. I was a piece of damaged goods at that time. For a while Joni came down and was with
Graham. We sailed down through the Windward Passage between
Cuba and Haiti and went to Jamaica. Had a wonderful, crazy
week in Jamaica. We got there a week after they had caught a
boat just like ours smuggling weed. They thought we were dope
movers. We said, "We don't have to smuggle weed. We're rich."
They said, "Yeah, sure." Eight guys searched us when we left,
but they missed everything: two or three pistols, a few rifles,
psychedelics, weed. We were fully provisioned for a long voyage.
There were five guys from Customs, two guys from Immigration,
and one from the police and they didn't want to get their uniforms
dirty. That's how we got away with it.

From Jamaica we sailed to Panama. It was fabulous. Going
through the Panama Canal was a total thrill. Absolutely amazing,
sailing through a three-tiered rain forest, a jungle two hundred

feet high, with parrots and monkeys and alligators and all that shit. You see that as you go down the side channel, what they call the Banana Channel, where the big boats can't go. From there you step down to the Pacific side. The great thing about the canal is that they charge you by your cargo space, which on my boat is practically nil. So going through the canal, saving five thousand miles of sailing around the southern tip of the hemisphere, through the Straits of Magellan and around Cape Horn, cost us about seven dollars, which is a real bargain. Nowadays, I think they only run yachts through there one or two days a week.

At the western end of the canal, I had one of the strangest experiences of my life; whether it was due to coincidence or my preoccupation with Christine's death, I can't say. I can only report what happened. At the Pacific end of the canal, the yacht club is on an army base. I went ashore that night to make a phone call. I was trying to arrange for Joni Mitchell to fly home. I went to the bar, which is where they had the phone that they would let you use. In the bar was this big crew-cut drunk, a mean, obnoxious guy. When I walked by him, he said, "Goddamn hippie son of a bitch. Why aren't you in Vietnam, you son of a bitch?" And more words to that effect. I remember thinking, "Gee, there's a nice cliff right there. I wish he'd just walk over and step off. This is somebody the world doesn't need." I ignored him. He got even more abusive, so I left. I remember distinctly thinking, "I wish he'd die." When I came back the next morning to pay my fuel bill, I asked the club secretary who the obnoxious guy was and she said, "He's the FBI head of security for the base." I said, "Oh my God! Thank God I didn't slap him with a beer bottle." And she said, "But he died last night of a heart attack." I wished he'd die and he did. Ever since then, I encourage everyone to be very careful about what they wish on other people.

Joni flew home from Panama. We continued up the west coast of Central America and Mexico. In Costa Rica there's a place where three humongous volcanoes loom right near the shore: amazing-looking gigantic cones. We made our first stop at the bottom of Mexico in Salina Cruz. And therein lies another funny tale. We were just a few days out of Salina Cruz and while checking the navigational almanacs, we find out that there's going to be a full eclipse of the sun, only visible in certain places, one of which is Salina Cruz, Mexico, which is where we're going. So we humped to get there. As soon as we tie up, Graham and Barry are setting up tripods on the dock, smoking their own filters over kerosene lamps, setting everything up to shoot this astronomical phenomenon. Bobby Ingram and I go to cash a few hundred at the local bank, so that we can stock up on food. But before we go, we smoke a couple of enormous joints of this Panamanian Red we had. Got totally ripped, then went to the bank. When we get there, not only can't they cash a hundred dollars, they look at me and Bob just like we're going to rob the bank. They think we're Butch Cassidy and Sundance because we've got long hair and beards and we're a little scruffy from being at sea. The guard is snapping and unsnapping his holster, he's looking at us weird, the whole management's weird, and the vibe is a little strange because everyone at the bank is making these little pinhole arrangements to look at the eclipse and it's getting darker outside, really dark. And we're still loaded.

People are acting real freaky and Bob's trying to make his Spanish work, but he overestimates his language skills, so we're in there, we're bonzo, we're trying hard not to break out in total uncontrollable laughter. Finally, we achieve part of our goal; they change one of our hundred-dollar bills into pesos. We exit the bank, it's high noon, almost dark as night, and we're in this little tiny dusty street in this little tiny backwater of a little tiny Indian fishing village in the poorest southern section of Mexico. We look at each other—we're still stoned—we look down the street and an elephant comes around the corner.

Bob and I look at each other and we go, "This is it. We finally cooked it. We've stripped our cranial gears." Bobby thinks we're sharing the same hallucination. I'm looking at him, saying, "Do you see the elephant?" And he's saying, "Do you see the elephant?" For a little while there, we were sure we'd absolutely lost it. Turns out there was a little tiny one-ring circus in town and that was their elephant. But in the middle of a full eclipse it just didn't seem right to see an elephant come around the corner.

From Salina Cruz we went across the Gulf of Tehuantepec, trying to miss the violent offshore wind that can nail you out in the middle of the gulf. Someone called it the "Tehuantepecker." Some sailors just run right along the beach the whole way, so they can drop anchor close in and be where it's safe. Not us; we were lucky and got across without incident, sailing right up to Acapulco. Acapulco was remarkable. There's a yacht club there where everybody stops, the Club des Yachtes or something; it was the first civilized spot we hit in quite a while, so we were out there, partying and having a grand old time.

Bob Ingram, because of his time in Coconut Grove and Miami, took his Spanish seriously, anticipating the time (now arrived) that south Florida would be a truly bilingual community, a cosmopolitan center where Spanish was a first language to more than half of the population. Now he reads and writes in Spanish and can use the subjunctive in conversation, which makes him as bilingual as anyone. But on that 1970 sail to San Diego, Bob Ingram's Spanish was not quite fluent enough, leading eventually to a pointed lesson in cultural and economic distances separating Americans from the Third World. Bobby recalls buying meat in Salina Cruz and donating it in Acapulco:

BOB INGRAM: *Again, my Spanish got us into trouble when we went to a butcher shop. I tried to spell out that we wanted meat, beef, trying to explain "sirloin, New York strip, T-bone, Porterhouse," to a Mexican butcher. He says he understands; he can give us what we want tomorrow. The next morning the guy shows up at the dock with a freshly murdered cow. So fresh it was warm. It had been machine-gunned. As for breed, it was Mexican Racing Cow. Real lean. He had cut it up and packed it in plastic bags. We had been up all night partying, so while we're hung over, he's passing these cow parts in little body bags to us on the boat and we're loading it into the freezer. We tried to make a stew out of it. We cooked it for a week, but it wasn't any more tender. Finally, in Acapulco, there was a gate outside the Acapulco yacht club where a lot of little urchins hung out. I met a kid there that was begging and I gave him the last of the meat. We carried it back to the shack where he lived with his family and when we got there, the kid started crying. I couldn't understand why he was crying, so he says, "Because my mother's gonna beat my ass." And I said, "Why?" He says, "We don't have a refrigerator." I gave this kid frozen meat and he didn't have a refrigerator.*

We tried to keep a fairly steady supply of weed and there was a bottomless film can of coke. However, coming up that coast, you want to thin it out as much as you can because you know that the farther north you sail, the more scrutiny you're going to get. By the time we got to Cabo de San Lucas [the southernmost tip of Baja California], we were keeping it pretty clean. We knew we were going to have to come through U.S. Customs eventually and the way we looked and the way the boat looked, it was a sure bet they were going to take us apart. After a little loafing in a remote bay north of Manzanillo called Tenacatita, we cut across the Sea of Cortez to Cabo de San Lucas. In those days it was quite a bit funkier than it is now. There was one hotel, not nineteen, and the way you got fresh water was to anchor outside the breaker line and swing your boat around, stern to the shore, and back in until you were just outside where the surf was breaking. The swells would come up under the boat and then break just behind your stern. The guy onshore had three garden hoses hooked up, end to end, and you'd have to row in, snag the hose, row it out to your boat, and fill your tanks. That was how you got water. Another great spot for laying out and goofing off. Somewhere around there Ronee Blakley's typewriter went over the side. She was a songwriter then, following in Joni Mitchell's footsteps. Ronee became an actress and got nominated for an Academy Award for her work in Robert Altman's film *Nashville*. But on the trip her typewriter was an incredibly irritating thing. A boat's a very small space and it's not an environment to listen to an old mechanical typewriter going *tappity-tap-tap-tappity-tap-tap-snappity-tap.* That's not a sound you want to hear for more than a minute and a half. Maybe she left it on deck and it got rusty, maybe I just threw it over the side, but one morning it was gone. The typewriter's demise was met with universal approval from the crew, except for Miss Blakley, who, no doubt, was probably angry.

Cabo de San Lucas is the last spot to relax when you're sailing north because from there on it's all upwind and you have to run on power, not sail, motoring all the way. If you have to do it, I recommend you do it at night. Wait until it goes flat, then run. In the daytime, go in someplace in the morning and hole up through the afternoon because the afternoon wind is right square in your nose. That's what you should do. That's not what we did. We powered into it head-on. On the way, we saw great stuff: little poisonous snakes swimming in the water; sunfish, big huge round fish that lie on the surface and soak up sun, ten feet across and circular; I saw a manta ray come out of the water, fly through the air, and smash back down again. This ray was the size of a car, with what looked like a fourteen-foot wingspan. Big for a sea creature. The biggest thrill was just south of San Diego, where we saw a blue whale. A genuine, actual blue whale, with a white patch under his throat, moving through the water ahead of our bowsprit, with flukes coming out of the water behind our stern. Which means that the whale was longer than my boat, which is sixty-five feet from tip to tip. Blue whales are almost extinct, the largest mammals in the history of the planet, and he was right there. It's the only one I've ever seen. I've seen lots of whales, but I never saw a blue before or since.

We managed to get just outside San Diego when we ran out of fuel—we had motored all the way up Baja from Cabo de San Lucas and spent the last reserves we had trying to stay with the blue whale, so the engine quit off San Diego somewhere. We sat there, drifting, waiting for the wind. When we got it, we finished the cruise right—tacked up and into San Diego harbor, sailed into the ship channel, sailed past the submarine docks, sailed right up to Customs, and docked without power, just sails and seamanship. We're feeling pretty damn proud of ourselves. We had gotten the boat from America through America, sailing a few thousand miles. We were feeling pretty salty. We pull in and everyone comes aboard: U.S. Customs, Immigration, the works. They're checking us out and I'm below, talking to them, when I hear the flap of canvas and the sudden loud sound of somebody's shrouds hitting our spreaders. Then this boat smashes into the bow of my boat and knocks the bowsprit completely off. Snaps it at its base. Now, we'd brought this boat five thousand miles without putting a scratch on her and here this guy knocks the bowsprit completely off. I wanted to kill him. You know who it was? The *boating editor* of the San Diego newspaper! I was tied up to a dock, minding my own business, with a boatload of Customs officers and Immigration agents as witnesses, so he had no choice but to be a gentleman and offer to pay for the damages, which he did. So I get a new bowsprit and pulpit out of it.

I had the boat in Marina del Rey for a short while and took it north to San Francisco. To Sausalito. That was triumphant. With that whole journey under my belt, I was feeling a whole lot better and lot less drug-oriented, much healthier and saner. A lot of the grief had time to go through me and I had figured out the mantra for handling grief; it's very simple. First you have to accept it. And then you have to release it. You have to accept that it's real. That was the first hard thing—to accept that it was real, that Christine was never going to show up again. That person on the table in the hospital was dead and that was her. She had her whole life ahead of her and I was first getting into thinking, "Hey, this isn't another infatuation or another great lay or something. This is somebody I love." I was just starting to learn how to do that. That was acceptance. Then, with the help of some very kind people, Nash, Anita, Debbie Donovan, Bobby Hammer, and some others, I managed slowly—and with great difficulty—to release the pain. The final act was to do what I had intended from the start; spread Christine's ashes at sea. It was the inevitable conclusion to the ritual of release.

Christine's ashes were scattered off the *Mayan* in the waters of the Pacific Ocean outside the Golden Gate. The boat found a mooring in the Sausalito yacht harbor and David began living aboard, dividing his time between Northern California and Los Angeles. There was a new mate and skipper, Bud Hedrick, a man of unique accomplishments who had met David in Acapulco. At the same time, *Déjà Vu,* the new Crosby, Stills, Nash and Young album, was being cut at Wally Heider's San Francisco studio. Bill Halverson, the engineer who had worked with the band on their first album, was back, but having much less fun on the job. His personal demon was alcohol and it was slowing his responses.

BILL HALVERSON: *I got up there while they were setting up to record Crosby's "Almost Cut My Hair" and he wanted to do it all live and I kept saying no, he couldn't do that. We set everybody up live and did it anyway. We were willing to take those risks. The feeling of the song sometimes demands that you do it all at once. "Almost Cut My Hair" needed that edge. I listened to it a couple of days ago and it still holds up as a performance. Back then I was living in L.A. and commuting to San Francisco. I lived alone in a motel, which didn't make for a very good marriage, but it wasn't a particularly good marriage anyway. That first CSN album was made on a real primitive board and machines and not only was I the engineer but I made coffee and cleaned the ashtrays and cleaned the backboards. I was a lot faster in those days. Now I rely on a good assistant.*

Such an assistant was Stephen Barncard, who had spent his lonely teenage years working in local radio in Kansas City. He sampled every end of the business locally, working as an on-air announcer, engineer, technician, jack-of-all-trades; whenever he recorded a local band that succeeded, they'd fly off to Los Angeles or Nashville or Chicago or New York and get "professional" engineers, leaving young Barncard grumbling about ingratitude. Eventually, someone told him the obvious: if he was going to succeed in the recording business, it wouldn't be in Kansas City, which had good music but not a whole lot of world-famous recording studios. Barncard went west.

STEPHEN BARNCARD: *In San Francisco the only thing happening was Wally Heider's. At the time, there weren't a lot of guys looking for jobs in the recording industry at the entry level. I asked the manager what should I do and he said, "Write Wally." I wrote Wally and I got a response. I did a couple of errands for him. He said, "Okay, I like you. When can you start working?" The next thing I knew I was learning the ropes at that studio and two weeks after that I was filling in with Crosby, Stills, Nash, and Young. They went to Wally's in San Francisco because they wanted to work up there. Dave wanted to be on his boat and Stephen was hanging out with the Dead and Graham was buying a house. There I was, at the very beginning of Déjà Vu. What a great time to drop in. It was one of the most scary and fascinating things I had ever seen in my life. With that much musical talent in one place burning up calories in the room, it was staggering. I had been in studios before, but nothing like that. It was an event. I was just the set-up guy, an assistant. I ended up doing a lot of tracking because Bill Halverson was late a lot and he would sometimes pass out. It was "Hey, Bill, listen. You know that Crosby, Stills, Nash, and Young are here and would you like to get up?" He was having a hard time and he got his life together later, but that's another story. I learned a lot from the guy and we never had a run-in or any kind of bad time. I thought he was creative. The major thing I learned from him about this particular group of individuals was a certain way to approach recording. First of all, you keep the tape rolling at all time. Record every fart, bleep, and squawk that happens. If you get it live, you try to get the first take. You try to save everything. You don't clip the beginnings and you don't take a lot of time getting the drum sounds. Live. That's why they got a live recording guy in the first place, for his background.*

There are various techniques of getting things recorded in the studio. One of them is being very social and just making sure every-

thing's covered. Another is to try and anticipate what might happen, keeping an eye out for things that might happen and making yourself very sensitive to the setting, more than anything else. You don't worry about what kind of microphone you are going to use. If you can't get to it, you don't stop the session; you don't stop the music because something technical isn't to your liking. That was another thing Halverson taught me, by doing. On "Almost Cut My Hair," which was recorded totally live, we had one shot at it and I hadn't patched in the limiter. I watched Halverson hot-patch the limiter in an interval just before the vocal got to where it had to be in and he had the levels preset. Now, in anybody's book on recording live vocals, that's a pretty dangerous thing to do. He made it. He got it right on and he needed that limiter because Crosby really belted it out later in the tune. That was an example of being on your toes, thinking on your feet, moving fast, the live recording technique that these guys always demanded.

BILL HALVERSON: *They were real efficient on that first album. They'd rehearsed all that time and they knew the songs and the first album was really fun to do. The next album was up in San Francisco and David and Graham would leave and go to a party and Stephen and I would stay in the studio and drink; I was doing uppers and we'd be up all night in the studio and they'd come back in the next day and we'd play them what we'd done. I got real obsessive, just keeping up with Stephen; it was hectic. We spent anywhere from five to seven hundred hours of studio time on the second album and a lot of that was rehearsal in the studio and trying to figure out what to do. Their success came so fast that on the second album the feeling was "We are going to get this right," only there was more and more dissension and there was a lot more distraction. The only time that David Geffen or Elliot Roberts could get the three or four of them together was in the studio, so they would show up on what was supposed to be a recording session with contracts and stuff to go over and there was such a negative vibe when they showed up that it would take four or five hours after they left to get back to being able to do something creative.*

ELLIOT ROBERTS: *After Christine died, David became guarded, afraid to give of himself. Before, he had been like a road map, wide open. Although he had a lot of possessions, there was nothing, outside of the Mayan, that was important to him. He had his collection of handmade knives, a few beautiful little boxes and a lot of crystals, his mother's silverware, and his guitars. Other than that, anyone could crash at his house, anyone could take his car or take anything that he had, really. It meant nothing to David; he was a real class hippie on that level. Before Christine's death, when David arrived, the party started: he'd be passing out jays, he'd be loud, he'd be the mover and the motivator. Once she was gone, everything stopped and he became introspective and shy. He was difficult to approach and he couldn't focus very well. You couldn't have long meetings with David. They had to be short, concise, and to the point. He didn't want to make decisions anymore. In the beginning, I would only talk to David and then we would tell Graham and Stephen what the plan was, ask if they had any objections, and if not, that was pretty well how it worked. After Christine's death, David didn't want to be the main guy anymore. Instead, Graham became the focal point of the group. It became hard to get David on the phone. There were long periods where you couldn't talk to him. You'd hear he went sailing or driving for the day and he didn't want to talk to anybody.*

Graham was living two houses down from me with Joni and that made it much easier. Graham took up the challenge and became the strength of the band. Obviously, anytime someone dies like that it's sad, but Christine's death was extra sad because David had been on such a run of good luck. When I first met him, he was tough and abrasive and had just been burned by all kinds of people: the Byrds kicked him out, managers took his money, a business manager left him broke. It took him a year or two in our relationship before he flowered again, for lack of a better term. When he got to that good level, he stayed there until Christine's death and then he started to regress, back to how he was when I met him: quick-tempered, tough, and hard. He didn't want to have emotional connections and he didn't want to have relationships that would burn him. It was extra sad for all of us around him who had to deal with him all the time, to see this other David.

Nevertheless, by the time *Déjà Vu* was in the can, there were two million advance orders for the album. In the jargon of the trade, "it shipped double platinum," which was a singular achievement. That kind of interest carried over into the concert arenas, where the band was able to command huge advances and fill stadiums and arenas, one of the first bands in history to accomplish that feat unaided. Their first venture out was the Carry On Tour, where new ground was broken. For the first time, a major group was leaving nothing to chance: they carried everything with them, stage monitors, public address systems, speakers, microphones, even a carpet for the stage, any stage. Everything traveled by air, in order to satisfy the booking schedule, which didn't take into account the complicated logistical requirements. That included air-freighting bulky, heavy speakers and stage platforms. Later, clever road managers and production teams refined the science of touring to the point where huge arena shows with complicated stage effects are common, shunting around the country during the concert season like so many gypsy caravans, fleets of eighteen-wheelers highballing from arena to arena while musicians follow in custom coaches or fly from city to city. But as 1969 turned into 1970, it was all new, exciting, and expensive. Fortunately, the money poured in and everyone was rich enough to buy whatever he wanted. It was the beginning of the glory years of rock 'n' roll, when new fortunes could be made by new players and anyone with a popular song to sing and any manager with a blank contract could elbow their way up to the table, claim a seat, ante up, and rake in a huge pot.

The game was not only lucrative, fun, and sexy, it offered a platform and a mechanism for effecting change. In an era when "consciousness raising" was a new concept, the unprecedented mass appeal of the new rock 'n' roll gave the singers a voice in public affairs. Ever since the folkie days and the "protest songs" of Phil Ochs, Bob Dylan, and Joan Baez, there was no doubting the power of voices raised in song. Growing out of that tradition, it seemed only natural that the new aristocracy of pop would turn to the headlines for material, instead of celebrating hot rods and teenage lust or repeating the "June-moon" romanticism of pop songwriting from a previous generation. The headlines didn't fail them; there was lots to sing about.

We have, all of us, over the years, written things that responded to the world as it slapped us in the face. Me and Nash, singing "To the Last Whale" and "Find the Cost of Freedom." Stills coming up with "For What It's Worth." These came right out of the news. People have accused us of taking stances and the truth is we don't. We try to respond honestly to what hits us. It's what Neil Young did with "Ohio." When we introduce politics into our music, we're using this wonderful multiplication of effort that happens when you enter mass communications. It seemed to evolve concurrently with the development of the music. We were no sooner in the Byrds than we were writing that kind of song and singing it. Obviously your awareness gets more sophisticated as you go along. I'm not a tremendously sophisticated person, but I've gotten smarter about it as I've gotten older. There was a period of time when I was so selfish and so completely concerned with myself that I really backed away from any kind of social consciousness; even if it was what I thought, I couldn't get outside myself enough to express it or do anything about it. I cared mostly about getting my next fix. I didn't care too much about people starving in Afghanistan. But that consciousness was still there; it was just dulled out.

When I speak about multiplication of effort, what I mean is that mass media is a power saw, compared to a hand ax. That power, that little gas engine, is really multiplying your effort. If you do that a hundredfold more, you approach the kind of multiplication of effort that takes place in mass media. How can we be effective? After National Guardsmen fired on students at Kent State and killed people, I watched Neil Young see, really *see* that famous picture of the girl kneeling over the dead kid, looking up as if to say, "Why?" I handed him the guitar and watched him write the song. We were up in San Mateo County, just above Santa Cruz, just me and him, Neil writing the song. I got on the phone and called the guys in L.A. and said, "Book the studio, man. This is it. Get the studio time tonight. I don't care where. This is important." I got Neil to the airport and we got on a plane and we flew down. We recorded it that night with "Find the Cost of Freedom" on the back of it. Gave it to Ahmet Ertegun at the end of the session. He happened to be in Los Angeles. He flew on the red-eye to New York and the record was out within days. It was on the street within a week of the event. With the finger firmly pointed right where the guilt lay: Nixon and the warmongers. At that point, we were powerful. We affected the world, right then.

BILL HALVERSON: *I happened to be working with Stills at the Record Plant. During the day we were rehearsing at Warner Bros. Studios for a tour. I got a call from one of the roadies, saying, "Set up for the whole band. They're all coming in tonight and that's all I know." I set up for drums and bass and all the guitars and all the vocals and they came in, set up, and sang "Ohio." When we finished remixing, they needed something for the B-side. They chose "Find the Cost of Freedom," so I set up four chairs and four vocal microphones. They went out and sat facing each other in a square with no frills or gimmicks. It was like they were sitting in a living room. They performed "Find the Cost of Freedom," which ends up a cappella. When they finished, I just pushed the talkback and said, "Now double it." They said, "You're crazy. We can't do that," and while I said that I was already rolling the tape back; before they could say anything else, I said, "Here it comes. Now, just double it." Then I switched it to eight other tracks and they did. They didn't even come into the control room to listen to it; they just doubled it without moving or anything. We ran the tape, they played and sang along, and we had the record cut in twenty minutes. They're amazingly talented. That's all I can say.*

There's been a huge frustration in me ever since I started to become conscious of the fact that the people who held most of the power—because they held most of the money—were so different from people that I liked. I always wanted to somehow compile a list of who they were and publish it and then everybody could say, "Hey, you have to listen to us. We live here." But it doesn't work that way. It's one of the things that's driven me throughout the latter part of my life, wondering what to do about it, because I see it as a key element, a primary cause of the problems that mankind has everywhere. Because we were famous, I've met senators and a president and some people who were very wealthy, but I never met the people that I'm talking about, the real Robber Barons, the real Captains of Industry. The guys who run ITT and Rockwell International, AT&T, GM, General Dynamics, Northrop, McDonnell-Douglas, Boeing, DuPont, and Dow. I've never met them, but I'm not misinformed; their actions are a matter of public record. The people who run the oil companies don't give a good goddamn. They make that clear. The people who run Westinghouse don't give a shit or they wouldn't be building nuclear plants after they found out that they have (a) no place to put the waste and (b) no way to control the damn things. So, if they had any sense of what awful poison they were spreading, they wouldn't do it. But they're ruled by the dollar, so they go ahead, all of them. It's not something that I have to prove; they've already proven it. You don't have to wonder, "Does Weyerhauser care about trees?" No, they don't. They're going to cut them all down. Boise-Cascade couldn't care less if you have a forest if they want the paper. Now someone is going to cut old-growth redwoods in California, the oldest living things on the planet, because they ran up a big corporate debt and need the cash. It's not a matter of establishing the truth of it; they are so completely powerful and so completely unchecked that no one can do anything about them. We're talking about people to whom Ralph Nader is a little bug buzzing around the butt of a rhinoceros. The rhino doesn't give a damn.

I wonder who they are
The men who really run this land
And I wonder why they run it
With such a thoughtless hand

What are their names?
And on what streets do they live?

I'd like to ride right over
This afternoon and give
Them a piece of my mind
About Peace for mankind

Peace is not an awful lot to ask

"What Are Their Names,"
Lyrics by David Crosby,
Music by David Crosby, Jerry Garcia,
Phil Lesh, Michael Shreive, and
Neil Young

These guys not only operate with a hyena pack mentality, they are also constantly looking to undercut each other. In the game of Big Corporations, they wait for one to be wounded: "Oh, look. There's one going lame. Let's drag him down and eat him." And it doesn't matter if it's a guy they played golf with yesterday and they were just saying how much they liked the dude. If he shows the slightest weakness, if his company's just a little overextended, they'll go in, cut his credit, buy his stock, take him down and put him out of business. Completely. Put the guy completely on the rocks, and say, "Hey, that's the breaks, babe. That's business." Well, that's not business for me. Business for me is people completing a transaction that leaves both parties wanting to do it again. Business is not the quick rip and the thorough rape. Business is doing something well enough and reasonably enough and asking a fair price for it, to the point where someone says, "Hey, that was a good deal." Then people come back together and you got a real business deal going. Guy trades you a fish for your vegetables and you keep doing it for life.

Back in the sixties, people were saying the music should be free. Hell, I don't think it should be free. I work hard at it, I love

it, and I intend to sell it. The music business seems out of propor-
tion; we make so much money because of the sheer mass, the
bulk of it. Mass media, that's what we're dealing with. We get this
multiplication factor. Everything's normal until it gets pressed,
then it gets multiplied by a million and it's totally different. If we
just went out and sang for our supper, we'd do well and we'd live
the same as everyone else. When you record it, press it, and send
it out, it's been multiplied by a million and we become millionaires—that's the amount of trading that's going on. I don't have a
problem with that as long as we don't just become millionaires.
The people that I think handle it well are people who realize that
if you don't have a sense of community, then there isn't a community. It's a very simple thing. If you have a sense of community,
then you're in one and it will be as good as you make it. If you
don't contribute anything back to the community and just take,
then you don't live in a community and when times get hard for
you or you get in trouble, don't look for anybody to help you
because you didn't help them. I've been helped already.

My community has tried to help me on a lot of levels: personal friends, the criminal justice system, the medical system.
I've been very lucky. I've been dealt with pretty fairly. My community of friends can be incredibly good to me. Consequently, I
like contributing my time and my energy and my efforts into the
general community, whether it's where I live or my city or state or
country or world. Once they started lobbing communication satellites up there, we entered an age in which the world is one community, where Muammar el-Qaddafi lives in your backyard,
where what happens in Paris tomorrow is as close to you as what
you eat for breakfast. A song I'm trying to write tries to make the
statement that there is no Third World. It's a misconception. The
Third World is your world. Those children are your children.
People anywhere are your people. Now, that's difficult to apply
because I don't like everybody. There are whole segments of the
world whose people I am not as fond of as I am of the people on

the island of Kauai, for instance. But they're still people and even if I don't want to be buddies with them and go hang out with them, I don't see that it's right to just deny them life. There are people in this world to whom we are denying life.

SEVEN

....

Everybody has been burned before
Everybody knows the pain
Anyone in this place can tell you to your face
Why you shouldn't try to love someone

Everybody knows it never works
Everybody knows, and me

I know all too well how to turn, how to run
How to hide behind a bitter wall of blue
But you die inside if you choose to hide
So I guess instead I'll love you

"Everybody's Been Burned,"
Words and Music by David Crosby

From its inception, the association of Crosby, Stills, Nash, and Young struggled to achieve an ideal: an ongoing commitment to combining talents without submerging identities or sublimating individual aspirations. The contracts reflected that and each member of the group was free to record and tour as an individual or with other musicians. This was a departure from previous music industry practice, where bands went on regardless of membership. Until recently, Ray McKinley was still conducting the Glenn Miller Orchestra, forty years after Miller's death and without a hell of a lot of the original sidemen. And, for want of contract language, there seems to be no limit to the number of original Ink Spots, Platters, Coasters, and Penquins working the oldies circuit. The philosophy underlying the "supergroup" sought to avoid this whole area of squabbling. The new loyalty was to an abstract: good music.

That concept put artistic goals ahead of loyalty to a single musical style or contractual obligations to a business entity that happened to play music. Which is not to say that the contracts weren't tough. Renegotiated many times over the years, the entities known as Crosby, Stills, and Nash and Crosby, Stills, Nash, and Young have an ironclad, bulletproof, ongoing association with Atlantic Records. Two decades of lawyering haven't opened any new loopholes and it's safe to say the boys have a mature contract that's been thoroughly examined, tested, and revised. They had learned the ins and outs of deal-making and now had David Geffen and Elliot Roberts overseeing every aspect of their professional lives.

The same freedom that permitted Crosby, Stills, Nash, and Young to pursue solo projects and to tour and record with other bands kept them from working together with the intensity required to deliver a steady flow of what the companies call "product." One of the reasons for the bands' long-time relationship with Atlantic Records goes a lot further than their cordial and familial relationship with Ahmet Ertegun. CSN and CSNY signed contracts that required them to deliver a quantity of albums. The magic number has never been reached and it may not be in their lifetimes. And yet, each player has been able to write and perform for two decades, carving out solo careers and lifestyles that are theirs alone. Their infrequent recombinations become events and festivals, ceremonies that commemorate a continuity of spirit, soul, and song. Still and all, they were individuals first and a group second.

ELLIOT ROBERTS: *When Neil went into the group, he was still with Crazy Horse, so at the same time he was recording and playing with CSNY, he was also recording and playing with Crazy Horse and having hits. As for the band, all of them—Stephen, Neil, David, and Graham—had been beaten for their publishing. When I first met Neil, his publishing was all with Cotillion and Atlantic and the Buffalo Springfield took all of his and Stephen's. One of the first things I did as a manager was start new companies for everybody so they all had their own publishing. We administered it and they ran it; Neil was a very big part of CSNY and was a motivating guy. His opinions carried a lot of clout because Neil's very opinionated and he began being an influence where David's opinion used to rule. When Neil came into the group, his schedule and time frame became the guiding influence on the band. We were always working around Neil's recording or touring. As for David, Stephen, and Graham, they waited for CSN as if it was their whole life, which of course it wasn't. But Neil had* Everybody Knows This Is Nowhere *which became a double-platinum album during this period, and followed that up with* After the Gold Rush *and then* Harvest. *As a consequence, CSNY played less and less because Neil had more and more recording and concert obligations and when Neil did that the guys did nothing. They took time off. They were groovy. They were cool. They posed. Eventually, it got so they could sense that they had better do another CSN album or even solo albums. Stephen started to do a* Manassas *album and slowly but surely the duo of Crosby-Nash evolved. David's solo album came out first. It came out around the same time as Neil was doing* Harvest. *David called his record* Does Anybody Know Who I Am or Any of My Relatives? So Where's My Cousin? Do You Have Any Papers? *[The album's title was* If I Could Only Remember My Name.*]*

It was a great album. It's one of my favorite albums, to be honest. So the problems started. Everyone had so much and when you have four strong individuals like that, it's not as if any one of them ever said, "This is all we'll ever do and that's it." They all had more material than they could record. Neil was writing fourteen or fifteen songs a year and could only get two or three on an album. When Graham did Songs for Beginners *[1971], he had a similar problem: he was writing a lot of material and could only get two or three songs on a CSNY album. Same thing with Stephen. David was happy because he only wrote two or three pieces a year and he could wait for the CSN or CSNY album. But when he had his own album, he wrote five or six songs, was very successful, and got another Gold Record to put in his bathroom.*

We always had a fair amount of conflict between us. The first time we broke up was when we were Crosby, Stills, Nash, and Young. The conflicts then were between me and Stills and Nash and Stills and a little between Neil and Stills. Stephen felt as if Neil had taken the group away from him in some fashion or other, even though it was Stephen who invited Neil to join us in the first place. We managed to get back together again, but without Neil. Then Stephen and Graham and I had real disagreements about stuff. I think, in all fairness to Stephen, that it wasn't all his fault or all anybody's fault. I think that Stephen has trouble being overly generous to other people about their contributions and Graham and I had a natural competitive problem with him because he's a lead player and he was always a dominant force. The idea was that we were equals in this band and that no one was the leader. That's one of the reasons we used our own names. The other reason was so that nobody could wind up owning the name and plugging different people into it; we all had experience with that.

I think Stephen always felt that Nash and I were resentful or trying to obstruct him. Nash and I always felt that Stephen was overbearing. I felt that he didn't really give us credit where it was due. In a thoughtless moment, he'd say things like "They're just my backup singers" to people. That would naturally piss us off. I don't think he ever really meant it.

In 1970 David began looking for a house in Marin County, living in the owner's cabin aboard the *Mayan* in Sausalito Harbor in the meanwhile. He still commuted to Los Angeles and his boat was becoming increasingly seaworthy. A new bowsprit and forestay had been acquired in San Diego and *Mayan* would be sailed down the coast to Newport Beach, where it would undergo an extensive refurbishing and upgrading. In Newport Beach, the Lido Shipyard enjoyed a reputation as an excellent wooden boat yard, with the kind of shipwrights, riggers, and carpenters that David wanted to work on his schooner. Now that he had an income, he could buy more and better homes, cars, toys, drugs, and boat. Unresolved grief over Christine's absence could still move David to sudden tears and he'd be plagued by bouts of melancholy and depression for the rest of the decade, but there were diversions, recreations, and work as a solo artist to occupy him. He negotiated a solo album deal with Atlantic and began to work on the first fully produced expression of his musical self in his career. The San Francisco Bay Area was alive with new music and besides his own album there were sessions with the Airplane, Grace Slick, Paul Kantner, Jackson Browne, and more. There would be talk of a screenplay, a movie deal, and ongoing contributions to the work of friends and collaborators, David's immediate musical family: Mitchell, Nash, Stills, and Young. Through the early seventies, David played, sang, sailed, and found more women to love. Jerry Garcia of the Grateful Dead was one of the players who enjoyed the Ubiquitous Cros for his political consciousness and for his sybaritic appetite for more and better dope.

JERRY GARCIA: *That's one of the things that doesn't come out very clearly in these retrospective looks at the sixties. They make it seem as though that was a period of aberration and since then everybody has gone back to normal. That's the illusion that the Reagan Generation would like to perpetuate, "Everything's like it was in the fifties. The sixties never were." They're not willing to say that stuff really happened. Drugs were our war. That's partly because drugs have always been part of music, part of poetry, part of art. Cole Porter sings about cocaine. Cocaine and hard drugs were certainly no strangers to the jazz musicians of the forties, thirties, and twenties. You go back to Charlie Parker and those guys, snortin' it up on the street corners when you could buy it in drugstores. I think it's part of the tradition of being a musician. Everybody has their thing. Part of it is the pressure of playing publicly. Part of it is the keeping your spirit fresh, "I need some air blowing through here. I need to put some energy through here." Drugs can do it if nothing else is around. If you're making it up as you go along or if you're having to reach into yourself, any aid is helpful. It's a matter of moderation, which tends to be the problem, since drugs have that thing of the more you take, the more you want and so on and so on.*

We had a little band called David and the Dorks. He was the star and it was his trip that we were doing and it was right around the time he was doing his If I Could Only Remember My Name *album and he was in the Bay Area a lot. [David recalls that the band also went by the name Jerry and the Jerks.] One time me and Phil [Lesh] from the Grateful Dead and Bill Kreutzmann and Mickey Hart, the drummer, we backed up David. We did maybe two of three shows. I think they were all at the Matrix in San Francisco. They weren't announced or anything; we just went in there on a Monday night and had a lot of fun and the sound was cool. In fact, that was the core of the band that played on David's album: David and the Dorks. It was a fine band and a short-lived band. Almost legendary. We had a lot of fun. David's one of those guys; it's really fun to play with him. He's a very giving musician, his songs are special and they're very different, so it's always a challenge to work with him. And the payoff is there when you hear it back. It sounds beautiful. Crosby has never gotten the credit he deserves as a musician. He's an uncanny singer. He has as much control as anybody I've ever seen or worked with and he's really gifted. He can do things that are truly astonishing if you give him half a chance and when he has his own head and he's in good shape, boy, he's fun to work with. He's an inspiration. I think some of the finest playing I've done on record is on his solo album. As far as being personally satisfied with my own performances, which I rarely am, he's gotten better out of me than I get out of myself.*

In no particular order, the next three years were occupied with sailing, women, and song. Reine Stewart reappeared in Sausalito with the title "ecstasy coordinator." Her duties continued through the completion of David's solo album. *If I Could Only Remember My Name* was recorded at Wally Heider's San Francisco studio during 1970 and made it onto the *Billboard* charts in March of 1971. It stayed there for eighteen weeks. The sessions were notable because of David's willingness to experiment, to explore new directions, and to involve his friends in his particular vision. The album took three months to finish, since work would be interrupted for sailing, for idle time to househunt and to shop for country property (a particularly choice chunk of Big Sur was being offered by its owners and that required a lot of on-site inspection), and for touring (David was starting to sing with Graham Nash and the two would work in concert in more intimate venues, always attracting a devoted following).

My solo album was made in the city, mostly at Wally Heider's in San Francisco. It was engineered by Stephen Barncard, produced by me, and we did it upstairs at Wally Heider's on Hyde Street. I was living on the boat at the time in Sausalito with

various people. Yes, there were a number of ladies and yeah, it
was me trying to get myself going again. And I had a lot of songs,
new ones and old ones. I did make what I think is a fascinating
album. It's very strange and it mirrored the strangeness in my life
after Christine died and I started to get it all back together, except
that dope was still a part of it, still a part of the daily currency we
used to negotiate with life. It didn't make it any easier when Janis
Joplin overdosed herself at the Landmark Motel in L.A. The Land
Mine, as we cordially referred to it, was one of those rock 'n' roll
hotels by which you could measure your progress. New in town?
The Tropicana. First real tour? The Continental Hyatt on the
Strip. Big Deal Established Star? The Beverly-Wilshire, the Beverly Hills, or the Bel Air. Staying for a few months to cut a
record? Two choices: Sunset Marquis, if you had a big budget,
the Landmark, if you preferred funk. [The Landmark, on Franklin Avenue in Hollywood, had the added convenience of being
close to the street dealers, who weren't welcome by the sheriff's
deputies and Beverly Hills police farther west.] Janis Joplin was
living at the Landmark, finishing an album with Paul Rothschild
producing; Jim Morrison also lived there, as well as Bob Neuwirth, Garry Goodrow from the Committee, a lot of people. But
Janis died there and Jim was in Europe and in a couple of weeks
he died too. It was grim, the first public dope deaths, and not the
last. But it didn't bother me. I was cool, I was making my album,
I had my shit together.

STEPHEN BARNCARD: *I was a totally unbiased, uncorrupted guy from
the Midwest and David never said a word to me. But at the end of
one of the dates when Paul Kantner was there and things weren't
going very well, David turns to me and says, "How come terrible
things happen when you're around? How does that make you feel?"
And I said, "Indifferent." It got a laugh. Next thing I knew, my boss
was telling me that he was going to do a David Crosby session and
would I like to engineer it? At first I said no. The boss kept calling
me and saying, "I want you to do this record," and I kept turning it*

down. I had to consult with my girlfriend and think about doing it. Why? Because David was an asshole. He was particularly nasty to me and I wasn't starstruck. I'd been exposed to enough talent. I admired his music for years, but I wasn't gonna put up with bullshit. But the job represented a pretty good hunk of studio time and recording engineers were better paid in those days. Plus, there was a lot of freedom and a lot of room for creativity and movement in that field. I eventually felt I was particularly fortunate to drop in at that microsecond in time. So I went for it. It meant double shifts, because I was also working with Creedence Clearwater in the daytime and then working with those guys until about 3 A.M.

It was a particularly wonderful time to be a recording engineer because the technology was in the hands of the technicians. It was like being a magician. You had status that inspired reverence. You were one of the people that could do this in an efficient way. You could record music. When I worked with David, I would set up everything. I would make sure I had machines in the room to do anything because I had no idea what we were going to do. We could cut a solo track or he might bring in the entire Jefferson Airplane and we could be cutting a whole chorale. We could be mixing a tune for the final mix for the record or we could be making a rough publishing demo. The only way you covered your ass on those kind of dates was to have a wall of machines and every mike and every option available, so that when they asked you for it, it was there. No questions.

In November of 1970, David and I started recording the solo album. Now, he had some stuff already recorded that he did with the Jefferson Airplane and some other folks, but it was still the most exhilarating project I've ever done in my life. We had a meeting of the minds and I was able to go through the project pretty effortlessly. There were times that I was real tired and didn't have a lot of patience. There was a lot of time frittered away and playback parties that I wasn't quite used to. It was a loose setup and I'd been doing some pretty tight projects before that. But I learned to relax with it

and before we knew it we were ready to mix. This was in January of
'71.

Along the way, some remarkable things happened in the studio. Some of David's old ways were reappearing and he was
again the facilitator, the host of the party, the guy cutting
new grooves and finding new ways of getting music recorded.
It was his own music, but it didn't hurt to involve his
friends, a virtual Who's Who of the San Francisco sound.
There were plenty of friends from the old folkie days and the
current word "networking" describes precisely the web that
David spun over the Bay Area, drawing in most of the singers and instrumentalists of any consequence. And what he
missed in San Francisco, he picked up in Los Angeles, rest-
lessly jumping back and forth, finding studio time and inviting friends and former lovers to join in the fun. People
wanted to play for him and on occasion he could be totally
vulnerable. David would be willing to bomb or succeed, he'd
go pedal-to-the-metal and balls-to-the-wall, and encourage
others to do the same. With the Cros's example shining in
front of them, people would mutter, "Hey, wait. Why
shouldn't I do it as good as that?" They'd do it better—or
worse—but always to the limits of their abilities and sometimes beyond, while the tape was always rolling. Steve Barncard was both witness and participant:

STEPHEN BARNCARD: *"Music Is Love" was an instance where record-*
ing everything pays off. David and Neil and Graham were down at
A&M in L.A. Neil and David were playing guitar on that tune and
somebody had a seven-and-a-half-inch mono tape machine running
as they broke into the changes on "Music Is Love." At the end of the
changes, they started singing the rounds that you hear in the final
product. It is basically the equivalent of making a track out of a
lousy cassette because it was just one mike open, across the room.
They stayed around and added vibes and congas and a bass part,
David put on a vocal, and out of essentially nothing a song was
created from the happy accident that a tape was rolling at the time.

"What Are Their Names" is another one of those things where we
had a jam going as the tape was rolling. David had some words
scribbled on an envelope that he wrote on an airplane. He put the two

DAVID CROSBY

together and that was the song, totally spontaneous, something we cut off the end of a jam on another tune. Then he got his friends in to sing the choruses. You know that big chorus where there's a lot of people singing? I didn't have much time to do it, maybe a ten-minute window to record all these people: Joni Mitchell, Grace Slick, Paul Kantner, David, Graham, David Freiberg, Jerry Garcia, Phil Lesh, Bob Weir, maybe Mickey Hart and Spencer Dryden, too. Immediately, I have to figure out how do I get enough headphones to get all of these people covered? In ten minutes? No way. So, I put a bunch of mikes out there and bussed 'em together and then put the track out in the speakers. That gave it sort of a washed-out effect, but I brought up all the faders on the board and made one or two runs: out of an impossible situation we got a spontaneous, timeless track. Once I burned through my frustration at the technical level, what I found was that if you let the music do the magic work, amazing things can happen.

It was at Wally Heider's in San Francisco and Stephen Barncard was using the chamber echoes. They had great chambers there and he had developed an EQ that created a fabulous echo for me to do something with; he had turned it up more than normal and I was sitting there, kind of goofing around, and then all of a sudden I wasn't goofing around. I was suddenly smitten with some kind of very strong emotion and the result was one of the most startlingly pieces of music I ever made and I had no idea where it came from. I never had sung anything like that before. I had no plan to do any such thing. It just happened. I knew something was happening, but I couldn't tell what. The music was coming through me, not from me, layer after layer, level after level. My memory of it was that it was six different voices singing together for about two minutes and it took about twelve minutes to record. Stephen says fourteen. I don't remember.

STEPHEN BARNCARD: *"I Could Swear There Was Someone Here" was the most amazing. I was recording David's vocal overdub with echo*

2 0 1

on one tune and while we were rewinding the tape, David started playing around with the echo chamber and he and I had quite a bit of echo in the headphones, so we put on a roll of fresh tape, turned all the lights down, and just started. David proceeded to lay down track after track after track after track. It was brilliant a cappella singing. It wasn't the usual cycle of "Work it out on the guitar, work out the parts, and punch in." On that track there are no punch-ins and no retakes. Everything is linear. Did it once, then did it again on another track, layered it and stacked it, and it was done in fifteen minutes. There were eight layers and each one had six voices on it and each one had its own echo track. We had all these tracks in this massive thing and we were just dumbfounded. Crosby was speechless when we got done and he said, "I don't know where that came from." It was like a bolt of lightning. I've rarely seen anything that intense. David and I have no explanation, but that's just the way he kind of gets songs. It just happened. I witnessed the creation of the song in real time and recorded it as we went along and it was probably the most remarkable event in my entire life.

After hours and days in the studio, David would drive back to Sausalito to his home, the schooner *Mayan*. Standing on the deck of the boat was "my way of keeping both feet on the ground and mixing a metaphor at the same time," David would say. The boat represented stability and order and the sea didn't care if you were a rock 'n' roll star or not; the ocean has no respect for status or ambition. It simply exists and you deal with it on its terms. The schooner was always a refuge and a comfort. In Sausalito, she was even more. *Mayan* was a pleasure boat in meanings that exceed the Coast Guard definition of that class of private vessel. A picturesque schooner with classic lines, it had enough room to house David, a permanent live-aboard mate and his companion, and enough spare bunks for a half-dozen visitors and ordinary crew. Most of the guests and live-aboards were female and they came and went with carefree irregularity. The men who came aboard and stayed were usually skilled carpenters or experienced sailors who would happily crew on a schooner of her stature.

The *Mayan* is a John G. Alden design, built in 1947 with

all the careful handwork that characterizes that bygone era. It's a classic wooden boat. She has teak decks and hatch covers and mahogany interior cabinetry, with leaded glass skylights, and lots of brightwork: brass lamps and railings and hardware. Throughout her restorations and renovations, she has been kept in period, with as few anomalies as possible. Unlike most schooners with deep keels, the *Mayan* has a centerboard that can be hauled up in shallow water, so she draws less than five feet despite her size and can sail into anchorages and inlets that would run most other boats her size aground. She is exceptionally broad in the beam, sixteen feet at her widest point, which makes her roomy and comfortable below decks. In all, a marvelous haven and a home that can hoist anchor and sail around the world. Or at least south from Sausalito to Newport Beach, by way of Santa Barbara, the Channel Islands, Marina Del Rey, and Catalina.

Just as press-gangs would roam the waterfront bars and snatch innocent youths to serve Her Majesty's Navy in the eighteenth century, David would patrol a Sausalito bar and restaurant called the Trident. Built on pilings over the water on Sausalito's main street, Bridgeway, the Trident was the proud creation of some Bay Area new money. One of its owners was a man who made his fortune managing the Kingston Trio in its glory years; among their other investments was the picturesque Triangle Building in San Francisco's North Beach, later acquired by Francis Coppola, when it was his turn to become rich and move to Northern California. The Trident was designed to take advantage of the new and natural all-wood look. It was a fern bar before there were such things. Elegant carpentry and expensive materials gave the place a bright upscale hipness, while the big windows and outdoor terrace fronted on San Francisco Bay, with a full view of the Golden Gate Bridge, the city of San Francisco, Tiburon, and Angel Island. Upstairs was a jazz club; downstairs was a restaurant and bar. The finishing touch was the help: short of the Playboy Mansion, there have never been so many exotic beauties assembled in one place for the humble tasks of serving food and taking drink orders. And, unlike Hefner's airbrushed cuties, the Trident women had rings in their noses and tattoos of flowers and butterflies where you could see them and sometimes where you couldn't. There was no house uniform, so waitresses could wear anything from Victorian velvet to see-through

Indian gauze. Some shaved, some didn't—it was a visual cor-
nucopia of delights and the line between staff and clientele
often blurred, as beautiful women would hang out waiting
for an interview or a job opening and female staff would
stick around after work, fraternizing with the rutting males
who could afford the tab (it was not a cheap place to eat). If
sex, drugs, and rock 'n' roll had caused a revolution, the
Trident was its Reign of Terror.

I've been through a lot of changes in terms of how I relate to
women. I didn't try to impose myself on them. I just told them
how I was and what the reality was. And it was fair—to me. It
might not have been fair to others and maybe there's some better
way I could have done it, but that's the way it happened. That's
how I was. You change as you go along; at that point I was still
very outgoing and giving and excited with life. The more I got
into hard drugs, the more I got self-indulgent. I got more selfish,
less giving, more into self-gratification, more into instant gratification, more into I-was-the-sex-object and the ladies performed for
me, which is not real nice, although I made it as nice as I could. I
think anyone who was a lover of mine in those days would confirm that this was true. It's not something I'm immensely proud
of; it's just how it was. It is again a part of what drugs do to your
personality. They make you more self-centered, more selfish, and
less sensitive. Early on, we went trolling through Marin County,
where the women were incredible. There was always someone
new and different: Big Gretchen, Susan Henke, Reine somewhere
in the background rolling joints . . . I can't remember all the
names. I was living on the boat and we were starting to really
work on her. There was another beautiful schooner down the
dock, *Sea Runner.* George Walker and I advanced the money to
buy her to her skipper, who was trying to keep her going with no
money and he had little daughters living aboard with him that he
had to support. Eventually, he sold *Sea Runner* and never paid us
back. At the time, however, he was a great help because he knew
a lot about traditional wooden boat construction and we were
really working on the *Mayan.* No matter how torn up she was,

there was always room on board for one more lady. I found them all over; some came looking for me, others I went after.

Shelly Roecker was an eighteen-year-old from Los Altos Hills in Northern California, with the same long straight hair as Christine Hinton and a similar background: Shelly had grown up on the Hamilton Air Force Base in Marin County. She had left home and was living out of her 1958 VW bug in Los Angeles on the Sunset Strip, working part-time at North Beach Leather, a custom leather shop that is still on the same block, still selling hip leather gear. In those days, it was fringed jackets, capes, and accessories and Shelly was trying to learn the basics of leathercraft as a hedge against poverty.

SHELLY ROECKER: *He walked into North Beach Leather and someone said it was David Crosby and I didn't know who that was. He sure was poorly dressed. They said he was rich. He wanted to buy everything in the store and he wanted me to make it for him. He invited me to dinner and North Beach Leather didn't pay too well for people who didn't know anything, so I hadn't eaten in about three days and there was no gas in my '58 Volkswagen. Hey, we're talking about having a good time at eighteen, although I might've been a little short on responsibility. David invited me to dinner and I was starved, so we ate in a pretty fancy restaurant and I finished all of mine and most of his and anything else I could find and then he invited me back to his boat in Marina Del Ray. I wasn't sure it existed, but it did. I stayed on the boat for a few days, not enough to lose my job. When I got onboard, he opened a hatch and a girl came up who looked just like me. I mean, twins. Her name was Jody, I think. It turned out not to be such a good thing later on because I got blamed for a lot of things she did, but it was kind of interesting then and David had twins for a while. I was pretty naïve, but I was starting to enjoy it. I always liked boats and he let me bring my cat aboard.*

The other girl may have left after a while, but Shelly stayed with David, on and off, for two more years. On and off was the only way to maintain a relationship, since there were a number of women and locations that claimed David's attention. There was also a lot of new money, thanks to the continued success of both the *CSN* and *CSNY* albums. David was not only a philanderer, he was a philanthropist; he was helping himself to sensual pleasures, but he was helping others help themselves. Time after unpublicized time, he would quietly aid a friend or acquaintance, staking them to tools or a basic education. His gifts were not just largess, although there was plenty of conspicuous consumption. They were gifts intended to make people self-sufficient, even if that independence meant they would leave his circle of influence and pursue their own pleasures or ambitions. Bobby Hammer and Salli Sachsi got quality cameras, open accounts at film labs, and plenty of backstage passes; they were able to earn a living taking pictures. Shelly Roecker got sewing machines and shop space in which to practice her crafts and fulfill commissions. Kevin Ryan was kept busy doing skilled carpentry. His personal abilities and work for David were enough of a recommendation to get him more jobs. Musicians were introduced to other musicians, to management companies, to record executives. It was a hippie meritocracy: if you could deliver the goods or show promise and desire, David would help in unexpected ways and with a generosity not usually associated with newly rich rock stars.

Me and Graham Nash put up the cash to start what was probably the first chocolate chip cookie enterprise. It was the Pine Street Bakery and we lent the money to Gretchen and Nancy, two women who had developed the concept, created the recipes, and found a location. No bank would lend them the money: "Two girls without collateral? A business loan? Forget it." Graham and I came up with the five thousand dollars they needed to start the specialty cookie shop. They opened the Pine Street Bakery and did very well. Sold a lots of cookies of all kinds. Eventually, they sold the place. I don't remember if they ever paid us back.

The generosity was in addition to the more normal philanthropic enterprises common to successful pop culture heroes: benefit performances, charity gigs, public service announcements for the usual worthy causes, and the fiercely ongoing concern for the environment and opposition to the escalating war in Vietnam. After Kent State and the furor over

"Ohio," Crosby's dark view of politics and the power structure was fueled by Kissinger's authorization of clandestine
CIA actions to destabilize the Chilean government, Nixon's
installation of tape recorders in the White House, the publi-
cation of *The Pentagon Papers*, the burglary of Daniel Ellsberg's psychiatrist's office and the subsequent indictment of
Ellsberg for conspiracy and espionage (for publicizing *The
Pentagon Papers*). David's onstage raps about "Who killed
the Kennedys" seemed less and less paranoid as the times
began to justify a certain suspicion of people in high places.

There was an ironic resonance to David's personal phi-
lanthropy. Ten years earlier, in a house in Venice, California,
David lived with Paul Kantner, Ginger Jackson, Sheri Snow,
Steve Shuster, and David Freiberg when they were all poor
folkies who pooled their money in a jar on the mantelpiece,
taking only what they needed each day for food and dope.
Now, David kept a drawer aboard the *Mayan* stuffed with
cash, upwards of two thousand dollars in every denomina-
tion. There was a similar stash of fifties and hundreds everywhere he lived. Ostensibly for "groceries" and "household
expenses" (which could include an occasional kilo of weed or
an ounce of hashish), the money was there for a nobler purpose. If you were close enough to David to live with him (a
definition that included at least a dozen people, though not
all at the same time) and you really needed money, you
could take some. He might grumble, he might curse, and he
could be coldly, harshly critical—if he was unconvinced of
the necessity of the appropriation. Most of the time, the
need was great and the capacity for giving equal to the need.
Shelly, as needy a girl as had come along in David's life,
became an intermittent steady girlfriend.

SHELLY ROECKER: *When we went up north, I stayed at Graham's
house for a little while, up on Buena Vista West in San Francisco,
and I got myself an apartment and a job. I was just a hostess at the
Trident. And I had my nice little car that David had given me the
last time I got mad at him. I met Gretchen on the boat, although she
was famous at the Trident. Gretchen was another one. There's was
always lots of them, lots of women around. I was supposed to think
that this was wonderful and take it in my stride, but I never did. I
tried. I made a good stab at it, but I hate that goddamn song*

"Triad" because a guy has one shot and if there's two women, one does without. Somebody stares at the ceiling all night and that was me. Why can't we go on as three? I just gave you one good reason. Why can't we go on as four? Why don't we go on with all three different kinds and everyone can stare at the ceiling all night. It's too one-way for me and I didn't really like touching girls and I didn't want them to touch me either. I went a long way trying to please David, but finally realized that's not me and I'm not going to like it and boy, we went around the room.

I'll tell you something: David is definitely worth waiting for, but he's not worth standing in line.

I went to New York once to surprise him, early in our relationship, and he got mad because he already had someone with him, but he asked her to move out and she moved in down the hall with the drummer. The three of us went out and had a pretty good time in New York. I quite liked her and I went back and stayed with her a couple of times later. She was okay. David let me stay in the room most of the time. It was a special room with mirrors—David went out of his way to be decadent. I met Peter Fonda that night. I drank wine for one of the first times in my life and Fonda carried me about twenty blocks on his back through New York. Interesting way to meet. A cute guy. David let me go see New York, but I could only go if I was with two other people he approved of because he said it was dangerous. We went to the Museum of Modern Art. We went to Abercrombie and Fitch and my eyes were so big. We spent money like water and I thought it was pretty neat. He made me go back after New York. I went back to my little job.

I used to crochet a lot and I used to do a lot of embroidering when I had that leather store. I was into string. I was a string person. I crocheted, I embroidered, I did macramé. I did tie-dying. I went into the leather business. David once told me that he wouldn't give me a dime for a dress, but he would buy me the sewing machine and all the material I wanted; and if ever I wanted to know something and he didn't know it, he would either find the answer himself or find someone who knew. If ever I wanted to learn something, he would

*buy me all the books I wanted and the tools, but he wouldn't buy me
the end result. I learned a lot. I learned to catch him in a weak
moment with his MasterCard and I got one dress that way. I had to
make all the rest. He built a lot of self-confidence in me, to the point
where I could go out and make money. I would take a deposit on
something I didn't know how to make, spend it, and when the money
ran out, make the garment, collect the other half, and everything
would be great. That was as responsible as I got for years.*

In answer to the record company's demand for more product, Crosby, Stills, Nash and Young came up with a double
live album called *Four Way Street. Billboard* charted the record first in April of 1971; it went to number one and stayed
on the charts for almost a year, despite the critics. They
condemned the record for the lack of new material, despite
the fact that David alone had contributed two solid new
songs: "Lee Shore" and "Triad." The rest of the album consisted of live tracks of songs from other albums and included
a lot of sloppy playing and vocalizing preserved by the escalating perfection of an evolving (and unforgiving) technology. Nevertheless, the record was embraced by the fans and
included a lot of dynamic performance tracks recorded in
concert under a variety of conditions across the country by
the everpresent Wally Heider mobile recording trucks or
trucks just like them. The mixing process was endless, with
each of the four principals revising each other's work until
marketing and sales pressures squeezed everyone to just say,
"Enough, already!" and put out the album. Stephen and
Neil went their own ways: Stephen with a band called Manassas and a side trip to England, Neil to his ranch in the
Santa Cruz Mountains and work with Crazy Horse and,
later, the Stray Gators. David and Graham hung together
and toured successfully.

Graham's house in San Francisco had four floors and a
recording studio in the basement. Upstairs was a little section called "Dave's room," which was, in effect, another
home for Crosby. It was a guest room permanently dedicated to one guest; it had David's books and clothes and
pictures hanging on the walls, his bedspread, and his knick-
knacks and crystals and scrimshaw and snuffboxes. When
David tired of the boat or was working late in the city or
flying in or out, he'd join the gang at the Nash house. Mac

Holbert, a knowledgeable and efficient hippie just off the road, signed on the CSN road crew. He gravitated to Graham and worked for him steadily in a variety of positions with escalating responsibility. By the eighties he would be overall tour manager and road boss, but in those days he was just hanging around and helping out for wages.

MAC HOLBERT: *After five years at the University of California, I left and went to New Mexico to live in a commune with a bunch of friends that had left college. I decided I was going to go to California to put together all my personal effects, sell them, buy myself a pickup, a dog, and a gun, and come back to New Mexico to live. In 1969 I ran into a gentleman by the name of Steven Cohen, who was visiting an old girlfriend on the commune. He and Leo Makota were production managers for Crosby, Stills, and Nash. He ended up giving me a ride back to California, hired me to do some work as a gofer, and by early 1971 I went out on the Crosby-Nash Tour, starting as a truck driver. I met David at Graham's house right before the tour. It was just after the first breakup of Crosby, Stills, and Nash and* Four Way Street *had already come out and there was a split: a Stills Camp and the Crosby-Nash Camp. We traveled a lot by commercial air and we did a lot of private planes, rent-a-cars, and limousines. But in terms of what we were doing out there, it's always been the same. We've always done a simple show: music and their personalities and that's the entertainment people want. They always toyed with the idea of doing a produced show, but when it comes down to it, six months before you go on the road and you have to sit down and start thinking about it, you can't get them to sit down and do it. They didn't want to deal with it. The only thing they can agree on is to get up there and do the music. Anything else is almost impossible to get past them.*

When things went wrong or when they weren't exactly the way David wanted them, he would absolutely blow up. If he walked in a hotel room and the maid had inadvertently not made the bed, rather than just say, "Hey, my bed is not made," he'd say, "We've got to move out of this goddamn place. This is the pits." The black cloud would descend on the whole group. Crosby had a way of doing that better than any person I know on the planet. Because when David is upset, he can pull a major storm down over the whole scene. But he can also do the reverse too. When David is happening, it's happening for everyone else and that's when it was good. When I started working for Crosby-Nash, David had just quit snorting cocaine. I remember once being sent to move some stuff out of his house to a place in Mill Valley and there were all kinds of containers: old snuffboxes and all the cocaine paraphernalia. When he sold the tubes and containers and everything that had all been packed away, he went right to pot.

Not exactly. David had been a cannabis devotee for more than a third of this life, but cocaine was always a close second, moving up to first as life got harder and he got older. Jackson Browne was a young songwriter who had been a favorite of the Geffen-Roberts office and would eventually sign with the company and its descendant, Asylum Records. He was one of David's favorite discoveries and was often included in recording sessions and the parties that preceded and followed them. The sessions themselves frequently became extensions of the camaraderie and social interaction that made the West Coast folk rock music scene so interdependent and self-perpetuating, even incestuous. Jackson would marry a beautiful model named Phyllis Major, who had been Bobby Neuwirth's companion for years previous. Phyllis would commit suicide several years later after bearing them a son.

JACKSON BROWNE: *David had said nice things about me in* Rolling Stone *and that was before I'd made a record. When I made a record, he sang on it and that was impressive. It was a very high recommendation that David would sing on someone's record. I have no doubt that the fact that David and Graham sang on "Doctor, My Eyes" was what got it played. It's not that great a record, but it was unusual that they would do that. One time I drove him to the studio. I was going with him and he had me drive. He criticized my driving the entire time because he says, "Look, I got a lot of drugs here. You have to drive really legal. You're a person that drives along with his head in the clouds, not thinking about how fast he's going, and I can't do that." David was a real careful driver and drove this 6.3-liter Mercedes that you couldn't get in America; it had to be snuck in somehow on the gray market; there were only about ten of them in the States. So I'm zipping along in this thing, doing about sixty-eight miles per hour, and Crosby's white-knuckling it. "Listen, are you crazy? Stop that! Drive right!" More than just a backseat driver, this was someone with a satchel of the purest Merck, of which I got a little. Crosby wasn't plying me with drugs. Any one of us could go and score our own drugs, except Crosby's dope was always a lot better, the quality was great, and it never occurred to me to say, "David, I'd like to buy some of what you have there."*

It was in 1971, I was waiting to go on tour and didn't have a place to live, so David let me stay on his boat. Those women! At one point, somebody's little brother was looking for his sister and poked his head into the main hatch of David's boat and Crosby flipped so heavily on this kid that it really was an indication that he was overwrought, overworked, and somehow off the deep end. The kid was just looking for his older sister and she was from some other boat or worked at the Trident or something. I know that a boat is your home and your castle and you shouldn't come aboard unannounced and stick your head down a hatch. It's like going up to people's houses and looking in the windows, right? But the kid didn't know any better. That was the first indication that David might be getting a little paranoid. After a few weeks of hanging out on that boat, it got so that I began to notice that people were willing to go to great lengths to get their next little hit. Crosby, noticing that too, began saying, "Okay, this is getting out of hand."

We all knew—because it was common, accepted knowledge—that cocaine was not addictive. The authorities screwed it up by overdoing it. Remember, they told us that if we took acid we would burn out our eyes looking at the sun and have bad babies. Those were lies and that did not encourage us to believe them when they said if you smoke marijuana it will lead to harder stuff. We said, "Fuck you. You're crazy." Well, it turns out that on the first two things they were wrong, but on the other thing they were right. I didn't know that. None of us knew that. And because they lied to us first, we thought everything they said was bullshit. Somewhere in the seventies cocaine became a Big Deal. It grew up from being a cottage industry where little independent operators would buy cocaine leaves or cocaine paste in Bolivia or Ecuador or Peru and would process it in little labs out in the jungle. One place would make putrid cocaine and another place would make fabulous cocaine. Peru made what was generally accepted to be the best because of regional differences in the plants and Peru was a more sophisticated place, where they had better chemists than you could get in Bolivia and Ecuador. By the eighties, there was so much money to be made that it all changed. When we first started seeing it regularly, the original suppliers were independent operators, independent smugglers, hundreds of different gangs that were smuggling and bringing it into the country and once it got here, there were hundreds of different distribution networks. Now there's so much money involved that it became the national product of at least four countries: Bolivia, Ecuador, Peru, and Colombia. And in these four countries, it's the government that's putting the cocaine out. It is the generals, the ministers of the interior, the heads of the country, the presidentes, the juntas that are doing the business. It's bankers who are the heavies. That's who's doing it. There isn't any question at all. And here's another thing—at the same time we devalued the dollar, they devalued the cocaine. Instead sending it up here pure, they started cutting it down there because they could make twice as much money and double their production—*bam*—just like that. And it's factories, protected by battalions of troops, not little independent operations. This Medellin Cartel, that's old news. That's the way it was before you started reading about it. I'll tell you later how I know all this.

The people who are trying to enforce the law are people who

make fifteen or twenty thousand a year, maybe fifty thousand at the very top. And the people that they're up against can afford to go in and plunk down a Halliburton aluminum briefcase with about a hundred thousand in cash inside, untraceable. They can do that all day. They can do it all day, all week, all month, and they're not even out of petty cash. We're talking about serious bucks here, billion-dollar operations. We're talking about the Colombian Government. I'll say it again. Quote me. Put my name on it: *the Colombian Government.* Down there we're talking about people who don't make anywhere near what they do up here. If you plunk down a hundred thousand dollars, they ask you, "Who do you want us to kill?"

If you want to bring cocaine into this country, here's how you do it. You buy everybody anywhere near the operation and you bring it in by the goddamn container load into Port Everglades. They do it all the time. They used to just bring the ships right up here off the coast. When you see on radar that a ship has stopped out there and twelve other little blips are moving around it and they all scatter so you can't catch them, you sure know what's going on. It's only fifty-five miles to the Bahamas and if you have a boat that does eighty, believe me, you can go to over there and back with a full load in one night, easy. Anytime it's flat. In the seventies, if you were anchored out there on a smooth night with no moon, all you hear all night is the roar of engines. I always thought it was cool. I was into the outlaw mentality and these smugglers were all outlaws. And I was doing the drug.

Now it's the industrial age. Cocaine is the national product of countries and it's billions of dollars' worth of dope and they don't run it in cigarette boats anymore. People started dying when the Colombians got involved and the whole thing went right down the tubes. The same that happened in Chicago during Prohibition with the gangs. Now they've knocked off all small operators. If any little guy manages to get hold of anything down there and get it up here, the big guys just tip off the DEA. They just drop a dime on him. They don't even bother shooting him anymore.

They have their own DEA agents. They have people inside the DEA, inside the Miami cops, inside the Marine Patrol, inside the Coast Guard, inside the Customs Department, inside Immigration, inside everybody. They've got people inside the military. They've got people in the AWACs radar planes. They've got people paid off everywhere. They've got judges: local, state, federal. They've got every kind of cop there is. It's just how it is: if you can afford to pay people off the way they can afford to pay people off, people can't hold the line against it. That's why they can get away with it at that level—because of the corruption. The millions and millions and millions of dollars that the government claims they are throwing at the drug problem are absolutely useless and totally bullshit. They're all cosmetic moves. The only way that they can do it is to go in and clean house. And they can't do that because the agencies are corrupt from top to bottom. J. Edgar Hoover, as strange as he was, knew this: that's why he never let the FBI go into the dope enforcement business; he knew his agents would turn and that there's no way you can stop the corruption that accompanies drugs.

It wasn't just the drug trade that was changing. The seventies began as an emotional, busy, productive, and confusing decade. The initial body of work created by Crosby, Stills, Nash, and Young had force and the power to speak to a huge audience. It also generated enough momentum to keep the machine rolling without much further collective creative input. True to the ideals of the group, everyone was free to do his thing. In David's case, it was an increasingly demanding chore: he had his work as a solo artist, his collaboration with Graham Nash, the technical demands of supervising the substantial investment required by the masthead-to-keel renovation of the *Mayan,* and the emotional stresses of personal relationships with women. He was also looking for a house in Marin, which would probably require either new construction or extensive remodeling of an existing structure.

As 1970 ended, Nixon commended a minor record executive named Mike Curb for purging his label of suspected drug users. Curb would go on to become a lieutenant governor of California, representing the California conservative coalition that had previously named Ronald Reagan governor. Unlike Reagan, Curb subsequently failed in every one of his later bids for elective office, but there is a Boy Scout headquarters named after him in Sherman Oaks, California.

Joni Mitchell's album was declared a Gold Record, having sold the required number of units, and David Crosby got a movie deal. The film was to be called *Family* and it was to be financed and distributed by United Artists, where an executive named David Picker was running things. The idea was an idealistic pastoral fantasy, without dialogue, elaborately scored with original music by Crosby and his friends. By any standards, it was original to the point where it might be considered uncommercial. However, a new phenomenon had come to the attention of the major studios: soundtrack compilation albums that included songs by pop groups stood a good chance of earning millions of dollars for a studio. Both the *Easy Rider* and *Midnight Cowboy* soundtracks had gone gold and *Easy Rider* had tracks by Peter Fonda's old pals the Byrds. There were also Byrds tracks on the soundtrack for *Candy,* another *Billboard* soundtrack album chart hit, and *The Graduate* had earned a fortune for Simon and Garfunkel. Soundtracks, being a new commodity, could usually be exempted from the strict exclusivity that welded artists to their record companies. For the price of a low-budget film (under a million dollars in those days), United Artists could have a Crosby-Mitchell-Dylan-Kantner-Garcia-and-Friends album for its UA Records label, which would be impossible for that company to achieve on its own, given the stature and normal unavailability of the artists. But David promised they'd help out with material, he pledged his own musically creative efforts, and it was a chance to make a movie, as his father had done before him so many times. And David would act in it, as well, fulfilling another long-standing ambition. Geffen-Roberts made the deal, with David Geffen dealing with David Picker for the services of David Crosby. It was a lot of Davids. This author was engaged to cowrite and direct. Crosby would produce, furnish the music for the soundtrack, and play a part.

DAVID GEFFEN: *David begged me to get him a movie deal, so I went to my good friend David Picker at United Artists and I sold him a David Crosby movie, under the assurance that he would be delivered a story movie for six hundred thousand dollars. That's the deal I made with him. In those days that was enough money to make a movie. David started hiring all these people to make this movie. I told him, "This is a friend of mine, I sold him this movie by promising him that you were going to professionally deliver a movie for which there was going to be a soundtrack, and blah-blah-blah . . ."*

When the movie deal came through, David and his coauthor went off to Hawaii to write the screenplay for *Family*. A working subtitle for the movie was *A Day in the Life* and it was a lyrical epic about a postapocalyptic or parallel universe in which a tribe of nomads arrives at a campsite, spends a night and a day, and moves on, leaving the environment lovingly unblemished. That was it. There was no dialogue, so expressive camerawork, semi-improvised performances, and wall-to-wall music would have to carry the narrative. It was a visionary and experimental film. To create it, the writers stayed for three weeks on Oahu's North Shore in a house on the sand: sunning, sleeping, smoking dope, and working for hours every day. There was a housekeeper recruited from the local hippie community who cooked plenty of brown rice and looked after the cleaning. A typical day would begin with a joint and a swim, during which the housekeeper would make breakfast. The creative team would emerge from the water, towel off, and eat fresh papayas, cereal, eggs, drink orange juice and coffee, and settle down at the typewriter. Instead of a normal screenplay, the script for the movie evolved as a series of three or four hundred four-by-six Rolodex cards. When they were almost done, the creative team felt that there was enough material written. Crosby and his partner and his partner's wife flew to the island of Maui to visit friends of David's who had emigrated to the islands because the Los Angeles lifestyle was too pressured and hectic. As one heads west, the culture left behind, to the east, acquires the reputation for being stuffy, pressured, class-conscious, and materialistic. New Yorkers feel that way about Europeans, Los Angelenos feel that way about New Yorkers, and in Hawaii if you seem at all concerned about schedules and deadlines, they wonder if you're "from the Mainland." In Fiji and Tahiti, Hawaiians are seen as scurrying, money-grubbing urbanites. The trend ends abruptly in the Far East (or the Far West, looking out from the Pacific Rim), where the bustling citizens of Hong Kong,

Taiwan, Singapore, and Tokyo are proud of being the most industrious ants in a world of less productive grasshoppers.

On Maui the screenplay for *Family* was put aside while a group of David's friends organized an overnight excursion to the bottom of Haleakala Crater, the world's largest volcanic crater, a moonscape of ethereal beauty. The trip involved an overnight stay in one of the picturesque cabins maintained by the National Park Service on the crater floor. The campsite is accessible only by foot or mule and the Maui contingent proposed the following sequence for the recreational outing. First, a substantial predawn dose of LSD. While that's taking effect, drive to the top of Mount Haleakala, a ten-thousand-foot-high dormant volcano and one of the scenic wonders of the islands. Second, once atop the mountain and thoroughly psychedelicized, take an hour or so to enjoy the sunrise, then hike down the Sliding Sands Trail, pausing to explore the lava tubes and caves along the way. Third, spend the night in the cabin. Fourth, hike out the next morning, spiritually refreshed. To add the final perfect touch, there was to be a full eclipse of a full moon on the night everyone would be in the crater. It was the night of February 9, 1971, and things went as planned. The crowd of local, transplanted, and visiting hipsters took the acid, hiked the trail, cooked supper, and stared happily into the dome of the sky overhead. The only bummer was a rumor, delivered by a hiking party of born-again Christians, that Los Angeles had been destroyed by an earthquake.

There were no phones, no radios, and no communications with the outside world. An old hand-crank field phone connected the cabin with the park ranger's office, which would not be open until morning. The only source of hard news was a band of night-hiking wide-eyed Jesus freaks, who happily informed the Crosby party that God had vented his wrath on the heathens and Sodomites of our hometown, that communications were cut off, and the National Guard had been called out. As it turns out, they were partially correct. It was the day of the Sylmar quake, a tremor that registered 6.5 on the Richter scale and did extensive damage to the Los Angeles area, dropping freeway overpasses, collapsing buildings, and inspiring the movie *Earthquake*. There was nothing anyone in Haleakala Crater could do, high on acid or straight. The consensus was that whatever had happened, it could all be sorted out in the morning. After the strenuous climb out of the park, it was learned that L.A. had survived; none of our friends had been hurt and the movie and record businesses were still in place. A quick return to the Mainland was organized.

Arriving back in Hollywood with a completed screenplay, David assumed his official role as producer. He employed his friend Bobby Hammer and Hammer's friend Jim Parks as production managers for the picture. Hammer had made a couple of experimental short subjects on sixteen-millimeter film, including footage of Christine and David shot during the *Mayan*'s Caribbean period. Parks's experience was more extensive—he had been production manager for some filmed commercials. Neither had any experience in feature films. The director and producer took an office and began casting, scouting locations, and interviewing cameramen and crew. A start date was set. The budget was revised continually as the professional production managers at United Artists pointed out areas where inexperience and enthusiasm had been substituted for hard-dollar production knowledge. Unbeknownst to the writers, United Artists was expecting more of a plot and probably some dialogue. *Family*, as rich as it was in imagery and ideas, didn't have a conventional story and the cast was composed largely of unknowns. The people who were financing the film began to get nervous. They wondered about the company's ability to complete the picture on time and on budget. They wondered about the soundtrack, which was the entire raison d'être for the film's funding in the first place. They wondered about the script, which was presented as a stack of Rolodex cards. Was this any way to make a movie?

DAVID GEFFEN: *All of a sudden I realized that all that money was going to get pissed away and I was not going to be responsible for this. I had, in good faith, made this deal with David Picker. I called him and said, "David, you know what I promised you? It does not look likely that you're going to get it. I want to tell you this because . . ." I had a relationship with the man. I urged him to pull the plug because I was not going to be a party to him being beaten for all this money and get nothing in return. I told David [Crosby] I did it. I didn't do it underhandedly. I called him up and told him so after begging him to get it together and get it organized. That movie thing was the major problem in my relationship with David. We got over it; we got past it. But he was pretty pissed off. It was just a nightmare. I took my relationships seriously, not just with the band but with the people we dealt with. I had to go back to those people. I had to ask them for favors. This wasn't going to be the end of the world. That's what they didn't get. They wanted me to lie on their behalf, which I was unwilling to do. There wasn't going to be a real soundtrack, by the way. That was all a scam. At that point, they insisted on the overages coming out of the Crosby, Stills, Nash, and Young money. The deal fell apart.*

David Crosby says that there was going to be a real soundtrack, there would have been a soundtrack album, and it would have had new and original songs. Yet, Geffen-Roberts (especially Geffen), who had made the deal in the first place, later advised their client to cancel it. Certain representations were made and developing circumstances drove United Artists to require David to pledge his personal royalty income as a completion guarantee for the movie. That was a deal breaker and the deal broke. Crosby and his film company might have lacked experience, but they wanted to make an original and experimental music film. United Artists was prudent and businesslike and wanted a movie with a salable soundtrack. The bridge between them should have been Crosby's management, but the bridge collapsed.

It was a time of escalating highs and lows, typified by the next event. The *Mayan* was raided by police while docked at the Lido Shipyard in Newport Beach. The boat had been sailed south by a crew that would become the nucleus of a little Great White Fleet. Besides the *Mayan* and Bob Wilson's *Sea Runner*, there was a magnificent schooner called *Flying Cloud*, owned by a gentle hippie who spent two inheritances refitting her to perfection. The plan was to sail south to Mexico, across the Pacific to Hawaii and Tahiti, and then decide where to go from there. First, everything had to be brought up to specs and the boats fitted out for extended ocean cruising, so *Flying Cloud* and *Mayan* wound up at the Lido Shipyard. By this time, Bud Hedrick had come to work on the boat as first mate and ship's carpenter. Hedrick was a good man to have onboard whenever emotional, climatic, or bureaucratic squalls blew up. A compact and genial man with enormous muttonchop whiskers and bright sky-blue eyes, Hedrick's face was lined and weather-beaten, but always smiling.

I met Bud Hedrick in Acapulco. When we got there, I was looking around, figuring on trying to find some weed. And I saw this guy hammering some piece of metal back into shape against a cleat on the dock. And I said, "That guy knows." I looked at him, I looked at the look in his eyes, and I said, "That man knows where I can get some of what I want." Sure enough, he did. Took me straightaway to his little room and he had it. His own self. Bud, it turned out, was a master sailor, an experienced diver, a motocross racer, and had studied bullfighting in Spain, a genuine novillero, on his way to becoming a full-out torero. He joined up with me in Sausalito, went right to work on the boat, and I never regretted that day for a minute. He's back on the *Mayan* even as we're writing this, overseeing her reconstruction as we make her ready for sea again.

BUD HEDRICK: *In 1969 I was in Acapulco, taking care of a boat for an absentee owner. My boat was anchored. It wasn't a very big boat and I had to borrow a skiff all the time to row out to the thing. That's how I met David. He was sitting on the dock beside a really rundown boat with hippies all over the deck. He was very much a hippie in those days. I asked if I could borrow a skiff and he said, "Sure. Go ahead." I figured maybe he'd like a joint, so I gave him a couple. The* Mayan *had everything stashed. They didn't want to have anything onboard because it was really tough in Mexico at that point. They would arrest you for having long hair and David had long hair; I had long hair and a big mustache. We rowed offshore to smoke 'em and that was the start of a long relationship. I joined* Mayan *in Sausalito and sailed her down to Newport. Shelly was with him then.*

Shelly was David's principal ladyfriend at the time, maintained in the curiously subservient-dependent relationship that he required and she conceded. As David's girlfriend, she was senior officer on watch when the authorities closed and boarded. The *Mayan*, by the way, is what is known in maritime law as a "documented vessel." This gives her certain rights under complicated laws dating back to the Age of Sail and predating the United States Constitution. A documented vessel (or any private boat, for that matter) may not be boarded without permission. The kids aboard thought that they could only be inspected by Customs officers or the Coast Guard in the lawful exercise of their duties. It's an extension of the rules that govern both private property and the absolute authority of the captain over his ship at sea. As long as the boat's afloat, the rules apply. One would think that this would rule out unannounced drug raids by the Orange County sheriff's office, whether or not they were based on anonymous tips about "the smell of marijuana" emanating from the craft. When the first deputies arrived, Shelly denied them any right to board; they sent for a U.S. Customs officer, Agent P. Green (his real name).

While waiting for the federal man, there was a standoff. The kids aboard *Mayan* started to get rid of any incriminating evidence, but they were landlubbers. Flushing your dope down the toilet might make sense at home, but aboard the boat, all that happened is quantities of leafy green material started burbling up and bobbing to the surface. The boat's "head" was being repeatedly flushed, each time discharging its contents through the hull into the waters immediately adjacent to it. In short order, a kilo of weed was floating in the water around the *Mayan*. (This was in the days before mandatory holding tanks.)

SHELLY ROECKER: *We were just sitting there, waiting for David to come home for dinner, and we weren't smoking any pot or anything. It was just that dinner had been held forever because David is always late. They weren't really supposed to come aboard the boat because it was a documented vessel, so I stayed like I was told to do and showed them the ship's papers. They didn't have a court order, a warrant, or anything like that. One cop thought I had a gun or something and he jumped aboard the boat because all he could see was my head coming out of the companionway, so he pointed a shotgun at me. I was thinking, "If I really did have a weapon, they'd be scraping you off the water. They'd be straining you now." What a dummy. We had guns onboard, David always had guns, and I probably would've been*

*within my rights to shoot at boarders, but I didn't. I'll never forget
all those shotguns pointed at my little head. I weighed about ninety-
eight pounds and was thinking, "Wow." They took me off with a
T-shirt and a bathing suit bottom and the ship's documents and my
passport and a bunch of sawed-off shotguns in my hand. It was like
"Adam 12," only the cops hadn't rehearsed too well and I laughed
so hard I cried. I got busted for pot and I don't even like pot. I've
never been a pot smoker. These cops were so corny and they had three
cars in a row and I'm in the last car, handcuffed to two other people,
and the guy in the last car lost the keys. They haul us all the way to
the station handcuffed together and then tell us to get out of the car
one at a time! Come on. The whole thing was just comic!*

David, at the same time, was arriving at the shipyard with
Graham and recalls seeing all the unmarked police cars. It
has been his sense for years that one should follow one's
hunches. This night was different from all other nights;
David didn't follow any of his instincts, despite a quantity of
clues and signals. Shelly, sitting in a police car handcuffed to
three other quaking hippies, watched it all go down.

Let me be clear about this. Always listen when you're trying
to tell yourself something! Graham and I rolled up to the boatyard
and as I parked I said, "Hey, look at all the four-door sedans with
the black sidewall tires. Must be the feds, come to bust me." We
both laughed. "Nah, I'm paranoid," I said. "Maybe I should
leave my bag in the trunk. There's a lot of stuff inside it . . .
Boy, am I paranoid." I laughed. Graham laughed. I walked past
all these cars, onto the dock, onto my boat, where Agent P. Green
put a pistol in my ear and told me I was under arrest. The moral
of this story is: when you have a hunch, *pay attention.* I knew it
was a bust. I knew there were federal agents at the boatyard. I
could've peeked inside any of those sedans and seen the radios
and special gear. I could've turned around and driven away and I
would have saved the twenty-five thousand dollars it cost me to
stay out of jail.

SHELLY ROECKER: *When they got David, I could see from where I was that he had his big shoulder bag he always had with him. He always paid for everything with cash and always threw the change in the bottom of the bag. The bottom four inches of this big bag was all small change and they had to catalog everything in it, which turned into a major trip. The reason he was late was because he had gone to the accountant's and gotten some incredibly large five-figure sum in cash to pay the shipyard, which was also in his bag, along with fifty ounces of gold and all his little magic bags of funny symbols with cute little rocks and stuff in them. They had to catalog all that crap. It took them hours and before they were through we were out on bail.*

BUD HEDRICK: *It was obvious that things were way too loose. I didn't stay onboard. I would go to Laguna to spend the nights. I was just working days. People were coming and going all the time. It was clearly going to come down. Newport's really an uptight place and you can't live there that way. When the bust came down, I wasn't surprised. I went into work one morning and one of the guys in the yard said, "Hey, don't go down near the boat. They had a big arrest last night and everybody's in jail." I called a bail bondsman in Laguna to get them out and he called me right back and said, "Somebody's already arranged the bail. They're releasing them right now." So I just parked outside the jail. I had a van that had belonged to a linoleum company. It said JACK'S LINOLEUM on the outside, but on the inside it was all fixed up for traveling. They got out of jail, piled in the van, and away we went.*

SHELLY ROECKER: *In the end, nothing ever happened with that bust. We went to court a couple of times and the assistant DA said he didn't have enough evidence. David punched some guy with a camera on the way out because he didn't want his picture taken and I guess there was a little trouble over that, but that got resolved too. Eventually, we got a call from a lawyer, met a secretary in an airport and signed some papers saying we wouldn't sue for false arrest, and the charges were all dropped and that was the end of it.*

Beyond that, all I remember is I had to wear a nice dress to court. The final kicker was this. What they said was the smell of marijuana was actually my cooking. I was burning the brown rice and the soy sauce and some fish that didn't turn out too well.

The headlines in the Newport Beach newspapers said ROCK SINGER PUNCHES PHOTOG, but there was little notice of the incident in the general press, which was just as well. David's parents were proud of their son's achievements and it would have done neither of them any good to see their son's picture in a story about contraband and scuffles in the courthouse. Aliph and Floyd lived very much apart. David's mother had a small house in Santa Barbara and it was becoming increasingly difficult to visit her. Her estrangement from Floyd had been complete, final, and irrevocable. She wanted no further contact with him. Floyd was retired from active filmmaking, teaching cinematography at UCLA and living with Betty in Ojai. Aliph lived alone and was becoming ill with what would eventually be diagnosed as a terminal malignancy. At the time, she was still being treated as an outpatient with chances for recovery. David would see her, then visit his father whenever he was in the Santa Barbara area. Occasionally, he'd make the drive up from Los Angeles, but the encounters with his mother were always stressful. Aliph was hurt and angered by the divorce, which she considered an abandonment. Floyd and Betty were settled in Ojai and Betty worked steadily as a script supervisor on major feature films. She was Barbra Streisand's favorite and worked on most of Streisand's pictures until Floyd's advancing years took their toll. By 1979 he would be frail and require Betty's constant attention. She retired from the business and stayed home after that, but not before experiencing Floyd's doting affection for his successful son and his anguish over Aliph's justifiable resentment.

BETTY CROSBY: *Neither Floyd nor I knew what a big success Crosby, Stills, and Nash was. I was going home one day from shooting on location with Howard Koch, Jr., and we were on Sunset Boulevard on the Strip and there was this great big billboard with the boys in their parkas. I said, "You know, that's Floyd's boy." And Howard said to me, "That's Floyd's boy? My God, Betty. Do you know who they* are?" And I said, "No." And he said, "They're only one of the biggest rock groups in the country." So I went home and told Floyd and Floyd was just as amazed as I was. We were so out of that rock thing. That's the first time I knew that they were so famous. He would visit us in Ojai and I was terribly concerned about his problem. He was so different from what he was as a youngster. I had the feeling that Graham was always an adult. David was on a terrific high and having a wonderful and marvelous time and I was scared because I felt that the things that he was doing were dangerous. And Floyd just wouldn't think about it. He really couldn't. I never felt I knew David. There was no rapport at all. I always felt he was putting on an act for me. Not for his father. His father loved him. Floyd was so proud. My God, after he knew how big David had become again, he'd go to the filling station and he'd say to the boy who put gas in the car, "Ever hear of Crosby, Stills, and Nash?" The boy would say, "Yeah, why?" And he'd say, "David Crosby's my son." He'd tell everybody. If they were young, he'd always do that. He was terribly proud of him. But it wasn't a happy time for Aliph. Let's face it. Floyd was with me, not her. We were happy, but he had guilty feelings, of course, and it always happens to a woman at that time in her life: the man decides he wants something a little different, a little younger. I'd been through this before. I had been married before and my first husband was in the motion picture business. I could've been Cleopatra and he probably would've left me. He did leave me, so I knew what Aliph felt because I'd gone through the same thing myself; I was jilted before I met Floyd. When we were married, neither she nor her sons came. But Floyd was very honorable. He never, ever missed a payment and was always concerned about the boys and I never interfered.

Money poured in from David's solo record and various tours with the band and with Nash as an acoustic duo. The relationship with Graham would deepen and intensify beyond what David shared with the other members of the band and the two men would record together, hitting the *Billboard* charts in April of 1972 with an album called simply *Graham Nash and David Crosby*. The record would stay on the charts for six more months, going gold like everything else the guys had done so far. David was working from a three-cornered base: the *Mayan* in Sausalito, his room at Graham's in the Haight-Ashbury in San Francisco, and the Lisbon Lane house in Los Angeles. Shelly would be around when she was in favor and elsewhere when David was with other women.

AHMET ERTEGUN: *A very special kind of bond developed between the group and myself. It's not that we hung out together all the time, but whenever we saw each other, whenever I saw Crosby, Stills, and Nash as a group or individually, it was a celebration. David was the person whom I knew the least and to whom I became closest in many ways. He was very straightforward and we could talk about things other than the music. There was a lot of political consciousness there. David was always facing reality. A pragmatist, except that he wasn't quite as methodical and clear-cut as Graham Nash. David was a person unto himself. He was already a kind of folk hero with his own following, not just of ordinary groupies but of special ladies who had a special relationship with him. David was a person who really enjoyed the rock 'n' roll life. Maybe too much, although it didn't seem like it at the time. It was a terrific time. All the artists who lived through that period must remember it with various different emotions. In a sense, it was just great. Maybe destructive, but great when it was happening. As a result of the success of CSN, David Geffen stopped managing CSN. I offered to start his own record label; Atlantic would finance it and that's how Asylum was born.*

DAVID GEFFEN: *I wish I could tell you that I thought David was basically a nice guy. He wasn't. Very early in the seventies he called me from New York. There was a Crosby-Nash concert at Carnegie Hall. Reine was flying into L.A.; I was going to New York and he wanted me to bring him some grass. I said, "I'm not going to carry dope for you. I'm not going to take a chance like that." And he screamed and yelled at me and abused me and was disgusting. He said that if I didn't bring the grass, he was not going on at Carnegie Hall. Right? So Reine brought me this manila envelope with grass in it. I put it in my attaché case and I went to the airport. I remember very clearly it was Yom Kippur. In those days they didn't have X-ray machines at the airport and they didn't check things all the time. But as I go through, they're checking. I thought, "Ay-yi-yi, what am I gonna do?" but it was too late. I opened the attaché case. This guy takes the manila envelope and shakes it and seeds roll out. The guy says, "What's in this envelope?" And I said, "I never saw this envelope before in my life." This, by the way, is the exact moment when I decided to give up being a manager. I was taken out of Los Angeles International Airport in handcuffs and taken to jail on Yom Kippur. Try and get a lawyer on Yom Kippur on the phone. I called my brother, who's a lawyer and who was the* last *person I wanted to call from jail. I said, "I've been arrested for grass," and he was really pissed off at me, but he got me out of jail. I got on the next plane, without the grass, of course, to get to the Crosby-Nash concert. I go to the hotel where they're staying, knock on David's door, and he says, "Where's my grass?" I said, "I was arrested and put in jail. I don't have it." And he said to me, "I'm gonna fucking kill you!" I had just gotten out of jail and went right to the airport so I could see them in concert, right? I said to Elliot, "I'm finished. This is the end." It wasn't just that I was finished with the management business. I was emotionally finished with David Crosby.*

Asylum Records became a power base for David Geffen, with one of the best artist rosters in the business. It became the home label for what was to be known as the California sound. Elliot continued running the management company, most of whose artists recorded on Asylum, whose corporate philosophy was "benevolent protectionism." The record company was different from other labels and was proud of its noninterference with the private and artistic lives of its artists, who in turn looked to David Geffen and company to insulate and protect them from the shocks and insults of commercially oriented sales and marketing types, aggressive promotion men, and demanding producers. The opening lineup at Asylum included Jackson Browne, the Eagles, and Joni Mitchell, with Linda Ronstadt joining shortly after. In 1974, the legendary Bob Dylan would leave Columbia and release two Top 10 albums with the company before re-turning to his original label. That didn't matter to David. Crosby, Stills, Nash, and Young were Atlantic artists and they were doing quite nicely, thank you very much. Besides, the new Great White Fleet was ready to live out the "Wooden Ships" fantasy and the *Mayan* was ready to sail to Mexico.

DEBBIE DONOVAN: *After Christine died, when David was living on the boat, we became lovers. I was around, but he really didn't want me around. He was afraid that all of a sudden I was going to cling to him, which wasn't the case. I went down and moved into the Lisbon Lane house. There was a little sex involved, but it was more on a friendship level. There was never any commitment on David's part. After a while I moved up to Elliot Roberts's place, up north in the Santa Cruz Mountains, near Neil's. He was rebuilding the place and needed somebody to caretake it. It was just something for me to do; it was a job and someplace to live and I loved the country and being out there. I was assistant teaching at the local elementary school and I was about to go to college and David called up and said, "Listen, we're taking the boat down to Mexico and you've been voted in." I said, "Huh?" I was just ready to go back east and take up teaching because I loved being with the kids. After some indecision I went on the boat, which may or may not have been a mistake, since at the time I was the odd girl out.*

In addition to the others, a carpenter named Gordon Abbott had drifted into Sausalito. Abbott was a transplanted Scots-man who had come to America after leaving a career as a stockbroker in Edinburgh and London. He fell in with Kevin Ryan and became the "third grunt" onboard, living and working on the schooner. A few slips down the dock was Bob Wilson and his family aboard *Sea Runner*. Wilson, the most experienced skipper of the group, was helping refit *Mayan*. Chronically broke, the feeling was that he was using the *Mayan*'s open accounts at the local marine hardware stores and ship chandlers to make his own boat seaworthy. Nothing was provable, but the bills kept mounting up for *Mayan* and *Sea Runner* kept getting new equipment. Despite that, the feeling was all upbeat and fanciful. David didn't begrudge Wilson at the time and *Sea Runner* and *Mayan* and *Flying Cloud*, three beautiful schooners, were going to sail off together on a great adventure. Two more crew had found their way aboard: Billy Martinelli and Dana Africa. Martinelli was a carpenter and a sailor and Dana Africa was a beautiful woman with unique sailing credentials. Her father had been a mate and mariner on sailing vessels since the 1920s and had been Sterling Hayden's first mate and sailing companion. His name was right out of boy's adventure fiction: Spike Africa. Dana had learned to sail as a child, cruising around the world with her father and brother, the Hayden kids, and Sterling Hayden himself aboard his schooner *Wanderer*. Their adventure was memorialized in Hayden's autobiography of the same name.

GORDON ABBOTT: *We loaded tools and equipment, canned food and supplies, and who knows what the hell we were doing? It was as if we were going to sail off and find an uninhabited island and set up on it. David endorsed this dream and Wilson verbalized it. He'd tell his kids, "We're going to sail off into the sunset and find paradise and live there." I don't think David believed it for a minute. But we set up and we bought stuff and off we sailed down the coast and there were some of the highest and lowest moments of my life on that trip, when I learned the true joys of big-boat open-ocean sailing.* Mayan *and* Sea Runner *sailed together out of Sausalito, with* Mayan *being the flagship and* Sea Runner *being the tender. I ended up on Bob Wilson's boat and fought with him all the way down. He was Captain Bligh. He wanted me to risk my life and the life of everyone on the boat. He was terrible. He probably resented being the junior skipper of the fleet, when he had been sailing longer than Crosby. We stopped in Santa Barbara, so that David could visit his mother in the hospital. I was taking a late-night walk when David came back and we ended up crying together on the dock about his mom. We walked and he smoked a joint and it was a foggy, wet night and my eyes burn right now, thinking of it. It was a very tender moment, one of the magic David moments. When we got farther down the coast I jumped ship, but not before I gained a lot of respect for him as a sailor. He was a safe sailor and a good sailor. He got the most out of a boat without drift and he was good at driving it. It was the perfect situation for David because democracy was not required. A benevolent dictatorship is absolutely the best way to run a boat and he ran the boat very well.*

BUD HEDRICK: *We left California on our way to either the Caribbean or Mexico. We didn't know where we were going; we just knew we were going. We had eight people onboard. David, Shelly, Debbie, me, Billy Martinelli, Christine McLenahan, Bobby Hammer, and Dana Africa. We got as far as Puerto Vallarta and everybody went to the beach except me. I was doing some work on the boat. They'd heard about a nude beach, which at that time was illegal in Mexico. There were also vigilante licenses in Mexico. You could go to the police department, pay a certain fee, and get a license that allowed you to arrest people. Then you'd take them in and get part of the fine. There were Mexicans down there who supported themselves that way and the nude beach was one of the areas they worked. There were two or three guys who worked the area from different points where they could see everything that went on down there. Including, as it turns out, the entire crew of the* Mayan, *except for me.*

The vigilantes watched them for a while until they saw them smoking some joints. That was a better bust than nudity because they'd get more money out of them. So they swooped down and everybody got rid of their joints by throwing them in the water. They said, "You can't arrest us. We don't have anything." The vigilante says, "Yes, you do. I brought my own evidence, just in case." He's got a little bag of dope he's brought with him, which he now says is theirs, and he takes them to jail. But he didn't have a car. They all had to hitchhike. In custody, thumbs out, waiting for a police car to come by so the local guy can flag it down and take his prisoners to jail. This struck our gang as funny, so they were laughing, which pissed off the vigilantes and the cops. So then when David or someone tried to pay them off, it was too late; they were definitely going to jail. David was saying to whoever spoke English, "Hey, tell the guy

I'll pay him the equivalent of a year's wages." But the guy wouldn't do it. He was really mad because they had laughed at him. Finally, everyone was in the habit of wearing big Buck knives on their belts, kind of a salty thing to do and useful. That was construed as carrying a weapon, which was still another charge. In Mexico, you don't just carry a serious knife around, not without getting into trouble.

Meanwhile, back at the boat, a lady came by with a VW van and told me about the bust. I speak Spanish, so I grabbed some money for bail and got a cab and I got over to the jail before they had arrived. Siesta time, so nobody was being booked before 4 P.M. They finally brought them in and none of the crew was smiling. They went into a big cell and we waited for the chief to come in. After siesta, it's his privilege to arrive a little later. Finally, he gets there and we go into his office and talk and work out a price, which turned out to be about seven dollars per person. Now the chief wants to give me back the evidence, saying, "Take this with you," which I was reluctant to do because after we hit the street, they could pull us back in and run the same number again. But the guy insisted. "No no. Take it. I don't want that in here." And I said, "Hey, this isn't ours. This is really garbage. We don't need it." He insists, "Take it with you." So, okay. Everybody got out. They gave them their knives back and we went out and drank margaritas and smoked the evidence. We had a good time.

SHELLY ROECKER: *The boat got real small real fast. Dana and I always got along pretty well. Bobby Hammer and I got along well. Before we sailed we went to the doctor and got a whole bunch of things in case we got sick in Mexico and one of the items he gave us was paregoric, which apparently has some kind of opiate in it. David always thought that I went in and drank the paregoric and I got in so much trouble. David, I did not drink the paregoric. But I know who did: Bobby Hammer. We had been out diving and David just dropped me at the Mayan and took off in the skiff, looking for some broad he'd seen onshore. I decided right then and there that I'd had enough. I didn't feel good. I wanted to go home. I caught some awful* *dysentery and had to be taken ashore, only we were anchored some-place where there were no roads except burro trails. I said "David, take me to an airport." He sailed to Puerto Vallarta and I made a decision. "It's time to reach into the money drawer and take a big handful." I wanted to go home. I had to put up with Debbie Dono-van all the way down there, who I knew he was sleeping with. She had been Christine's best friend, so that made her higher up on the ladder. I went back to L.A. and stayed in his house. I felt self-righteous at that point and I needed a place to stay, so I just went with the key and opened it. I knew he wouldn't mind and he didn't. I went back once. They were all out of meat. The boat was still in Puerto Vallarta, so I took a big load of meat and fresh foods that they didn't get down there. Got off the plane and took a cab to the boat, lugging a suitcase full of steaks. Then I came back and got my teeth worked on and sent the bill to his accountant.*

Shelly eventually turned her back on rock 'n' roll and went into horse racing. She rode as a jockey in minor races at the Aqua Caliente racetrack in Mexico and on smaller tracks around California and was injured several times in severe falls. She met and married a doctor, and eventually got di-vorced. Now she raises imported German shepherd dogs in Yuba City, California. She hasn't seen David for many years.

SHELLY ROECKER: *I haven't made any major significant contribution to society and probably never will, but every once in a while, I help somebody a little along the way who probably doesn't deserve it and sometimes I get screwed for it, but I'd rather have done it than turned my back. David encouraged me to pursue my curiosity and showed me ways to find out what I wanted to know. That's a tool that I got from David and I'll always be grateful for it. I probably learned more in those two years with David than any other two years in my life; for positive and negative reasons, he's responsible for the forma-tion of most of the values and ethics by which I live today. He taught me to be honest, to try to be creative, to continue trying to learn, to pursue knowledge. He gave me a lot of tools that are still with me. Maybe it was so hard to get close to him because there was always a crowd. It probably contributed to his problem that he gave so much of himself and was being somebody for so many other people that he lost himself. He's back to being David again. The Cros. I think that's all I have to say.*

After the arrest, Mexico seemed a far less hospitable place. Maybe it wasn't such a good idea to anchor the Great White Fleet South of the Border. Bud Hedrick had met a girl in Puerto Vallarta we'll call Ms. Lucky. Lucky had helped Bud clean up the boat, off-loading all the drugs so that the *Mayan* could withstand an inspection by Mexican authorities— if it came to that. The satchels full of contraband were taken to Lucky's grandmother's house and stored there temporarily while Bud dealt with the police. The grandmother never knew. The new plan was clear: get out of Mexico. As soon as the *Mayan* could be provisioned and made ready for sea, she set sail for Hawaii, her longest deep-water adventure yet. David was at the helm, Debbie was in the owner's stateroom, Bud Hedrick was first mate and senior sailor, and Lucky had joined the crew. Bobby Hammer and Dana Africa stayed on and Jim Dickson, back in favor, flew down from Los Angeles to help sail the boat west into the Pacific. Billy Martinelli and Christine McLenahan returned to San Francisco. *Flying Cloud* and *Sea Runner* made their own preparations and followed. All three boats made the Pacific crossing without incident and arrived in Hawaii within a few weeks of each other. Bobby brought his sixteen-millimeter film camera and took movies of the voyage. On a royal blue Pacific stretching endlessly to the horizon, the crew can still be seen, taking on-deck showers out of canvas buckets of seawater, climbing the rigging, bathing naked in the sun, and enjoying what must have been an idyllic sail. There was even a storm at sea, a real Pacific squall at night, with waves crashing on the deck and filling the cockpit, and enough wind to blow out the spinnaker, which is an "all hands on deck" emergency for a sailboat. The ship survived. In all, they were at sea for twenty-eight days and David was responsible for the celestial navigation that plotted the ship's course and position. They made landfall on time and within ten miles of their final destination, as projected. Crosby had sailed *Mayan* across three thousand miles of open ocean and reached his destination dead on course. They sailed into the old whaling port of Lahaina, on the island of Maui, just as generations of sailors since Captain Cook and the square-riggers of the nineteenth century had done.

That was the most wonderful journey. It was spectacular. We had a compatible crew, with experienced sailors like Bud and Jim Dickson and Dana Africa. I had learned how to navigate and I did it. It was a major thrill when I hit it smack-on. I learned to navigate from a guy named John Kapelowitz, a small, bearded, marvelous man. Very bright and extremely patient with me. I studied in Sausalito and forced myself to learn it. It's not that hard, I studied the Air Almanac and the 249 System. People make navigation out to be this arcane art, usually just so that they can aggrandize themselves, make themselves seem tremendously wise, powerful, and magical. In fact, what you have to know how to do is some simple math and, in particular, how to take sights. I can take a good sight. The rest of it is knowing how to work a stopwatch and a radio and how to use tables. It's a fairly complex process. I know that I never smoked a joint before I tried to do it because there were about twenty-three steps in the method I used and you have to be meticulous about it. I'm not normally a methodical or orderly person and in those days I was pretty chaotic in managing my life. Yet, I managed to learn to be careful and thoughtful about two things: making records and navigating.

It was mystical, sailing under the clearest skies in the world. At night more stars than you'll see anywhere, even in the desert. In the daytime the trade winds, slowly building up towers of cumulus from utterly clear marble-blue sky in the morning to two and three layers of cumulus clouds by evening, followed by the most spectacular sunsets. We were running handlines out over the stern, fishing for mahimahi, cooking them within thirty minutes of pulling them out of the water. Heaven. Just heaven. By the time we'd been out there a couple of weeks, our eyes got acclimated to seeing all this stuff. You can spot birds working fish, miles away. You can see the ripple of wind on the water, miles away. You can see the slightest change in things. You get attuned to it. You get attuned to the schedule for standing watch. Sailing in the trade winds with the wind over your shoulder, there were at least four of us who stood watch and as captain I took advantage of the privilege of rank. I scheduled myself for the best watches, six to nine, A.M. and P.M. That way I got both sunrise and sunset on my watch. We did four watches of three hours each, which is really just the nicest possible way. You get three hours on and nine off. I loved it. It was probably one of the happiest times in my life, ever.

We wound up in Maui. Lahaina harbor was tiny and packed and it was very difficult to get a slot. We spent most of our time anchored off Mala Wharf, which is a good spot. When we weren't sailing around, we were diving from small boats. The boat stayed in Lahaina for almost two years and I joined the Lahaina Yacht Club. I would fly back to the Mainland to do business and then fly back to Maui to sail and swim. That's where I learned to dive too. Bud taught me. Once I learned to dive, I took pictures underwater, brought Graham with me and got him diving. I went as deep as I could. I remember once I went two hundred and thirty-five feet at Kealakekua Bay near Captain Cook's monument off the big island of Hawaii. Major thrills, absolutely. We were after a brand-new Danforth anchor that someone had left down there and we got it. Jim Lindersmith, a sailing buddy we used to call Captain Fathom, was a good diver and I think he found it on his first dive and he took the rest of us there to get it. I had some spectacular dives, seeing whales and dolphins. A whale is as big as a locomotive underwater. If you drop ahead of them, they'll go right by you and put that big eye on you, look you right in the eye, with no hostility. They're remarkably friendly and quiet and peaceful creatures and they sing. You could hear them even when you couldn't see them. Humpbacks love to sing. One time Bud discovered a humpback hanging head down over a spot where it liked the resonance, just singing away like we do when we're in the shower. You could hear them for a mile or more away when you were underwater, clear as a bell. I'm sure that's what the ancient Greeks thought the Sirens were. Whales, singing. I'm sure when they heard those songs through the hull of the boat they said, "Oh-oh. Trouble. Big trouble. Something not usual here. Ocean is talking to us, so we'll have to invent a mythology for this." I'm sure that's what it was. Whales. And that's just one of the reasons they are too beautiful and noble and important creatures to be exterminated. During those times, whenever I was on the boat, it was, at the same time, the most peaceful and the most exciting existence that I've ever encountered. Even though I could only commute for short periods of time from the Mainland, I was always at my happiest and healthiest on the *Mayan*.

The Hawaiian sojourn was an idyllic setting for the other members of the group as well. Graham frequently joined David and learned to dive; the two of them spent hours underwater with Bud Hedrick and others. Graham so loved the islands that he eventually left his house in San Francisco and moved to Kauai with his wife, Susan. To this date, he's still a resident there and carries a Hawaiian driver's license. Stephen and Neil found their way to Maui in 1973, where Neil had rented a house and written a song that seemed a natural title tune for a Crosby, Stills, Nash, and Young album: "Human Highway." In the laid-back Aloha State, songs that each member had accumulated were taken out and examined. They had obviously been saving their best for the next CSNY album; perhaps this would be the time. They played and sang together in the peaceful atmosphere, rehearsing tunes that they could record back on the Mainland. After weeks of fun in the sun, all four made their way back to California and began to record. In theory, it should have worked—they had even gotten a perfect cover photo for the album in Hawaii, lined up in a clearing, palm fronds overhead and a blue sky behind them, out of order, as usual: left to right it was Stills, Young, Crosby, and Nash. Yet, nothing came of the sessions, there was no aggreement as to whether to tour or record, and everyone went their own way again. The time wasn't right.

What had started as a two-week cruise down Baja California turned into a two-year odyssey for the *Mayan*, which stayed in the Pacific under Bud Hedrick's command. Lisica left, Bud met Cassie Mimbu, the woman he would eventually marry, and she moved in with him on the boat. David didn't get back to California for three months. When he did, he kept his options open, flying to Hawaii to go sailing and diving at every opportunity. Bud and Cassie were both sailors and loved life aboard the *Mayan*. They became a dedicated and professional crew of two. George Walker kept *Flying Cloud* in Hawaiian waters and made the mistake of lending her to an underqualified friend, who took the beautiful schooner and ran her aground. *Flying Cloud* was pounded to death on the rocks, where she broke up and sank. Bob Wilson kept *Sea Runner* in Hawaii until he ran out of money and Dana Africa returned to Marin County, where David bought her tools for metalworking and jewelry. Later, when she made a career change, David also helped her get an education that made her first a medical technician and finally a registered nurse. She now lives and works in the Pacific Northwest with her husband and family.

In Mill Valley, David finally found a house that he could make into a home. It was an ordinary house on a large secluded lot on the slopes of the hills above the redwood groves behind the village. Kevin Ryan and Gordon Abbott got the assignment to remodel and reconstruct the place. They assembled a crew of a few hands who had worked on Graham's house and some untried woodbutchers who were long on creativity and good vibes and short on real experience. David's architectural inspirations were eclectic: the woodsy Lisbon Lane cottage, the elegant Nouveau Hippie Carpenter Gothic of the Trident, and the California Craftsman architecture of Greene and Greene. Mostly, it was David's desire to have a comfortable place to hang his hat at last. The property was ideally situated on a winding street that snaked up the side of a hill just outside the town. It was a large lot and could be fenced entirely around its perimeter. Set off below the street there was a pool and a gatehouse sat over the garage on an upper level. David added Hawaii to his regular itinerary, creating a flexible trapezoidal route whose four corners were Graham's house in San Francisco, the Lisbon Lane property in L.A., Mill Valley, and the *Mayan*, wherever she was docked.

GORDON ABBOTT: *I was off boats altogether after Mexico. I came back in awful shape, with dysentery and God know what all. I got a job as a busboy in the Trident, which was where one fell in love, found substitute parents, brothers and sisters, scored dope, got work, found a house, found a car. One day David came back to town and while I was bussing dishes he came into the place. I hadn't seen him in six months and all eyes turned to him as he walked across the restaurant, grabbed me in a huge bear hug, and gave me a huge kiss on the cheek while everyone was looking. We talked and we were old pals again. Then, along came the new house. David took us up and showed me and Kevin around the place and left. Kevin and I stumbled around up there because neither one of us were truly builders. This was David at his best, where he took somebody and said, "You've got the raw material to do anything you want. Here's the money. Become a builder." Basically, David made a cabinetmaker out of me and a finishing carpenter out of Kevin. He also took various other people who were thundering in the arty-building business. He knew all about Greene and Greene and knew all about Maybeck, knew all about this and all about that. The house was a redwood-sided ranch house on a beautiful lot. When we were finished with it, it was another Trident; It was another Nepenthe [a wooded cafe and restaurant nestled on a cliff in Big Sur]. In our own unconscious way, we blundered through and made this little tribute to those guys and to Frank Lloyd Wright. My only quibble was that the kitchen was designed by David and Kevin, neither of whom could fry an egg, despite whatever Debbie wanted.*

KEVIN RYAN: *I had lots of arguments with David about the gatehouse or guest house. I always said, "Your guests deserve as good as you" or whatever. But all the effort went into the main house. After about six months, I had the worst cocaine habit of my life. I was a fucking wreck. I weighed ninety pounds. I had a weird construction budget, you see. In the bank account there were certain checks that could be written for a mythical Jose Gonzalez. The Gonzalez checks were used to buy quarter ounces of cocaine, which would be broken down into grams for the guys who wanted to buy it at cost, which worked out pretty well for everybody. David couldn't stand the muss and the fuss and there was no place for him to live. He would show up and stroll around and light a joint and pretty soon everybody on the work force was sitting around. David was rapping and everybody's high and that's the end of the work for the day. He did not have anything to do with cocaine and the crew at that time. He passed out joints right and left, but he didn't toot with the toots. I was the cocaine source on that job and he'd stay out of it. Dope was the candy given to the troops and cocaine was just one of the perks of the job—under the guise that it got things going. We all believed that; we were all relatively innocent about it. Anyhow, after six months on that house, it was basically complete. The shell was done, the trim was in, the deck was more or less done, and I was exhausted. David wanted to move in and Debbie was pregnant or about to get that way.*

GORDON ABBOTT: *David created the illusion that cocaine could do work, but all that cocaine did, of course, was produce a lot of talk about work. It never produced any actual productive work, except maybe for menial jobs: unloading lumber and whatnot. It never really produced construction; it never really produced carpentry work.*

> With the house under construction, David returned to Hawaii and the *Mayan*. There was time for one last long good sail and every sailor knows that the run from the Hawaiian Islands to French Polynesia is one of the best cruises there is. The winds are kind, the weather is perfect, and the destination is the Tahitian Islands: Tahiti, Mooréa, Bora Bora, Raïatéa, Huahiné—names that recall Gauguin, the *Bounty,* and a hundred other tropical delights under the Southern Cross. It's the ultimate destination when sailing the Pacific. From California, where he had been touring with Graham and Neil, David was able to call and get the crew to get *Mayan* ready for the trip. On the appointed day, David boarded the boat and they cast off for the South Seas.

It took us nineteen days and it was absolute heaven. Couldn't have been nicer. Bud and Cassie did the provisioning and preparing. My strongest input on getting the boat ready for a voyage is making sure that it's got a lot of spares, a lot of ways to jury-rig things. That she can be in the best possible shape she can. Even though the sea is not out to get you personally, it's not very forgiving. On that particular cruise, I was working right up until just before I took off. So I flew from the coast, drove from the airport, got on the boat, and we left. It took a little while to get used to being back at sea, but fortunately it takes a day or two to just get clear of the islands. After that, it's an absolutely wonderful feeling, getting up in the morning, early, no sight of land, having a great breakfast. Rolling out of your bunk at 5:45 A.M., snatching some breakfast, a cup of hot coffee from the Thermos as the person goes off watch, and taking the wheel at 6:00. And then you watch the dawn. You're there alone, everybody else is asleep, and you're just scooting along with the sun lighting the sky and the ocean and the day.

BUD HEDRICK: *Debbie went, once again, with David. And it was Cassie and myself. Who else? Patty Montgomery and Steve Elkins and Jim Lindersmith [Captain Fathom]. We weren't in Tahiti very long before David had to fly back and go to work. He said, "Just take care of the boat and I'll get back and we'll sail the islands." Well, he didn't get back. And it was very hard to talk to him. You know, it's not easy to call him anyway, but try calling him from Tahiti, it's really difficult. He didn't get back in a year. And at the end of the year I got a telegram, saying* I CAN'T MAKE IT. I'M TOO BUSY. BRING IT HOME. *Everybody had already gone home except Cassie and myself, so we picked up a crew down there—people off the dock that wanted to sail the islands and were willing to work just to get a chance to see it. And that's what we did. We'd work half-days and the boat was continually coming up and getting better and better until it was in great shape. David sent Jim Dickson's brother Bob down to navigate on the trip home and he's a real good sailor. We went back to San Francisco, by way of Hawaii. We lost the centerboard somewhere on the way to Hawaii. You have to start back from Hawaii in the summer before the winter storms set in, so we took a lot of fuel on deck and got good winds out of Hawaii, sailed into the North Pacific High, which is a big flat area and no wind at all, and motored right across until we got up above it and picked up our westerlies and sailed right into San Francisco in twelve days. It was a real nice trip.*

While this was going on, life took on a decidedly grimmer cast. Graham had been going with a girl named Amy Gossage, the daughter of a legendary San Francisco public relations executive. The affair ended with bizarre finality; Amy was murdered by her own brother. The case was made for San Francisco's exploitative dailies, since investigation revealed that it was a drug-related killing. Graham was not involved and was spared adverse publicity, but the tragedy was heartfelt and cut deep. David's mother, Aliph, was already in the final stages of her terminal illness. In the midst of all this, David and Graham were asked to join Neil Young, who was finishing a lengthy and difficult tour; they went. David's brother, Ethan, was in Santa Barbara, visiting Aliph, when the call went out to David that he had to see his mother.

ETHAN CROSBY: *When my mother started to die, I was commuting every week from Big Sur to see her and it was a long grind. David was out with Neil and they were touring in a Lockheed Electra, which is a four-engined turbo-prop airliner. That was close to the end. Neil lent David the plane and David flew to Santa Barbara. The airliner landed and rolled up to the terminal, the ramp came down, and David came out. The ramp went up and the plane wheeled away and parked with the engines running. That was because they didn't have the machine to restart those engines at Santa Barbara Municipal Airport, which at that time was not into four-engine airplanes. I took David to the hospital, he saw Ma, we hung out, had lunch, whatever, and went back to the airport. The crew came running out of the coffeeshop and David mounted up and flew off into the ozone. I don't know what that must have cost Neil.*

There was no way to calculate the cost and Neil didn't care. It was a simple gesture to a friend and partner at a time of need. Aliph died during the summer equinox. Ethan recalls David attending the funeral in a bright red shirt. Floyd was excluded and neither he nor Betty attended the services. Aliph was cremated and when the *Mayan* was back in San Francisco Aliph's ashes were scattered beyond the Golden Gate in the same waters that had received Christine Hinton's last remains. The deaths—and the feelings they inspired—mark one of David's most touching songs, a celebratory anthem that's informed by both depression and elation. It's called "Carry Me" and it's a song that is uniquely his.

> *When I was a young man*
> *I found an old dream*
> *It was as battered and worn a one*
> *As you have ever seen*
>
> *And I made it some new wings*
> *And I painted the nose*
> *And I wished so hard*
> *Up in the air I rose*
>
> *Singing Carry me*
> *Carry me*
> *Carry me above the world*
> *Carry me, Carry me*
> *Carry me*
>
> *And I once loved a girl*
> *She was younger than me*
> *Her parents kept her locked up*
> *In their lives*
> *She was crying at night wishing*
> *She could be free*
>
> *Course I mostly remember her laughing*
> *Standing and watching us play*
> *For a while there*
> *The music would take her away*
> *And she'd be singing*
>
> *Carry me, Carry me*
> *Carry me above the world*
> *Carry me, Carry me*
> *Carry me above the world*
>
> *And then there was my mother*
> *She was lying in white sheets there*
> *And she was waiting to die*
> *She said if you just reach*
> *Underneath this bed*

And untie these weights
I could surely fly

She's still smiling
while she's dying
She'd like to hear
That last bell ring

You know if she still could
She would stand up
And she would sing

Carry me, Carry me
Carry me above the world
Carry me, Carry me

"Carry Me,"
Words and Music by David Crosby

Appearances to the contrary, the middle verse is not about
Christine Hinton. The young girl wishing to be free was another long-haired, long-legged teenager named Nancy
Brown. She had been friends with Graham Nash for a few
years, since dropping out of high school. Nancy had always
wanted to meet Graham's partner, David. But for one reason (or another just like it), Graham never made the intro-
ductions. However, on a day that David flew into San Francisco, soon after after attending his mother's funeral, Nancy
met him for the first time. She had just turned eighteen.
That day or the next, they watched the sunset from Mount
Tamalpais, near the new Crosby house in Mill Valley. Soon
after that, they would see each other regularly, but not at
David's house or the boat, because Debbie Donovan was
there first. Debbie had spent enough time with David to
settle in as his principal ladyfriend. She was a veteran of the
Mayan's Pacific voyages, from Puerto Vallarta to Hawaii to
Tahiti, and when the house was finished, she moved in with
David and became the First Lady of Greenwood Way. In the
rustic wood and plaster house with the decks overlooking
the redwoods, she became pregnant, survived a shootout
with intruders, and gave birth to a daughter, Donovan Anne
Crosby.

EIGHT

. . . .

The year 1974 opened with a rush to the gas stations. For the first time in anyone's memory, there were lines at the gas pumps as the oil cartel tested its strength for the first time. Patty Hearst was kidnapped by the Symbionese Liberation Army and the Watergate affair continued to unravel as investigations tugged the Congress toward impeachment hearings in May. It was a good time for paranoids and anyone with a conspiracy theory because there were, in fact, a lot of conspiracies being revealed. David Crosby carried a gun. He had always carried a gun and loved weapons. Later, he would speak of the death of John Lennon as a rationale for going armed, but he had always owned guns and frequently carried them on his person or in an ever-present shoulder bag that contained wallet, cash, change, papers, address book, varying quantities of dope of all sorts, and a loaded Colt .45 Commander in nickel finish. A practicing pistolero, David owned a number of handguns, including several nine-millimeter Browning Hi-Powers, with their fourteen-shot magazines. He favored automatics, although he had a beautiful Smith & Wesson Model 25, a revolver conveniently chambered for .45 auto ammunition. (Most revolvers don't accept automatic weapon cartridges; the Smith Model 25 is the exception.)

I was raised around guns from the time we moved up to Carpinteria. I always wanted a gun. My brother had a couple of guns and I got a .22 when I was ten years old. I got to the point where I could shoot a lemon off a tree at a distance and I joined the Junior NRA and went through their whole riflery program, earned all the badges, and became quite proficient at it. I've always had a fascination for well-crafted machinery. I love things that people build or make that are better than they have to be. Handguns and guns, in general, are very often made by people who take a lot of trouble to make them flawless. Knives too. I collected knives because there was an extraordinary variety of wonderfully handmade knives available, really excellent work. I can appreciate guns as finely crafted pieces of work. I also subscribe to the theory that is embedded in the Constitution: that an armed populace is one that cannot be easily ruled by a dictator. I know that in every dictatorship, in every totalitarian government, the very first thing that they do is take away everyone's guns. That tells me something. It's not a matter of theory; it's fact. Now, there are places where the idea of everybody having guns is carried too far—that's an extreme that becomes anarchy. Witness Beirut. But I don't say everybody should have assault rifles and anti-tank weapons.

I believe very strongly that it is our constitutional right to keep and bear arms. I will argue that point and defend that point as long as I'm alive—I'm convinced that it's absolutely true and right. When you pass laws against guns, all you do is remove them from the hands of the people who obey the laws. Again, this isn't theory. It's fact. All the criminals will have them anyway. I don't really believe in gun control. I think it's absurd. As a matter of fact, in the states where it's legal to carry guns, you don't see a lot of bank robberies. You don't see a lot of armed robberies because if somebody pulls out a gun and says, "Stick 'em up," the nearest five people will drill the son of a bitch.

Weapons of mass destruction are an entirely different ballgame. I do not approve. In *The Wind and the Lion,* a movie written and directed by John Milius, a man who understands and appreciates weapons, there's a wonderful speech about guns delivered by Sean Connery. He talks about guns that tear up the earth and guns that fire many, many times and says they have no honor. Well, they haven't. In a society where people can go armed, it makes everybody a little more polite, as Robert A. Heinlein says in his books. I can't see how anyone is ever going to convince me that I should relinquish my ability to defend my hearth and home and my children and my wife from some goddamn crazies who want to come in and do a Manson on us. If they want to just take the TV, I'll help them load it in the car. It's insured; I don't give a damn. But if they want to rape my wife and cut my kid's hand off and then stick me with a bayonet, they're going to have to do it through a hail of gunfire. It's not conjecture —I've been assaulted in my own home and I did shoot at the intruders.

I'm not a pacifist by any stretch of the imagination. I'm antiwar, which is an altogether different ballgame. War is an extension of politics and war is usually based on a massive greed for power. War is guys who never risk themselves going in and forcing a situation to happen: men and women with no choice then have to risk their lives and lose them. I'm totally antidraft. I believe that any politican who wants to start a war should have to lead it. Physically, personally, and as the point man. Then I'll listen—any guy that wants me to get into a battle and is willing to lead me into it, I'll listen to him. But if someone says, "You boys go fight for this cause because your government says it's right," I know he's a crock of shit.

I'm fascinated with war because of its historical significance. If you don't study history, you're a fool. Wars have shaped history; they've been the decisive turning points. Most real human changes of course have been decided in conflict, except for the occasional time when somebody sits down after a war or during a war and writes the Magna Charta or the French Constitution or our Constitution. Great documents, but all written either directly during or on either side of war and revolution. War fascinates me because of what it does to human beings; it calls up the very worst and the very best in them, as most extreme circumstances do. Human behavior fascinates me—I want to understand more of why everyone does what they do. I will always be curious. I study war, particularly recent wars. I read about them, watch movies about them, and I confess to being excited by the effective portrayal of the heat of battle. I'm not excited by it in a morbid way. I don't love seeing people get shot; it's not cool or glamorous or glorious or any of that crap. I'm excited by human courage and I'm fascinated by the turn of events.

I love airplanes. I love ships. I love technology. I am a techno freak. As a dilettante, I love to keep up with the current edge of technology because it fascinates me. Technology dictates what our world's going to be like next year. What they're developing now is what we'll be using later. I would give anything for a ride in a military jet fighter, particularly a Grumman F-14, which is probably my favorite. But that's because of the airplane, not its destructive power.

It may seem strange to other people, but I don't see any conflicts in my rationale; I have a very definite set of opinions and I've had to question them and test them over and over again. When Charlie Manson and his gang committed the Tate and LaBianca murders, I started thinking about guns. There were direct connections: the Tate killings occurred in a house owned by Terry Melcher, who had been my producer with the Byrds. There was a theory that Manson had gone to Melcher's house looking for Terry and killed the other people there by grim mistake. I had been to Melcher's house on Cielo Drive many times and I lived less than a half mile away in Beverly Glen Canyon. For all I knew, I had been offered Charlie Manson demo tapes, same as Melcher. Living in the hills, I subscribed to the hippie ethic and didn't have any weapons around, despite my childhood familiarity with rifles. But when the murders happened, I said, "Oh-oh, the rules of the game have changed," and I started keeping a twelve-

gauge shotgun around, that being the number one contender for
the best home defense weapon in the world, the second being a
Colt .45 automatic. I trained with a .45 and I'm an accomplished
handgunner. I can hit a torso-sized target with a Colt .45 automatic, retarget over 90 degrees, and hit a second one in about one
second flat. And I can do it almost every time.

> Even in the fast lane of the rock 'n' roll lifestyle, there was
> rarely the kind of provocation that would require a firearm.
> In all the years that David carried a gun, he only pulled it
> once. Guns was never brandished or displayed. They were
> discreetly concealed while out of the house and stored in a
> prudent way at home. Nevertheless, during the time the
> 1974 CSNY Reunion Tour was taking shape, there were
> auto burglaries on Buena Vista Terrace, right outside
> Graham's San Francisco house. Graham's Mercedes lost a
> couple of tires to the entrepreneurs from Midnight Auto
> Supply. David was a light sleeper and decided to watch the
> cars from an upper-story window—after all, his Mercedes
> was parked out there on the street too. Mac Holbert,
> Graham's friend and tour manager for the various Crosby-
> Nash, CSN, and CSNY tours, remembers the time, before
> David moved into the Mill Valley house.

MAC HOLBERT: *One night, when David was staying at Graham's,
somebody came and took a tire off one of the Mercedeses. Crosby was
real pissed. So a couple of nights later, David was looking out the
window and he sees this guy studying the Mercedes. Then he sees a
hippie with a long blond ponytail get out of his car and start to rip
off the Mercedes. David yells at the guy and he runs away. David
runs to get his gun and waits for the crook to come back, figuring he
left his car parked somewhere nearby. How far do you want to walk if
you're carrying a set of Mercedes wheels and tires? Sure enough,
after a while, when he thinks it's quiet, the guy sneaks back and gets
into his car. Crosby sees him and yells at him to stop, but the guy
doesn't. David stands up on his balcony and puts a bullet right
through the back of this thief's car as it's speeding away.*

David fired straight down, deliberately punching a hole in the trunk of the would-be felon's car, as a warning. Shortly after that, it was time to move into the Mill Valley house: 21 Greenwood Way was finished enough to become home to David and Debbie Donovan. Gordon Abbott, the carpenter, was living in the little gatehouse over the garage and was part of the family that was being assembled by luck and circumstance. It was to be David's permanent home and he treated it as such, furnishing it with handmade one-of-a-kind wood furniture made by the craftsmen and women of Northern California. Stored under the house was a stock of rare hardwoods, seasoning against the day they'd be used for some future project or renovation: rosewood, spruce, teak, coca bola, lignum vitae, Circassian walnut, luxurious woods from all over the world. It was a place where the best was expected.

DEBBIE DONOVAN: *The house on Greenwood Way was a real home. It was something that David had been seeking for a long time. He's always been a homebody. Beverly Glen was his little abode; he'd take care of it; he loved to water the lawn. Reine and I would go visit him in the early days and he'd be out there stark naked, watering ivy, which, of course, doesn't need water at all. But here's David; he's domesticated. I think he always wanted that. I think that the couch camping had gotten him down and the boat was something he wanted, but he couldn't live on it all the time; he really needed a home. David, as crazy as he likes to seem, is basically very, very straight. I offered that. We started with a conventional relationship that didn't make many demands.*

GORDON ABBOTT: *At the time, David had no real magic woman in his life. He settled in with Debbie, for a variety of reasons. First of all, she was the perfect duchess and it seemed to me that David was making a big effort to be like an old-fashioned Hollywood star; to set up a scene. There were magnificent nights while I was living up there, when cocaine was probably used to excess, but it didn't seem like it at the time. There were nights with dinners with good wine and good food and great conversation and no coke until after dinner,*

*then brandy and coke and chess games and guitar and piano playing
and backgammon. But mostly chess . . . maybe two or three chess-
boards set up at once and winners playing winners and women sewing. And there was an awful niceness to it. There was something that
was really magic. But that was undermined, I think, by David's
sexuality.*

The sexuality was driven by David's constant explorations of
the limits of permissable behavior and by the sheer quantities of fun made possible by a major rock 'n' roll tour. Two
things were coming together at the same time: the house and
a Crosby, Stills, Nash, and Young Reunion Tour. After several years apart, after the abortive attempt to make an album called *Human Highway*, after all the separate trips and
tours and records, the pressure to reunite the band tri-
umphed over the individual ego thrusts that kept pushing it
apart. The American supergroup was guaranteed the biggest
and best tour ever organized. They would play only stadiums, nothing under thirty thousand seats, with some venues
holding seventy thousand or even two hundred thousand
(Ontario Motor Speedway in Southern California). The proceeds from ticket admissions, T-shirt sales, programs, and
merchandising would be stupendous. Ben Fong-Torres, writing in *Rolling Stone*, had authoritative estimates of a gross
between six and ten million dollars, with eight hundred thousand to a million paid admissions, at a time when the most
expensive tickets were eight-fifty (adjusting for inflation,
that would be a twenty-dollar ticket in 1988 and today's
gross would equal twenty-four million dollars). The ameni-
ties on the tour would be unparalleled; every detail would be
more than anyone had a right to expect.

MAC HOLBERT: *It was a stadium tour, a Monster Big Deal. I think we
did thirty-four stadiums and it was the largest tour in the history of
rock 'n' roll to that date. The largest grosses and probably least
returns to the artists of any tour that has ever gone out. It was an
exercise in excess on every level. You would go to your hotel room and
you would pull back the cover on the bed and there would be your
pillows, which would have custom-made pillow cases on them with a
Joni Mitchell logo for the 1974 tour, silk-screened in five colors on*

your pillowcase. You would go to dinner backstage and there would be a teak dinner plate with the tour logo burned into the wood. Everyone was going, "Wow! Bill Graham is just an amazing guy. What a wonderful guy he is!" We did Learjets, helicopters, a huge backstage scene every night, with twenty or thirty people just cooking and serving food to the whole little village. That was the first tour that had that. It was Bill Graham's opportunity to really try something out and he did. In every hotel, we'd have a suite that was open around the clock, twenty-four hours, with shrimp on ice and hors d'oeuvres and champagne and wine and drinks. There were little double-ought capsules available every day, filled with about a gram of cocaine, if anyone wanted it. We had everything we wanted. We had parties where there were hookers in the closets giving blowjobs— dancing girls in the hotel rooms—it was astounding. Everything that everybody thinks about rock 'n' roll actually happened on that tour and the amazing thing is that a lot of that excess was not utilized by the principals or even the band; it was utilized by a lot of the people that were surrounding the scene. The press agent, for example, had a blank check to fly out press people first-class and put them up in suites. Everywhere we went we had parties. Oceans of money surrounded the guys and not a lot of it got back to them.

It was a new era in popular music and the power and influence of the big groups was just beginning to be perceived for what it was. Musicians like Craig Doerge were discovering what it was to play with superstars and supergroups. Craig was a pianist and keyboard player who had come to California to play rock 'n' roll. After knocking around playing pizza parlors and demo sessions, he made his way into James Taylor's band, joining Leland Sklar, Danny Kortchmar, and Russell Kunkel. Eventually, the group would be known as the Section and would play behind Jackson Browne and Crosby, Stills, and Nash. With the addition of such lights as David Lindley, Jim Keltner, Larry Carlton, the loose-knit association of superior session players and musicians became known as the California Mafia and was responsible for a disproportionate share of historic rock 'n' roll rooted in the California folk rock tradition. Craig plays with Crosby, Stills, and Nash to this day, has written songs with David, and has been a producer on his albums. Although he didn't play on the 1974 Reunion Tour, Craig's observations are worth noting:

CRAIG DOERGE: *I don't think musicians were aware of their power throughout the seventies. I think all of us in show business have a greater responsibility than we realized at the time. We weren't aware of how much show business influences teenagers and the rest of the world, so when Jackson Browne was singing that song "Cocaine" on his album, it was an influence, even though Jackson would be the last person to suggest that a kid should do any kind of drugs at all; he's very much against them now. When you played colleges and that song came up, the kids were all yelling and screaming and it was getting them into it. The musicians—James Taylor, and Jackson, and certainly Crosby, Stills, and Nash and all of us—we still thought that after age thirty-two or something like that everyone would throw away their rock 'n' roll stuff and do more serious things with their lives. The idea that rock 'n' roll would be an ongoing lifetime pursuit hadn't really sunk in.*

NANCY BROWN: *I was born in Montana and my daddy worked on a railroad and when I was seven we moved to San Francisco. When I was nine years old, he killed himself because he had lung cancer and my mom remarried. We moved to Marin County. I was walking down Union Street in San Francisco during school hours and I was the only juvenile around and I heard somebody yelling, "Hey, you! Hey, girl! Hey, you there!" I looked around and there was this guy hanging out the window, yelling at me and waving his arms, and it was Graham Nash. We had a friendship for a couple of years and Nash somehow always made sure that David and I would never meet. It's kind of like he knew what would happen if we got together. But we did—Graham and Joel Bernstein were picking David up on his way up to see his new house in Mill Valley after he had wrenched his knee right after his mother's funeral. Since my dad had died of cancer and his mom had just died and I had my eyes on him anyway, we kind of hit it off and our first date was that day and we went up and saw the sunset on Mount Tam. Always a romantic sight. When I met David, he tried to get me to finish school. I was surprised at that because I'd always been hanging out with older people and none of them ever put much effort into that. I never did graduate.*

Debbie lived with him for the first two years that I was on the road with him. She was at home; I was on the road. That's why we fit together so well. David and I had the same belief about where I belonged: right on the fringe. It was a comfortable place to be. He took real good care of me. He paid my rent. He paid all my bills. I didn't have any money, but I didn't have any bills either. My emotional immaturity had me sitting around waiting for him to call all the time. My heart would just go forty thousand times faster if I heard a Ferrari or a Mercedes of the right pitch go by. He took very good care, not just financially; he was a very caring person. If you can maintain a contact with him, he's very dear and very supportive. Goldie was on the road with us. Goldie Locks. That was her name. On the CSNY Tour we were both there. David got a lot of guff from people on the road because they couldn't afford to bring their wives and here he had two real pretty ladies with him, all humility aside, and we were having a good time. We were always laughing together. On the inside, as far as the whole "Triad" thing, like somebody else said, it's always a one-on-one, no matter how quickly you try to go back and forth, it's still one-on-one and it basically came down to "Whose turn is it?" or "Why don't you guys go ahead and have some time together and I'll have some time alone." It would even get well enough balanced to where it was Goldie and I having time together, being like sisters, and saying to David, "Don't you have something to do? Are you still here? Don't you have somewhere to be?" It would have been emotionally better for either one of us if the other one hadn't been there because that way one of us would've felt more loved. Yet we were a comfort to each other because being on the road is boring at certain times and in certain ways. You're on an airplane and you go to the hotel, you check in, you order room service, you go to the sound check and then get some food stuffed in your face, then there's the concert, and then you go back to the hotel.

*More room service if it was arranged ahead of time. If not, the
roadies have to scramble at 2 A.M. to come up with a greasy burger
and then you go to sleep and then you wake up and do the same
thing the next day.*

MAC HOLBERT: *He was hanging around with all of us more in those
days too, so he was more visible, except for the time he spent in his
hotel room. His room was his cave and there was always an army of
room service trays coming down the hallway. I would get a call from
Crosby. "Listen, I need some money. Can you come on down to my
room?" And I would go down to the room and Nancy would be there,
she'd be doing him, and I'd have to sit there and try to do business
while that was going on. I'm not a voyeur by nature, so it didn't get
me off.*

That's not true. I wouldn't have asked her to do that and she
wouldn't have done it. We were outrageous—I'm not going to try
to say we weren't—and there were other ladies that got involved,
on and off. They were all very pretty and we all had a lot of fun;
I'm not going to deny that. It's no good asking about details about
the largest pile of bodies and who did what and with which and to
whom. That's irrelevant; that's not fair. I've never been into or-
gies or large-quantity high-volume group sex. I was always too
selfish for that. I wanted to be the center of attention and I was—
because the girls loved me and wanted to make me happy. I love
them for that. I can only tell you that because the motivations
were on a pretty high level and the people were of a high quality;
it was not gross or obscene. There was a lot of absolute joy. We
got off, heavily. I don't want to get too technical about what we
did, but I'm a very inventive guy and used a lot of imagination.
Nobody was idle. Waste not, want not. We had a great time for a
long time. I was not into being monogamous—I made that plain
to everybody concerned. I was a complete and utter pleasure-
seeking sybarite. A greed head for pleasure, I did what I had
done before: manipulate the situation to where people would do

what I wanted. And whatever it was, it was done out of love, although I'll confess that it was probably very selfish on my part. Look . . . I had a great deal of fun. When we went out on tour, it caused dissension and raging envy in the ranks. There were a lot of guys on that tour who didn't bring their wives and here was I, with Nancy and Goldie and others, living a life of absolute decadence. There are people who still haven't forgiven me for that.

The hard part was realizing I had come to a point where I didn't want to keep going with Debbie. It wasn't what I wanted to do and I found myself loving Nancy Brown. She was scrumptious. She was wonderful. She was great. She still is. As soon as I made the decision, I started to disconnect, even though Debbie was pregnant. That was tough. Debbie had been my very good friend for a very long time. She helped save my sanity when Christine died and has always been a great friend to me—before, during, and after, even now. Always a friend. I couldn't see my way clear to ditching her when she was pregnant with our child, so I stuck around for a year after I had made the decision while she went through the pregnancy and had the kid. I went to Lamaze School and I helped deliver the baby. I was involved. I was good, although I admit that I put Nancy in a little house across Mill Valley and snuck out a lot. I dealt with it the best I could.

Dr. Robert Belknap is a physician in Mill Valley who'd be considered a healer in any culture. Because he practices conventional Western medicine, he's an M.D. He practices family medicine, he's board-certified as an internist, and he makes house calls. It's his chart that's reproduced in the prologue to this book; Dr. Belknap is the one who had David admitted to the detox section of Ross General Hospital in Marin. A tall, fit man who's losing his hair, he wears glasses that do nothing to conceal the bright intelligence in his eyes. Whenever he discussed David, he reviewed his office medical records and recalled every entry in the Crosby charts, which cover the period from 1974 through 1984. Dr. Belknap has seen David as a patient and as a human being troubled by more than medical problems.

DR. ROBERT BELKNAP: *On the positive side, I will say I've delivered about two hundred and fifty babies and although I didn't have a big obstetrical practice, I practiced obstetrical medicine until about 1981. My experience with David and Debbie was that they were very devoted to the child; they took making a baby very seriously. They attended child-care classes, Lamaze exercises, they paid attention to the details of Debbie's pregnancy. I must say that's the one thing they did very appropriately. More than appropriately—they were devoted to the idea and it really did evoke a kind of remission in the other aberrant behavior.*

> It was a difficult pregnancy, not made any easier by David's sneaking out to see Nancy Brown, who was living across town in a house he rented for her. The infidelity might have been easier to handle if it was the only problem, but it wasn't. For one thing, Debbie developed kidney stones and had painful second and third trimesters. She took a lot of Percodan for the pain and the birth was delayed almost a month; it was a ten-month pregnancy. Percodan is a strong opiate-derivative painkiller and is a Schedule III narcotic, which in California requires prescription forms filled out in triplicate.

DEBBIE DONOVAN: *We didn't have the group classes so we went to private classes. We went through the whole program together and David was very good. I could not have made that delivery the way that I did if it hadn't been for him. David was right there for me the whole time. I had kidney stones at the same time, so I was on Percodan for the last four months of my pregnancy, which I believe lasted ten months. I think it was extended because my whole body chemistry was slowing down because of the drug. It was a really painful period and I was ready to be knocked out because my kidney was enlarged and all during the delivery I couldn't tell if it was labor pain or kidney stones that was causing all the discomfort.*

It's one of the few things I ever did right. I went to classes with Debbie so I could be in the delivery room. Dr. Belknap is one of the best doctors I have ever met in my whole life. He is also one of the people who tried repeatedly and sincerely to get me off drugs. I didn't have to personally experience the pregnancy—men are spared (or denied) that—but I wanted Debbie to have the baby if she wanted it. I love Debbie and I have always loved Debbie. I still love her; she's one of the nicest human beings I know. I never intended to stay or cement the relationship, but it wasn't the right time to leave a friend, so I stuck around and we went through the pregnancy and the delivery. I was there for the whole thing and I was the first person to hold Donovan; the doctor pulled her out and put her in my arms while he cut the cord. That was absolutely the hottest magic ever. Higher than the highest exalted feeling at the end of the best concert ever, more exciting than the best sex, just the most wonderful magical trick there is in the world: to watch a woman give birth to a child and be a part of it. I couldn't have been happier about it.

There was another difficulty encountered during the time that Donovan Anne was in the womb, about at the end of Debbie's second trimester. It's not a normal hazard of pregnancy and it wasn't covered in all the well-baby books and new parent counseling that David and Debbie had been receiving. On the other hand, it wasn't an unanticipated emergency; there was a drill for it and everyone had practiced against the day when the privacy of the compound and the sanctity of home and hearth would be grossly violated. It was in the hours near dawn, when everyone was asleep. David's custom was to keep a loaded .45 Colt auto on the nightstand. It's a practice that drives the Coalition to Ban Handguns crazy, but on this winter night, it was a prudent choice.

DEBBIE DONOVAN: *I was six months pregnant. I felt somebody there and I thought it might've been David because he used to prowl around the house at night; he'd wake up and go out and patrol the area, just walk around, checking on things. I looked up and I* thought, "Oh, there's David again. He's out patrolling." Then I put my head back down and I thought, "Wait a minute. David doesn't wear a ski mask when he patrols. Nope, I don't think this is right." And I sat up in bed and stared at the guy and he stared at me; I slid back down and tried to get my hand under the covers over to David to wake him, but he wouldn't wake up. That's when the guy started breaking through the glass in the french doors. He said, "Roll over. Both of you. Now." I looked at my six months' pregnant stomach and I said, "You've got to be kidding!" and I rolled over onto my side; that was as far as I could go. At that moment, David woke up and was instantly on top of the situation. He grabbed a gun he kept on the nightstand, went down over on his side of the bed, and started shooting. His reactions, coming out of a deep sleep, were amazing. We had worked this thing out before, practiced what to do if there was an intruder in the house, and David had instructed me. I knew where the shotgun was. I knew how to reload the Colt. I knew how to count the rounds. David went out over the broken glass on the floor, chasing the guys, and by the time he came back in, I had the shotgun ready and a full clip for the .45 in my hand. I handed him the shotgun, took the pistol and reloaded it, then followed instructions when David told me where to stand. It was all a very neat little scene.

GORDON ABBOTT: *We had various codes on the intercom. One buzz meant: "Hey, if you're not busy, come on by." Two buzzes meant: "Whether you're busy or not, pick up the phone." And three buzzes was the general quarters alarm: "Prepare to defend yourself. We're under attack." We never used that. One night there'd been company and they'd gone and we'd gone to bed and I was briefly asleep when I heard gunshots. I was armed with Kevin's carbine and an Attica riot thing, a twelve-gauge pump shotgun that was the ultimate self-defense weapon. I heard the gunshots and I grabbed the M-1 and the shotgun and galloped to the bathroom, which I'd rehearsed in my stoned dreams a million times. There's a big window in front and as I was galloping across the floor naked, with the guns, the three buzzes went off. When I looked out, I saw three guys with warm-up suits, guns in their hands, running across the yard, freaking out. At a moment like that, you're living right on the second. Guns had been fired, but I'd heard the buzzer, which I computed meant that not everybody is dead down there—but somebody may be and I may be next. I'm looking around the corner of my doorway and I decided, "Well, unless they come running toward the foot of my stairs, I'm not going to shoot." The guys were in disarray, so I fired a shot into the air to add to the disarray and pumped another one into the chamber and they took off; they were gone.*

When Debbie woke me, the first thing I saw when I opened my eyes was a guy in a ski mask at the french doors, knocking the glass out of the window with the barrel of his .38. He must've seen too many Westerns; you don't have to break glass, you can shoot right through it; that's what I did. I grabbed my piece, rolled off the bed, and opened up: put the first one through the wood and glass right next to his head, sprayed splinters all over him. I shot first and I won. I drove them off. A guy pointed a gun at me and told me to roll over and, in essence, submit and I tried my level best to blow his brains out. Fortunately for my karma, I didn't kill him, but I was trying and I sure as hell scared him and his partner. They took their ski masks and their .38s and went somewhere else. I don't feel ashamed of it at all and anyone who wants to point a loaded gun at my pregnant old lady in our bed is going to get the same exact response and maybe this next time I'll drill the son of a bitch. I'll certainly try and I see nothing wrong with that.

DEBBIE DONOVAN: *David and Gordon went out looking for them, but they ran and never came back. They had a car waiting down below; the driver heard the shots and took off, leaving the other guy alone. He flagged somebody down who was going down toward Mill Valley and had told the guy, "David Crosby just shot at me." The guy in the car didn't say anything; he just dropped him off then went to the police and said, "Hey, there's something going on out there." I think there had been other reports of gun shots. The cops didn't come to the house until a few days later. We cleaned everything—by the time the police came, we had had the glass replaced in the french doors, the bullet holes had been patched and painted, and all of the dope was out of the house. We had just gotten a rather large haul from Hawaii and all of that was gone. There was still blood on the floor from where David ran through the broken glass in his bare feet and cut himself up. He didn't notice it until after he and Gordon had gone out and gone through the entire area. It was frightening. After that, we couldn't sleep. We had to bring a friend over from Hawaii, Patty Montgomery, because David and I couldn't sleep at the same time. One of us had to be awake all the time. It was these kids, who probably figured out that there was a stash at the house, but the police don't tell you anything. We don't really know if the guy was ever caught or not and that made us very uncomfortable for a very long period of time. We were sure that they were going to come back. Our friends kept saying it was our fault because David had all these guns and all that dope. He never had to have that amount of drugs. One person couldn't smoke that much. On the other hand, he was always giving it away.*

The police had responded immediately to the "shots fired" call, but couldn't tell at first which house was involved; David had appeared and played "confused homeowner," saying things like "I dunno. I heard them too. Maybe it was over the hill." After a few hours, local cops were able to place the location of the gunfire at Crosby's. It was obviously a great convenience to have a skilled carpenter and handyman on the premises; fueled by the adrenaline rush, all signs of the shoot-out (except for David's bloody footprints) were covered over, patched, and painted. Only the blood-stains on the floor from David's feet remained and those were cleaned up by 8:30 A.M. when the police finally arrived. Debbie recalls that one of the investigating officers speculated that the intruders were local Marin County bad kids. Young thugs barely out of high school had begun a routine of locating drug dealers' homes, invading them at gunpoint, raping or assaulting the women present, and stealing the cash and contraband. In Miami, Detroit, or New York, the little banditos would have suffered grim and final retribution after the first rip-off; luckily for them, most Marin dealers were laid-back hippies, amateurs. For David, who was always accused of being overly suspicious, it was an unwelcome reinforcement to a basically paranoid wariness. From now on, he could say with absolute certainty, survivalist handgun training was a necessity. Charles Tacot, a handgunning friend of David's who had worked for Cass Elliot, sent him a plaque commemorating the event, welcoming David to that elect fraternity of shooters who've faced an enemy and hostile fire and discharged a weapon in anger at a human target. Good handgun practice had saved David's and Debbie's lives and the life of their unborn daughter. For the next eleven years, David carried a gun. Even paranoids have enemies.

DEBBIE DONOVAN: *David and I had straight sex. It was not all that exciting. Nancy Brown offered a lot more adventurous alternatives. David would come home from the road and tell me what he had been doing. I'd start crying and he'd say, "Why are you crying? You're supposed to be happy for me." I didn't see it that way. The breaking point for me was during my whole pregnancy. Sex completely turned him off. He did not want to have anything to do with me while I was pregnant. He came back to me one day when I was ready for sex and he wasn't and I said, "Okay, what's the deal?" He said, "What I want is for you to be here and take care of my home and I'll go out on the road with Nancy." I was free to go out and have whatever affairs I wanted to have. I just had a baby! That's not me; that never was me. I was ready for a family and I always saw the David that David said he never could be. That's what I always wanted, and he'd say, "No no no. I'll never be that way." Eventually, I said, "No thanks. Goodbye, I'm leaving." And I got my bag right then and there, packed, took Donovan, and left.*

Debbie moved out shortly after the baby was born. She knew and she moved out. I got her a place and I moved Nancy in and I must say the early part of my relationship was absolutely wonderful. We were very, very happy.

NANCY BROWN: *Debbie left and I moved right in. I was the new mistress of the house and "mistress" is the appropriate phrase for a lot of that time. I always felt as if I was camping out there. For the whole four years that I lived there, there was one whole room full of clothes that Debbie had left. I never packed them up and got them to her and she never came and got them. I probably waited for two years before I even emptied out the drawers under the bed to have a place to put my underwear and there were shelves in the bathroom that had her clothes and I just wouldn't touch them. It's as if I didn't belong there either. Once, he did actually ship me out to L.A., so that somebody else could be there; a couple of other ladies came and one of them laundered my clothes that should've been dry-cleaned and that's what made me the maddest—she messed with my clothes. She shrunk them. But I came back because David's world revolves around David and as his lady, you're eager to let that happen. In my case, I found his world fascinating and fun and he's a kick. It's easy to get involved in what's going on around him. Because if you don't, you have to have a real strong identity on your own . . . and I didn't.*

I'm just a small-town kind of kid. Living with David and touring with the band was definitely "Lifestyles of the Rich and Famous" and I think I got to ride on the peak. I want my kids to experience that for a day. On the 1974 tour, I had my eighteenth birthday at the Plaza Hotel in New York and the next show was in Washington, so we flew there in a Learjet. We went up and there were little teeny cottony orange and pink clouds, around sunset, with lightning playing between them, and we were flying through it and it was just gorgeous. There were two Learjets: Nash and Stephen and their friends in one, David and the managers and me in another. The other Learjet sang "Happy Birthday" to me over the radio and when we landed there was a whooping crane that was taking off. Nash said, "It's incredibly good luck if you see a whooping crane take off on your birthday," and he dedicated "Our House" to me that night and it was as if I was flying. It was just great and I'll never forget it.

At the conclusion of the big tour (David started calling it the Doom Tour), Crosby, Stills, Nash, and Young had so much topspin that centrifugal force was scattering the group in all directions. The complexities and nuances of their contracts made it possible for David and Graham to go to another company to make records; they chose ABC, where their former business manager had been named head of the company. It also seemed natural for the two of them, always friends, to tour as a duo. It was the natural extension of the affinity between them and the pressures on the band were felt equally by management.

ELLIOT ROBERTS: *We did twenty-four or twenty-five stadium shows and they were all-sold-out. Very successful dates, but they left a bad taste in the band's mouth. They wanted to do smaller things. It had seemed like a great idea to play stadiums but after you played the first four or five, it didn't matter whether you were in Kansas City, Minneapolis, or Detroit; it looked exactly the same. Neil immediately wanted to go into a Crazy Horse tour in small halls, which we did, and Crosby-Nash went and recorded an album. Stephen left the management group shortly after the big tour. By this time we were managing Jackson Browne, the Eagles, Poco, America, Joe Walsh, Joni Mitchell, CSNY, and some other acts I don't even want to think about. Irving Azoff was working for me, along with John Hartman and Harlan Goodman, so we had five managers in the company and David Geffen and I had just started Asylum Records. While I was out on the stadium tour, my eye started to twitch, a little nervous tic that at first only I could feel. I'd go over to guys and I'd say something like "Dave, look at my eye. Do you see it vibrating?" And he'd say, "No, I don't see anything." A week or so later it was getting worse and people could see it. I stuck it out on the road until the end of the tour and as soon as we got back I went to a Beverly Hills eye doctor who examined me, did a big physical, and said, "Absolutely nothing wrong with you. One hundred percent nerves." That blew my mind and when I walked out of his office the twitch was gone and it never came back. That day I called a meeting of all our clients and I dropped everybody but Neil and Joan and I split up the management company. The Eagles and Joe Walsh went with Irving. Hartman and Goodman took America and Poco. Stills was already gone, so I*

talked to Crosby and Nash about us not working together. I ex-
plained what I was going through and that I really wanted to scale
down and just keep Neil and Joni and that's what I ended up doing.
For me, Crosby, Stills, Nash, and Young were over.

We dissolved our relationships at the height of everybody's ca-
reer. Jackson was just starting to happen. The Eagles were in the
studio recording Hotel California. *Everyone was at his or her zenith.*
Joan had just recorded The Hissing of Summer Lawns. *The real*
breakdown was not because things were going badly, but because I
couldn't cover it all properly. Everyone had such tremendous de-
mands because of success. Most of the calls I got from people I
represented were at night. Late at night. David getting an idea at
two in the morning or Neil thinking of something. Everyone was up
late in those days, so I was up late myself. I took it all very person-
ally: everything was life and death and real important. That was
probably to my detriment. Going to the eye doctor saved my sanity
because I realized I was taking it all much too seriously. After all,
who cares? If I'm dead, will any of this stop for a second? I think
not. Then David and I got bitter with each other. David actually
called me up to his house to tell me that he was firing me, which
made me livid, because (a) he could have done it on the phone, I
didn't have to make the trip, and (b) it was just so stupid because it
was totally out of greed. What he said to me was "Our old record
deal's out and we're making a new record deal and I'm just going to
get a lawyer and save the fifteen percent that I pay you." I said,
"David, that's totally fine with me," because we already had discus-
sions about my not representing them anymore.

At a much lesser fee, David and Graham engaged a woman
named Leslie Morris, who had worked as a personal assistant
to Elliot and David Geffen from the very beginnings of
Lookout Management (Elliot's company). Lawyers could attend to the details and hardball of contract negotiation,
business managers could manage the budget, and agents
could book the tours and concerts and personal appearances.
All that was needed from a management office was expedit-
ing the details of touring and recording, and lots of attention

to personal services. Leslie was the perfect choice. She was one of a small band of submanagement elite; her counterparts hold down the fort and run the shop everywhere in the entertainment business. They are the senior production assistants in television and the movies, the number one underlings who can speak with the authority of the boss and never be questioned. They guard the palace gates, know the secret passages, and can get you on the guest list with the stroke of a pen. People like Leslie are quietly backstage in the center of the maelstrom, unsung heroes of rock 'n' roll. She packed her bags and moved to Northern California to begin a two-year stint working for Graham and David.

LESLIE MORRIS: *I had been working with Elliot for four years at that point, so I knew all their business. I knew the record deals, I knew the publishing, I knew basically what was going on with them and the people around them, so they asked if I would manage them for a couple of years. I had a little office in Mill Valley because Graham was living in San Francisco and David was living in Mill Valley. The office was in my house. I had a desk made, we opened a bank account, and we started moving agents and lawyers, but we didn't move accountants. We changed everything that we felt was a conflict of interest between Elliot and the guys. We no longer wanted to have the same lawyers and agents. The problem was that I'm a woman. David is a blatant male chauvinist pig. He never really gave me the responsibility or the respect. He could never call me a manager; he couldn't bring himself to do that. Instead, he called me the Big Cheese; that's how he put it. He could live with that. And yet I booked the tours. We negotiated a deal with the agent Howard Rose for him and I functioned as the manager. I was on a salary. I didn't take a percentage. They paid all my expenses: rent, everything. But I couldn't make a decent living.*

As I recall, we put a two-year period on it and it ended short of that two years, with me and David in a raging fight. I didn't realize how much drugs they did until I'd left them because I had been doing drugs every day for two years. Drugs were an everyday occurrence and we had no idea there might be a problem. It wasn't a problem for me. I had no trouble stopping, but if I had gone on at

*that rate, I certainly could've had as much of a problem as anyone
else. It was just like "Let's have a burger. Let's have a milkshake.
Let's have a line." Especially through that period. Cocaine was
peaking. Pot, at that point, was just to bring you down. At Elliot's
we smoked dope all the time, but by the time I moved to Mill Valley,
it was just a tranquilizer. Dope is not a good thing. It didn't help
David; it hurt him very much. The funny thing is that I stayed
connected to David—couldn't help it. Debbie Donovan was my good
friend, still is, and little Donovan Anne was my goddaughter, so it
never really ended between us. I rented David's Lisbon Lane house
for years after that.*

Two fresh albums by David and Graham came out of their
association with ABC Records: *Wind on the Water* in 1975
and *Whistling Down the Wire* a year later. They also toured
extensively together, with a band that was distilled from
some of the best players around. They were called the
Mighty Jitters, mostly for fun—they were anything but jittery, every member being a veteran session and backup musician with a long history in rock 'n' roll. The Jitters included Craig Doerge on keyboards, Russ Kunkel on drums,
Tim Drummond on bass, Danny Kortchmar on guitar, and
David Lindley on all the stringed and fretted instruments he
could carry. David and Graham were frequently singing with
Carole King, whose album *Tapestry* was fast becoming one of
the most popular records in the history of popular music (six
years on the charts, including fifteen weeks in the number
one position). She'd join them onstage in concerts on the
road and they'd all meet on one track or another in recording studios around the country as everyone pursued his or
her vinyl destiny. David remembers it as a time when they
went out and sang with anyone with whom they wanted to
sing. Their harmonies turned up on albums with James Taylor, Jackson Browne, and Elton John, while the *Wind on the
Water* sessions were an extraordinary indication of the developing power and maturity of David and Graham as recording artists.

My relationship with Graham Nash has been absolutely wonderful; it's an affinity that exists despite our character, instead of

because of it. We are totally different and yet we manage to agree on whatever it is that matters. In 1975 we felt very good about each other and we put together a marvelous band—the Mighty Jitters. We made two amazing records and another live one, *Crosby-Nash Live,* and that was some of the absolute best of the creative process that I've ever been through. We had almost no impediment to doing the very best work we could. There was no bone of contention between us; we didn't compete, except in the healthiest possible ways. There was a lot of love there. I was snorting a fairly large amount of cocaine but was not debilitated by it yet. I felt great, I was very happy, I was with Nancy Brown, I was excited with life. I was being both egotistical and determined, but I felt good about what I was doing. There was no compromise in it—Nash and I would try anything to do the best quality that we could and we were managing ourselves. This was another important factor.

Leslie Morris was our assistant and our calm center. She wasn't a secretary; I'd say she was sort of our junior partner while we managed ourselves. We had a good lawyer, Gregory Fishback. We had a good agent, Howard Rose. We had a very good scene happening. No compromise! The recording was incredible! We were at Village Recorders in Westwood when James Taylor came to help us on a couple of songs, playing acoustic guitar. On the session were James, me, Nash, Craig, Russell, Leland, David Lindley, and Danny Kortchmar. This was an awesome amount of creativity to pack into one room. We cut four songs in one afternoon: first was "Marguerita." Next one was "Mama Lion." Then came "Carry Me," followed by "Wind on the Water." These were masters, complete tracks with lead vocals in place, and we cut them all in one day.

CRAIG DOERGE: *Crosby and Nash showed they could create almost as powerful an energy by themselves with* Wind on the Water *as Crosby, Stills, and Nash ever did. It was a terrific record. There were moments in there when David and Graham came to the studio radi-*

ant. One day on that album, we cut four master tracks, with James Taylor playing on one and singing on another. All four songs in one afternoon, top to bottom. There was no overdubbing on any of it. It was all live. That was a great day because, as you know, albums since then have taken a little more time to make—you don't knock out four masters in one afternoon. I think there's a move to go back to that kind of recording. David's aware that live performance is often his best work and on his new album the live stuff with the band in the room is as good or better than things that take two weeks to do. Nowadays most singers work out of the control room and get the rhythm track first and then overdub everything; the vocals come in last. It's much more difficult to get vocalists genuinely psyched-up to feel like it's a performance. David's really an instinctive musician on a lot of levels, so he likes to hear that interplay—you can hear it in his vocal performance if he's excited.

Touring was the same. Graham and David wanted to actually make the Jitters a firm unit, except for the fact that CSN was always looming in the wings. It probably would have been very similar to Springsteen's E Street Band or Seger's Silver Bullet Band. We would've been an actual entity, a band with a name, if it wasn't for the policy of staying away from band names. [The continued existence of one incarnation of another the Byrds or Buffalo Springfield still rankled. The reason the band had been called Crosby, Stills, and Nash in the first place was so that there'd be no way to continue it without any one of its founder-members.] We played some amazing shit with that band. There were some concerts and reviews that were unbelievable; not only did they have the material—the Wind on the Water *album was every bit as good as top CSN stuff—but what they did in live performance was astounding. And they gave us the opportunity to stretch as musicians, which no one else had done. Most artists hire the band and tell you, "Just play what you played on the album and don't step out too much." David and Graham were just the opposite. They said, "What can you do for us? Perk up. Play and give us as much as you got," and that made everybody in the band feel a little bit like an artist themselves, maybe on the second tier, but artists just the same, not just schleppers; nobody felt like he was only a background musician.*

Cameron Crowe, writing in *Rolling Stone*, covered the Crosby-Nash *Wind on the Water* Tour. Reporting from Dallas, he wrote: "The Crosby-Nash band's three-hour performance is intended to bury the stigma of their laid-back CSNY image. The acoustic close-harmony balladeering is still there, of course, but so is a stream of double-fisted metal music . . . [They] all cook with the assurance of a cocky rock 'n' roll band. A Dallas disc jockey puts it another way as he waits outside their dressing room: 'I'm impressed.' He shrugs. 'Truly impressed. Between you and me, I always thought of these guys as the George and Ringo of Crosby, Stills, Nash, and Young . . . I was wrong.' " Crowe's report covers sold-out performances in Dallas and Miami, where Carole King joined them once again. *Wind on the Water* eventually stayed on the *Billboard* charts for more than seven months, until after *Whistling Down the Wire* appeared the following summer.

CRAIG DOERGE: *The only letter I ever wrote to* Rolling Stone *was after a review they did of a concert that we did in New York. That was one of the best concerts of all time and the crowd just went bananas. This thing was sold-out: there were fifteen thousand inside and twenty-five thousand out on the lawn, listening because they couldn't get in.* Rolling Stone *[not Cameron Crowe] reviewed that concert and said that the band was better than Crosby-Nash. It was the only time I was really pissed off at the paper because there are very few artists who have the nerve to allow bands to really stand up and do something for them and the last thing you need is for reviewers to say, "The band is doing too much more than you." It's also bullshit because the reason the concert is great is because the artist and the band meet each other. If the band is more than the artist, it won't be a good show and the crowd'll pick up on that. We didn't steamroll them. David and Graham were supplying the material, the energy, the amazing vocals, and creating an opportunity for us to play this stuff and we reached this amazing point where it was so phenomenal because both sides met. In other words, they gave us the freedom and we gave it back and it locked in this special place.*

While the record and tour were doing well, the studio and live recording of the music reflected the normal chaos and tension of making music in the public eye. David and Graham were fighting for their individuality, creating a dual entity they believed was separate and independent from their quadratic involvement in CSNY. Life in the darkness at the console was a lot more complicated than just tweaking knobs and setting levels. Stanley Johnston was a young assistant engineer who had come to work for Don Gooch when Gooch was engineering in the studio in Graham Nash's basement. Stephen Barncard had been with the group since *Déjà Vu* and had worked at Wally Heider's in San Francisco.

STEPHEN BARNCARD: *The tour was first-class all the way. It was a great tour and there was the whale consciousness at the time. We had the Cousteau guys going along; they had a booth that they opened up at the shows to raise money. They had given Graham and David some exquisite underwater footage to use with* Wind on the Water. *It was in the summer; we played all these indoor-outdoor places. They were concert venues, originally designed for orchestras, and they held about five thousand people, which made for good acoustics. It was small enough to be intimate, but it was big enough to rock. We were recording all along the way wherever we could get equipment together and at the New York gig in Central Park the partnership between me and Don Gooch came to an end. I had had a bad day and Don had had even a worse time. He had volunteered for the tour before he knew we were going to record. He'd signed up to mix the house PA, which is a lot different than making a full-fledged album recording. So he got Stanley Johnston to do house and he was working in the truck with me. But Don was never one to relinquish the mixing position either way and he's a big guy. He asserted himself in the middle of the console and obviously was not going to allow much input from me. So I was really feeling kind of tired of this because it had been going on for a couple of years, so I told him he was asshole. I said, "Don, you're an asshole," and he exploded into a frothing frenzy of fit, grabbing at my glasses, smashing my glasses, had me down on the floor. Dave Hewitt had to pick him off me. I said, "That's it. I can't work with you anymore." That was it. Meanwhile, the tape's rolling and I knew it would end up on the record.*

STANLEY JOHNSTON: *I came out of radio and I met David at Graham's house, where Graham was working on his solo album,* Wild Tales. *David was living in Marin and was there a lot, hanging out. It was like a family in 1973. Gooch was the engineer at the time and I was just learning what was going on. I had never seen tape two inches wide before or anything with that many knobs on it. I hadn't dealt with artists like that. I had done a lot of live recording for radio, but I had never dealt one-on-one with any recording artists. I thought it was a lot of fun. David was a nice guy, kind of stand-offish, a little hard to get to know, but he saw that Graham and I got along, so I think he must have decided that at one point or another I was okay. Eventually, I wound up one of the regulars and was on the road with Crosby-Nash, running monitors, when the struggle went down. It was in the old Record Plant-New York sixteen-track recording truck and David Hewitt, who has since worked with us a number of times, was running the truck. There were complaints from way down in Central Park about the noise. It was quite a show, but Steve Barncard and Don Gooch were not getting along and in the middle of the recording of "Lee Shore," they decided to wrestle a little bit on the floor. On the next song, Gooch is suddenly up onstage with me, so I said, "Gooch, what are you doing up here?" And he tells me that him and Barncard just had a big fight. I was busy mixing monitors and I couldn't really stop and get into it, but the track that's on the live album, part of it is from the Central Park performance. The first part was recorded at the Syria Mosque in Pittsburgh, where we had a power failure, true to Crosby's karma. It was the very best live performance of "Lee Shore" ever and toward the end of it there's a building power failure and everything goes off, so we have this incredible performance of "Lee Shore" up to where the power fails, after which, of course, there's nothing. I believe Gooch did the edit. It's a magnificient edit on the* Crosby-Nash Live *album at the end of "Lee Shore," where it cuts from the interior of the Syria Mosque to the exterior in Central Park, and you can't tell the difference and you certainly can't tell that all through those last ten bars the machine is rolling unattended while Gooch and Barncard are wrestling on the floor of the truck. Quite a day.*

DON GOOCH: *David was paranoid about strangers. Once we came back from a concert and we were at Graham's house, sitting around the living room, and Russ Kunkel had come over with the limo driver and this guy wasn't in a limo outfit. He was just in a suit, standing in the kitchen, when David suddenly sees him for the first time and says, "Who are you? What are you doing here?" And the poor guy didn't know what the hell to do. "I'm Russell's driver," he says. David turns to Russ. "Is that true?" Russell says he's the driver and David cools out, but it was a very intimidating moment and Dave was real paranoid, real wary, and it wasn't even his house. He could also be a pain in the ass, but if you stood up to him, it would all work out. We'd be doing a session and he'd be right up on top of the mike and I could hear his nose hairs batting together. I'd say, "David, can you back off from the mike?" He'd get real defensive and say, "I've been making albums for sixteen years. I know how to work a microphone." I'd say, "I've been making them for about sixteen years too and I know you're too close to the mike." He said, "If you can't handle it, get somebody else who can." No problem. I got up, went out and got Barncard, and he's wondering what the hell's going on. I put Steve at the console and told David, "Here's somebody who can handle it." And I left. That kind of thing got David and me real close, I think, and we worked tightly together all during* Wind on the Water *and* Whistling Down the Wire.

The place in Graham's basement was a great little studio, but we had to get out of it and go to L.A. to finish the album. We just didn't use it. When you have your own studio in your home, it gets a little sloppy. If it's booked at noon, you don't necessarily have to show up at noon. "It's our studio. No big deal. Let's go shopping for a

*while." So they'd go shopping and we'd drift in around four, then
we'd have some tea and stuff and get in the mood. Once we were in
the mood we'd wander down into the studio, about which time Walter
Cronkite came on with the news. Well, we couldn't miss the news, so
we'd go back upstairs and have a bite to eat and watch the news.
Then it'd be time to really go to work. Okay, we'd go downstairs, but
you couldn't really get going somehow. The food hadn't settled and
we hadn't relaxed afterward. So we'd relax for a while and then try a
few things and somebody'd drop by or the phone would ring or
something and by the time it really got wound up to doing something, it was getting late. "Well, we'll get an early start tomorrow.
Let's knock off early tonight so we can get a fresh start tomorrow."
Tomorrow would be a nice day. David would want to go sailing or
Graham would be at an art show and we never really got into doing
it.*

So, in the interests of efficiency and getting the record out,
the scene shifted to Los Angeles, where most of the musicians lived and where everyone could settle in at some hotel
like the Chateau Marmont: picturesque, private, traditional,
and forgiving. In 1975 the Marmont had more than rock 'n'
roll stars and movie actors from New York in residence. A
small crowd of hot new writers had set up camp: Carol East-
man, author of *Five Easy Pieces,* was there, as was TV producer and headwriter Lorne Michaels, fresh from an innovative special starring Flip Wilson and with "Saturday Night
Live" still a dream to come. There were poker games and
late nights to spare. David and Graham weren't in the main
building; most of the time they took a bungalow together.

The Chateau Marmont has a very large mixed bag of memories for me. I think it must be the actual original "Hotel California" that the Eagles were singing about. I lived in a bungalow,
with great joy. Later it would become famous as the place where
John Belushi OD'd and died. Graham lived in one room, Nancy
and I were in another, Arthur Garfunkel was next door. We would
drop across the street to Schwab's Drug Store for breakfast,
Schwab's is where Graham met Susan Sennett, the girl he'd

marry. If we couldn't get the bungalow for an extended stay, we'd live in one of the suites upstairs. At one time while I was staying in one of the suites, my rental car was stolen out of the garage, which pissed me off mightily. I was sure that it was an inside job because the garage attendants were in there twenty-four hours a day. Nobody could've snuck a Cadillac Seville out of there without them knowing about it. So, still smarting from losing the car and going through all that hassle, Danny Kortchmar and I are coming back from a session, totally zapped, tired, drained, and this guy says, "You can't park here."

I said, "I'm staying here and I'm already parked here, so don't tell me I can't park here. I just did." So this guy started giving me some lip and I said, "Hey, fuck you, as in read my lips. Fuck you!" He grabbed a piece of pipe, to which I have a witness. Kootch was there. The guy takes a length of iron pipe and comes at me, so I took the Colt .45 automatic out of my waistband and put it against his rib cage and said, "Do you really want to die now? Here? Just like this? Do you really want to hit me with that pipe? Are you sure about that?" I just got right up in his face and said those things and I scared him to death. He dropped the pipe, ran away, got the security guard. In the meanwhile, I tucked the .45 in the back of my pants, underneath my jacket, and walked up the stairs, cool as a cucumber. The security guy comes down and the little attendant with the pipe is babbling to him, saying, "He's got a gun! He's got a gun!" I said, "Gun? What gun?" I opened my coat and I showed him I didn't have a gun. I said, "This guy's nuts and beside that, he stole my car." The security guard didn't know what to do. He didn't see a gun. Me and Danny didn't look like we were raving. He couldn't put it together, so we made it through that one. I will say in self-defense that in carrying a gun for, like, ten years I never used it. That was the only time I even threatened anybody with it and that was because the man pulled a piece of pipe on me first and was probably going to try and knock my brains out. Justifiable or not, there's something else operating here and I think that what they tell you about cocaine psychosis is true. The world is just as violent a place now as it was then—if not more so; I am just as much of a target as I ever was—if not more so; and I don't feel the need to carry a gun. I think that it was largely part of the cocaine psychosis, the paranoia that comes naturally with being high too much of the time and not getting enough sleep. I have to tell you that a large part of where you get the hallucinations and the psychotic behavior in drug abuse is from lack of sleep. If anybody stays up a week, they'll be completely crazy. That's a fact.

Nancy and I were staying up a lot, on the road and off. I did get to sail the *Mayan* from Sausalito to Santa Barbara, where it was closer to L.A. The schooner became a symbol of sanity and clarity, life at sea was clean and healthy; the obsessions and dependencies of the rock 'n' roll life on land could be left at the dock. From the first day I owned a boat my feeling was "Well, if it's all going to come unglued, I'm gonna sail away into the distance." Which is not only unrealistic but not right, as Jackson Browne pointed out when he asked me, "What about all the people that can't afford a yacht?" Jackson had a conscience. He said, "It's not cool. You just can't leave them holding the bag. It's our right and duty and proper place in things to stay here and try to make it better." And he was right. He wrote "For Everyman" as an answer to "Wooden Ships," one more example of the way we would communicate and exchange information in song. He's still right and what happened along the way, of course, is that I found out how much fun it was to go sailing.

NANCY BROWN: *The boat was like a crystal in our lives, something that we looked forward to and made us anticipate a change in our inner feelings and chemistry, even though we did our best to wreck them. There were always vows to stop taking drugs when we went on the boat and I remember the first time; we threw an ounce of cocaine overboard. It was a wonderful feeling, but unfortunately we did that a lot of times. It was no big rebirth like it should have been, like we hoped it would be. It just happened over and over and over again.*

Going on the boat was always a a good time because there were no pressures. David would have to go to a pay phone to make his millions of phone calls, so that got cut short. It was a special time; it was finally a time for a relationship. On the road we would put on this act and be strong, which is something I'm very good at, personally. I can put on a front. We would try and maintain for a year and stay together and then go to the boat and actually have a relationship. The only place that I felt that I was part of a relationship was on the boat. There was always too much business and too many phone calls and drugs everywhere else.

One of David's new sailing companions was a recently divorced manufacturer of diving equipment named Bevly Morgan, whose company in Santa Barbara still makes a bewildering variety of state-of-the-art deepwater diving helmets and underwater gear. Bev Morgan has spent enough time underwater to have webbed feet and has done everything from commercial diving with a hard helmet in the North Sea to recreational spearfishing around the Channel Islands off Santa Barbara.

BEV MORGAN: *Bevly is the first name. I just go by the name Bev—it's been a problem all my life, getting mixed up with the feminine gender and all that, but after a while you learn to live with it in the business. Everybody remembers it. I manufacture commercial diving gear and was a commercial diver myself, years ago, and at one stage of the commercial diving, I dove with Bud Hedrick, who wound up working on David's schooner,* Mayan. *I was flying in and out of the South Pacific doing some commercial stuff when Bud invited me to come diving with him, to look for whales. So I went over to Lahaina and went diving and had a good time and later on, when they brought the boat back here to the coast, we got a diving thing going using my boat, a twenty-four foot Radon, working with it off the* Mayan. *The Radon made a real handy dive boat while we lived on the schooner. I got to know David because of his love for diving. Bud was taking care of the boat. I was in the process of a divorce, traveling and moving around a lot; a nice big sailboat with a lot of pretty girls was definitely a magnet. The boat was a getaway from all the fat life. David's day would start late in the afternoon. It took about a week out on the boat to get him shifted over to making a first dive in the morning. He'd put in for the second dive. We usually had a good cook onboard and we'd let him eat breakfast while we'd go for a quick dive. David's a very competitive guy and within four or five days he was getting up in the morning like the rest of us and hitting it. He'd get restless at night. That was the only fly in the ointment. We'd be anchored in some beautiful place, full of a nice dinner, and he'd get restless. "Let's move it," he'd say and we'd agree: "Yeah, okay, Dave." Because we got used to it. We'd move around the corner and anchor up again. And he'd pace the deck like Captain Ahab. It was a classic scene, but eventually he'd adjust and settle down and get a nice sleep.*

NANCY BROWN: *Mostly I remember the lobsters, which we called "bugs." And problems getting tanks. You can't get tanks with compressed air in them unless you have your little diving certification card. We didn't have those. David and Bev Morgan taught me how to dive. Bev Morgan wrote the first diving manual for the Navy, so he didn't need a card. David bought a compressor and installed it on the deck of the* Mayan *and we could compress enough tanks for everyone to have two dives a day. Whoever had the physical stamina to do two dives in a day would get up and do the morning dive to get lunch. We'd go bugging and get lobsters. David was always so cute in his wet suit. He looked like this big huge round seal with his little mustache sticking out on both sides of his regulator and underneath his mask and he had this big long shark spear. I'd stay real close to him. For one thing, I didn't even know what sharks looked like, so I'm going to stay close to somebody who can protect me. David would stab the lobsters and I carried the bag and we'd stick them in and go up and have the freshest lobster you could have for lunch and I've got some pictures of the table in the cabin in the boat set with steak and lobsters. It was beautiful. It was a wonderful way to eat. We'd just sit and hang out and every once in a while, if there were more*

*females than myself onboard, we would get buzzed by a military
helicopter full of eager young men and they would tip it so that all
of them could get a full view of us, because we rarely wore anything
more than shorts or a swimming suit bottom and we had fun with
that. It was such a comfortable free life and even when I was the only
female onboard sexually there was no threat. Bud and Bill, Bev and
David and myself and every once in a while, Bud's wife, Cassie,
would come and Billy had a girlfriend for a while named Helen,
who I think was there more for entertainment than anything else. She
was a nurse and the thought of her having anything to do with
keeping someone from death was frightening. This woman was such
an airhead they all just watched her bounce around the deck. "Hey,
Helen's suiting up. Let's all go watch." Abalone divers would come
out in special boats and we'd trade fish and we'd have lots of lobster
and abalone and they'd have tuna or something like that and it was
just such a comfortable fun environment and so healthy. We actually
got exercise. On the road, the only exercise we got was chasing each
other around the bed and locking each other out of the bathroom.
And, for variety, every once in a while we'd get a viatmin B12 shot
at the beginning of a run and feel great.*

Bill Martinelli is a tall, blond carpenter of great skill and
reputation in Sausalito, where he works out of a shop near
the water. In the seventies, he was one of the rootless
craftsmen who lived by trading on their skill and per-
sonability. He had been working on a schooner named
Wanderbird when David found him and asked him to work
on the newly arrived *Mayan*. Billy became a trusted
boatkeeper and worked with both Bud Hedrick and Bob
Wilson. Personable, attractive, and good with his hands, he
was a natural choice to crew when *Mayan* sailed to Mexico
and back and he went with her to Santa Barbara in 1975.

BILLY MARTINELLI: *I had some good times on that boat. David was
very generous. He treated me like gold. One Christmas he asked me,
"Bill, what would you like for Christmas?" And I said, "Well, I
could use a few more pairs of Levi's, you know?" and he said, "Go*

out with me," so we drive over to the city to Johnson and Joseph and he buys me a sextant worth a thousand dollars. He was a good sailor. He could carry on a conversation about that boat with anybody. He could talk about every stick of wood, every piece of machinery in detail. He's really knowledgeable, but don't let him out of the cockpit. Just let him point his finger and say, "Hey, get that up" or "Get that down." He knew the boat that well. Once, on a dive trip with just me and David and Bev Morgan, we're stepping, kind of high off the dive, and David was getting off the rubber boat onto the Mayan and there's a little bit of a swell and both boats are kind of bouncing together and David's laughing away and all of a sudden he steps between the rubber boat and the Mayan; he goes down and the boats come together, his head flies back and he gets this giant gash under his chin. He's bleeding like crazy and Bud's telling him, "You're going to need stitches. You should have it sutured up." So I volunteer. I get the sutures out and I'm ready to sew the wound, but David's saying, "No way!" So we taped him shut, but he still has a scar under his chin from that one. I was married to the boat; I was in love with the boat. That was my main focus and I told all the gals that and some of them really got pushed out of shape. David would come back out after a tour in the late summer and we'd do a cruise on the boat and no more hard drugs, no more coke. Just diving and strong black coffee and some good smoke. For the first week or so, David was kind of grumpy. After the second week, he really started to enjoy himself. He was really healthing-out. And I think he felt so good after two or three weeks on the boat that he had to go debauch himself again.

The diving I remember was the Channel Islands diving. The theme was underwater photography and he had cameras and strobes and we'd go down and take pictures of lobsters and abalone and all kinds of stuff. He'd take his buddies out there; we'd meet his other musician friends who'd come out on the boat and do weekend trips with us. Sometimes we'd meet him in Catalina, in Avalon Harbor. He'd fly into Avalon and then we'd go out to San Clemente Island and do some diving there. A lot of good times on that boat, the highest times in my life, so far. Not drug-induced highs, just good times. I remember my twenty-ninth birthday on the boat. Nancy Brown was there and Goldie and David said, "Why don't you girls play Get Bill?" I couldn't believe it, but they did. They got me; I wasn't quite sure what I should do for the first ten minutes and pretty soon I didn't have to do anything and then when they were done with me, I just sat there in awe.

It was a wonderful way to balance the craziness of what I did on land. It gave me equilibrium, between being big on shore and having all the attention centered on me and being out on the water, just another person on a boat, trying to keep my shit together. The ocean never heard of Crosby, Stills, and Nash. Or Young. It doesn't give a damn. Not even a little. The ocean, although it's not out to get you, is remarkably unforgiving; it won't let you make more than two mistakes in a row, never three, and usually just one. It was phenomenal for me; it was a discipline. And for a person who grew up with hardly any discipline at all, it was a powerful influence. It helped me gain confidence in the real world and taught me a lot. It's still teaching me a lot. Sailing? Very, very, very good for you.

Joe Walsh was born about as far from the ocean as you can get and still be an American: Wichita, Kansas. A quintessential California rocker, he joined the Eagles in time for the historic *Hotel California* album in 1971 and enjoyed a career as a solo artist after the Eagles broke up. He found himself the owner of a boat and sought out Crosby.

JOE WALSH: *I had a forty-one-foot sailboat and I lived in Santa Barbara, California, and I was in the Eagles. We came off a tour and I was on my boat, wishing I knew how to sail it or how it worked. I heard, by word of mouth, that David's boat and David were in the harbor. There had been amazing sea stories about his ability to handle any situation that Mother Nature and/or the ocean could come up with and I had heard from Jimmy Buffett that David Crosby was one of the finest sailboat captains. Humbly, I walked over to his boat, met his crew, and later that day, while I was sitting on my boat, David stopped by and introduced himself, looked at my boat, hung out, and said, "We should go sailing sometime." A year later, in 1978, David was in the harbor again with his boat, found me, and invited me to go sailing for about a week so he would teach me how. I said, "Okay." Boy, did he teach me how.*

I got to go to the grocery store and get a bunch of groceries and carry 'em from some station wagon about a half a mile down the docks to his boat and I got to help him put all the groceries away. Then he said, "See this? This is a halyard." And "See this? This is a this. This is a that. This is an anchor. This is how you do this." He showed me his boat, which is one of the finest sailing boats I've ever seen. Finally, he says, "Be down here at five in the morning 'cause that's when we're leaving." I got on my boat and all the groceries we had were potato chips and M&Ms and stuff. At about five-thirty the next morning, I left the harbor in my boat and followed David to an island called Santa Cruz. We went over there and anchored in a harbor and dinghied over to his boat later in the afternoon and were invited to stay for dinner, which was good because after a hard day of sailing, potato chips and M&Ms are not enough. I wished I had at least bought some hot dogs or something, but that wouldn't help 'cause I couldn't get the stove lit. So we went over to his boat and had dinner and he told me all about sailing to Tahiti, showed me a sextant, and gradually I learned how to sail.

Then we went to Catalina Island to a place called Avalon. We stayed there for a couple of days. I learned how to go buy groceries and put 'em in my own boat, which is a good thing to know. Next we went to another island called San Clemente Island, not to be confused with Nixon's West Coast White House—this is an island, fairly remote. We went around to the far side and David warned me about how much fun it was going to be. We pulled into a beautiful little harbor and I got anchoring lessons. When everything was secured, we went over to his boat and he said, "Come on, we're gonna go scuba diving." And I said, "I don't know about that. Aren't there sharks and stuff?" He said, "Yeah!" So the next thing I know, I have a wet suit on and I'm underwater, breathing air out of some tank, and I guess I did pretty good. I passed. The next thing I know after that, we're back onboard, eating a bunch of really good things like lobster and mussels and abalone. I also learned how to pound abalone so you can eat it; if you don't pound it right, it's like chewin' on a balloon. It's kinda like getting a pizza with rubber bands and balloons on it.

Toward late, late, late afternoon, a naval patrol boat, like a PT boat, pulled up and a bunch of officers broadcast over their PA system that the harbor had to be evacuated. There were one or two other boats there, some lobster and abalone fishermen. What I didn't know was that you can't go onto this particular island 'cause for the last fifteen years it's been a target for the Pacific Fleet, a firing range for battleships and destroyers. The Navy guys said, "You have to get out of here because at twelve, seven . . . nineteen-thirty zulu," or something, "we're going to have target practice." And all these other boats left. And I said, "We better get out of here, don't you think, David?" And he said, "No problem." Then they came around to tell us that we had to go, but they wound up saying, "Hey, Cros!" The entire U.S. Navy knew David Crosby. He sent over a few six-packs and introduced me and they knew my tunes, so I was okay with them. Then Cros says, "Where's the best seat in the house?" and they say, "Over here by us." We pull up our anchors and go over near them, right? Once we're there, Crosby says, "Now the fun starts." It was almost dark—the sun had just left the sky—and we could hear these Navy guys next to us talking to all these big battleships just over the horizon.

It looked like lightning at first, twenty miles away. Then we heard the shells coming and a flare went off, a sighting flare, and shells the size of a Volkswagen start to hit the cliffs of the island. The object of the game was to get the three shells as close to the sighting flare as possible. And it was like the Fourth of July and it went on for, like, an hour and a half. The guns would go off on the horizon and you'd catch a glimpse of a destroyer or cruiser or something, *then in about ten seconds, shells would come screaming overhead. We were maybe three football fields away from the cliffs on the island and they would slam in there. Ka-blam! The last thing that you heard was the actual sound of the shells being fired. The guys in the PT boat would say, "Aim a little more to the left." Or "Try a blue flare this time." "Hey, Cros, you like that one?" I was very nervous. It was the most amazing thing I've ever seen or heard and it went on for an hour and a half.*

The last thing that the battleships did was to fire a sighting flare directly over my boat, when they were supposed to be aiming into the cliffs. The inference was that there were three shells coming next! I remember standing on the deck, yelling at a battleship twenty miles away: "No no no no no no no!" Yelling at the top of my lungs, which the Navy thought was hilarious because they had a microphone open and all the guys on the battleship were listening to me going berserk because I thought three Volkswagens were going to land on my boat. Cros had it set up with the Navy guys! I got set up pretty good on that. I didn't see David for quite some time after that, but by then he wasn't David for a while.

David and Graham were also touring together with great success as an acoustic act, without a backup band. They could go out with a carpet, a couple of high stools, and perhaps one accompanist. Usually that would be keyboardist Craig Doerge, who had begun to contribute his compositional skills and was a credited collaborator on a few of their tunes. Sometimes it was David Lindley, with his surprising fluency on a variety of stringed instruments. Crosby and Nash went to Japan, to Europe, and had fun all over.

CRAIG DOERGE: *David was fun to be with on the road in those days. He had a lot of enthusiasm and we could get real crazy on the road, because it can be pretty monotonous. Count Basie said this about it: "They don't pay me for playing." That's always how I felt too. They don't have to pay us for the two hours we get to play; what they're paying us for is the twenty-two other hours in the day, the Holiday Inns and buses and the airports and waiting around and the lost luggage and bad food. It's really not easy on the road. It's usually not easy for anyone.*

NANCY BROWN: *I never sought a second opinion on anything David told me in those days. For one thing, there was no way physically, logistically, to seek a second opinion because to stay with David, even when we were home, was full-time. I rarely went from the bedroom to the kitchen without him or without him talking to me while I was up there. We were never ever separated unless it was for him to conduct business and then I got dropped like a hot potato. "I know you'll stay right there. You'll be here when I come back." And I was. I was right where he left me every time, even if it took days—or weeks. I remember the European tour because I didn't get to go. I was ticked. I got left home from Japan and Europe and I was there when he came home. I got to hear about all the wonderful European ladies he'd met.*

By 1976, there was once again a confluence of forces moving David toward a reunion with the others for a genuine Crosby, Stills, and Nash record, their first studio album as a trio since their debut album, eight years earlier. They had never been long out of touch. The mechanics of the business kept them within rumor distance, they were friends, and they could always find a way to meet backstage, onstage, in a studio or hotel, or on the telephone. Just as David and Graham had been working as a duo, so had Stephen and Neil, in the Stills-Young Band, which had a parallel hit record, *Long May You Run*, on the charts for eighteen weeks in 1976 and early 1977. Eventually, David and Graham added vocal tracks to some songs recorded by Neil and Stephen. The intention was honorable on both sides; the results could have been another Crosby, Stills, Nash, and Young album. That would have been a major music event and would've earned millions for the quartet. At the least, it would have been the historic reunion of a great American band. It wasn't to be. Conflicts in schedules and disagreements over priorities resulted in a nearly heretical act: the Crosby and Nash vocals were physically erased from the master tapes and never heard. It would've permanently destroyed most other relationships; it caused bad feelings for a long time between the opposing duos. Yet, in the end, they came back together. The location was North Miami, Florida, at a studio called Criteria Sound.

We already knew about Criteria. It's a great place. Stephen had made records down there on his own and two producers we liked worked out of there, the Albert brothers. Graham got together with Stephen, then came to me and said, "Stephen's got songs." The music's always been the bottom line of attraction between us. If I can sit down and play a song for Graham that is startling, arresting, a noticeable piece of work, something that reaches out and moves him in some fashion, he can't deny it. That's something that I love about me and Stephen and Graham and Neil—and many other artists that I truly appreciate. At a certain level of quality, music is an undeniable force to us. We can't ignore it, can't deny it. We're powerless before it. At that level, it's so good it's intense—and Stephen had some great songs. I had some great songs. Nash had some songs that were even greater than ours.

> Graham's tune "Just a Song Before I Go" was a hit single, jumping into the Top 10 on *Billboard*'s charts. The long-awaited Crosby, Stills, and Nash reunion album was titled, simply, *CSN* and it went platinum, easily selling more than a million units. "Just a Song" was on the charts for twenty-one weeks and *CSN* stayed up there for thirty-three weeks; it was a triumphant return for the trio and its success spoke from the heart.

Nash was the real stunner. I had "Shadow Captain," of which I was very proud, and I had "In My Dreams" and "Anything at All"; I love all of them and I think they're great, but Nash had "Cold Rain," which is one of his very best ever. If you want to understand Graham Nash and Manchester, England, and a British lad from a poor family growing up in a factory town wanting to do something better, listen to "Cold Rain." It's the most completely honest and unpretentious nakedness on Graham's part. It's that simple and it's a brilliant song. He had some other beautiful ones: "Carried Away" and "Cathedral," which is a major work. Stephen had good ones too: "I Give, You Give, Blind," "Run from Tears." He had good stuff. I'm not belittling his contribution, which was excellent, even outstanding. But I thought Nash's songs really stood out on that album. The whole album worked well and making it was wonderful. For weeks we lived in the same house. We went to the studio every night together. We worked. The vocals were excellent. The work went well. The pictures for the album cover were taken aboard Joe Maggio's schooner, which at that time was called the *William H. Albury.*

Joel Bernstein was the photographer selected to record that particular episode in the history of Crosby, Stills, and Nash. A talented friend of them all, he had stumbled onto the scene as a songstruck teenager from Philadelphia who dabbled in photography; he had taken some shots of Joni Mitchell during a local appearance and they'd impressed her. She invited him to New York to shoot her Carnegie Hall concert when he was seventeen. He stole away from high school to make the pictures and they were so successful that Joel was invited to shoot the whole Lookout Management stable. He moved to California and together with Henry Diltz is responsible for most of the authorized photos of Joni, David, Graham, Neil, Stephen, and the others. Besides being a talented photographer, Joel's an accomplished musician and has worked on the road with many of the permutations and combinations of Joni Mitchell, Crosby, Stills, Nash, and Young.

JOEL BERNSTEIN: *I went down there to do an album cover and found that they were recording in the evenings, living in the same house, and staying up until at least dawn every day. David was doing a lot of drugs. Too much cocaine. He and Nancy would be up all night and she looked terrible. I was there to do an album cover and it was important; it was the first time anyone would see them together since the first* Crosby, Stills, and Nash *album in 1969. I was going to the studio with them every night and I wasn't going to use a black-and-white, low-level light, studio picture of them for this album. I wanted it to be color, I wanted them looking good. This was Miami. There was no reason I couldn't get some sun in the time that we were recording and get a healthy-looking cover shot, one that would make you say, "Hey, they look pretty good." David, in the meantime, would stay up all night. David got up during the daylight hours twice in the two and a half months he was down there. I wound up doing the album cover on a boat, after most of the album had been recorded and they had started mixing. We took a break for a week and sailed to Bimini and the Bahamas.*

That was a hell of a sailing weekend. First thing we did was run aground. Then we got over to the Bahamas and almost drowned Joel Bernstein, showing him how to dive for the first time. It was just one fantastic time. On the cover photo for the album, we did a great thing. The shot that was used shows the three of us on-deck, looking properly serious and artistic. There was another picture taken ten seconds later in which we're cracking up, laughing our heads off, same exact shot except we're yucking it up. When they used up the first run of covers, we switched cover pictures so the second run of album covers show us laughing where the first one had us serious. There are two different covers circulating on that album. It was a funny thing. I'm very proud of that record. I loved it. I thought it was innovative and gratifying and it had really fine vocals on it. More important than anything else, however, is the fact that at Critera Sound I met Jan Dance.

Jan Dance is now Mrs. David Crosby. In 1976 she was living with her mother, Harper, after abandoning a failed relationship in Atlanta. The two women lived in a house that Harper was renting from Bobby Ingram; it was the house Ingram's parents had left him when they died. Jan was working at Criteria as a girl-of-all-work, Harper was the night receptionist and the first sergeant of the studio, running traffic, catering, arranging a little of this and a little of that. Jan was a bright, bouncy, enthusiastic apprentice, loving every aspect of work at the studio. She liked David at first sight, but knew he was there with another woman. David noticed her, but had other problems: his relationship with Nancy was entering a final phase and his nasal septum was about to give way after years of processing an awful lot of snorted cocaine. Peter Fonda, who had taken a beach house in Malibu, remembers that after a visit from David, the wastebaskets were full of blood-stained Kleenex; David never said anything about it.

NANCY BROWN: *I carried the drugs and David was much bigger than I was and he would tell me that he got to take more drugs because he weighed more than I did, which was a crock. But there would be times when I wanted to get high and I couldn't because I didn't have permission, so I started stealing. You might say he was using it to control me, but he owned it. I wasn't working. I didn't buy it. I didn't acquire it at all. I was just carrying it and I would process it and make sure that there was some ready to use and I would roll the joints and we would sit around and process all the different drugs and call them "Dave's Pharmaceuticals, a subsidiary of Dave's Drugs," and giggle about it and have a good old time. I didn't get as much as I wanted, so I started to steal from David. I would have his little container and I'd put some in a container that he didn't know I had. So from the very beginning, drugs were bad because I was stealing from somebody I loved. There was a whole trust lost and a whole lot of self-esteem lost because I was doing that. I don't remember the physiological effects or any of the effects of the drugs at all. I just know that in my life it was bad from the beginning. We had quite a few times when it got real ugly and I would get sent home from the road because I'd been a bad girl, because I'd stolen, but home wasn't home, home was David, so you could say I got sent away. Exiled, the supreme punishment, "I will send you to this place where you don't feel comfortable without drugs." So I got to come down all alone, dumb-dumb. You know, having somebody sexually involved with David didn't threaten me. I don't know if I could count how many women were in bed with him while I was there. Didn't faze me much. Toward the end, it got to a point where I said, "Fine, you baby-sit him. Maybe I can cook breakfast now."*

It was a time of replacement. A new girl might be a replacement for Nancy Brown and there might be a substitute for sniffing coke. In Florida, David was introduced to Jan Dance. In California, a month or so later, he was introduced to smoking freebase cocaine.

NINE

················

I could feel something was wrong with my nose. I went to a plastic surgeon who specialized in noses and he examined me. Looking up into my nostrils, he shook his head, moved some tools around, and said, "Here, we'll remove this plug of crust . . ." He did that, then he looked some more and gave me the news: "Yes, you have a hole that goes all the way through up there." I had a perforated septum.

> *The Merck Manual of Diagnosis and Therapy* says this about septal perforation: "Ulcer and perforation of the septum oc-cur occasionally in the source of systemic diseases such as syphilis, tuberculosis, diphtheria, and typhoid fever; as a re-sult of exposure to chromic acid and tetryl arsenic, and simi-lar compounds; and commonly because of trauma from an intranasal foreign body . . . crusting and bleeding are fre-quent symptoms."

That was me, Ol' Crusting and Bleeding. How that happened is this: cocaine is a vasoconstrictor. Your septum [the internal division between nostrils] is cartilage; it doesn't have its own blood supply. It gets it from the mucous membranes that are on the surface, rich in blood vessels, which is why it's a choice place to ingest the drug—the mucosa are useful in osmotically transmitting stuff in and out. The problem is the constriction of the blood vessels. You do it one hour out of the day, no problem. Two, three hours, not much. If you do it all the time for a very long time, you're shutting down the blood supply too much of the time. Vasoconstrictor means it shrinks the capillaries, reducing [and, in extreme states, shutting off] the blood flow, thereby inducing the frozen nose condition described earlier in this very book. The problem is that if you deprive the tissues of proper blood supply, they necrose, they die, and they do it at the point farthest from the edge, in the middle, and when they do that the cartilage underneath them is deprived of its blood supply and also dies and you get a hole in your nose. It's not terminal. It's not even dangerous, but it is an obvious warning sign to those of us who can see it. I saw it and it scared me to death. Other people had it happen and kept right on snorting until it chewed a hole in their turbinates, into their sinuses, and in at least one case that I know about, right through to the brain. I mean, right up into the ol' cranium. That's the physical damage from sniffing cocaine. Psychologically, we have to go back to Sigmund Freud and start before that.

PETER FONDA: *I was living in a rented house up on Woodrow Wilson Drive, finishing postproduction on* Outlaw Blues. *I was visiting with David at his house and drank six or seven beers. Dave couldn't snort coke, so he was drinking it, dissolving it in little vials of distilled water. I told him that his stomach was going to get a habit. When it was time for me go home, I had a little buzz going. At first, Cros wouldn't let me drive. When I insisted, he kept me there for a while, talking, letting me process the alcohol and come down a little. Then he insisted, absolutely insisted, that instead of driving my rent-a-car I should take his 6.3-liter Mercedes because it was a safer car. Safer! It was a tank, there weren't more than a dozen of them in North America at the time, and it was a rare and beautiful piece of machin-*

ery. His entire concern was for my health and not for himself or his possessions. Or his own health and safety, for that matter.

NANCY BROWN: *David's nose got trashed snorting cocaine, so we started drinking it. He started drinking cocaine in wine or tried to find all sorts of other ways. He would never shoot. I doubt if he ever did because he felt the same way about needles as I do. I can't stand them. I can remember snorting mescaline to come down. Unfortunately, we were among the pioneers of freebasing. Or at least we were given this deadly information by the pioneers. Exactly when we started freebasing is lost to me. It seems like years and years because it was such a terrible time in my life. I was still stealing from David and was much more addicted. We would buy whatever we could get. At this point, we were making the buys ourselves. Later, that's what the gofers would do. It became the job of whoever was living in the gatehouse. There were a few people who sold dope who came to the house but even if they were dealers, when they came to visit it was more of a social call and the dealing rarely happened at the house. It became somebody else's job to provide for him. And us. One time David even let me buy and it turned out to be 100 percent cut. It was great. I ran all the tests and it passed them all; we took it home and started preparing the base and we washed the whole ounce out. All gone, nothing left, no dope in that dope. It was funny and I was high enough to laugh.*

At first, what we put in our noses was cocaine hydrochloride. The stage before it becomes cocaine is an alkaloid stage called "basa." Then it's washed with hydrochloric acid, which makes it acidic. Finally, it's rinsed with either acetone or ether or some other wash. But if you take cocaine and use a strong alkaline precipitant, you can switch its pH back from acid to just over alkaline, converting it to cocaine base or freebase. The first time I saw that demonstrated was by a guy who used to live in Sausalito. It came at the perfect time; I was desperate for some way to do coke without sniffing it and this new trick came along. A friend named Patrick showed me how to make freebase, using ether as a medium and water. It was a dangerous way to prepare base because you had to make sure you got all the ether out. Ether is terribly volatile and flammable. There were fires. I set myself on fire, ignited the entire front of me at one point. Luckily, ether burns fairly cold and all you have to do is roll over. If you panic like a certain comedian friend of ours, then you're in real trouble. Especially if you're wearing a polyester shirt, which is what really burned him.

What they call "crack" now is just degraded freebase. Real freebase is made entirely from cocaine. Crack is made mostly from cut and that's one of the reasons it's so dangerous. That's the reason that it's cheap. They're using stuff that isn't even illegal and is totally bad for you. Street "crack" is total shit base with almost no cocaine in it. Regular freebase got you very high, very fast. Crack makes you jittery and weird and agitated, so you know you've smoked something, and the addiction level is just as strong; all of the habit and none of the high. Very, very bad.

What amazed me, when I thought about it, was how compulsive people became around freebase. All basers are obsessed with it. They all think they know everything about it. Basers imagine they're chemists, scientists, doctors, and pharmacists and everybody has a slightly different theory about how to make it right. I studied it pretty carefully. I talked to people who were knowledgeable about chemistry and I think I probably understand it pretty well. But it becomes an obsession. You collect junk for it. You have a million little pieces of glass. You have little tubes and bottles and stoppers and screens and pipes and pieces of rubber. You have all kinds of little metal tools to scrape the pipes. You have a zillion little containers to keep liquids and powders. We carried around bags full of stuff. I carried little pH papers to check the acidity and alkalinity. I carried bottles of water, little containers of ammonia. I carried bags of baking soda. I always carried a shoulder bag. At first it just had pretty boxes and Buck knives and crystals and a carpet of loose change on the bottom.

Then it got to be a bag that was entirely occupied with base parts and pieces. I used to say, "Have I got all my parts and pieces?" I'd have a pipe and a spare pipe and then parts to fix the pipe and all kinds of strange shit. The torch became a part of the things I carried with me, the way people carry car keys or a wallet. I always had a lighter even though I don't smoke because I had to light my torch. I had little torches and big torches, the big ones were more dangerous; I burned holes in furniture, I burned holes in myself. I have numerous scars from overheated pipes or torches; they'd touch me and burn me. It's further evidence of the psychosis involved in drug use that you can do such obvious repeated painful damage to yourself and not understand what the message is.

NANCY BROWN: *We would smoke it on tinfoil with a little foil straw. When it went through the straw, it would leave a residue and you could smoke the residue—I'm getting a stomach ache just remembering this stuff. It wreaked havoc on your digestive system. I would steal the straws from David and stuff them in the couch in the kitchen and then frantically try to find them when he was asleep. It was terrible: I had to have something because I couldn't sleep. When he wasn't home, I would stay up all night, smoking opium, too terrified to go to sleep because I was so paranoid. I could see things. My eyes aren't all that good anyway, but I saw many things. I would stay up all day because you don't sleep during the day and then I'd stay up all night. I helped. I helped it all start to fall down. When David started to use ether to process the base, I started to separate myself from him. Drugs brought David real close to hitting me about twice. It got ugly. It got so it wasn't a relationship outside of the drugs anymore. It got to a point where at night when we would be contemplating sex, we got ourselves so loaded we couldn't function. Then I'd tease, saying, "Yeah, I'll do that. Gimme some coke," and just tease my way through the night. Tease my way through the ounce. We'd go through massive amounts of drugs. An ounce didn't last long for us. When we were freebasing, we were lucky if it lasted two days. We did an ounce a day at times. Up to twenty-four hundred dollars. That ounce I wasted cost twenty-four hundred. The mind boggles. We were so disgusting to be around that nobody ever came around. Even bad junkies didn't come near us. David was so ornery and stingy with his drugs and I was frightening to look at. I was emaciated. I had sores on my face. I never got them as bad as he and Jan, but I've got a passport picture where I look like a motorcycle mama. I've still got those scars.*

While this was going on, Jan Dance was still safe in Florida, working at Criteria.

JAN DANCE: *I began as a receptionist and graduated to traffic co-ordinator [the person responsible for booking studio time for artists and their producers]. I was so in love with music. It was a great open door for me. The Eagles recorded at Criteria. And the Bee Gees, Eric Clapton, and Aretha Franklin. I wore a lot of hats and gained a lot of confidence. My mom worked the graveyard shift and was very close to a lot of artists. It was a unique time; the studio people and the people who came to record grew together and I could actually see a song and an album be born. To me, that was one of the greatest gifts there was. There was also an outfit in Miami called Home at Last, which made life a lot easier for anyone who came down to record with us. They'd rent mansions on Miami Beach—several at a time— and put up musical groups and their families in these houses and cater to their every wish: provide meal service, rental cars, whatever people needed. They began as a catering service at the studio. I worked for them, too, before I started full-time at Criteria. They arranged the house for Crosby, Stills, and Nash.*

David and the others were doing the CSN album and I was thrilled by their music. I met them by sneaking in and doing things for them in the studio; I thought I could get myself noticed that way. I was just thrilled to pieces that they were working in our studio and I wanted to hear what could be born. Ron and Howard Albert [the producers] were very kind to me and I'd stay as late as I could after I was off my shift, just so I could glimpse one of them or be there and hear something new because I was fascinated by the lyrics they wrote and how they could put that to music. I didn't know anything about building a song or building an album of songs and I was just thoroughly fascinated and I thought if I could get a chance to talk to David Crosby about some particular lyrics of his, that I could somehow get a better grasp of myself. Finally, it happened. David came out of the room and I didn't realize it, but he had a girlfriend at the time. He sat on the couch and I started to ask him a bunch of questions. Right in the middle of feeling all this excitement and finally being able to talk to the man, Nancy Brown showed up. She came out of the studio and then they both got up and went in the bathroom and I thought, "How unusual." I'd never seen two people, male and female, do that before; they were in there for the longest time, and I thought, "Well, I guess they're having a good time and I better leave," so I did.

Now, I didn't realize at the time what kind of fascination I was building up for the man personally, but I did know that I stopped any idea of pursuing my personal interest for him because he had a girlfriend and I was of the mind where if people have mates or spouses or girlfriends or boyfriends, then it's not a kind or human thing to do to try and chase one away. So I sat back and didn't pursue my feelings.

NANCY BROWN: *Jan was around a bit at Criteria. She was a sweet, friendly, shy girl whom everybody had gotten to know because they had been at the studio more than I had. I heard about her a bit and I only met her once or twice, but David brought her home and introduced her to me as he did with girls he was interested in. Jan was not interested in partaking of "Triad" sex, which indicated a little brains on her part. A lot more guts than any of the other girls had— especially me. David and I got to where we were arguing about stupid things and didn't trust each other about anything. One day we were on our way to Nash's and David started yelling at me about the wrong kind of bagels. He said I had bought the wrong kind of bagels. I was stupid. I said, "Let me out of the car. This is close enough to home. I'll hitch a ride back home. I don't need to finish this." He let me out of the car and I didn't see him again for six weeks. I didn't hear from him; I didn't know where he was. He had kept his appointment at Nash's and late that night when he didn't come home, I called Graham. Nobody knew where he was. About four days later, I got a call from an operator in Colorado who said that he wanted to charge a call to the home phone. I figured that he was heading for Miami and I knew Jan was there and so I thought, "Fine. You can have him." I started to move out while he was gone. I never really did divorce myself from him. What I did was divorce myself from the situation. We had tried to get straight many times with psychiatric help, with drug substitutes, and I saw that we couldn't do it.*

JAN DANCE: A year later they came back to do another album and, as it turned out, David and Nancy had split up. When I found out, I went for it. I made myself as available as I possibly could and I dressed as sexy as I could. Back then, to know me and to think of me as a sexy woman, that would be very funny. But I had this great fascination for David and I wanted to get close to him and, lo and behold, I was standing there one day when he happened to come out of the studio. He was standing with Graham and I caught him staring at me. I thought, "Good. It finally happened." A few days after that, on April Fools' Day, 1978, he took me out for our first date and we went to the International House of Pancakes. We were both hungry and it was the closest place. We could have gone to Burger King for all I cared and I would have been just as happy. I was thrilled to be with him at all. One thing led to another and I let him know right away what my intentions were. I fell head over heels in love with him and found out that he was falling in love with me.

NANCY BROWN: I realized I needed to get out of there. I was not going to live if I didn't and a lot of people who loved David dearly were doing everything they could to help me. Graham and others were calling me, saying, "Nancy, you've got to get out." I had it set in my mind to leave Greenwood Way. I started dating somebody who helped me move, but basically what I was doing was coke-whoring. I was being with people that I would never have been with if they didn't have drugs. I didn't sleep with them, but they didn't know that I wasn't going to sleep with them. I'd string them out all night long.

Eventually, I just prayed. I said, "Whatever You are, if You're out there, get us out of here alive and if You pull that off, I'll come looking for You." Something happened in us and one night I realized that I didn't need David. It was in the middle of a real emotional thing that probably neither one of us knew we were having. It was a big old fight and all of a sudden I realized I didn't need him and I felt real peaceful. When David came back, I hid from him. I hid up in the gatehouse. He called up there and asked me, "Are you leaving or what?" I said, "Well, as a matter of fact, yeah, I am." For the next few days, I would still be getting high with David because once you freebase, you have to keep it up until you pass out. Coming down is too frightening. While David was stuffing his little mouth with freebase, I'd be in the other room, filling pillowcases with things I wanted and putting them outside the window. Then I'd go outside and put them in the car. It took me quite a while to move that way. I got a lot of things that weren't mine. Lots of things I forgot to mail back. I sure wouldn't have done the kinds of things to him that I did without freebase. I wouldn't have gotten as cheesy; I wouldn't have stolen. I was just mad for drugs. David is somebody who you never stop loving. You just have to leave.

Nancy moved out and lived with a bartender in San Rafael. Eventually, she overcame her substance abuse. She made a decision for Christ, fulfilling the promise she made when she prayed for release from her drug dependency. Today, a born-again Christian, she lives quietly with her husband and children in Modesto, California. She neither smokes nor drinks nor uses any drugs and hasn't for years. David found himself able to accept the loss.

I felt I was destroying Nancy and Nancy felt I was destroying Nancy, so she finally just wasn't there the next time I came back and that was a very good thing. It was a survival move on her part and took a great deal of courage and I admire her for it to this day, although it was very painful at the time. I had a lot on my mind and I went back to Florida with Stills, Nash, and Young to try and repeat the *CSN* experience. We tried to put it together with Neil, but it wasn't happening. Let's be diplomatic and say that it was a conflict between me and Stephen or me and Nash and Stephen. For whatever reason, it didn't work. The rapport between us did not transcend our personal problems. Musicians and groups have a lot of stuff pulling them away from the central issue, which is the music. I call it "peripheral bullshit." We have traditionally gotten too drunk or too loaded or too high or too screwed up to keep our shit together. We all have egos or we wouldn't be performers. Most of the egos are large. Sometimes when you're screwed up, they're way too large. We all had other people telling us, "Oh, you're the heaviest, baby." Any time somebody wants to insert himself into the scene and attach themselves to a successful rock artist like a remora suckerfish, what they do is tell that person, "Wow, sweetie baby, you're the real heavy. You don't need those other guys. They're nothing without you." This is a classic syndrome. There was ongoing tension between us from previous encounters—emotional scar tissue had built up. It would be easy for me to try to assign blame, but I don't think it's fair to do that. The blame has to be shared. We just didn't transcend ourselves that time. Stephen and Neil made a record as the Stills-Young Band, *Long May You Run,* but it didn't achieve its potential. Stephen and Neil went out on the road and had an enormous tour of sold-out dates. They got through a few of them, so the story goes, when on the way to a gig Neil said, "Turn right," and Elliot said, "It's left to go to the gig," and Neil said, "Turn right anyway." They never made the gig. Neil wasn't having any fun, so he just split.

In Florida, I had the opportunity to meet Jan Dance, which turned out to be one of the smartest things I ever did. She was an incredibly vivacious, funny, bright, happy, smiley human being

ABOVE: William Beebe's schooner, anchored off San Miguel, Haiti, 1927. Not as nice as the *Mayan*, but a lot bigger. *Crosby Personal Collection*

RIGHT: Proof that sailing and a love for the sea are inherited traits. Floyd Crosby at the wheel of Beebe's schooner, 1927. *Crosby Personal Collection*

CLOCKWISE FROM TOP LEFT: Floyd and Aliph Crosby, overlooking a waterfall, on location in British Guiana, 1931. *Crosby Personal Collection*

Holding a ball, watching my mother, 1947. *Crosby Personal Collection*

The Littlest Charro, Los Angeles, 1949. *Floyd Crosby*

A happy nuclear family. The Crosbys at home: Aliph Crosby, seated with needlework, Ethan playing the guitar, Floyd watching, and me playing the recorder, 1950. *Shirley Burden*

As far downstage as I can get, toes over the edge of the stage, singing in *H.M.S. Pinafore* at the Crane School in Santa Barbara, 1952. *Crosby Personal Collection*

Captain Floyd Crosby, hands in a changing bag, loading film in a B-24 bomber, World War II, Roberts Field, Liberia, 1943. *Crosby Personal Collection*

RIGHT: John Lennon, me, Paul McCartney, and George Harrison at the Abbey Road Studios, London, 1966. *Apple Corps Ltd.*
BELOW: Ethan, the cool jazz head, and his kid brother with the rock 'n' roll haircut, 1965. Notice the Coltrane influence. *Jim Marshall*

RIGHT: The Singing Cossack. This is when I played with the Byrds, 1967. *Crosby Personal Collection*
FAR RIGHT: Here I sport a new hat at the Monterey Pop Festival, 1967. *Crosby Personal Collection*

ABOVE: With the Buffalo Springfield—Richie Furay (center) and Stephen Stills (right)—at the Monterey Pop Festival. *Crosby Personal Collection*

LEFT: Three of the original Byrds at a reunion. With Roger McGuinn and Gene Clark, 1968. *Crosby Personal Collection*

The playback process. In the studio, listening through a headset, 1969. *Henry Diltz*

OPPOSITE RIGHT: The full ensemble of Crosby, Stills, Nash, and Young; drummer Dallas Taylor, bassist Greg Reeves (with a flower in his teeth), Stephen Stills, me, Neil Young, and Graham Nash, Laurel Canyon, Los Angeles, 1969. *Henry Diltz*
OPPOSITE FAR RIGHT: Out of order. Stephen Stills, me, and Graham Nash at the Santa Barbara Bowl, 1969. *Henry Diltz*

ABOVE: Before the tragedy. Christine Hinton smiling over my shoulder, Los Angeles, 1969. *Bobby Hammer*
BELOW LEFT: Our favorite way to be. Christine Hinton and me, naked in the surf, somewhere in the Bahamas, 1969. *Bobby Hammer*
BELOW RIGHT: Christine Hinton floating in the pool at Shady Oak, 1969. *Crosby Personal Collection*. Swimming on acid in a swimming pool *somewhere* in space and time, 1969. *Bobby Hammer*

LEFT: Graham, Stephen, and me in front of the old house that was photographed on our first album cover, West Hollywood, 1969. *Henry Diltz*

FAR LEFT: One of the few times we're arranged in the right order. Me, Stephen, and Graham, Los Angeles, 1969. *Henry Diltz*

CENTER: Here I introduce the fringed and beaded leather look for some devoted fans, Balboa Stadium, San Diego, 1969. *Henry Diltz*

LOWER LEFT: Looking one way while a dummy looks the other, Los Angeles, 1969. *Henry Diltz*

BELOW: At that point in time, I felt the government had a gun pointed at my head. Naked, smoking something (my customary state during 1970). *Henry Diltz*

BOTTOM: The contents of my pockets, 1970. Two kinds of marijuana, two guitar picks, two knives (Buck and Swiss Army), gold coins, inlaid snuff box, roach clip, matches, keys, Bambu rolling papers, glass bottle with white powder, tiny spoon, semiautomatic pistol, hairbrush. *Henry Diltz*

Same group, new support personnel. Stephen Stills, Graham Nash, drummer Johnny Barbata, me, bassist Fuzzy Samuels, and Neil Young. Rehearsing at Warner Bros., Burbank, 1970. *Henry Diltz*

Lined up correctly, with a friend. With Laura Nyro, Stephen Stills, and Graham Nash, Los Angeles, 1970. *Henry Diltz*

Old friends, new songs. Me, Laura Nyro, Neil Young, and Graham Nash, Los Angeles, 1970. *Henry Diltz*

LEFT: Debbie Donovan. *Crosby Personal Collection*
RIGHT: Relaxing together in Mill Valley. Debbie Donovan and me, 1973. *Crosby Personal Collection*

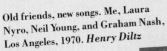

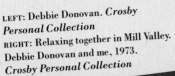

Singers, songwriters, friends. With Carole King and Graham Nash in performance, 1975. *Stephen Barncard*

Clown and Cros. Wavy Gravy and me. *Henry Diltz*

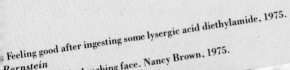

Feeling good after ingesting some lysergic acid diethylamide, 1975. *Bernstein*

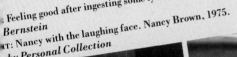

T: Nancy with the laughing face. Nancy Brown, 1975. sby *Personal Collection*

BELOW: Making a point about the music with Graham. *Joel Bernstein*

ABOVE: Observing nature with elephant seals on a beach with Bud Hedrick. *Bev Morgan*

RIGHT: One of the ways to try to get straight: sailing. The *Mayan* under full sail off the coast of California, 1977. *Bev Morgan*

Preparing to dive, on Bev Morgan's *Radon* boat, with the beautiful Nancy Brown on the stern. Bud Hedrick, me, Nancy, Billy Martinelli, and Dana Africa. *Bev Morgan*

RIGHT: The intrepid duo. Frogpuss and Octoman (Graham and me) underwater. *Bev Morgan*

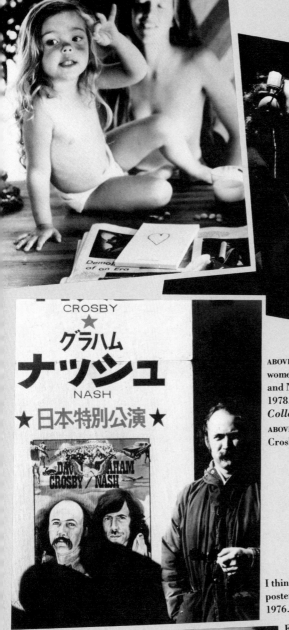

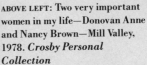

ABOVE LEFT: Two very important women in my life—Donovan Anne and Nancy Brown—Mill Valley, 1978. *Crosby Personal Collection*

ABOVE: In the studio in the right billing order. Crosby, Stills, and Nash. *Joel Bernstein*

I think I'm turning Japanese. With a wall poster in Tokyo, touring with Crosby/Nash, 1976. *Crosby Personal Collection*

Enjoying the nourishing health food provided for us at the Florida house while recording the 1977 reunion album. Around this time I met Jan Dance. Me with peanut butter sandwich and glass of milk, Stephen in his bathrobe, and Graham with toast in Miami. *Joel Bernstein*

CLOCKWISE FROM TOP LEFT: Graham: the Sculptor at Work. Graham (in the flesh) and me (in marble), Miami, 1977. *Joel Bernstein* Navigating aboard the *Mayan* at sea, using a sextant to take a noon sun sight. *Crosby Personal Collection* The former bullfighter relaxing on the rail. Bud Hedrick on the *Mayan*, 1978. *Bev Morgan* Bev Morgan of Santa Barbara, California, and the Deep Blue Sea, 1978. *Crosby Personal Collection*

My coauthor, Carl Gottlieb, and friends—
Mimi Fariña, Carl, Joan Baez, and
Howard Hesseman—backstage at a benefit
performance for Bread and Roses,
Berkeley, 1982. *Henry Diltz*

I was always able to make the gig. Onstage
during the CSN Tour after my arrest in
Dallas. *Henry Diltz*

Singing with Graham, something
we've always done well.
Henry Diltz

LEFT: A Leo and a *Felis catus domesticus*, Mill Valley, 1981. *Henry Diltz*
RIGHT: Attempting to swallow a healing crystal to cure myself of a sudden resemblance to Salvador Dali.
Henry Diltz

CLOCKWISE FROM TOP LEFT: Not at my best. At a press conference while in custody in Dallas a week and a half after my Moment of Decision in Florida, 1985. *UPI/Bettmann Newsphoto* In a holding cell in Dallas with an unidentified black prisoner, 1985. *UPI/Bettmann Newsphoto* Singing with the prison band, Huntsville, Texas, 1986. *Gregory Gathwright* The mustache is back and my sideburns are growing in fast. With Jan Dance after getting out of prison, 1986. *Chris Chenard* Feeling a whole lot better. With an unidentified guard at the actual moment of my release after being granted parole. *Houston Chronicle*

CLOCKWISE FROM TOP LEFT: Reunited after satisfying Jan's Kansas City judge and the California probation officer that it was safe for her to see me, 1986. *Crosby Personal Collection* Healthy, happy, whole, and sober. Back together with Graham, Burbank, 1987. *People Weekly* The Coauthor and His Research Assistant: Carl Gottlieb and Maryann Zvoleff (dressed up for my bachelor party). *Henry Diltz* Trying on the All-Breasts Headpiece at my aptly named Vulgar and Tasteless Bachelor Party, Los Angeles, 1987. *Henry Diltz*

Jan and me with Donovan Anne on our wedding day, May 17, 1987. *Crosby Personal Collection*

Famous profiles and happy fronts. Jackson Browne, Bonnie Raitt, Judy and Gary Busey, and Jan and me at our wedding reception, Encino, 1987. *Crosby Personal Collection*

Another passion: my Harley-Davidson. This was me when I was riding off to score, 1985. *Henry Diltz*

Jan, my wife, as I will always know and love her, 1987. *Chip Stone*

In the wind. Mr. and Mrs. David Crosby on my bike, Encino, 1987. *People Weekly*

Jan and me, post-recovery, 1987. *Roger Ressmeyer–Starlight* and I fell in love with her. I fall in love with her probably two, three times a day nowadays. I also turned her on to base and eventually heroin, which was not a real nice thing for me to do. She had a strong constitution and lasted a long time before it got to her, but eventually it did affect her very adversely. I'm probably guilty of using drugs as a mechanism for controlling. The only mitigating factor was that we loved each other. We went down the tubes together, but we did it with our hearts intertwined.

JAN DANCE: *My personal cocaine consumption didn't start until the last year or so that I was at Criteria and it was miniscule. It took me about three weeks to snort a gram all by myself. Every once in a while I would turn on a fellow employee: I would share about a fingernail full, it would supply three or four people, and the quality of the stuff that I had wasn't very good, which is why I never got a buzz from it and didn't experience any kind of recognizable high. I just was too naïve to notice, but there was a great deal of pot smoking. It wasn't until later that I found out what parties were about and what using drugs was about. I would go to a place where they would have piles of it out on mirrors and people all around the tables, snorting it, and I had never seen any of that at the studio. The closest we came to heavy drug usage was when some Rastafarians came in to do a record and the whole place smelled like pot because smoking ganja is part of their religion.*

Joel Bernstein and I were sitting up in this second-story building that was being built as the new studio for Criteria. I was attracted to Joel and felt as if I was falling in love with him—this was before David paid any attention to me, but it was happening at the same time. I didn't think David could ever see anything in me and Joel fascinated me. I was sitting on his lap and he said, "Look, don't go out with David because he can be a real jerk." I thought, "Okay, that helps me decide." If Joel hadn't have said that, I might be with him right now, but because he warned me about David, I decided I was going to be with David. Other people said the same thing, cautioning me about him, but naturally I didn't want to believe what they were saying. I was beginning to have a relationship with a man who seemed more honest than anyone else I'd ever met in my life; I just let my heart guide me and fell in love with him. When David told me he loved me, it was the first time a man ever told me that, so I felt myself believing it. It was a very strange sensation and I chose to believe he really meant it. I would play some game so I could get him to come to my house and he'd show up and I thought that if I could get him to come to my house then he must really feel something for me. I had all the normal fantasies about musicians at the time. I thought of them as rock stars; I thought of them as extraordinary people who didn't really pay any mind to us peons. When he finally left Florida to go back home, he told me he had a situation that was very uncomfortable for him, that his old lady of four years was leaving him, he didn't want her to go, he loved her very much and that he wasn't going to try to stop her if that's what she really wanted to do. I thought, "God, for the first time in my life, someone was that honest with me about their relationship with someone else." I had to admire him for it, so I hoped for the best for him and underneath that hope I really hoped that it wouldn't work out. He said that when he got home he'd see how it was and if it wasn't working, he'd send for me. Immediately, my mind went on this trip about living with David and being with him all the time and I just fantasized about it constantly.

One day he said, "Have you ever smoked any freebase?" I said, "What's that?" And he says, "Come here. I'll show you." I smoked a little bead of something on some foil and I had no knowledge at all of foil or beads on foil or dope in general. The heaviest thing I knew about was a little white powder in a little brown bottle or some reefer and that was it. I knew a little bit about acid and Quaaludes and those kinds of things, but heroin and freebase cocaine I knew absolutely nothing about and I wasn't a drinker ever. Never did like alcohol, so I didn't go that way. When David introduced me to freebase cocaine, I didn't really feel the power of it the way I did later when I tried it in a pipe, but I do remember that that's how it began.

It's hard to appreciate the addictive potential of smoking freebase cocaine; the urban horror stories of crack users finding themselves hooked after a single use are not overstatements and crack (as David pointed out earlier) is degraded base with very little real cocaine in it. The impact of a carefully prepared base, made from relatively pure cocaine, is unimaginable except to those who've smoked it. The comparisons articulated by adults who tried base and who had experience with other illicit substances are uniform: "Too good." "I took one hit and never took another because I knew I'd like it too much." "No other comparable rush except maybe shooting speed [i.e., intravenous injection of Methedrine or amphetamines]."

David had experienced virtually every other form of recreational and contraband drug. He was already psychologically dependent (but not yet physically addicted) to substances that altered his consciousness. The druggie Prometheus (Patrick) who introduced David to freebase brought the gift of fire to a pyromaniac living in a powder keg. Jan Dance was drawn to the flame.

JAN DANCE: *After David left Florida, he called me from Hawaii. He called me from all over and I was thrilled. He finally called me from California and said, "Why don't you come visit me?" I knew right then that I wanted to come to California and be with him and never leave, so that's what I had in my mind when I came to Mill Valley. I visited a couple of times, then I had to go back to Florida, but California had fascinated me from the very beginning because I had heard all these stories about what an up place it was and how they were centuries ahead of everyone else and I wanted to find out about it. While I was in Florida, between visits to David, Patrick happened to be there at the same time. I hung out with him for a while and he turned me on again to base. That was my third experience with it and I knew there was something very dramatic about it, something very serious underneath the playfulness of it, but I couldn't put my finger on it. I didn't think I was in any real trouble.*

Jan became the First Lady of Greenwood Way in 1978. Nancy Brown's brother Ken was living in the gatehouse and her sister Susan was working as a part-time housekeeper. Jan and David began spending time together steadily and basing became part of the lifestyle in the house on the hill.

SUSAN BROWN: *I wasn't making any money and Nancy told me, "David needs a housekeeper and I think that you could do that." She talked to him about it and he thought it was a great idea. I went up there one night with my boyfriend and my kids in the car. Left them in the car and went to talk to David. I'll never forget it. It was one of those turning points in your life. He was at his best. When David wants something, David knows how to get it. He was so charming; sat me down at the piano and played "Delta," a song he had just written. Then he gave me my first hit of base, which totally knocked me for a loop. The combination was the most seductive thing that I have probably ever experienced, so I went to work for him.*

When I started, I thought, "This isn't going to get any more complicated than we can handle." At first I was working part-time and teaching Montessori in the mornings. I'd do my teaching, come over, do gardening while they were getting it together, then come in and make breakfast in early afternoon. Jan was intimidated by me because she was very insecure about herself and she was real insecure about her relationship with David. She didn't know she was the lady of the house; she acted as if she thought she was filling in for Nancy. And there was plenty for me to do. I was not heavily involved in drugs; I was a very social user. It was okay with me if I didn't get loaded, but it was more okay if I did. I wanted very much to do a good job. It was a challenge to be there and to take care of everything so that David and Jan didn't have to do anything.

A lot of time was taken up with music and Don Lewis was around, basing pretty heavily; he scared me a lot. Partly because he liked me and partly because David did this number where he asked Don what he wanted for Christmas and Don said he wanted me. I got really angry when David told me that. I said, "Fucking pimp. What do you think this is?" It took a while for me and Don to develop a friendship, but we did. We spent some really interesting times together, to say the least. That's a whole other book, about getting loaded with Don Lewis and his bird. Have you heard about the parrot? This bird would say, "Pass the pipe. Pass the pipe." We'd all be sitting in the bathroom and the bird would be on the shower curtain, squawking, "Pass the pipe. Pass the pipe." Eventually, the pipe would get around to Don and he'd put the rubber hose up to the bird's beak and blow through the pipe so that the bird would inhale through the hose. The bird's claw would hook onto this hose and it would not let go. Once the pipe was in the bird's claw, forget it. You had to get him really looped before he'd finally let go. He had to get the hit that he wanted. Then the bird would spin around, still clinging to the shower curtain rod, and hang there upside down, totally zonked.

The nature of base smoking is that once you get started, you do it a lot. After your first taste, the next day you do it a lot. It's a peculiar drug that way. You become obsessive with it immediately. It doesn't take a week and it gets worse. You get obsessive and want to do it until you fall out. A lot of times it happens to people the very first time—base gets you loaded if it's made properly. It's a quick rush and then it's gone. So you want to do some more right away and then you want to do some more and then you want to do some more and some more and some more. In all fairness to myself, I did want badly to get away from cocaine and get away from the pipe and get away from all of it and I tried repeatedly to do it. My usual method was to go to the boat. I'd figure that I wouldn't take any with me, I'd be able to get away from it, and the problem was that I would come back and I would want it just as much as the day I stopped, so I'd go right back to it.

In 1978 and 1979, there were some sails aboard the *Mayan*, the final intention being to sail her south, back through the Panama Canal and into the Caribbean. There, in the balmy islands, David might recapture the magic and ambiance of the Tahitian and Hawaiian sojourns. The secondary purpose, which was fast becoming a primary concern, was to escape the influence of drugs, especially the pervasive cycles of smoking cocaine base. The emotional angst caused by Nancy

Brown's departure was another onion in the soup. Bev Morgan sailed with David to Mexico, bound for the Caribbean and the Bahamas, where some of David's old friends from the Coconut Grove days would join them.

BEV MORGAN: *Bobby Ingram joined us when we got to Acapulco. I had to fly back here and do a couple of things and then go back and rejoin the boat. The plan was for David to stay on the boat; we figured the whole idea of the trip around the Bahamas was to kidnap David through his own volition and keep him on the boat for two or three months to clean him up, totally. By the time we got to Acapulco, he was really antsy. I had to fly back to the States on business, but when I went out to the airport in Acapulco and got on the airplane, here comes David. He's going back too. That scared the hell out of me because we had to go through U.S. Customs and he had a bag; I didn't know what was in it. By the time we got to L.A., I'd figured out that he had a limo waiting for him with a stash. As we go up to the Customs counter, he hands me his bag and says, "Hey, Morgan, do you mind?" I'm holding his bag and he's walked right through Customs. He's gone and I'm holding the bag. I looked around and saw everyone reacting to David, saying, "There goes David Crosby." I went to the next inspector and said, "Here, you want to look at Crosby's bag?" And the guy says, "Ah, go ahead." So I went on through. What I didn't know is that Bud got him an unblemished new bag in Mexico, without any leavings or scrapings or residue, and they had sent him to the airport clean. All that fast thinking on my part . . . wasted.*

Bud Hedrick, by now the full-time mate and master aboard the schooner, had partnered with Cassie, the woman who joined the boat in Hawaii. Together, they saw to the boat and to David when he came aboard.

BUD HEDRICK: *We had been off the boat for a couple of years and had moved to Santa Barbara when David said, "Do you want to move the boat down here?" and asked if I'd go to work for him again, so I said, "Sure." We cruised waters around here for a couple of years.*

That was really enjoyable. Bev Morgan was a big part of that. All that time we were talking about going to the Caribbean, going to the Caribbean. One year [1978] we almost made it, but the engine had to be replaced. The old Mercedes finally gave up the ghost and it took too long to get it in. The weather was no longer sailable. We would've gotten there during the hurricane season and that wouldn't do. David's a good sailor; he's cautious. He's not careful about much else in his life. After a while, we didn't hear much music. He didn't play that much. Remember, he'd usually be coming down to clean up. In the early days, he used to play a lot; there was a lot of good music going on all the time in the salon. A lot of good guitar players would show up in San Francisco. Jerry Garcia would show up in the afternoon. You could see the changes in David. He always had respect for the boat and now you would see him start doing things like dropping his torch on the boat and burning the side. He burned the overhead over his bunk a couple of times. It was just dangerous. The thing was liable to go up in flames at any moment.

The year 1979 was one of tumultuous public events, beginning in January when the Shah left Iran to fundamentalist Shi'ite Moslems led by the Ayatollah Ruhollah Khomeini. Then came the Three Mile Island nuclear accident in March, the SALT II treaty in June, and the success of the Sandinistas and the fall of the Somoza dynasty in Nicaragua during the summer. There was turmoil in Cambodia under Pol Pot. Park Chung Hee, the President of South Korea, was assassinated in October, the American Embassy in Teheran was seized and its occupants taken hostage in November, and the Russians invaded Afghanistan in December. As a group, Crosby, Stills, and Nash were in one of their recurrent quiescent states, lying dormant, except for the occasional benefit performance. Much of that was Graham's doing; he and Jackson Browne organized a series of performances throughout Southern California, culminating in a massive concert at the Hollywood Bowl, called Survival Sunday, on behalf of MUSE (Musicians United for Safe Energy). Graham and David tried working together at Britannia Studios in Los Angeles on a new album for a new company. The deal at ABC had fallen apart, along with that label; they would try making an album for Columbia.

Recording studios are my playpens. I love them all and I've worked in a great many of them. When I started with the Byrds, we worked in a recording studio the size of a football field— gigantic and ridiculous. It was at Columbia and their engineering union wouldn't let anyone touch the board or have anything to do with anything—and they would take breaks in the middle of the session. If you made a mistake during the session, they would hit a big buzzer. *Bzzz! Clinker!* Just wrong. But it got better and better as time went on and the technology grew at a phenomenal rate. By the late seventies, all that union crap was over. The artists got their hands on the tools and when we made an album, we sang, played, produced, mixed, and mastered everything, with engineers and assistants who were responsible to us and, by extension, the music. In most cases, they were our friends as well as our collaborators in the creative process. We got control of the album covers, got our choice of pictures and artwork, supervised the color separations, checked the printing, rode the process all the way through. You could delegate responsibility or keep it all yourself. Graham actually left a label because of a disagreement over the use of the bar code label on his album.

> The incident was famous in music circles; Graham had total artistic control of his album, including the choice and placement of cover art. He had selected a photo with a rainbow and, unbeknownst to him, the record company had just begun printing a Universal Product Code on all its releases. The bar code is a little black-and-white square filled with vertical lines of variable width and computer-readable numbers that signify the name and price of everything. The record company chose to stamp the bar code on the album photo right at the end of the rainbow, destroying the composition and making an unwanted artistic statement. In a legal dispute, Graham insisted that the inclusion of the symbol destroyed the aesthetic of the album cover and violated his contractual rights to control the artwork and design. The violation enabled Graham to break his contract. That's how serious artists were becoming about the nature and extent of their control in the studio.

Studios are a time machine. They allow you to take a moment, stop that moment, replay it, divide it up, analyze it, dissect it, restructure it, play it again, analyze it, change it, restructure it, and then play it once more. You can do the most amazing work in the studio. I've done so much in studios that made me so happy. I've had some of the most wonderful creative experiences in my life in recording studios. There's a special kind of gestalt that takes place between a team of people accustomed to working together in a studio. You acquire an almost telepathic rapport with each other, functioning in a context where a shorthand develops that enables people to communicate whole volumes with just a look or a gesture. Before computerized mixing, we had so much fun; we'd "fly" a mix on a forty-eight fader board, rolling a take that required ten different things that had to be changed during the mix. It would take five people to make the mix (or four people switching around) and if you blew the take, you'd have to go back and do it again from the top of the song. It was a lot of fun. The camaraderie and the level of communication between people who are making a record in a studio can develop into some of the highest and most joyful kind of work with each other. I had that with Graham Nash to a truly intense degree and with Stephen and Neil and with a number of people and it's just one of my best, most favorite pleasures.

The fact is that all the recording science and technology in the world is no substitute for a good song or for real feeling. Music is about feeling and if there isn't any genuine feeling, if the song isn't about anything that anybody gives a damn about, there's nothing you can do. All the technique that exists won't make it any good; it'll just make it technological. All the production values you add won't do anything except make it glossy. If it's shit to begin with, it'll still be a piece of shit. Perhaps it will be a highly polished turd instead of just a dull turd, but the essential quality won't change. We're not anti-technical—we use the most advanced technology that's available, the most advanced synthesizers, the most advanced digital recording systems. We use highly advanced studio gear and we have people who can take it to its limits. Nobody has anything against technology. What we all feel unanimously and very strongly is that music isn't technology. Technology is in support of music. The essence of the thing has to be that there is a real song there, that somebody is singing it as if they care, as if they had something they want to communicate and that there is something to be communicated. For that, we'll use any technology there is—whatever we need. We move notes around. We bend them, we change them, we harmonize them, and we run them through processors. We process signals in the most astounding way sometimes. In the Crosby, Stills, Nash, and Young album that was recorded as this book was written, the tracks were sung live, performed more or less simultaneously by four guys singing into one mike, and the tracks themselves were cut by live musicians playing together in a room where they could see, feel, hear, and smell each other. We may accomplish all kinds of technological marvels, but we start with real music and that's the key to the deal.

In 1979, Nash and I went in to try and make another record. We had tried a little bit in San Francisco and we tried again in Los Angeles. By that time I was severely addicted and Graham was very resentful about it. Rightly so. I was very crazy. I was obsessed. I would lie. I would show up late. I would be fucked up. When I would show up, I'd fall asleep. I was impossible. We went to Los Angeles and got a house in the hills. We were able to make a record deal and got the Mighty Jitters to play on it. The potential was there. It always had been there before—whenever we got together. Finally, at Britannia Studios after a couple of weeks of trying to do it, Graham said, "Look, I can't handle it. It's madness." I remember him using the word "madness." He said I couldn't do it.

GRAHAM NASH: *Where it all finally broke for me was at Britannia Studios, down on Cahuenga. David's pipe was on his amp and the Jitters were jamming. David and I were in the control room while* they were playing, jamming on some changes, sounding pretty good. I noticed that because of the vibrations, the pipe was slipping closer to the edge of the amp and on one particular chord it went over and shattered on the floor. David stopped everybody playing to pick up a pipe that was way beyond repair and I knew that the drug then was much more important to him than the music. Previously, I'd done lots of things to try and moderate his intake, but he's a grown man, a very powerful being, and certainly he could live his own life. But we were getting to the point where we couldn't sing harmony anymore! When David's standing on my left, the entire left side of my being is open to him, with the kind of a preknowledge that enables me to know when he's going to make a mistake so that I can make that same mistake myself. To the audience, of course, it's not a mistake because we sing exactly the same thing without apparent error. I'd know; he'd know. That was the kind of communication we had and behind the vast amounts of cocaine, that ability stopped. I couldn't pick him up anymore; I couldn't vibe him out; it was as if there was no one transmitting.

Now, at the same time, I was not myself. I wasn't smoking the stuff, but I was snorting and maybe I wasn't receiving to the same degree. It wasn't all one-sided, but whatever it was, the communication between David and myself stopped and that was terrifying to me because I thrived on it, same as he did, and all of a sudden it was disappearing. Was it gone forever or was it just a temporary thing? What was going on here? I tried various things: I tried snorting as much as he was smoking. I tried to smoke more dope than he did. I tried abstaining from cocaine and marijuana. I tried to set an example by being intensely, creatively straight. I tried everything. After the pipe went down that night, I decided I would play my big card. My big card, I always thought, was the intense musical relationship that I had with this man, so I put that on the line. I told him that I would no longer sing with him, write with him, or record with him. "I'm done," I said. I was finished. After what went down, I told him exactly why I couldn't do it anymore. I tried musical abstinence from David and it made no difference whatsoever. That shocked me be-

cause I always thought that David was a musical animal; he was insatiable in his appetite for music in any form. He loved anything that was good and I thought that my trump card in trying to salvage this relationship was to take away the music. It made no difference. He didn't stop at all. It didn't even faze him. He was intensely upset by it, but he couldn't control his intake.

CRAIG DOERGE: *There was a musical loyalty between all of us and one of the great things that comes out of loyalty is the ability to not worry about impressions you're making, but to just open up to the best in everybody's playing. At Britannia we were jamming and it was getting to that magic space where it's really becoming something else beyond what any of us were doing. The whole was greater than the sum of its parts. That's it. That's the best that happens. We're getting to that point and the room was starting to vibrate and all of a sudden David's pipe landed on the ground. David stopped everything immediately and I'll never forget it as long as I live because Graham and I looked at each other and we knew then that he had crossed the line. That wasn't the David that had been leading us down adventuresome paths for the past ten years. This was a different David, someone who'd would stop a hot jam because his pipe was broken.*

JAN DANCE: *At Britannia, he had been up for three days with not enough drugs to stay up that long. He kept nodding out. While they were in the studio, he had put his pipe down on a speaker and gone into the control room. When it went on the floor, I'll never forget the moment because I saw a side of David that only I could understand because I was closest to him in that mode. Other people there weren't as involved in the drug side of David as I was and they didn't have the empathetic nature to understand that something else might have been going on. All they could see is the surface of it, so when the pipe hit the ground, I felt badly for David because I knew he needed it to stay awake, to do the session; I knew that if he didn't do the session they might stop working with him. There were other times when they would try to put studio time together and it would go well for a while and then fold. It happened at Wally Heider's in San Francisco; it happened at another studio in L.A. Things were on edge and David was pushing himself to extremes, trying to meet deadlines and appointments after not having any sleep for many days. I know that a person can't do that for long and operate as their normal self.*

I saw Graham come to a decision and heard him say "Okay, motherfucker, you're out of here," or whatever it was he said. "We don't want to work with you anymore. You're out." It was devastating for David. With all his pride, he got his stuff together. He said, "Okay, if that's the way you feel, I'll leave." He left the studio and went to the car and as I followed behind him, Graham pulled me aside and said, "If I were you, I'd get that son of a bitch to a doctor right now." Graham was always pulling me aside and saying heavy, heavy things to me, like "This man is killing himself. Why don't you do something about it?" Or "You're killing yourself and I don't dig it. Do something about it. If you want me to help you, I'll help you." He was never really able to stand there and watch it go down without being affected by it and I know it was hard for him. Most people spoke about our problem behind our backs. Graham was the only one who would come to my face and say something real.

We sped away in the car, David's normal way of expressing anger. When David gets angry, he does it right away. He doesn't wait until moments later or hours later or days later. He expresses his feelings right when they happen. I was holding the dashboard, swaying back and forth in the car, begging him, "Please slow down. Let me drive. Let me drive." He said, "No no no. I'm driving home." I knew I could drive better than David right then, but David wasn't going to have anything to do with that. He was speeding up into the hills, on the kind of a street where cars are parked every few inches and you've got to be careful. I saw David nod out at the wheel and an instant later we were smacking into the back of a parked car and that woke David up. He said, "Oh shit, what happened?" I said, "We had a fucking crash, you asshole. Do something. We've got to stop and get out and go apologize or tell them who we are." David said, "The fuck we will," put the car into reverse, backed up, and drove out of there. I had never done anything like that in my life and my little heart was pounding so fast just from the experience of crashing and all this emotional stuff. I thought, "My God, this is too crazy. This is really too crazy." I begged him the whole way home, "Please turn around. We've got to go back. You just don't hit someone's car and leave." We never told anyone. We drove out of there in such an upheaval of emotions. We had been up for several days with no sleep and we couldn't really be rational.

As it turned out, he found a way to get a road manager to reimburse the people whose car we hit and later on it started to make sense to me. If the people whose car he hit had found out who hit them, they probably would have asked for more money, thinking that David had lots and lots of bucks—that happens with him a lot. When we got back to the house, David drove right into the garage, closed the garage, and went upstairs like it never happened. That night we had a long talk. I had hit my head on the dashboard, but that was no big deal either. He saw the best musical and personal relationship in his life dissolve before his eyes and he knew it was his fault. It made him fall into a blue funk about his music. We went home to Mill Valley, where he brooded and brooded. He'd say things like "I really want to play music with those guys. That's who I want to play music with."

It was tremendously painful because to me it wasn't that big a deal. My pipe fell down, so I picked it up. But they all saw it as "He stopped playing music to take care of his damn drug paraphernalia." I understand how that must have looked to them, but to me it was no big deal. That's how blind I was to the situation. It was a terrible, painful moment when Nash finally called a halt to it. I don't blame him. I totally understood, but it hurt me so bad. That was it. My last remaining friend said, "This is just not working, Dave. Call me when you get straight." It was terrible. It was painful. Graham went off to make *Earth and Sky* and I was all alone. I went back up to Mill Valley with Jan. She got me back on my feet and put me back working again.

In the fall of 1979, with time on his hands, David and his coauthor from the ill-fated *Family* project sold another film script. By this time, the collaborator had accumulated significant screenwriting credits on major feature films *(Jaws, The Jerk, Which Way Is Up?,* and others). The two of them received a substantial fee to write an original movie called *Push Play* for Warner Bros. As before, a major sales point was the possibility of an impressive soundtrack album delivered by the Cros. David flew down to L.A. from his home in Mill Valley to attend the preliminary meetings at which the concepts were discussed and the deal pitched; there would be a mandatory pre-meeting break in the car during which he would toke up on the base pipe, smoking enough to get him through the next hour or so of studio executive chit-chat.

The subject matter of *Push Play* is revealing: as envisioned by Crosby, the story begins when a member of a supergroup dies, leaving as his only legacy an unfinished master tape that is clearly intended to be the reunion album for his former band (which has long since scattered to pursue a variety of lifestyles). His surviving ladyfriend takes it upon herself to see the project through to completion, moved by the power of the music. Her immediate obstacle is the rocker's ex-wife, who has a legitimate claim to the tape as part of her and his children's estate; they become reluctant allies when the forces of commercialization and exploitation seek to put the record out without the other members of the band. Fighting against the odds, the ex-wife and the girlfriend struggle to find the former band members and get them into a studio to complete the dead songwriter's vision of a reunited group. His ex-partners must work together again to add their voices to his on the unfinished tracks. Interestingly enough, David wanted to play the part of the musician who dies (and who is never seen alive onscreen, except in a brief prologue).

When it came time to write the screenplay, David's writing partner would have to fly north. David was getting to the point where he would rarely leave his house. He'd still go out for meals, to tour or record, or to attend mandatory meetings to sell product or raise money for a project. In all cases, his ubiquitous bagful of cocaine paraphernalia would accompany him, complete with glass pipe and propane torch.

CARL GOTTLIEB: *Here's how the screenplay for* Push Play *got written: I'd take a Friday night flight from L.A. to San Francisco, rent a car, drive to Mill Valley, get to the house around dinnertime (any time between 8 and 11 P.M.). We'd smoke a little grass, watch the late news and maybe a movie; I'd have a little base, then come down and go to bed. Saturday I'd get Cros out of the bedroom (never knowing if he'd slept or not) and we'd go to Sausalito for breakfast at the Lighthouse, a favorite of David's. Around one or two in the afternoon we'd sit down to work, me typing while we both talked through the story and created dialogue for the scenes we were writing. During this time, David would only take an occasional "maintenance" hit from the pipe. I had objected early to him being too stoned to work. It was a waste of my time and I didn't have a lot of time to waste. I had a wife and a life in the film business in Los Angeles. My trips to Mill Valley were a compromise to get the show written.*

After six or seven hours without a break except for a sandwich and a soft drink for lunch, I'd see David hitting the pipe more and more often. At the same time, after an intensive afternoon of creative effort, the idea of a brain-burning, mind-numbing all-engrossing smash of base seemed like a terrific idea. I'd say something like "Cocktail hour," or "Break time," we'd find a convenient place in the script to stop, usually an act break or the end of a scene or sequence, and I'd take my first hit of base of the day. I couldn't work behind it. My wife used to call freebase "dummy dust" because whenever we smoked it conversation suddenly ceased. I'm a loquacious and occasionally funny guy when I'm high; on base, I was silent, uncommunicative, and would usually just sit and gasp for air between hits—that's how powerful a drug it was. In fairness to Dave's generosity, he was as open and sharing with base as he had been with weed in the sixties. In 1979, there was plenty to go around (in the immediate family, anyway), so I would get blasted.

Sometime before dawn, if I wanted to get any work done on Sunday, I'd have to crash, so I'd take a Valium, three aspirin, and a thousand milligrams of vitamin C to counteract the effects of the drugs. I'd pass out and wake up around noon, when we'd begin the cycle again. On Sunday nights, I knew enough to taper off sometime around 11 P.M., so that I could make the run to the airport and catch a 3 A.M. flight to L.A., where I'd resume a more normal life. After several months of that, the film was finished. I'm not an addictive personality. When I was with David, I'd smoke base. When I wasn't, I didn't. I never needed it, except if I had just had some—then I wanted some more right away. But when there wasn't any, there wasn't any, and I had enough sense to never ask him to show me how to make it for myself.

In due course, the screenplay *Push Play* was submitted, re-written according to contract, and dropped from further active development. It suffered the fate of ninety-five out of a hundred movies commissioned by the studios every year and it languishes to this day in the vaults at Warner Bros. The screenwriter went on to write and direct a movie that starred an ex-Beatle and had no dialogue *(Caveman)*, while David went to work on a solo album. He and Graham had invested in a small studio facility called Rudy Records. Located in a quaint office complex in Hollywood with the grandiose title Crossroads of the World, Rudy played host as David struggled to get material recorded to satisfy a contract he had made with Capitol Records. David also began touring as a single and working acoustic. He was interested in finding new musicians; Mark Aguilar met David in Florida.

MARK AGUILAR: *Ingram had talked to him and played him my tapes and he came down and saw me play with Van Dyke Parks, Fuzzy Samuels, Paul Harris, and Vince Martin at the Coconut Grove Cinema. I saw the change in David because in 1978 he was only snorting and the next time I got with him, he invited me back to the room and that was the first time I ever saw base. There's a lot of shit down in Miami, but that wasn't there yet. He was having a hard time getting along with the other guys because of his problem and he was looking for other things, so he came down to my house and he brought all of his gear. One morning I go out and I see a STUDIO INSTRUMENT RENTALS truck outside and they brought in road case after road case, everything of his. His Mackintosh, all his twelve-strings; we sat there and tried to get something together, but Cros could only play for about fifteen minutes at a time. In '78 he was snorting and smoking the great green ones and he was really a cool guy, witty and intelligent man that he is, but as soon as he got into that pipe it took a little of the wit away and a little of the smarts.*

I made him buy an air conditioner for my room, so we could all work in there. This was when he was making base with ether. I just inhaled ether. My neighbors came over and said, "Hey, Slick, I smell ether, man. Is Cros in there? Man, you guys better be cool, I can smell that out in the front yard." I'd walk out and burp and my wife would ask me to get away from her. We tried to get it together, but his attention span was just too short. I was ready to go, but he couldn't. The next thing I found out was that David was addicted to heroin.

There is a human mechanism that says, "I want it, I want it, I want it, I got it!" It's the one that gets built up in humans when we want cigarettes or sugar or any of the other addictives. You can build an addictive cycle on a lot of different stuff. I'm just now being able to beat the one on sugar. I beat the one on cigarettes many years ago. Beating the one on heroin was difficult because it involved physical illness. You get very sick when you kick heroin and your endorphins are nonexistent so you feel terminally fucking awful, but the psychological dependency on base is the most obsessive of all. I used to smoke some base that wasn't good, feel sick, and want some more. That's totally fucking crazy. The point that is best learned from the whole experience is the craziness, the completely illogical short-circuiting of the normal human mental process that takes place in obsessive addiction. You no longer have control of your mind or your spirit or your choices. You just don't. When you become severely addicted you do stuff that doesn't show any sense at all. There are definitions for addictive behavior: one of them is doing the same thing repeatedly and expecting different results. Another is doing something that you know is self-damaging and doing it anyway. Another is deliberately destroying your social circumstance, knowing that you're blowing your job, you're wiping out your savings, you're smoking yourself out of house and home, you're selling the car, and you're doing it anyway—just so you can do more dope. That's what being an addict is really about.

I had chippied with heroin for a long time, but that's when I started doing it more seriously. I started scoring from different people: coke from coke dealers and smack from others because heroin dealers generally deal only in heroin. I can even remember one heroin dealer that I liked, a nice man who eventually committed suicide because he didn't like what he was doing. Heroin dealers are usually not nice people—to put it mildly. Heroin became serious for me when I discovered Persian or Pakistani dope: it's called Persian Brown. I was turned on to a way of smoking called Chasing the Dragon. I've always been terrified of needles. Toward the end of my addiction, I overcame my fear and became an intravenous drug user, as well as snorting China White (which I had done all along). I have probably shot up a couple of dozen times in my life. I had somebody else do it because I couldn't do it to myself. One time I overdosed in Novato; I turned blue and was dying and woke up to find my friend's old lady with her hand down my pants with a handful of ice cubes. I heard angel's wings. That's what you hear when you're going out: a rushing noise, like wind in the trees, as you lose consciousness.

Heroin has always been the big villain, the bottom-line worst drug of all time. It's not. In my opinion, cocaine is more dangerous than heroin because you can kick heroin faster. You get sick, but you can beat it. Freebase cocaine is more addictive on a more dangerous level. The numbers say I'm wrong; figures on recidivism and the ability of people who are addicted to kick are worse for heroin than for cocaine. But if you factor into the equation people who are smoking base, not snorting cocaine, the base smokers' rates of recovery are even worse than those of people on heroin.

The brain has a lot of voices, a lot of levels, and apparently they all get to have a vote on your behavior. What I have found is that my verbal crystallization level, the one that's speaking here, is the articulate one. In most people, it's the one closest to the steering wheel and has the biggest vote—or one of the two or three biggest votes. You have a lot of other levels in your head: emotional, spiritual, imaginative, intuitive, clear back to baby ones, just saying, "I am." What happens with hard drugs is that they take over, level after level. They're like a little guerrilla unit that moves through a big apartment building, taking over floor after floor, until you can't stop your elevator on those floors. You open the doors on those levels and it's not good. More and more levels of your head will vote for: "I'll do whatever I have to do to put some more drugs in my face," without looking at the situation or what the drugs are doing to you or how your health is deteriorating or how you're not doing what you want to do.

On the conscious level I'd say, "I can't do this anymore. I'm going to put myself in the hospital." Then I'd pick up the pipe and take another toke. Now I'm not sure who in my head said, "Let's go to the hospital," and I'm not sure who said, "Let's take the next toke," but they clearly weren't talking to each other, not those two. I would take my life's steering wheel and turn it to the right and my life would veer sharply to the left. That's a helpless feeling. Jan and I tried to change because we didn't like how it was. We had frequent moments of utter despair. I thank God that neither of us is suicidal because I most assuredly would have committed suicide. The depression that hits you when you've been doing cocaine for twenty years and during the last year, let's say, you haven't stopped once, just the minimal amount to get enough sleep to enable you to pick up the pipe again. The only limiting factor is that after six or seven days you'll nod out with the pipe and a lit torch in your hands and burn yourself with the torch. I have scars from those burns all over my body.

Bobby Colomby was a record executive who saw those scars firsthand. Known now for his work as an on-camera music reporter for "Entertainment Tonight," Colomby has had three different careers in show business. At first, he was the original drummer with the hit-making group Blood, Sweat, and Tears. After he left that band, he became a successful executive with Capitol Records, only the third musician in history to make the leap from recording star to record company executive (the others were Herb Alpert and Mitch Miller). At Capitol, Bobby got the job of supervising David Crosby.

BOBBY COLOMBY: *Capitol had said to me, "Okay, let's hear what he's done," so I went to a studio in the Valley and when I walked in I smelled formaldehyde or ether—whatever it was. I got a sinus headache for two weeks after that. I thought my brains were going to come out of my head. I couldn't physically sit in that room. You could smell a vile chemical. I went in and I met David. "Hi, man. How ya doing?" "Oh man I'm glad," he said. "I know you care . . ." But it just sounded like a con. And he had open sores. He had sores on his face and on his hands. I said, "Christ! What happened?" And he said, "Oh, I was diving in Hawaii and I got scratched by some kind of coral." Then Jan came in. I knew her from a studio in Florida where I recorded when she was in charge of traffic. She was a pretty little girl, but this time I could see she had the same sores on her face and her hands. I looked at David and I said, "I know . . . skin diving, right?" They were emaciated and for two people who were coming from Hawaii, they were awfully pale. It looked just like a vitamin deficiency. I don't know what it was. It was terrible, really unfortunate. David brought me in the room, then he'd leave every once in a while. He was always leaving. I sat down and I listened to a couple of gorgeous pieces of music. I thought there was one song that actually could have been a hit record. The aesthetic on some of this stuff was so beautiful and then there was absolute crap. The absolute crappola was as if someone ran a two-track in a live gig somewhere he played in New Mexico or Texas. It was junk. It was "Let's stuff this record and get it over with." They'd run out of money, I'm sure. It was "Well, let's use this." There are some times you can get away with it, but when there was such a difference between the good stuff and the crap, it was too obvious. It was just shoehorning songs on an album. I really felt bad for him, to tell you*

*the truth. I said, "Well, I'm going to go back there and I'm going
tell them that you're doing what you can. Maybe I'll get you more
money to finish this record." That's what I wanted to do, so he could
develop the record right, give it a shot, but Capitol had no interest for
this guy. I mean none. None!*

Bobby was convinced his company didn't care about Crosby;
Graham and David had come to Capitol as a result of a
corporate decision to acquire popular names, regardless of
their current draw in the marketplace. They had been mildly
interested in Graham, but from Colomby's perspective, David's contract as a solo artist was an afterthought, a favor
granted by the company to assure favorable terms with Nash
. . . and perhaps Stills.

BOBBY COLOMBY: *For some reason there was this theory at Capitol
that we had to get names. I don't think they gave that policy much
thought because the next thing I heard is that they signed Graham
Nash and David Crosby. They signed these guys individually, even
though their names—Crosby, Stills, and Nash—were still Atlantic's
property. CBS had obviously grown very dissatisfied with Crosby,
Stills, and Nash as individuals. If they were happy, they'd never let
them go and there was no reason for anyone to voluntarily leave CBS
Records. They were a very good label. What I'd heard, streetwise,
was that the head of the company was relieved to get rid of them. He
liked Graham and didn't want anything to do with David. So, here
we are at Capitol with Graham Nash and his best friend, David
Crosby. It was basically a case of Crosby being a passenger.*

When the recording industry changed and singer-songwriters
moved into the ascendancy, they began to enjoy a creative
authority unmatched in the commercial performing arts. No
filmmaker, no journalist, no theatrical talent enjoyed the
absolute autonomy and control of the successful album-
maker. They went from being highly compensated employees with few contractual rights to outright owners of their
creative effort who licensed (not sold) their work. A record
company would, in a conventional "fund" deal, advance the
artist a sum of money against his future royalties (at a nego-

tiated rate) and for that money receive a finished master recording, complete artwork, and the promised cooperation of the artist in touring to promote the album. No rights of approval, input, comment, or direction; the company could reject the master or refuse to spend further bucks marketing or distributing it, but outside of that, the "suits" had no recourse. Normally, the system worked. In David's case, Capitol was being difficult.

BOBBY COLOMBY: *The word had already been everywhere that he was unfit to make records. Everyone had said, "This guy's not ready to do it." Nevertheless, Capitol somehow made a deal with Crosby that was ridiculous. They lent him money with his house—or some property—as collateral. Which is very unusual for a record deal; normally it's an advance against royalties. I think David went beyond that and asked for a sizable cash advance with his home as security. Now I've been a recording artist and the idea of the local promotion man from my company moving into my home with his family is pretty wild—"Hi, I'm your local L.A. rep. I think I'll take your bedroom. And my kids are going to sleep over there . . ." Insane.*

CRAIG DOERGE: *That was a painful project because we were starting with tapes that were as old as 1977 that he did down in Florida. He was really in trouble with his drug problem and Stanley [Johnston] and I spent some long nights in there. It was traumatic just trying to get things on tape, doing tough vocals where David had to be good enough to sing it in one pass. We would have to comp to work around his problem. Comping means that you sing a song ten times and out of all the vocals pick and choose and make one track out of the ten times he sang it. We'd have to do that to just get one pass and then, with that one pass, it would only be a place to start. We played some songs for Bobby Colomby: "Delta," a song that my wife Judy and I wrote that David was going to do ["Might as Well Have a Good Time"], and a song David and I wrote called "Melody" that we're still doing; that came out great. We played these things for Bobby and he got us the extra money.*

That was the worst part. When we finished the album, Stanley and I went on the road with Jackson [Browne]. David remixed the album and Capitol wasn't happy with it. We were having good luck with our tracks, we just weren't getting the vocals done. Stanley and I were so unhappy with it we didn't know what to do. We wanted to take our names off the album. We didn't want it to go out. It wasn't David's best work. Capitol took it out of all our hands because they didn't want to release it, even though "Delta" and "Might as Well Have a Good Time" turned out wonderfully well. It really gave us goosebumps to hear David sing "Delta" because he was living that life. We were always waiting for that final phone call from someone: "David's gone. He didn't make it."

It was in Montecito, while visiting Debbie, that "Delta" was written. I had been fooling around with a phrase had been in my head for some time; it had come from nowhere, as lyrics and phrases often do. I was telling it to Jackson Browne, who had come to visit with an expression on his face and a look in his eyes that meant worry—unexpressed, but palpable. To his credit, Jackson didn't dwell on it; he brought a strong, untainted energy with him, a pure creative force that's part of him. I mentioned the lines that had intrigued me. Jackson was excited and encouraging at the same time. They were embryonic lyrics, but he saw the promise in them or sensed the need in me to bring out more than was already there. He ragged me, got me to my feet, dragged my butt out of the house and into a car. He got me to Warren Zevon's house in Montecito, where there was a piano and, luckily for us, someone home. He sat me down at the piano and once I got going he told me not to get up. I wanted to get up. I wanted to smoke the pipe and my attention span at that time had the duration and constancy of a drunken butterfly's. But Jackson wouldn't let me up or let me at the pipe. He just stood there, looking over my shoulder, holding me at the bench, forcing me, slowly and painfully, to give birth to the song, not the lyrical fragment or the convenient phrase. The whole song. He kept me into it, threatened to break my arm if I got up. (I outweighed him, but he's a wiry guy. Politically a pacifist, creatively he was an implacable fascist.) It was an act of love and great caring; he showed concern for me, for my work, for seeing me get my work done. "Delta" was the last complete song that I wrote for years. I was the child, crazy for the deep. Without Jackson, the song would never have happened.

Waking, stream of conciousness,
On a sleeping street of dreams.
Thoughts, like scattered leaves
slowed in mid-fall
to the streams
of fast running rivers
of choice and chance

And time stops here, on the Delta
While they dance, while they dance

I love the child
Who steers this riverboat
But lately he's crazy for the deep

The river seems dream-like
In the daytime
Someone keeps thinking
In my sleep
Of fast running rivers
of choice and chance
It seems as if time stops here on the Delta
While they dance, while they dance
While they dance, while they dance

"Delta,"
Words and Music by David Crosby

JAN DANCE: *It became difficult to have a house to stay in while he was recording. It was too expensive and we had sort of built up a bad reputation that we weren't able to take care of places. It was not that we deliberately went to trash a place, but after several days of neglect of your human body it would take its toll, so you can imagine what our surroundings would look like. Garbage would pile up; laundry would pile up; things would just not be clean. It's very startling for most individuals to come upon a scene like that; it throws their psyche out of whack and says, "This is the wrong picture. They made this picture, so they must be wrong too." We got that from lots of people who were close to us. It seemed to bother everybody that we were using drugs. People were talking behind our backs about how bad we were and what criminals we were becoming and how the drug abuse was totally out of hand and something had to be done. At the same time it was very strange because these same people would come and ask us for dope. I'm ready to admit that I became an addict and I abused my body and I abused my health in ways that were beyond normal behavior and I'm sorry that I did it, but I can't go backward and change what I did, I can only try to be a better human being now. The funny part was that I would find ways to build excuses and fabricate reasons, since people were coming to us and asking us to share our drugs with them; it happened again and again, often enough to where I could use that for a reason or an excuse to say, "Behind our backs, when you get real with them, these saintly people are asking us for drugs."*

STANLEY JOHNSTON: *Jan was a sad case. She was so dependent upon David for everything that the only thing she did on her own was breathe. I've always loved Jan, but it was very sad. At one point I told David, "Jan's really a distraction. If you're not thinking about doing drugs, she is. Maybe you shouldn't have her here." He didn't like that and I didn't like asking him, telling him he couldn't have the person he loves with him. God, what a terrible thing. She stayed out of the studio after that and I remember going out of the double studio doors out at Devonshire and finding Jan curled up like a little puppy against the door, waiting for it to open. On the floor in the hallway of the studio, just miserable, coming down. She was being abandoned and left and separated and she didn't understand because it wasn't her thinking about it, it was the drugs. They were bringing a whole new kind of behavior to all of us.*

   It had gotten to the point where David was singing in the control room, right at the end of the console, next to me. I thought that if I had him close enough it would be easier to communicate; he didn't have to leave the studio to come into the control room to listen to the playback. If he did, he'd pass a bathroom where he would do some more drugs. The control room was where his little drug setup table was; it would be five minutes of singing and half an hour of playing with drugs. It was not moving the album forward and it wasn't getting the vocals done. I found those drugs to be very enjoyable. If you're enjoying the drugs, it's not a drag. But if you're responsible for getting the vocals done, you're seeing your time go away and you spend hours and hours being high but not doing anything. I didn't mind being high, but I minded not getting the work done. In that state, I hadn't completely put two and two together, although the number "four" was beginning to come into my brain. One night the determining factor on how much he sang was determined by how long it took the tape to go from STOP *to* REWIND *and back into* RECORD. *If there was too much time between* REWIND *and* RECORD, *he'd stop thinking about the song and think about drugs and go for the pipe and it would be another fifteen or twenty minutes before I could get him singing again.*

As Stanley Johnston reported this next event, his eyes misted over and he was moved to tears, recreating the night in the studio when David's solo album died.

STANLEY JOHNSTON: *David's a master singer, but he wasn't turning in master singer vocals. We were doing one line at a time and it was breaking my heart. We got to the end of this one phrase and before I could get back to "record," David picked up the phone and called somebody who owed him money. A hundred dollars. He needed it for drugs and the guy either didn't have it or didn't want to pay him and David was incredibly abusive and unpleasant to the man. I looked at this entire forty-five seconds of event and David looked at me and knew exactly what I was thinking. I got up and took the tape off the machine. I said, "David, this session's over. We have to stop. This is not working and you know it. One of the things you pay me for is to tell you when it's not working, so I feel obligated to tell you*

*it's not working. You're not concentrating! You're not on these songs.
It's a battle between the drugs and the songs. The drugs are winning
and I can't compete. We should stop doing this, stop wasting money,
stop wasting studio time. You go do whatever you need to do. I have
to go away for six weeks; you go on your boat and clean out and get
your head straight. Let's meet somewhere: in Florida at some studio
down by the beach or in Martinique at George Martin's or someplace.
You'll do all these vocals in a day and a half and we'll finish this
record and it'll be fine."*

*He didn't want to stop and he looked at me and we both cried.
We were both in tears and it was a horrible night for me. The man
was my close friend and I loved him dearly; he brought me up in this
business and gave me my chances and believed in me. He was letting
me down and I felt I was letting him down. It was really fucked up: I
remember him sitting in this chair next to a table with all kinds of
half-empty and empty vials, tears running down his face, asking me,
"Are you going to hide these tapes?" I said, "No, David. It's your
album. You can do whatever you want with it. I'm not going to hide
it. I can't stop you from working on this album, but you're not
singing. You're not doing as well as you can. I can't be a part of it
anymore. I'm nuts and I can't stay here!" Working in that studio was
like a tomb—it smelled of ether and all those chemicals and although I don't know what morgues smell like, I bet it's close. There
was death in that room—for all of us.*

JAN DANCE: *I wouldn't let people get close to me. I had a way of
being in a room and not being there at the same time. I wanted to be
invisible so that I could get the enjoyment that I wanted from just
being there and at the same time not be in anybody's way. I'd
pretend I wasn't there and make myself very inaccessible while I was
sitting right next to a person. I would just not be there for them and
make it hard to talk to me. I didn't mean to do those things. Now
that I'm a little clearer, I know that wasn't a nice way to be with
people.*

There were times when we didn't have enough stash for both of us to smoke that much and I knew that David knew what he was doing and could pace himself. If he had drugs, he knew exactly how long they'd last. If I'd ask, "Do you have enough for me too?", he'd be honest with me. If he didn't have enough, he'd say so. If he did, he'd say so too. There were many times when he didn't have enough for both of us and I tried really, really hard all those moments not to beg him for some, but there was a side of me that wanted it desperately, so I'd beg him anyway and put him on the spot and make him uncomfortable. I'd do awful things to make him share his stash with me.

BOBBY COLOMBY: *David went into his car and cried, with his head on my shoulder. He said, "I've lost my best friend. I've lost my family. I'm broke. I can't kick this." I mean, I'm an A & R guy, you know? For him to break down and just open up was a little unsettling. It was almost as if he saw someone for the first time who didn't want to take anything from him, who wasn't there to berate him or give him a hard time. I just said to him, "This is no secret. It's not like no one knows what you're doing." He drove me back to the office. Now, I don't know what freebasing is, but he had, like, a Gilbert chemistry set in the car. And all the time he was telling me how horrible it was and how his life is destroyed and he didn't know what to do, he was smoking this stuff. It was so sad, like a train out of control. You knew he still had talent. I was honest with him, I told him, "They don't give a shit. They don't care. I don't want your hopes up, thinking this thing's going to be a bonanza for you, because they won't lift a finger." And they never put the record out anyway. They even tried to take his house. David called me and said, "Jesus Christ, they're gonna take my house." I said, "I don't know what to tell you. What's going on?" Then I went into the front office and said, "You're not going to do that." I pleaded his case and pointed out the publicity would look bad for the company if we actually repossessed his home and evicted him to get our advance back. It would have been just too unbelievable.*

I was trying to do my second solo album and there's the key to the whole thing: *trying* to do. I've blown the whistle on myself before getting out two sentences. That's the truth. "Trying to do." You don't try to do something; you either do it or you don't. On that second album I did some credible work. "Delta" was a good recording that I made, with the help of other talented people: Craig, Stanley, and Stephen Barncard. The rest of the album was spotty; some of it was fantastic, some of it was not fantastic. I don't apologize for that album. But Capitol was looking for hits, they wanted me to be like Devo [a techno-pop New Wave art band that has since dissolved]. Devo was what they wanted me to be, which I'm not. I've always been on the fringe of the musical community, doing things that were ahead of most of what was being done, I like to think. At least people tell me that that's true. Anytime anybody ever rejected any work of mine, they were reacting to me, not the record. Bobby Colomby knew what was going on and that was what prompted their reaction. They had talked about it; other people had talked to them about it. If I'd recorded it in the Bahamas and nobody'd been around, then nobody would have seen me. And if a well-dressed representative had delivered the master and I'd have cleaned up and put on a suit, they would have put it out. No doubt in my mind. I retreated back to Mill Valley with Jan.

JAN DANCE: *I looked right at him and I said, "Look, if they don't want you to play with them right now, play by yourself or put your own band together, but don't stop playing." He said, "I can't do that." I said, "Of course you can. You're perfectly capable of bringing this thing back together. It's going to be okay. Don't worry about it." I'd do that constantly to him and he couldn't believe it, didn't want to believe it. In his heart he didn't ever want to play without them, but after one thing led to another, it turned out they weren't going to play with him anymore. Stephen and Graham even started to do an album by themselves [eventually, it would become* Daylight Again]. *That hurt David tremendously. He was crushed. That's when he said, "Okay, I'm going to go do my thing until something else can happen. I might as well." He started singing solo. He would do acoustic shows. He did a benefit for Bread and Roses, Mimi Fariña's organization that brings entertainment to people in hospitals, jails, and convalescent homes. Then David Scott came into the picture and I'm glad he did.*

When Jan told me I should put my own band together, I said, "Ummmmm, I don't know if I could do that," and she told me she was sure I could, that I should have done it a long time ago. Jan told me, "You should put your own band together and you should play your own tours; you should make your own record. If that's the way things are going to be, you should do it and do it great." Right. She told me straight out that if I could go out and prove my own worth, others would see it. They'd see I wasn't a total and complete mess and they'd all come back to me. Jan said it and was responsible for my doing it. It was difficult, mostly because of my debilitation behind the drugs. I hired people to rehearse. We'd work for a half hour and I'd have to go and take fifteen minutes off to go smoke it. It wasn't quite like starting over because I had done solo work before and I knew I could do it. I just hadn't ever put my own band together. I couldn't call the people I always worked with, I had to find other musicians to jam with. I assembled a pretty good little band: Jay David on drums, Tony Saunders on bass, and a guitar player named Carl Schwindemann, who didn't work out. He was followed by a wonderful guitar player named Slick, who did. Slick was Mark Aguilar, a guy I had met in Florida. He was and is a fantastic guitar player and real good friend. That turned out to be a damned good band. We booked ourselves, agents booked us, David Scott booked a few gigs.

DAVID SCOTT: *I was into rock 'n' roll since I was a kid in the late fifties. In England our heroes were people like Georgie Fame. I went* on the road with Gene Vincent and Eddie Cochran when they came to England. I got to America around 1973 and opened a blues and jazz club in San Francisco called the Green Earth Cafe. By the time I met David, I had started to do some bookings in England. A friend was running a club in London called the Venue, which I think was the biggest nightclub in Europe, seated a thousand. I was living in Mill Valley and hanging out with Dan Hicks, Maria Muldaur, and lots of San Francisco artists. My friend was interested in booking them into the Venue, so I did. I brought all these American artists to England: Dan Hicks, Commander Cody, McGuinn and Hillman from L.A. I was booking clubs around the Bay Area and dealing with artists that I really liked, that I wanted to bring back to England because they were really loved there and hadn't been seen for a long time.

David and I were introduced by a mutual friend who was on the board of directors for the Palace of Fine Arts, which needed a new roof. I asked David if he'd do a benefit for it and he said he would. He did the Palace of Fine Arts and he did it exceptionally well. We played it for two nights. It holds a thousand seats and we sold out both shows, which was very gratifying for David because he hadn't played solo for quite a while. He liked it and said, "Shit, this is good. I'm having a good time. Let's do it again. Where can we go now?" I said, "Let's go to England," and he said, "Well, that's a bit scary. I haven't been there for years." And I said, "I know what you'll do there. Four shows, two shows a night for two nights, we'll have fun, and you'll get eighteen thousand dollars." He liked the idea and he asked me, "Can you get me half the money up front? Then I'll sign the contract." I said, "When do you want it?" And he said, "I want it now." This was Christmas Eve. I asked him, "Where are you?" And he said, "I'm in Santa Barbara." I was in San Francisco. One of the partners of the Venue was in Los Angeles on her way somewhere else, so I called her and said, "I need nine thousand now." I hopped on a plane and met David on Christmas Eve at midnight at a large rock between Los Angeles and Santa Barbara, somewhere by a military installation, and gave him the cash.

Then we both got pneumonia. David was in hospital in New York for a couple or three days. I went on to England. We had to postpone the gig for a month, which was cool at that particular time; the Venue and David's people had lawyers in common. The only thing that scared me was that 30 or 40 percent of the tickets were sold to kids in France and Germany and Italy and Spain, so I spent my first night in England on the phone at the Venue's office, calling people, telling the kids not to worry, they could have their money back if they wanted to cancel or if they wanted to wait a month, David had pneumonia and blah-blah-blah. We never had one cancellation, which was wonderful. Plus, we sold out every show and he got rave reviews. The only thing that was weird was seeing Jan and David pack for the trip. She couldn't go to England, so I moved in with them in Mill Valley two days ahead of time to make sure we got on the plane okay. I wasn't stoned, I was just sipping my little brandy; I'd smoke a joint, but I was together. I wasn't where they were, so I could just watch the whole thing. I watched them pack that suitcase twenty times. Jan was making sandwiches to pack, putting them in the suitcase, in case he needed a snack on the way.

Here, the club owners loved him. David wanted to play for the good guys and they always fronted the money and would give it to us immediately. That was David's thing. They'd wire it immediately to Mill Valley. I took 10 percent of everything that came from the gigs and when I went out on the road David paid my expenses. I'd get my percentage at the gig and David always got his front money. That was the beginning of a relationship between myself and Jan and David that went for five years. It became the worst time of his life. Looking back, we had some fun times. But we weren't dealing with a very happy individual. The happy parts were when he was on the stage, performing. Then it was great, really great.

One of the musicians in David's band was a drummer named Jay David, who had a long background in pop music and was a second-generation hipster—his parents had run a club in the Northeast when he was a child and he had started playing drums early on. Formerly with a band called Dr. Hook and the Medicine Show, he had played on a number of albums that made the *Billboard* charts. When David was putting together a band, Jay got the call.

JAY DAVID: *My folks managed a nightclub in Massachusetts during World War II; Louis Belson passed me my first pair of drumsticks. I was with a band that sold thirty-five million records. I had seen David's picture on the cover of* Rolling Stone, *which is funny because that happened to be one of my hit records ["The Cover of Rolling Stone" by Dr. Hook and the Medicine Show]. I thought to myself, "I'd really like to play with that guy. I really like his music." Then British David Scott told me he was a friend of Crosby's and I mentioned that I'd like to play with the dude and he'd say, "Yeah, you know, one of these days," and one of those days finally occurred in July 1981. Scott said, "Would you like to come up and do some playing with David?" I went up to the house on the hill in Mill Valley and was in the garage, setting up my drums. I turned around and there he was. He looked a lot bigger, a lot sluttier, and a lot dirtier than the guy I remember seeing in the picture on the cover of* Rolling Stone. *He flogged some chords, turned around, and said, "Hi, man." It was him all right, but he looked rather grotesque. He started playing some rhythms and Scott was beaming because Crosby was beaming and I was beaming; the first thing I said to Crosby was "Gee, it's nice to do it with somebody who knows how." We sort of got it on with each other and before you know it we were sitting down talking and he said, "Did you ever do this before?" and flamed it up and I said, "No, what is it? . . . Oh, is that what that is? Huh, yeah." We had a nice conversation when we found out we were both Welsh and we got on rather well.*

So, with his new band more or less rehearsed, and Jan firmly in tow, David hit the road as a solo artist, playing short tours that enabled him to stay afloat financially. The solo outings with the David Crosby Band were different from all the tours that came before, but some things never change.

With Crosby-Nash, we used to fly commercial and get rent-a-cars. Crosby, Stills, and Nash got conned into using an airplane a couple of times and it used up all the money, a total mistake. Unless you're U2 or the Rolling Stones and making twenty-five million dollars in thirty days, using an airplane to tour is just not practical. Making the money we did and splitting it three ways, the only practical way to tour was to use buses. I wouldn't do it any other way, even it were practical to use airplanes. I love airplanes, but I don't like using them for touring. It's just not realistic. Even though you can fly when you want to, you have to file flight plans and when you do get to where you're going, you wait while the roadies go to the commercial part of the airport and rent cars—if they have any—and bring them back to your part of the airport so that you can drive to wherever it is you would have been going in the bus anyway. I can sleep on a bus very comfortably. I like seeing the countryside. It's the only way to go. Besides, you could turn on in tour buses. Country and western people have been using them for years. You can rig them to carry up to twelve people, although at that point, they're crowded. I used to hole up in the stateroom in the back, smoking my pipe and watching the scenery roll by.

Before David graduated to the big tour buses, he economized. The first time he sallied forth on his own, he rode in a van. Jan was with him and their stalwart road boss from the CSN days, Mac Holbert, went along as tour manager.

MAC HOLBERT: *The problems were real severe at that point. I told David, "I'll do the tour for you, but I really want you to show me some sort of effort in terms of trying to clean up your act." So he said he would. My girlfriend at the time was a singer; Crosby took her as the opening act, so it was perfect. I'd be able to go out with my old lady while working for David. We were doing about five shows a week. We'd go around in a van; we removed all the seats from the back and Crosby and Jan had a little mattress and it was an incredible scene. We'd get in the van and he'd smoke base all day. We had to stop at every Dunkin' Donuts and every McDonald's, and by the end of the tour the back of the van was filled with McDonald con-*

tainers and old bags of donuts and there was a hole burnt in the mattress and old propane tanks—it was disgusting.

That 1981 tour was distinguished by another crisis, which led to a surprising resolution. It began in a motel on the East Coast while Mac was sleeping after a show.

JAN DANCE: *We were back east between gigs. David had just done a show. We came back to the hotel and we were smoking. He said, "That's enough. We have to go to sleep." He lay down, but I wasn't ready to go to bed. I wanted to do some more, naturally. So I sat up on the other bed and took some. I didn't think of myself as stealing it, but I was helping myself to some that he wasn't offering me, so I guess you could call it stealing. It was right then that David had his first grand mal seizure due to overtoxic saturation of drugs in his body. I fell apart when I saw this thing happen in front of my eyes— a grand mal seizure—I never saw anything like that in my life and I was sure he was dying in front of my eyes. The only thing that mattered to me was saving his life. I didn't think about anything else. I was prone to panic and didn't know how to help him. I tried to get his mouth open and put a stick in there to keep him from biting his tongue or swallowing it, but I wasn't very successful at it and he bit my thumb. I decided to run down the hall and get Mac. I needed somebody who knew what was happening.*

MAC HOLBERT: *One night, at five in the morning, there's a pounding on my door and Jan is just screaming out of her mind. "Mac, Mac! You've gotta come help. David's dying! David's dying!" I leaped out of bed, threw my pants on, went running down the hall a couple of doors down, and went into a room where David was lying on the bed, naked, flipping around like a fish, having a seizure. There was blood pouring out of his mouth because he'd bitten his tongue and Jan was completely and utterly gone. I'd had a little bit of experience with people having seizures before, so I did what you're supposed to do: turned him on his side and made sure that his breathing passages were clear and all that and just sat there until it was over. When he finally came around, it was ominous. It was as if David Crosby was not in that body anymore. His eyes were pinned and he was completely gone. I went back and told my girlfriend, I said, "Man, you know, I hated to see that happen, but it's probably a good thing because there's no way in the world that this man could ignore what happened."*

JAN DANCE: *I'm sure I alarmed Mac and that probably started a bad feeling inside him toward me unless it started before that. I don't really know. What was weird was the very next night we went to another hotel and I had a seizure! David had to deal with it and he saw what it was like to watch someone go through it—he saw me experience the same thing he went through the night before. When you have these seizures, you don't know you've even had one unless someone tells you or you wake up with your tongue bitten and bleeding.*

MAC HOLBERT: *I had been in telephone contact the whole time with Graham, keeping him apprised of the situation. The whole tour was about David, me, and money. I was hiding money and telling him there wasn't any or that I hadn't cashed the check, saying things like "They paid us and I couldn't get the check cleared." I was trying to save, but he was constantly on me for money to buy more drugs. He was going through a few thousand dollars—or about an ounce of cocaine—every day. We were almost at the end of the tour, doing an outdoor show in the afternoon at some college in Boston. It was nickel-beer day for one of the fraternities, so there were thousands of jock types running around, out of their minds on beer. My girlfriend did her set and went over great because she was beautiful and sang well. Then Crosby got up there. He looked like hell, he wasn't taking care of himself, and Jan looked like the walking dead. He started to sing a song, being totally oblivious to what was happening out in the audience. That was truly unusual because as a rule he was pretty sharp on that level. He'd pick up things like "Hey, this is a pretty rotten crowd. I'd better play something that they're going to relate to." This time, he didn't. He opened with "Guinnevere" or something like that, completely inappropriate. They started yelling at him. Screaming, then booing him. David said, "You've gotta be quiet. You've gotta be quiet." He started an altercation with the crowd, then stopped and walked off the stage, back to the dressing room; we grabbed our stuff and had to run the gauntlet to get out of there. There was a line of students yelling things like "You're washed up, Crosby. You're a has-been." Spitting at us. It was an ugly, ugly scene. I got him into the van and we took off and didn't even go back to the hotel. We headed right for Boston, where I booked some rooms, and from there we went to Chicago and did one last show. I had been in touch with Graham, told him everything, including, "This has gotten out of hand." Graham was setting up an intervention in Mill Valley.*

When David and Jan came off that road trip, in May of 1981, Don Lewis met them at the airport and drove them to the house on Greenwood Way in Mill Valley. He hung back as David walked through the door, happy to be home at last. David dropped his Halliburton suitcase on the floor and shouted, "Hello, House!" To his surprise, the house answered back. Twenty of David's friends, a physician, and a professional psychiatric social worker were waiting for him in his living room as if they were guests at a surprise party. The party was for Dave and the surprise was that they wanted him to stop doing drugs and check into a hospital.

TEN

··············

That was the cause of the intervention. I had some seizures out on the road and Mac told Nash about it. Everybody said, "My God, he's actually going to die. We've got to stop him." The stuff we did on the bus was driving my band crazy, so you can imagine what a completely weirded-out scene it was. It seemed normal to me and Jan. We were about to be surprised.

In the inexact and emerging science of managing addiction, a "crisis intervention" is a militant confrontation for a benign purpose. The subject's family and closest friends assemble en masse to plead, threaten, cajole, and otherwise influence the addicted person to a point where he or she will voluntarily take some action to improve his or her condition. Graham had gotten the news from Mac that David was having seizures. Bob Wilson assumed the responsibility for calling everyone. It became a case of "more is better" and eventually more than a dozen people assembled at David's house to meet him when he came off the road. With them was a professional caseworker who outlined the procedure and introduced everyone to the form. A doctor, Gene Schoenfeld, attended the planning sessions, but declined to attend the intervention itself. He was an old friend of David's who had his hip credentials completely in order: Dr. Schoenfeld was "Doctor Hip-pocrates," author of a popular sixties column on contemporary medical problems, most of them having to do with drugs and sex. He understood counterculture medicine as well as any practitioner could and he could provide a referral to a medical detox facility, should David choose that method of rehabilitation. By consensus, the group felt that the goal of the intervention would be to get David away from Jan and into a hospital for a prolonged stay. Graham, generous to a fault, offered to underwrite the cost, which would be considerable. Rock 'n' roll performers usually didn't have medical insurance and most insurance carriers in those days wouldn't cover substance-abuse recovery programs. (It wasn't until the rules changed and insurance money became available that professionally operated treatment centers began their aggressive marketing—in 1981 there weren't a lot of commercials on television urging viewers to call their local rehab clinic or "care unit.")

The event was a reunion of friends and lovers, people who shared an abiding affection for David and a deep concern for his current condition. They came from every closet and compartment of his segmented past. Attending were: Paul Kantner, Grace Slick, Jackson Browne, Carl and Allison Gottlieb, Stanley Johnston, Joel Bernstein, Nancy Brown and her sister Susan, Graham and Susan Nash, Don Lewis, David Freiberg, Girl Freiberg, Bob Wilson, Uva Gunnerson (the facilitator), and others. Allison Gottlieb characterized it as "the first drug love-in I ever attended."

By that time, the conventional wisdom shared by all of David's friends was that Jan's continued presence was detrimental to any recovery. David and Jan were considered coaddicted. If one could be cured, the dependency of the other would drag the partner back to using. Susan Brown was charged with the responsibility of removing Jan from the event and managed to detain her in the gatehouse on some pretense while the intervention went forward.

JAN DANCE: *I didn't have any idea what it was all about. We got off the plane and met Don Lewis, who was picking us up at the airport and was supposed to have had some stash for David because we had been out for days. Don very coolly said, "Look, I got your stuff at home. Let me take you home and everything will be okay." He had* just the tiniest bit of Downtown [heroin] for David and nothing for me, but that's okay. We get home and we walk through the gate and we go into the house and there are about twenty people there. The first person that I remember seeing was Susan Brown, followed closely by Graham Nash, who picked me up and hugged me and said, "Same old Jan Dance," and I felt a shiver go through my body; I didn't know what he meant by that. I had a feeling that Mac had maybe called somebody and told them about these little seizures we had and that maybe that was why this room full of people was there. Susan took me by the hand and said, "Jan, I have to show you something." I told her I didn't want to go anywhere, but she insisted that I go with her to the gatehouse. She locked me in there and said, "All those people want to talk to David and they don't want you there." I got very angry. I had been told time and time again by various people that someone didn't want me to be with David and I was fed up with it. If I wasn't supposed to be with David, David would tell me. It wasn't cool for all these people to be pushing at us and saying, "Don't be together." "Don't be together." "This is crazy." "You're hurting each other." "You're this." "You're that." I never really felt comfortable around other people when I was with David and I was always with David, so I didn't want to be around them by myself, for sure.

A doctor came up and said, "We've decided to take David to a hospital to try and help him. Now if you'll just be calm and stay here, we'll come back after we take him away and talk to you about what we can do for you. What we have in mind is to take you to another place, out of the state, and see if someone else can help you. Maybe we can do it tomorrow. Do you think you'll be all right here by yourself tonight?" I felt pieces of me fall away and I thought, "My God, how can these people come in my home and say to me, 'We're taking your old man away and you have to stay here.'" It didn't compute. I thought, "Okay, if David tells me that this is what's going on, then I'll go for the idea because I want him to get well. I want him to have help. If that's what it takes, if this is the point in time where we need that help, then I'll go for it, but he has

*to tell me." Then I broke away and they were screaming at me,
saying, "You can't leave! Come back here!" I went to David and I
said, "Talk to me."*

*David explained, "All these people want to take me to the hospi-
tal and I really can't turn them down. They've gone to a lot of
trouble to do this and maybe they really can help me." I said, "Is
that what you want to do?" And he said, "I'm not going without
you," so I said, "Let's go together." I was willing to do that. I was
willing to say inside that we needed help, but I didn't want anybody
to take him away from me. I didn't want to be put aside, separated. I
thought it was awfully wrong of them to think that they could have
the right to do that. It never occurred to me that they were trying to
save someone's life.*

The group, this author among them, went through the intervention ritual. One after another, in formal order, every participant stated his or her personal and private reasons for
confronting David. Paul Kantner and Grace Slick had overcome their own demons; Grace was a recovering alcoholic
who had tried most of the other available chemicals, herbs,
weeds, and fungi. She confronted David on every level of
substance abuse. Crosby was a frequent houseguest at the
Gottliebs', they had witnessed his deteriorating physical condition, and Allison reminded David of his edema (excess
fluids causing a swelling of the legs and ankles). Graham
reminded him of their failure to make music together. Jackson chided him on his inability to write meaningful songs
anymore. (David's last viable solo creative effort was
"Delta," which Jackson had practically forced him to finish.) Every person there, friends who went back more than a
decade, urged David to cut back, stop, seek help. There were
tears; there was shouting; there were accusations, recrimina-
tions, and exhortations. It lasted for hours.

GRACE SLICK: *When we eventually get into heavy-duty drugs, all of
our worst attributes not only get magnified, but come right straight
up to the surface and go plowing right through everybody around us.
At the intervention, for a while, David was semicontrite and had*

little tears coming out and I believe that was real. Then he went in the back room and we thought he was packing, but he was freebasing. After which he came out and said, "No, I don't think I need it," and that was real too. Everyone threw up their hands and said, "Oh Jesus Christ," but those two people were very real—because you feel contrite and you know you're killing yourself, but you can't really stop at that point. That was David.

David heard from everyone, each speaking in turn. Some were excited, some were sad, everyone was keyed up to the highest possible pitch of personal intensity. By the end of it, he was in tears. He agreed to seek help; that wasn't good enough for the group. They wanted him to commit to a time (now) and a place (Scripps Hospital in La Jolla, California, where there was a formal inpatient drug detox program). About three hours had passed since the first "Hello, David," and it was night. David excused himself from the group and went into his bedroom, ostensibly to unpack and use the bathroom. After a few moments, Graham followed him into that part of the house. There was an eruption of angry words.

Graham's a wonderful person, but he has a flaw in that he will bury stuff and hold it in. He doesn't always react when you piss him off. He's a gentleman. He's nice. He doesn't tell you. Graham had been carrying around a huge ball of burning resentment about my fucking up everything. I had been his friend and I had deprived him of our friendship—and a wonderful partnership to which he was committed and which he loved. Then, in the middle of the intervention, I did exactly the wrong thing: I snuck off into the bathroom and tried to smoke some more freebase while twenty people were begging me to stop. Graham chased me in there and blew his stack, which is how Graham does it. He holds things in until something wrong happens and then he blows his top—volcanically. He knew it was a mistake, but his anger was valid. My actions were wrong, he had every right to be mad, and I used it as an excuse to back away.

JACKSON BROWNE: *After he finally said, "Okay, great. I'm gonna go. I'm gonna go," he excused himself and went into the room to hit the pipe and Graham flipped. You can understand why. They were standing there screaming at each other and Dave was trying to get him off his back and Graham was outraged. Then me and Gottlieb kind of second-staged it, right? We became the people that were gonna wait with him. I took him to score the next morning because he needed to be assured that he would not be going through withdrawals on the trip down. What a joke. I don't know how I actually did that. I was pretty dingy by that time. I remember it was late. Or early in the morning. We were supposed to stay up all night so David wouldn't disappear.*

CARL GOTTLIEB: *I wasn't able to make it through the whole night with David—my wife had to be back in Los Angeles to supervise a looping session, so I took her back to where we were staying, drove her to the airport, took a shower and changed clothes, and (still without sleeping) went back to David's in Mill Valley to help him pack and get on a plane for San Diego. It was like a dull movie in slow motion. David had his suitcase, he had just come off the road, it wasn't as if he had to do a lot of packing, but it took forever. We kept changing plane reservations. San Francisco to L.A. is a commuter run. There are flights at least every hour, sometimes more. We made reservations for ten, changed them to noon, then to three in the afternoon, then five-thirty. David kept hanging back, kept smoking, and everyone else had gone home to bed. Jan was going to go too, so she did the same slow dance. Jackson and I were baby-sitting the two of them, moving them ever closer to the door in tiny, incremental steps until it started to get dark again. That's when David broke down and tried to plead that he couldn't make a commercial flight. He was too grungy, too sick, they wouldn't let him and Jan on the plane, ya-ta-da, ya-ta-da. Jackson called his bluff and said, "Okay, if you can't fly commercial, we'll go charter." Next thing David knew, we were at Butler Aviation Terminal at San Francisco International, getting on a Cessna with a flight plan to Palomar Airport in*

Carlsbad, California, only a few miles from the Scripps Hospital. Jackson and I rode up front; David and Jan huddled behind a curtain in the back. They actually freebased in the plane, lighting their pipe with a propane torch at twelve thousand feet. The pilot never knew and I wasn't sure. David told me later.

Despite the invitation to fiery disaster in the air, the flight was made without incident. A limo and driver met the plane at the darkened little private field in Carlsbad in a scene that must've looked like a clandestine operation; to avoid the press, the driver hadn't been informed of his passengers' identities. Nobody was supposed to know that David Crosby was checking himself in for rehabilitation, accompanied by his companion Jan and escorted by Jackson Browne. Unfortunately, the driver was a long-haired rock 'n' roll fan who spotted Jackson and David instantly. He was tipped to keep his mouth shut and ominous hints were dropped that if the *Enquirer* got this story, responsible people would assume it was the poor driver who leaked the details. He agreed to keep quiet. The quartet got to the hospital after the evening meal and began the tedious process of getting David and Jan admitted. There was no Blue Cross or medical insurance, just a personal check for thirty-five hundred dollars, written by Graham Nash to the facility. It took a while for Graham's check to be verified and approved by the business office (they had gone home for the day), but eventually David and Jan were qualified as patients. The head of the drug rehab program arrived to take David and Jan's histories and give them the "new patient" orientation. He knew they were high, understood and accepted it, and told them he was a recovered addict himself, an alcoholic doctor who had gotten into the habit of writing himself prescriptions for speed and opiates (apparently a common problem among physicians). Sincere and committed to helping other addicts recover, his conversation revealed that he didn't know a whole lot about freebasing.

The hospital's policy was to separate coaddicted couples; Jan and David wanted to sleep together, a couple of wounded interdependent dopers. They were assigned to different rooms. David spent a restless night. Jan may or may not have experienced improper treatment at the hands of the admitting physician; she's not sure herself.

JAN DANCE: *I think he came on to me. It's just something a woman knows. He took me into a room and he said, "Take off all your clothes. I want to examine you." That didn't sound funny, so I did. Then he started to touch me, not like a doctor would, and I said, "Hey, this is not cool," and he says, "Okay, okay, we'll finish this later." I either shook him up or jumped to a conclusion, but I don't think I was wrong. They separated us. David was in one room, I was in another, and I didn't like that. I thought, "If I'm really going to accept that I need help, please, God, let it be together." I was so frightened that the separation was going to last forever. Somewhere in the back of my mind, that's what it signified. The next morning when I got up, I went straight to David's room and I said, "Look, this is what I think happened to me last night and I don't want to stay here. Would it be okay if I left?" He said, "I don't really like it here either. I'm going to leave too."*

After David and Jan had gone off to bed, Jackson and this author made their way back to the airfield where the plane was still waiting, the meter running. The pilot had to fly back to San Francisco and the two weary escorts would ride as far as Burbank, back in their hometown of Los Angeles. Jackson's number one man, a road and tour manager called Buddha, met them at the airport and drove them home. After nearly forty-eight hours awake, baby-sitting and hand-holding David and Jan from Marin to Scripps Hospital, they were exhausted. At nine in the morning, after only a few hours' sleep, the phone rang with word from La Jolla. David and Jan had checked themselves out of the hospital without telling anyone their destination.

JAN DANCE: *We packed our stuff and instead of going to the first class —or whatever they had scheduled for us—we went to the elevator and this nurse comes running over to us and says, "Wait! Wait! You can't leave. You're signed in and everything," and David says, "Well, now I'm signed out." I'll grant that I could have made up three-quarters of my vision of what happened in order to leave because I obviously wasn't ready to accept help at that time; that was my own personal world in a nutshell. But I do believe, with all my heart, that the doctor did something improper and that David made his own decision. There were many times that we each came to our own conclusions, then came to each other with those conclusions; we may have fed each other.*

JACKSON BROWNE: *After the intervention, it was clear that we did everything we could. That was when I realized I was double-parked with my own family and I could be towed away. I didn't have the time to spend indefinitely with somebody who really didn't have the desire to change. You begin to write somebody off and say, "This is a terrible waste, but I can't invest any more hope or belief. It's too painful to stand around, hoping that he gets his act together. Maybe I won't even worry about it anymore and go do my other stuff." No matter how much we talked, we'd come to the same place: "Well, you know, like, what more can anyone do?" All I could do was be angry because my deepest feelings of friendship were being turned away.*

CARL GOTTLIEB: *We were dragging ass by the time we got back to L.A.; we had to stay awake without drugs in order to set an example for David and because of the politics of the situation—we couldn't very well exhort him to quit doing dope and stop ruining his life if we were doing anything stronger than black coffee and No Doz to stay conscious. It was almost dawn by the time I got into my own bed and I hadn't been sleeping more than a couple of hours when the call came from Bob Wilson up north with the bad news: David and Jan left Scripps, they were on the road somewhere, no one knew where, and the whole intervention was a big bust. That's when I gave up on David. The whole event was a dead loss; we spent time, effort, and emotional resources and got nothing in return. Not only that, it cost us all money. Jackson had to pay an enormous bill for the private airplane charter and the limo, I don't think the hospital refunded Graham's thousands, and Bob Wilson never paid me back whatever I lent him in anticipation of some grant money he was expecting for a musician's recovery and resource center. David was supposed to be the first in a series of dependent musicians and artists that would be*

helped by this foundation, to be called—seriously—Chopped Liver.
I'm sure the name had some significance then. Today, I can't figure
out what the hell it was supposed to mean. After David's failure,
nothing much happened and I heard that Wilson eventually moved
to Hawaii. Nobody offered to reimbursed me for the bribe I paid the
limo driver.

We were always glad to be home and when I said, "Hello,
House!", I meant it. When twenty people said, "Hello, David!"
back, it was a bit of a shock, and then when we saw who it was,
we knew what was happening. It was awkward in every way that a
thing can be awkward. We were instantly on the defensive, naturally, because we knew what was coming. Apparently the game
plan involved splitting us up, which is never a good idea with me
and Jan. It doesn't work because we don't split easily. The accepted wisdom of recovery is to divide couples. Very often one
will make it and the other will not or one will succeed at a different rate than the other or one slipping pulls both of them down.
Consequently, it was difficult to get a recovery facility to accept us
as a couple. The intervention was well intentioned and incredible
painful. It was obvious that those people loved us and I was
moved to tears by that and by having to confront what it all
meant. It's a very painful thing to have all of your friends—one
after another—tell you, "Hey, look. This used to be good about
you and it isn't anymore." "That used to be good about you. That
doesn't work anymore." "We're all terrified." I remember Carl's
words: "I hate to think about your fat little feet drumming on the
floor." He knew about the seizures and I remember the looks on
everybody's faces when it came up.
    The flaw in their plan was the fact that nobody wanted Jan to
go with me to the hospital. I don't think anybody really understood how much we loved each other and I also think they made
the mistake of trying to find a scapegoat, loving me and thinking
it must be all Jan's fault. The truth is that I turned Jan on to base,
not the other way around. It wasn't her fault. We were coaddicted

and we had no intention of being split up. The whole confrontation had inherent problems: for one thing, there was a stranger in the middle of it, the guy who was supposed to be an expert. He was not good at communicating, was not powerful, didn't understand me or the situation real well, and wasn't the right guy for the job. For another, I was totally lost: I didn't believe I could quit; I didn't want to face trying to quit; I didn't have any idea of how to quit. I didn't think any of the people at the intervention knew anything about what we were up against. I didn't think that people who were supposed to be experts on drug recovery in those days knew anything about freebase or the intensity of addiction involved or how to deal with it. I felt frustrated because if you said "freebase" to somebody in the rehabilitation and recovery business, they would say, "Yeah, cocaine." And you'd say, "No no, freebase," and they'd say, "Right, cocaine base. We understand." And you'd say, "No no, *base*. Cocaine is one thing. Base is another thing." And they'd say, "It's just cocaine." They didn't know. They're starting to learn only now, years later.

The whole episode served a purpose—it rattled our cage. I had built-in cop-outs: they shouldn't have tried to separate us; they should have realized this was not a normal situation. Those would be my excuses to not do anything. By morning we got to a point where I said I would go if Jan could go with me. We would go to Scripps because they'd take us both, even though we'd be in separate rooms. It might have even worked—if we'd been ready and willing. Carl and Jackson were so patient and tried so hard; they agreed to Jan's coming along and I couldn't think of any more objections. I delayed and dragged my feet as much as I could because I wanted some stash so I could get high on the way to quit drugs. Eventually, we went in a private plane and Jan and I sat in the back where you could pull that little curtain. We smoked all the way there.

When we got to the hospital, we found that doctors and counselors were pathetically ignorant about base and what it does and how it works. That tied right into my cunning as an addict. A person who is severely addicted is looking for every possible way out. He's looking for an excuse. He's looking at you, saying, "You're going to fuck up. I'm going to get to go get high." They didn't stand a chance. We weren't ready. We were looking for them to be wrong, looking for an excuse to leave. We knew we could. I was so severely addicted that if I could leave a place, I would. I would hit a peak of anxiety and a trough of despair and a wave of addictive compulsion would overwhelm me and I couldn't handle it. The next morning we split. We were very crazy. We got in a cab, made friends with the cab driver, and said, "Fuck going to the airport. Drive us to Los Angeles." He drove us to Los Angeles while we freebased in the back of the cab. I had hidden enough dope and paraphernalia and the hospital had missed it. The only thing I did right in the whole intervention was to call up the key people afterward and say, "Look, I'm sorry I messed up. I know you did it out of love. Thank you for caring." That was the only correct moment in the whole damn mess and even that was just more pain to all of them. It cost me what was left of my old friends.

JAN DANCE: *It was such a shock to us; first to have gone on the road and then to have had those seizures. What we wanted was for it to be David's first major solo tour. If it came out right, we could've said, "Look, see? He can still do the music." Instead, we had massive amounts of really bad cocaine that made us have those seizures and then we came home to our house and were seriously confronted by all our friends and then we had this episode at the hospital. One way or another, we got total strangers to help us get home. God only knows what happened. I'm not real sure. I guess we hitched a ride to the nearest dealer, which was our nature. We'd run out of drugs. We'd been, like, a couple of days without them. Our bodies were screaming for that medicine. We knew not to go to any of those people who'd been at the intervention, so we went somewhere and copped and then dealt with life as it dealt with us.*

For a few days they stayed underground, traveling from dealer's house to dealer's house, making their way laboriously up the coast back to Mill Valley, where they sank back into the same dismal routine of scoring, cooking, fixing, smoking, and looking for money to repeat the cycle. For the rest of that spring and summer, David rehearsed with his new band and played solo gigs and benefits in the Bay Area. Cameron Crowe, a reporter for *Rolling Stone*, went with Joel Bernstein to see David perform solo at the Great American Music Hall in San Francisco. Joel went home to sleep; Cameron went to David's house afterward. He had been writing about Crosby, Stills, Nash, and Young since his first days on the paper and was no stranger to Crosby. He had conducted many interviews with David over the years and considered himself as much a friend as a journalist. David was always open with Cameron and permitted him full access onstage, backstage, and offstage. Crowe's piece on Crosby was never submitted; it was only written as a way of exorcising the unforgettable encounter.

In it, he describes a life that most of Crosby's friends no longer saw because of their increasing alienation. The Mill Valley house was dusty, the pool was stagnant, and the place reeked of old cat food and used cat litter. David would disappear for half an hour at a time and was clearly getting loaded. He was mouthing the defensive lines that everyone else had heard: "I know what they're saying about me. That I'm fucked up. That I'm a junkie. Well, a junkie is only a junkie if he doesn't get the work done. I get the work done . . . Well, let me tell you. I have a drug problem. But I've always gotten high. I've always gotten as stoned as I could get for all those songs, all the favorites. It's not that different now." David mentioned that Stills and Nash were doing an album without him; that hurt. Obviously in psychic and emotional pain, he excused himself to get high and was gone another half hour. When David came back into the untidy room, Cameron noticed his eyes were glazed and darting. Crosby asked him to stay the night so that they could continue the interview in the morning. Cameron declined, but offered to come back and see David the following week, when he would be performing with his new band. David thanked him. Cameron asked if there was anything he could do to help. David said, "Write a review. Tell everybody I was great. I was great tonight, wasn't I? Just tell them I was great."

CAMERON CROWE: *He clasped his arms as he sat at his kitchen table. I caught a glimpse . . . there, in the crook of his arm, was something much different than a simple needle mark. It was as if a divot, a wedge of his skin, had been cut out. Fresh blood dripped down his arm, almost onto the table. He had just shot up. "You can't drive to the city tonight," said Crosby, eyes flashing. "You'll get busted." "I gotta go." I had never turned the tape recorder on. "I'll walk you to your car." Crosby got up, walked the steps of his house and gave me a quick tour of the garage, where he was rehearsing with his band. Old CSNY Gold Records gathered dust, lying around half-cracked. "I keep the records out here," said Crosby. "That's how much I respect them." He smirked. "I was great tonight, wasn't I?" "You were." "I was," said Crosby. "I was great."*

The show had been good. The smallish audience included fans who knew every song and followed David's career. It was not an impartial crowd. The level of self-delusion was high and it was a fundamental problem that had no solution. As David is fond of saying to friends who are the same shape now as he was then: "Denial is not a river in Egypt." Denial was what David was practicing every day, despite his continuing physical problems, his mounting addiction, and Jan's inevitable physical decline. Both of them were increasingly less healthy and small sores had become large infections. Cameron had noticed both Jan and David using heavy pancake makeup to cover the nickel-sized lesions that were starting to become apparent everywhere to everyone.

David's self-esteem and historically strong ego might have been tested that summer, but just when it would have been useful for Crosby to confront his situation, Stills and Nash came back into his life. They didn't want to, but a series of business and professional decisions made it necessary. Keeping to their intention to record without David, they had proceeded to fashion an album themselves for delivery to Atlantic Records, the company with which they had the longest and most successful history.

I knew I could still function as Crosby, Stills, and Nash—if only I could get them to be willing to work with me as I was. At that time, Graham was disillusioned and offended by the extent of my obsession and addiction and hurt by the fact that it took me away from him as a friend. Graham had already said, "You've got to get some treatment and quit before I can work with you again," and he meant it. He and Stephen had even started making an album by themselves. When Graham and Stephen went into the studio to try and make a record without me, I was crushed. I actually thought, "How could they do that? I'm wonderful. I don't have a problem." Nevertheless, they went into the studio and did some work with a bum band that wasn't any good. When I heard it, I said, "That's not good enough. You guys are kidding yourselves," and I walked out. I was right; they got a better band. They probably had about half a record. Atlantic had thought that they were going to try and involve me and when it became clear that it was just Stills and Nash, Ahmet told them, "That's not what we're paying for. We don't think it will sell." Our respective managements wanted money and pressure was brought to bear on Nash from all sides. It culminated with Atlantic Records saying flatly that the company didn't even want them to turn in a record without me, that nobody wanted a Stills-Nash album, that nobody would buy a Stills-Nash album, and they had better involve me— or forget it. Graham didn't have much choice, so he eventually made the call. I was totally triumphant. I said, "Aha! You see, you couldn't do it without me. You have to have me." It was the worst kind of ego stroke at exactly the wrong time. Graham and Stephen had gotten themselves into a situation they couldn't back out of. Stephen needed the money desperately and Graham had gotten himself contractually obligated. He had to finish the thing and he had taken all his money. He couldn't just pay it back. They were stuck. They had to do it. Graham changed his stance as gracefully as he could and invited me to Rudy Records in Hollywood. I was asked to bring some tracks from my aborted Capitol project. I brought "Delta" and "Might as Well Have a Good Time," which was to have been—ironically—the title tune of my solo album. I wanted to say, defiantly, that it was okay to be high all the time, even though for me it was degenerating into being low all the time.

I finished the record with them. I had been working on my solo album, so I had some good stuff. "Delta" was the last song I wrote before I came unglued. Graham and Stephen had been trying to carefully construct an album that would sound as much like the three of us as the two of them could make it. They used the considerable talents of some of the best singers in the country: Michael Finnegan, Timmy Schmidt, Arthur Garfunkel, and others, but nothing sounds like Crosby, Stills, and Nash except Crosby, Stills, and Nash, which is why, when Graham and I made duet albums earlier, we deliberately didn't try to emulate the sound of CSN, but tried to develop a sound of our own. It's my opinion that because Stephen and Graham were afraid of rejection and criticism, they made most of the tracks of the new album too carefully. They were seamless and finely crafted. By being the last one involved, I managed to bring some specific qualities of liveliness to the tracks and I was able to add my own peculiar harmonic sensibilities. There was one notable exception, the title song "Daylight Again," which is a haunting, beautiful piece about the Civil War and war in general. Arthur Garfunkel, one of the finest harmony singers of our times, did a beautifully fitted and uncanny piece of work when he added the third part to that song. I heard it in the studio and said I wouldn't touch it. I could've (I suppose) replaced it note for note, but it deserved to stand as it was and I doubt if I could've matched it, particularly at that time in my life. I wound up adding a fourth part at one point in the song where it really worked well. We added Stephen and Graham's vocals into the harmony stacks on "Delta" and they replaced my harmonies on "Might as Well Have a Good Time."

Of any group album I've ever made, I'm probably least happy with that one; I can admit now that it was my fault as much as anyone's. The album wasn't a genuine example of the Crosby, Stills, and Nash creative chemistry, regardless of how much chemistry was involved in my coming to the project. We work best when we work together, in various combinations and permutations, pulling each other up, bringing each other along, driving each other to a level that generally eludes us when we struggle alone. It's my fault that the three of us weren't there all along, bumping heads and hearts to make the best album we possibly could. Due largely to Nash's heroic efforts, it's an album of which I'm now proud, even though it included a song that made me very uncomfortable at the time, a song of Graham's called "Into the Darkness," whose title was a turnaround on a song that was written by Graham, Craig Doerge, and myself, a beautiful tune called "Out of the Darkness." "Into the Darkness" was a powerful and deeply felt indictment of me and my behavior; in hindsight, I'm no longer uncomfortable with the song and I can only love Graham for caring enough to write it.

> While *Daylight Again* was being finished, David continued to play small solo acoustic dates booked by David Scott. Jan was with him constantly, a small shadow at his side.

DAVID SCOTT: *He was pretty normal. It took a couple of grams to get him out the door; in those times it was a sustaining joke between us that David always knew I could always get mine. I could go out and get two or three ounces. Then to David, I'd say, "There's only two grams." It got us to the job. When we got there, he'd want to score an eighth immediately and maybe another eighth to get home, but it was not like ounces and ounces. I booked the gigs and went out as road manager, which made it fun because I could hear the music. We played all over California. We went to New York in '81 and played Town Hall. David sold it out. He also fired me there. He got up off the chair at the end of the set and the place was going nuts, it was fucking great, he was getting an ovation. As he stood up, the chair went over and a Colt .45 slid out from the inside pocket of his coat and would have been seen by the whole audience, so I leaped across the stage and knocked into him, fell over on the chair, and put the gun up in the coat and took the coat offstage. He came back raving.*

"You motherfucker. That was mine." Fired me on the spot. I held up the gun and he went, "Oh."

> At the same time as all this was going on, as the Mill Valley house was slipping into decay and dissolution, David still had the problem of dealing with Debbie Donovan and the daughter they had. Debbie had moved south to Santa Barbara and it was getting increasingly difficult for David to play even a minimal role as a parent.

Debbie had a problem with booze and with Valium, which led her to get help, join a program, and beat it seven or eight years before I did. She quit completely and has never gone back. I'm eternally grateful to Debbie for the wonderful job she's done at one of the most difficult things that's ever presented to anyone: being a single parent. There were times when I used up all my money on drugs and didn't send her the child support that she needed. There were other times when I was flush, when I bought her a house in Montecito and a brand-new BMW. For a couple of years, Graham paid for my kid's schooling because I simply spent everything I had on dope. It's something of which I'm ashamed, it's difficult for me to deal with it, and I've had to look it square in the eye and say, "Right, I did that. That's part of drug behavior and one of the reasons I don't do it anymore." I deal with it and move on. I can't sit here and beat myself over the head with it because it's unfortunate and painful, but that's what happened.

Even though I'm sure Debbie was hurt that I had fallen in love with somebody else, she never hated me and she never did what normally happens between people who split up after they have a child. Normally they fire the child back and forth at each other like a missile, like a shuttlecock with a bomb on it, saying things like "That lousy bastard. Let me tell you what he did!" and "That no-good bitch. Why doesn't she understand?" The poor kid is taught by his or her parents to hate his or her parents, a totally destructive thing. People do it all the goddamn time. Thank God and thank Debbie Donovan that she didn't do that to me—and she could have. I was wide open for it. I was a drug addict. I was a perfect target. Debbie could have absolutely raised that kid to hate me, arranged things so that Donovan would have never even spoken to me, but Debbie never did that. She always made it possible for me to have contact with the kid in whatever was the best way at the time. Early in Donovan's life I wasn't so screwed up. It got worse as it went along, so the contacts became more difficult. Donovan would come and be with me for a weekend or something, but she would be out there in the other room with some stranger and I would be off in the bathroom with the pipe. She was just a kid, but she saw what was going on. She's very honest. She'd say, "I love Daddy, but he's always in the bathroom."

DEBBIE DONOVAN: *I definitely felt uncomfortable when she was with him. She'd go for a week at a time; she was still so young that it didn't matter if she left school. David would call and say, "I wanna spend some time with Donovan." I'd say, "Well, how're you doing?" And he'd say, "I'm doing the same." I'd ask him, "How do you feel about having Donovan around there?" That would end the conversation. I dropped her off once and I heard they had worked for two days to clean it up and it was a mess when I walked in. If that was cleaned up, I can imagine . . . No, I don't even want to imagine. It was the last time that Donovan went to visit. My awakening made me want to distance myself from David and his problem and I wanted to heal my child and get back on the straight road to myself. She was still too young to ask about things. I knew that whenever he'd be around, she'd be uncomfortable; she wouldn't know who her daddy was. I always told her that Daddy was sick. That was how I dealt with it. If Daddy acted strange, it was because he was sick. He had a problem with drugs and I had a problem with alcohol. Donovan was still very young, so it was only by repetition that I could keep telling her all this. The last time she went to see him, she was uncomfortable up there, but at least she knew that Daddy was sick. At least she was able to take that with her. David was sick.*

3 5 7

DONOVAN ANNE CROSBY: *I went to his house once and there was this guy who came to visit in the night and after he came I didn't see my dad much. In the morning, after Daddy was awake and I was trying to get some cereal, I told him that there was no milk. He said, "Oh, it's real easy. You can take anything, water even. Personally, I enjoy apple juice," and he poured apple juice in the cereal and he started eating it. I thought that was pretty weird. Another time I woke up one morning and there was nothing to eat and I told him and he said, "You want some ice cream?" That was cool because I never got ice cream for breakfast when I was living with my mom.*

When David passed through Santa Barbara, he would stop to see Debbie and Donovan. Sometimes he'd be alone; sometimes he was with Jan.

DEBBIE DONOVAN: *He'd say, "As soon as the freebasing stops, we'll get back together again." He said he wanted to have a family and help raise Donovan and that kept me going for a long time, although I'm sure that as soon as he went out the door, he forgot about it. When he came here he wanted Donovan to believe that we lived together and that whenever Daddy was gone it was because he was on the road. David wanted Donovan to believe that she had a daddy and a mommy and that there was a nuclear family, even though we had the agreement that he would go off and live with Nancy or whoever. I didn't see any point in it. I'd hope that we could get back together at some point, but eventually the whole thing got very old and stale. When he was with Jan and he came to visit, she would sit and wait in the car. For hours at a time. Talk about neglect. One time they showed up in the middle of the night. Just—bam!—him and Jan needing someplace to stay. So I just folded out the couch in the den and started to go to my bedroom and David followed me, all ready to come and sleep with me. I said, "Wait a minute. You can do this to me, but you're not going to turn around and do that to her. You sleep out there." Then the checks stopped coming and the lies started. "I'm gonna be there at three." Seven o'clock would come. No phone call, no nothing. It was tough for Donovan 'cause kids don't have much of a sense of time and she'd be upset if I made other plans because she'd believe that Daddy was coming. After a time, I stopped telling her. When he did arrive, we would be freebasing and we'd lock Donovan out of the room because he didn't want to have the baby around. I would say to David, "Okay, let's just stop this for a day and play. Let's go to the zoo. Let's go to the beach. Let's spend some time with Donovan." I remember talking to him on the phone one time when he was coming to town and I said, "Let's plan on having a day where we can not smoke it." He said, "What are you talking about?" and I said, "You know, have a straight day. You've done that before." And he said, "Don't you realize? I never stop."*

It wasn't an exaggeration. While David was awake, which was for inhumanly long periods of time, he would be smoking freebase. He would smoke in airplanes; not just on private charter flights, but on commercial airliners, sitting in first-class. He could ignite a propane torch behind his parka and, under the pretense of sleeping or pulling the coat over his head, take hits from a glass pipe between meal and beverage service at thirty thousand feet. David could smoke at the wheel of a car he was driving; using both hands to manage torch and pipe, he would steer with his knees. "I'm the best no-hands knee-steering driver in the world," he would reassure startled passengers, this author included, as he took a hit from the pipe while doing seventy on the highway. As disturbing as this might have been to others, it was a way of life to David and Jan, even though they had both experienced grand mal seizures while basing. On March 28, 1982, Crosby was driving a rented car to Orange County to play at a No Nukes rally outside the San Onofre nuclear power plant in Southern California. He had been smoking freebase, although he probably had both hands on the wheel when the seizure took him. Police reports describe what happened next:

STATEMENT BY WITNESS: *Witness related he was southbound on 405 approx. 20 car lengths behind V-1 [Crosby's car]. V-1 was in one of the righthand lanes when it suddenly went to the left, as if to change lanes. V-1 kept going left and struck the center divider. DR-1*

[Crosby] made no attempt to brake or swerve. Witness thought DR-1 had a heart attack or fell asleep.

OFFICER BAECKEL (COSTA MESA POLICE DEPARTMENT): *I arrived and saw Crosby sitting in the driver's seat of the red Granada, which had collided into the center divider fence. I asked Crosby if he was all right [he had blood on his face]. Crosby told me he was late for a "gig" and had to go. I told him he had been involved in a collision. Crosby said he hadn't. He then started the car and was preparing to leave. I reached in and turned off the car. Paramedic assisted me in taking Crosby out of the car. Crosby did not know what today was or where he was or what had happened. I looked inside the car and in plain sight, on the driver's floorboard, I saw a propane bottle and "bong." I left these in place. Highway Patrol arrived and took over the collision scene and investigation.*

CHP OFFICER GLIDDEN: *When I looked in the vehicle, I noticed a glass bottle with two pipes extending from it and a glass tube sitting on the driver's floorboard. Both had a brownish residue within them . . . When I went to the right passenger door to look for registration, I saw a leather zipper bag on the right floorboard. The center portion of the bag was open, exposing a chrome .45 cal. automatic (#310543). When I lifted the bag, I noticed in a side compartment several small glass bottles containing a white powder residue . . . Bag contained numerous drug paraphernalia items (razors, glass tubes, matches, instruments, etc.). A gray plastic film canister was found to contain a white powder, which was later determined to be baking soda. The contents of the bag and the items found on the floor are commonly used for "freebasing" cocaine . . . based on the nature of the T/C (drifting off the road into c/d fence), witness statements on the subj's incoherent manner and the drug items found, I determined the subj was possibly under the influence of drugs. He was placed under arrest for 20152(A) V.C.*

From the emergency medical facility, David was transported to the Orange County Jail in Santa Ana, where he was formally charged with driving under the influence of drugs or alcohol and carrying a concealed weapon. He was released on twenty-five hundred dollars' bail, but he missed the gig. Graham and Stephen went on without him.

I had a seizure from toxic saturation in the fast lane doing sixty-five miles an hour on the San Diego Freeway. One minute I was driving along, going south to play a concert. The next thing I knew I was parked facing into the center divider fence, talking to a California Highway Patrol officer and a paramedic and there was about a hundred yards of fence torn up behind me and the front of my car was a mess. The worst part was not being busted or having a gun or being charged with possession of drug paraphernalia, but realizing it wasn't just me that was in danger. What if I had jumped the fence and crossed into the opposing lanes of traffic? The luckiest thing that would have happened would have been dying alone. What if I hit a family and wiped out three kids? Could I have lived with that? Seizures from toxic saturation were not only a danger to myself and Jan. If I had one in a car, I became the kind of menace that I dreaded, someone out of control who could cross the center line and hit my daughter or my friends, someone who could kill innocent people. I had a night in jail to think about that, then I got bailed out, but not without notice by the press: the story made the wire services.

WASHINGTON POST: *Rock singer David Crosby, who was arrested and charged last weekend with driving while intoxicated and concealing a weapon, will face narcotics charges as well, according to authorities in Santa Ana, Calif. Crosby's rented car hit a freeway divider while he was en route to a demonstration at the San Onofre nuclear power plant. He was to perform with rock singers Graham Nash and Stephen Stills, his partners in the 60's group Crosby, Stills, and Nash. Lt. Wyatt Hart of the Santa Ana Sheriff's Office said that in addition to a gun, Quaaludes, cocaine, and drug paraphernalia were found in the singer's car. Asked why he was carrying a loaded .45-caliber pistol, Crosby said simply, "John Lennon."*

David hired an experienced criminal lawyer to handle the case and went back to Mill Valley with Jan, in order to prepare for a road trip with his band. This time they were going to Texas to play dates in Dallas and Houston. Jan had dental problems relating to her car accident; she wasn't going. She had also blacked out at the wheel of a car, driving back to Mill Valley from the San Francisco Airport. In Jan's case, she was alone, late at night.

JAN DANCE: *The first time I passed out at the wheel of an automobile I might have had a seizure; I'm not sure. I was barely awake when I rode with David to the airport. I was to drive the car back home and I was so sleepy and lethargic from having been up all night and from not having any drugs that when I started to drive home from the San Francisco Airport I felt myself falling asleep so I pulled off the road a number of times to get some rest. When I got about a mile from our house, I felt myself falling asleep again. Instead of pulling over, I tried to keep going. I woke up having hit the steering wheel with my mouth. I cut my tongue, so deep they had to sew it back together, and I lost all of the bottom teeth in my mouth. They just popped out from hitting the steering wheel. I was taken in an ambulance to an emergency place; they wouldn't give me anything because they thought I'd done it on purpose and that I'd come to the hospital for drugs. They told me that. They referred me to a dental surgeon, who they called first and told I was on my way and probably wanted drugs. I got there and the guy gave me some Novocain, told me he didn't want to work on me—I don't know why. He was mumbling throughout the whole ordeal that he didn't want to be working on me. It was awful!*

What was worse was that Jan would be alone in Mill Valley while David left to play clubs on the road. In Dallas, there used to be a club called Cardi's; a long room with a bar and some pool tables and a rough stage at one end, with a dressing room/backstage area off to one side. It was a sleazy joint, but it had a loud and steady clientele who appreciated live music. Cardi's liked to book name entertainers, when the club could afford them. David Crosby and his band were a good act for the joint and they were booked during the Easter holidays; the first set was scheduled for Monday, April 12. It was exactly two weeks after his release from the Orange County jail on the drugs and concealed weapon charges, which were still pending. Tony Saunders, a large black bass player, doubled as road manager and assistant to David. He was standing in front of the dressing room, blocking the entrance, when Officer Chris Rinebarger of the Dallas Police Department arrived.

COURT OF APPEALS, FIRST SUPREME JUDICIAL DISTRICT OF TEXAS: *The appellant [David Crosby], a well-known nightclub and recording entertainer, had contracted with Cardi's, a Dallas nightclub, to perform on the night of April 12, 1982 . . . Cardi's was a club licensed to sell alcoholic beverages by the Texas Alcohol Beverage Commission. Further, the contract between appellant and Cardi's provided that appellant was to be furnished with a private dressing room secluded from the general public . . . . Between 11:45 P.M. on April 12, 1982, and midnight, Dallas police officers received a call that a man was refusing to leave the Medallion Shopping Center, which is in the immediate vicinity of Cardi's. Two police officers, Officers Rinebarger and Holly, responded to the call; however, they shortly thereafter received instructions to disregard the call because other police units had sufficiently covered the situation. Notwithstanding, Rinebarger and Officer Holly decided to proceed to Cardi's as a backup unit. Upon arriving at the nightclub the officers discovered that the other police units had indeed resolved any problem which may have existed outside Cardi's. Nevertheless, Rinebarger and Holly decided to enter Cardi's to conduct a "routine investigation, inspection for liquor violations," presumably pursuant to T.A.B.C. s101.03. After entering Cardi's and inspecting the customer area of the premises and during an intermission, Officer Rinebarger stepped upon the stage and approached an adjacent room, whose entrance was covered by a drawn opaque curtain. As Rinebarger made his approach to this entrance, he was intercepted by a man who placed his fist in Rinebarger's chest and said, "You can't go in there." Rinebarger responded by pushing the man aside and walking around him, pulling the curtain back, and entering the dressing room. Upon entering the dressing room he observed several people seated on a couch and Crosby crouched on the floor with a propane torch in one hand and a glass pipe in the other. Rinebarger also testified that he then noticed an unzipped athletic bag on appellant's lap, and when he [Rinebarger] looked inside the unzipped bag he saw a Baggie which contained a white powdery substance which he had reason to believe was cocaine. Rinebarger arrested the appellant, zipped and confiscated the athletic bag, seized the torch and pipe, and transported the appellant to the Dallas City Hall. While on the elevator riding up to the jail Rinebarger believed the seized athletic bag felt unusually heavy, whereupon he searched it and found a .45 Colt automatic pistol. This was the basis of the weapon offense.*

JAY DAVID: *It was a one-nighter. A very long night. Cardi's was a long, thin hall and down at the stage was a dressing room. They had built a false wall which did not quite go up to the ceiling of the room so you can hear people walking to the men's room and the ladies' room and there was the thinnest of plywood doors and a little curtain separating the stage from the dressing room. Open a little door and you're right on the stage. David had done the acoustic set, after which we'd take a break for anywhere from five minutes to an hour, depending on how much he had. I'm drumming on my knee and I hear* bang, bang, bang, bang! *"Get the fuck out of the way, you nigger cocksucker," I look up and here's this cop in all of his fuckin' finery. He looked almost angelic. He was beaming with this glow of the spider that caught the fly and he looks at me and says, "Where is David Crosby?" Crosby's smoking now; he's got his fuckin' hundred-dollar gram and he's puffing away. I jump up and I put my back to the cop and go over to David in the corner and I'm saying, "David, get rid of it. Get rid of it!" And the motherfucker's trying to get around me. I'm trying to slap the pipe out of Crosby's hand. He's*

fighting for the pipe, saying, "What are you doing that for?" The
cop got around me, me not being the biggest guy in the world, looked
at David, and just grinned. He said, "David Crosby, don't you
remember what happened to Richard Pryor?" He reached into a blue
bag, I'll never forget it, and said, "You're under arrest." At that
point I'm nuts. The whole place crowded in with the cop. What am I
going to do? Who's going to tell the crowd, man? What the fuck's
going to happen now? So, I tell 'em. "Show can't continue." "Booo-
ooo!" "But we're going to give you your money back." "Yaaa-aay!"
"I don't know what's going on, but you'll definitely see it on TV
tonight or tomorrow, kids. Now, please leave." And that was it.

David was out on bail in four hours; he left the next day to
play a job in Houston. Again, the press picked up the story.
This is the UPI wire account: "Authorities are preparing
formal drug and weapon charges against rock singer David
Crosby, who was arrested in his nightclub dressing room between performances. It was his second weapon and drugs
arrest in three weeks. Police spokesman Bob Shaw said cocaine was seized from Crosby and a .45-caliber pistol also
was confiscated, he said. Crosby, formerly of the Byrds and
Crosby, Stills, Nash, and Young, was arrested early Tuesday
at Cardi's rock club. He was released on a writ of habeas
corpus and directed to return for a court hearing, May 6."
Texas gun laws reflect that state's frontier heritage and it's a
felony to carry a loaded firearm into a place licensed to sell
alcohol beverages. It's another kind of a felony to be in possession of contraband drugs. It escalates the prosecutor's
zeal when you're charged with both felonies in the same
instance, especially if you're a long-haired rock 'n' roll performer from out of state. Knox Fitzpatrick, an assistant district attorney in Dallas, appeared for "the people." Jay Ethington, a prominent Dallas criminal defense attorney, was
engaged to represent David in *The State of Texas* v. *David
Van Cortlandt Crosby.*

JAY ETHINGTON: *I got a phone call at home around midnight that*
some guy named David Crosby had been arrested in Dallas and,
candidly, I was half-asleep. The call was from some lawyers in Cali-
fornia whom I'd met at a seminar or something; I'd heard of them,

they'd heard of me. I told them, "Thanks. Fine. I'll look into it,"
hung up, disconnected the phone, and fell fast asleep. The next day
several younger lawyers in Dallas were all a-buzz about the big fight
that several lawyers had had at the police station that night, trying
to post the bond for Crosby. There'd been quite a struggle. I thought,
"Oh shoot. I've lost an opportunity to represent somebody in a high-
profile case," but the phone messages in my office from California
indicated that they wanted me to represent Crosby, so the next day I
started looking into the case. I appreciate music and all that, but I
really hadn't spent a lot of time thinking about David Crosby in
many years. The name didn't really mean that much to me. But in a
day or two, I realized that it was an interesting case and I wasn't so
much concerned about the personality as I was about the case because
I could sense that this case was a setup. Something stunk about it. I
knew there would be plenty to work with that would be fun—maybe
the police would overreach. It was going to be worthwhile getting
involved, so I did.

When David was arrested, everyone ran for a phone and
called someone: managers, lawyers, agents, friends. Everyone
who was contacted got in touch with a law office in Dallas
and there really wasn't anyone in charge. As a result, there
was a hassle of lawyers (much like a pride of lions or a gaggle
of geese) quarreling over who would get to bail David out of
the Dallas City Jail.

Conventional management types were starting to put
some distance between themselves and David; his difficulties
made involvement with him an increasing burden with a de-
creasing rate of compensation. The more trouble he got into,
the more time and effort would have to be spent on coordinating legal teams, arranging bookings around court
dates, and paying for defenses and the appeals that would
surely follow if there were (God forbid) convictions. At the
same time, David was less and less capable of generating any
substantial income and he had his own priorities as to who
got paid first. He would always show up for the gig and that
made him feel marginally in control. As long as he could
stand up to play and sing, he could earn enough money to
pay for the necessities of life. Those were, in descending or-

der of importance: drugs, drug paraphernalia, drugs to counteract the effects of other drugs, more drugs, then legal fees, tour expenses, food, shelter, medical care, and taxes. One business manager quit, another simply said, "There is no more money," and delivered all of David's records in a cardboard box to one of his many attorneys. Someone had to step in and help David with the details of his increasingly complicated and frustrating existence. Unfortunately, synchronicity was working against David. The man who came into his life was a classic case of the wrong guy in the right place at the worst time.

I met a guy we'll call Mort for legal reasons. Mort was the man with the smile and a very slippery fish to catch. He had done time, knew what the score would be if he was ever rearrested, and was determined to not get popped again. At the time we met, he had successfully avoided the law, despite years of smuggling and moving weight. Mort knew how to keep his profile down and his guard up and his only vice was the pipe. Except for that tragic flaw, he didn't use his own product. [The pipe finally got him.] His theory was that you could get away with anything if you kept up a solid front; he could see plainly that Jan couldn't keep up a good front. He wanted me clean-shaven and in fresh clothes and looking presentable. Then we could go smoke the pipe in back, like he did. That's how he handled it and he did handle it; he was a functioning baser then. If there's ever been such a thing as a functioning junkie, it was Mort. He was anti-Jan because she looked like a junkie cripple about to die and he wanted her out of the way. He also wanted her out of the way because she didn't trust him and she told me so. Mort would've preferred me more malleable. If he could get me alone, he figured he could manipulate me. I would've been controllable. He would have loved it if I had taken up with his sister Myrna; then he would have had me. But I was too much in love with Jan. I did spend some time with a short brunette we'll call Deedee (once again for legal reasons), but that was because she pushed herself into the scene.

Deedee wanted to be with me and although Mort didn't gener-

ate the attraction, he approved of her because she could be controlled. If Mort could have substituted Deedee for Jan, it would've
made his job easier. He was filling a self-created vacuum by becoming my personal manager. Deedee came to me via one of the
guys who worked for me and lived in the gatehouse. I pinned her
for a dummy, which she wasn't. Jan hated her because Deedee
would call and say things like "I wish you'd leave, so I could
move in." Deedee was nice. She cared about me, but I wasn't in
love with her. In point of fact, I don't think she was ever in love
with me; I think she wanted my house and the position. She liked
what she imagined the role could be. She had a vision of being
able to get me healthy and together so we could cruise into the
sunset together. Deedee put quite a bit of effort into trying to put
me with people who would try and help me get off drugs or try to
get me to a particular place or get sympathetic people to me. For
that, I thank her. For the next couple of years, Deedee was in and
out of my life, although my first and only commitment was to Jan.

Mort was a major supplier. He was Little Fred's connection
and Little Fred was one of my many dealers. Little Fred was a
flamboyant, funny, completely outrageous mover in the drug
world of Northern California. One of his houses was once raided
by twenty-one members of the law enforcement community, who
had the misfortune to miss the main stash. Fred introduced me to
Mort and that was that. I was glued to Mort like a tic because he
had kilos. Once I got involved with Mort, I sold dope for him. I
sold pounds and kilos. I had a scale. I had customers. I became a
minor wholesaler, dealing to retailers, although I never retailed. I
just sold pounds and kilos. I never did anything less than a pound
and I didn't step on it; I just marked it up a little bit. I don't like
stepping on dope. The retailers and distributors who dilute it are
the ones all strung out themselves. In order to support their habits, the normal profit isn't enough. They have to double and triple
it by cutting the dope in half, which they did and still do. I was
just as strung out, but I had other income, so I wasn't reduced to

adulterating what I sold. The normal markup of 400 percent worked perfectly well for me.

How did I get to move so easily in the world of dealers and movers and smugglers? Simple. Over the years, I had established myself as an immediately recognizable well-known doper with a positive public stance on drugs. That way I got to meet a lot of people in the dope business. Why would these dangerous paranoids admit me into their confidence and share their secrets? Because they all knew that I was not—could not—be the heat. Big-time dope movers have one chief worry in life: a cop or informer on the inside who's clean, someone who is not just another crook who's made a deal with the prosecutor in the hopes of buying a reduced sentence. Clean, credible evidence can destroy them. Anyone who could not possibly be an agent was—had to be —a friend. I was a known quantity. People knew who I was and where I had been since the sixties. One thing I wasn't was a cop, a snitch, or an informer. Since I was also a member of a major rock group, I had a certain status. That, by the way, rapidly faded and disappeared as I became known as a voracious base head. For the most part, people in the dope trade shun basers like the plague because basers, like locusts, will consume everything in sight, refuse to leave until it's all gone, promise anything to get more, never pay up on the promises, and are usually (in the terminal stages of their addiction) hotter than a two-dollar Mexican pistol.

Mort and David opened a joint bank account and Mort (ever the entrepreneur) structured some kind of deal: he'd advance David money and drugs, in exchange for a large ownership position and share in future income and royalties from new David Crosby projects: solo albums, tours, even David's share of CSN and CSNY income. Whatever income David had would go into their mutual enterprise. With the successful release of the *Daylight Again* album, Crosby, Stills, and Nash were once more on the charts. By June, "Wasted on the Way" was a *Billboard* Top 10 single and there had to be a tour. There was just too much money out there to ignore, the group hadn't worked on that scale for years, and everyone could use the money. Peter Golden was a personal manager who had been with Jackson Browne and had come up in the "traditional" way (from the William Morris Agency mail room). He became associated with a manager named Bill Siddons, who had inherited what was left of Crosby, Stills, and Nash. Bill Siddons handles Crosby to this day. Peter Golden is enjoying his retirement and remembers 1982.

PETER GOLDEN: *There was a conversation about "Wouldn't it be great if Crosby, Stills, and Nash did it together?" All I knew about Crosby was that he had a very bad reputation. He was reputed to be one of the foulest human beings to deal with and I knew people who had walked away from him even though they had made a lot of money from him and now he was a drug addict on top of everything else. We decided to have a meeting with the band and David came down for it. It was the first time I'd experienced Crosby: I think he was late and I'm not sure if he missed the plane and it was the next day or if he demanded a limo and we had to send him money to get him down here. We laid it out: "If you want to sing, if you want to be a part of this, you have to get clean." He was shocked that we would say this. "How dare you? I can perform onstage." So we issued a mandate: "If you're not clean, you don't perform." Later, Crosby, Stills, and Nash sang at the Rose Bowl and he wasn't clean. We were all-sold-out to whatever degree you want to say and it was magical. Good or bad, it was magical.*

Graham had organized a massive political demonstration and concert at the Rose Bowl in Pasadena. Among its many distinctions, the concert marked yet another public reunion of Crosby, Stills, and Nash. The event took place on Sunday, June 6, 1982.

PETER GOLDEN: *It was obvious that the way these three guys were going to earn a living was as Crosby, Stills, and Nash. I put out some feelers. "What do you think we can get?" I was astounded to find out we might get fifty thousand a night if we put them out on tour.* Daylight Again *was a record that was being put together for years in the worst way and it was not a great Crosby, Stills, and Nash record, but there were some possible hits on there—if anyone knows what hits are. We started to put the tour to bed and we're still laying out mandates to David. David was saying he's going to clean up and we all secretly knew he wasn't. We even prepared telegrams to send to promoters, saying* THE GROUP IS PREPARED TO GO ON, EVEN THOUGH DAVID IS: (A) HOSPITALIZED, (B) UNABLE TO APPEAR TONIGHT, (C) DEAD. DAVID WOULD HAVE WANTED IT THAT WAY. *You know, you spend three to five hundred thousand dollars preparing a tour and making commitments; it's not too easy just to walk away from it if David doesn't show up. We knew he was doing base, which wasn't charming. We got three buses for three guys. Then I started getting to know David, spending time with him. We would keep having the same conversation: "You gotta stop these drugs." We slowly became whores, watching David feed his habit, getting him the money, giving him the money. Except . . . he was the most charming person. He was always lovely. I don't know what that other David was. I never witnessed it. In a way, it was funny—I'd get a call from him, and he'd say, "Peter, you're the best manager in the entire world. Can I have three thousand dollars?" And I'd say, "David, you should at least take a beat between 'You're the best manager in the entire world' and 'Can I have three thousand dollars?'"*

The tour had two legs, one in the summer, the next in the fall. It was a typically successful CSN tour and for the first time new fans were beginning to show up. The group had always drawn a sixties crowd, young (and not so young) adults who had been teenagers and college students, rocking to "Woodstock" and singing along with "Teach Your Children," songs that were already more than a decade old. On the 1982 CSN Tour, it became obvious that there was a whole new generation of record-buying teenagers who were discovering Crosby, Stills, and Nash all over again, kids who had to have been preschoolers when Woodstock happened. They saw quality shows, but they didn't see what was going on backstage. Michael Finnegan, a tall and handsome keyboard player who had toured with Stephen and came from a long and honorable background in blues and rock 'n' roll, was a bemused observer. Currently enjoying his third year of sobriety, he speaks from the perspective of a former user when he recalls that tour and others.

MICHAEL FINNEGAN: *David used to attract the damnest group; they would be pretty fucking far down the scale. I used to call the people on his bus "the Manson Family" because he had this collection of ne'er-do-wells, guys like Mort and various types that would come and go, just hangers-on, people that were using with him mostly. Anybody that didn't use the way he used, he didn't want them around. He wouldn't let anybody else in. Me, I'd cluck and shake my head a lot and have another toot. Graham was the least judgmental of all of us because he's the only normal motherfucker in the whole bunch. I think the rest of us, especially the rest of us that drank and used, found a lot wrong with David so we could reinforce how right we were and how okay we were, when, in fact, we were just as sick as he was. When I started using drugs in the early sixties—marijuana, psychedelics, a little speed here and there, stuff like that—we were being told that the shit was going to kill us and we knew that it wouldn't. But gradually we decided that if this is okay, then this other must be okay and so on and so forth and eventually you wake up and you're a fucking drug addict. But nowadays it's a little different because the things that people are fooling with in terms of drugs are a lot more serious than what we did, I think—just in terms of how quickly they can kill you.*

Mort and I seemed destined to enjoy a long and tortuously involved relationship. I liked Mort because he was intelligent, ballsy, funny, and kind to me. He was one of the only people in the eighties who didn't think that my career was over. Because he was similarly addicted, he had an interest in proving that one could be a functional base head. But rather than looking at my sad state of affairs and drawing the obvious conclusion, he looked as his state of affairs, which was pretty much still in order at that time, and tried to get me to emulate him. He tried to get me to shave, dress better, and in all ways to keep up a good front. He believed me when I told him that I could still function with Crosby, Stills, and Nash—if only I could get them to be willing to work with me as I was.

PETER GOLDEN: *Mort wasn't a real manager. He didn't participate in our commissions, he didn't participate in the tour at all, he didn't have decision-making authority, he was just David's man. I never saw him doing drugs myself, but it was obvious from the people around that they were both basers and that while he supplied David with a lot of money and David owed him money, it was hard to know what their relationship was and where it went. The rumors were that he was a major drug dealer out of Northern California. I don't really know. He was a vile-looking person. I mean, he was a seedy-looking guy. But if it wasn't for Mort, I don't know if David would have been able to make the dates.*

In September 1982 David was arrested a third time. It was right after the closing concert of the summer leg of the Daylight Again Tour. As he walked off the stage at Irvine Meadows Amphitheater, police from Culver City took him into custody on an arrest warrant dating back to 1980, to an altercation with two women in a Culver City condo. It was a bogus charge, a harassing tactic common to celebrities who make themselves vulnerable by intemperate behavior. Because of the exigencies of the tour, paperwork and court dates had not been met and technically David was subject to arrest on the outstanding and unanswered warrant. That charge was eventually dismissed. The Orange County arrest had been plea-bargained to a nolo contendre settlement, in which David paid a seven-hundred-and-fifty-dollar fine and court costs. In return, he received probation, with the requirement that he complete a drug diversion counseling program. On the other front, the Dallas case had resulted in a formal indictment and would proceed to trial. In November 1982 Crosby, Stills, and Nash played two nights at the Universal Amphitheater; the performance was carefully videotaped for a national cable television special and the footage of "Wasted on the Way" was released as a video to MTV. There are very few close-ups of David in it.

GRAHAM NASH: Daylight Again *was a patch job. David probably did 80 percent of the record, but there were a couple of cuts that he wasn't on because he just couldn't cut it. On the tours in '82 and '83, there were times when Mike Finnegan, without the light on him, would sing David's parts, while we turned his mike down. Not that David didn't make the attempt; I always had faith that he would come out of it, so I covered my ass. I recorded him separately. I have a tape of David attempting to sing that's disgusting. He's never heard it and he never will, but by God, if he ever comes back to me and says, "I could have cut it," all I have to do is play him this tape and show him the famous* Daylight Again *video from the Universal Amphitheater. It was bad enough he got there so late for the first day that we thought he wasn't going to make it at all. If we're doing a CSN show, then we need Crosby songs, Stills songs, and Nash songs and we need the people who are singing those songs. We were personally involved in making that show because we took the cash advance and we employed the people that did it: Neal Marsh and Tom Trbovitch and their wonderful crew. In the editing sessions afterward, I kept having to say things like, "I'm sorry, you can't use this shot of Crosby. He looks like Dracula," and "You can't use that one. I'm not letting Crosby be seen like this." The patch job that we did on the visuals on David's songs was remarkable and even so it's obvious to anybody with half a brain that he's out of it—the stare in his eyes, the vacant faraway expression, the almost comatose way he went through the tunes. He certainly tried his best, but he just didn't cut it. That was an incredibly painful thing for me to deal with.*

CARL GOTTLIEB: *I visited backstage at the Universal concerts, both nights, because I was working at the studio and it was easy to drive up the hill from my office, through the back lot and into the backstage area at the Amphitheater. Seeing David was a huge disappointment. Before, at a comparable show, the adrenaline of performing would bring David offstage in a rush of good feeling and real joy. He would still have to get high almost immediately, but the boost he got from ten or twenty thousand people screaming approval would carry him through at least a half hour of backstage mingling and polite chit-chat, some banter with the band, autograph signing, the usual after-show dressing room schtick. At the Universal shows and every performance I saw after that, he'd come offstage and make a beeline for his bus or a secure dressing room where he could light his pipe. The show adrenaline couldn't buoy him up for the time it took for him to walk from the stage to the wings. That was depressing.*

That winter Stephen Stills's song "Southern Cross" climbed onto the *Billboard* charts and Crosby, Stills, and Nash stayed in the public's eye and ear. There was a new development that lent fresh popularity to veteran rock 'n' roll groups with historic accomplishments. It was called "classic rock" and it was a playlist format that swept FM radio as the Yuppie Eighties unfolded. Classic—or "album-oriented" —rock was a euphemism for records that weren't "golden oldies," but had the distinction of being hugely popular across a broad spectrum for many years. It enabled FM stations to play music that rocked a little harder than "middle-of-the-road" album stations, who tended to play a lot of the Carpenters. "Classic rock" was a format that favored the California sound of Jackson Browne, Linda Ronstadt, the Eagles, Joe Walsh, and, of course, Crosby, Stills, Nash, and Young in all their permutations and combinations. CSNY had a lock on the format and were being played nationally, extensively, and on stations with a strong audience share in every market. They were becoming a hot hit group with songs that were almost fifteen years old, as well as with their latest tunes.

Meanwhile, the proceedings in Dallas continued; David's lawyers had made motions to suppress the evidence found in his dressing room on the grounds that it was inadmissible, the fruits of an illegal search and seizure (what David used to call "seize and suture." Remember?). The motions hearings had taken place in 1982 and Judge Pat McDowell of the Dallas Criminal District Court had ruled that the evidence would stand. That would be the basis for the appeals, later. But first, David would have to stand trial; he elected to waive a jury trial and have his case heard by Judge McDowell.

JAY ETHINGTON: *He was addicted to drugs; I knew that. I knew that I'd have a problem getting him in and out of the courtroom and I wanted to make sure that he didn't get arrested in the hallway of the courthouse by sheriff's deputies—because they're chickenshit like that and they would've loved it. By then I relied quite a bit on Smokey Wendell; he'd give me almost daily reports on schedule changes or security precautions or problems that Crosby was going to have with what Wendell called his "personal problem." He'd say things like "He'll have to deal with his personal problem after he gets off the plane, but before he gets to your office." Wendell and Armando and some of the others developed a code among ourselves. I lied to myself intellectually by trying to ignore all this, keeping some professional and personal distance between myself and all that. Smokey and Armando would deliver Crosby as if he was a package and I would carry the package to the courtroom. There were times when Crosby literally needed cleaning before we could get him in the courtroom. He smelled bad, as if he'd slept on the plane for three or four days. I would tell Armando or Smokey that the hearing was expected to last three or four hours or the trial was expected to last two or three days and that would just create great alarm because we didn't have a rider on our contract to provide a secure area next to the courtroom like you do onstage.*

Smokey was Robert G. Wendell, who came to the world of rock 'n' roll from improbable beginnings. He had served with the U.S. Secret Service and as Agent Wendell he had guarded the President of the United States while working for the Executive Protection Agency of the federal government. Smokey had seven years in government service and was a tested "professional watcher, a proven drug enforcer," as Robert Woodward noted in his biography of John Belushi. Wendell started in the music business taking care of Joe Walsh; Walsh referred him to Belushi. A chain of referrals that included Stephen Stills hauled Smokey into David's camp. Armando was Armando Hurley, a talented singer and songwriter who submerged his own talents out of affection for Crosby and in deference to his job as David's road manager, companion, and guitar tech. Taking care of David was a full-time job.

JAY ETHINGTON: *The coffee breaks in the morning and the afternoon were less than twenty minutes and I had to get the judge to agree to extend that to half an hour. We used the excuse that we had other business to attend to. Crosby didn't realize he was even in a court-house sometimes. He couldn't differentiate between my office and the courthouse; he was that far gone at some stages. We were lucky in getting the court bailiff to give us the jury room as an on-site office facility. That way the sheriff's department provided security in the jury room for our hearing and trial conferences, but unfortunately Crosby wouldn't attend or participate in those. He went immediately to the bathroom in the jury room. What nobody knew was that David was probably committing a felony within a few feet of bailiffs who were standing guard to see that he got confidentiality in the prepara-tion of his case.*

Back home, Peter Golden and Bill Siddons were trying to take care of business. Jan was becoming further withdrawn and addicted and was not always invited to accompany David on the road or to Texas. The house in Marin County was falling into decay and disrepair. The Lisbon Lane prop-erty was leased to Leslie Morris while agents looked for a buyer so that David might have some cash. The *Mayan,* still in southern waters, was drifting out of reach as money got short and Bud Hedrick decided to quit as skipper. David was running out of things to sell.

The basis of all drug deals is cash: convenient, untraceable, liquid cash. When I could no longer convince someone at the other end of a phone to send me money, when I had spent all the money I earned, including what was supposed to be set aside for the government and the Internal Revenue Service, I started sell-ing things—things I had bought with a connoisseur's eye or on the advice of knowledgeable people. It's a common step along the junkie trail, that moment when you start to trade anything you have of value for drugs. I didn't like selling guitars, so I didn't do much of that. But I did leave a number of guitars as collateral for "fronts" of drugs. [Fronting is a dealer term for "advance," as in a cash advance or getting an advance on your paycheck or your royalties. Drugs are put forward in the anticipation of recovering their retail worth. Commonly, drugs are fronted to dealers short of working capital or to any trustworthy user, which is practically an oxymoron. The drug world being what it is, "trustworthy" is a flexible term with a range of interpretations, most of them situational.]

I had a Ferrari which I wrecked. I sold the wreck for twelve thousand dollars. The most interesting story is the saga of my 6.3-liter Mercedes, a dark blue sedan that I had picked up myself at the factory in Stuttgart, Germany. I drove it for years. It even had a secret gun stash built into it—a spring-loaded panel under the dash would deliver a cocked and loaded .45 auto to your hand when you pulled on it. That was a perfect example of high technology in support of low paranoia. The 6.3 sedan was supplanted by a later and grander model, the ultimate Mercedes: the 6.9-liter sedan. I had two Mercedes Benzes and I didn't sell the 6.3 until the day a dealer whose name I can't even remember offered me an ounce of cocaine and four thousand dollars for it. He gave me the ounce of cocaine, went to the house of a nearby ladyfriend, overdosed on heroin, and died—all in the same evening. The lady woke up with a dead dealer beside her in bed. The tenant in my gatehouse got the panic call and went to the ladyfriend's house to remove the drugs and money before the police and authorities were called. He also brought back my Mercedes. Since the transaction had never been formally recorded, the car was mine again and I didn't have to give back the cash or the cocaine.

The second time I sold the same 6.3 Mercedes, it went to another dealer friend, named Dennis. He had it for a few days, having traded me a couple of ounces of cocaine and some reduction in the amount of money I already owed him from a time when he had considered me trustworthy. The transmission went out, the car blew up under him, and he had it towed back to my driveway, expecting me to make good on it. He had taken the car in good faith, expecting it to be in superb running condition, which was always how I boasted about keeping my cars. That was Dennis's mistake. Once the car was back in my driveway, people assumed it was mine. I sold it a third time to dealer named Don, this time for three ounces of cocaine, flat. It took Don a long time to get the Mercedes towed to a shop where it could be fixed. While it was still in my driveway, I would offer to swap it to anyone who was interested for any combination of drugs or money. After a while it became obvious the car wasn't drivable—it had a thick layer of dust and the tires were going flat. I could've washed and waxed it and kept it looking fresh and sold it a few more times, but I wasn't washing myself that often, so I wasn't about to trudge up the stairs to the driveway. I couldn't put together any more deals using that car. Dealers could see it wasn't running.

The 6.9 wound up in the hands of some very big dealers, wholesalers who moved dope on a scale equal to the car. There was a sixteen-thousand-dollar dope debt involved. A musician friend named Drew, who is still a friend of mine because he's quit doing drugs, lent me the sixteen thousand I needed to redeem the car, to get it back from the heavy movers who had it. I got it back, but later, when Drew ran out of money, I gave it to him, trying to do the right thing and keep business straight between us. He lost a lot of money on the deal, but like me, he's glad to have gotten through the drug experience alive. There were a lot of shady transactions. I had a lot of collectibles to lose and they went singly and in lots, like at an auction, to the highest bidders, who bid money, drugs, or any worthwhile combination of the two. The whole time, I never even considered selling the *Mayan;* it was a deep-rooted escape hatch. If everything got too bad, I could always sail away. If I could find the boat.

BUD HEDRICK: *I brought the* Mayan *back from the Bahamas. Didn't want to leave it in a foreign country. We got a good spot for it. I*

called David and told him what was going on and that I was leav-
ing. He was supposed to arrive on a certain day and he didn't. I
hung around another four days. He still didn't arrive. Every day I
talked to him, he'd say, "Yeah, I'll make it tomorrow. I missed the
plane today." And tomorrow he'd say, "I have an abscessed tooth.
I've got to go to the dentist and he can't get me in till tomorrow."
Meanwhile, I had thirteen thousand dollars of my own money tied up
and I wasn't about to put any more money in the boat. David's new
accountants wouldn't take calls. They wouldn't let me know what
was happening. If I could have talked to an office and gotten some
kind of answer, like "The money will be in the mail next Monday"
or "We can send you dock fees and a little something to keep the boat
going," I could've stayed on. But at some point, everybody felt there
was no hope. It took me seven years to get my money back. It's all
paid off now, so I take that as a real strong sign that David's well.

Bud had to spend his own money toward the end of the time
he was on the boat because I didn't send the money one month
and then I didn't send it another month and the third month he
said, "Hey, David, this ain't happening. I'm not going to spend
my own money on this boat. Either send me the money or I'm
leaving." I didn't send the money, so he left. I went down to
rescue the boat and once again was on the *Mayan,* trying to kick,
in March Harbor in Abacos in the Bahamas. A sailor named
Robbie Smith came sailing by on his little boat with some fish and
asked, "You guys want some fish?" and we said, "Sure." We
invited him onboard and he was a personable, funny, nice guy
and as we got to know him and like him it became obvious that he
was a knowledgeable sailor. We needed somebody to help and he
stuck around and helped. In some ways he was great and in
others not so great. I have no bad feelings about him, even
though he let the boat go completely to shit. I can't blame him for
it because I didn't send him much money. A couple of times I was
able to send him ten grand, but those times were a couple of years

apart and I don't blame him for letting things fall apart. I figure I'm lucky the boat is afloat.

Bud is a less forgiving seaman. David didn't visit the *Mayan* much during the eighties and the boat was left in Robbie's care. In effect, it became his boat, his home. He used it to make money any way possible, taking out an occasional charter if it could be arranged, selling parts for salvage if it came to that. When Bud returned to the *Mayan*, many years later, it was almost a shell; even the plumbing was gone.

BUD HEDRICK: *It's hard to blame Robbie for what happened to the* Mayan, *since there was no money coming to him. But, on the other hand, he sacked the boat. He took stuff off the boat and sold it or hid it or gave it away or allowed it to be stolen. That should never have happened. He even sold the ship's sextant. When I finally got back on the boat, everything of any value was gone, except for the winches and sails. That's not right. I've also heard lots of stories about him running aground. Joe Maggio told me a whole bunch of times that he saw the boat fast aground in the Bahamas and Robbie trying to get it off. There's no need to run that boat aground because it only draws four and half feet. You wait for the tide and you're off. Robbie made a lot of errors; maybe he wasn't a knowledgeable sailor. I know he knew how to sail little plastic boats; I'm not sure what he knew about wooden schooners.*

In May 1983 a new Crosby, Stills, and Nash album was released. It was called *Allies,* and there was a major European tour planned for the summer. In New York, three guitars were stolen out of the van used by David on the road. In Texas, David ran out of continuances and a date was set for *The State of Texas* v. *David Van Cortlandt Crosby.* Assistant D.A. Knox Fitzpatrick made a strong case for the prosecution. Jay Ethington mounted an eloquent defense, working hard to perfect the record for an appeal, should it be necessary. It was.

JUDGE PAT MCDOWELL: *The record will show this is a case in which, on both of these causes, on June 3, 1983, after a plea of not guilty in front of the Court, the Defendant having waived his right to a jury trial, the Court heard all the evidence. Having heard all the evidence, found the Defendant guilty in both of these causes.*

UNITED PRESS INTERNATIONAL: *Rock musician David Crosby, who dozed and snored in court while a judge found him guilty of cocaine possession and carrying a loaded pistol into a nightclub, will be sentenced July 15. Crosby spent most of his day in court trying to stay awake. But several times he fell asleep and snored loudly, his head tilted back and his mouth open. When the snoring became too loud, one of his attorneys leaned over and shook him awake . . . Crosby was convicted of two felonies. The forty-one-year-old singer faces a maximum penalty of thirty years in prison and fines of up to fifteen thousand dollars on the two counts. His attorney asked the judge to put Crosby on probation. Crosby, who gained popularity as a member of the Byrds and Crosby, Stills, Nash, and Young, also was arrested three times last year, twice on drug and weapons charges. He is serving three years' probation from a California misdemeanor conviction for reckless driving. The pudgy singer wore dirty tennis shoes, baggy corduroy pants, a work shirt, and a black-and-white plaid jacket to Friday's nonjury trial. His graying tangled hair was pulled back in a ponytail.*

The sentencing was postponed until after David returned from the Allies Tour of Europe. The band was going to tour using a prop-jet private plane that held forty-five passengers, mostly band and techs. There were no wives or girlfriends along, for budgetary reasons and because Jan's appearance would be certain to draw the attention of Passport Control and Customs officers. The tour would be crossing lots of international borders and going through Customs inspection every time a venue was in a new country. Concerts were scheduled in Paris, Rotterdam, Hamburg, Berlin, Rome, Milan, and in London at Wembley. Additional dates were booked in various smaller cities in France, Spain, Italy, Germany, and England. In addition to the normal heavy preparation required as advance work for a major rock 'n' roll tour, a trusted road manager had to be sent ahead to do special advance work for Crosby. The tour couldn't be jeopardized by the chance that one of its principals might be arrested for possession of contraband substances; everybody had to travel "clean," yet David's considerable needs had to be met.

The solution to the problem was a special advance person who was hired for a very specific purpose. He or she would go to Europe well ahead of the band, traveling inconspicuously as an anonymous, affluent youthful tourist. In each of the cities where the band would play, he or she would obtain drugs from local suppliers and stash them in a safe deposit box in a local bank. When the band arrived, the advance person would retrieve the drugs and deliver them to the hotel or backstage. Nobody had to carry; nobody had to go out and score. It was neat, expensive, crafty solution to a constant problem. Yet, people continued to carry small amounts for their personal use.

MAC HOLBERT: *When you go to Berlin, you have to fly into East Berlin if you have a private plane because that's the only real landing field. So here we are, flying into East Berlin, and I'm going, "Hey guys. C'mon. Don't fool around with me. We need to get rid of every bit of drugs that we have because I don't want to spend the rest of my days in a prison in East Berlin and neither do you." I'd walk down the aisle with a box and all of a sudden, an hour before we were landing, little bits would come out. Ten minutes before the landing, everybody started dumping stuff. We ended up with five or six grams of cocaine as we were coming in on the landing pattern, getting ready to touch down. We were doing the old Woody Allen, sneezing into it, taking all we could because we had to get rid of it before landing. It was terminally stupid.*

In Berlin, David insisted on renting a car and driving into East Germany, where they were stopped for speeding. Chances are that David was holding. It was the moment that everyone had always feared. Armando, a light-skinned black man, extricated them. He spoke perfect German! His father had been a black U.S. Army serviceman who had married a German woman; Armando was the product of that union and had been raised in a bilingual household and spent time on American bases in Germany. Crosby got off with a speeding ticket from the German Democratic Republic. It's probably never been paid.

The Allies Tour was not particularly successful for several reasons. Management or the promoters (each blamed the other) had overemphasized the band's popularity and large venues had been booked: soccer stadiums, sports palaces, arenas. Wembley Stadium in London was a perfect example. Originally booked for three nights, ticket sales required that the three dates be collapsed into one well-attended performance. That's a respectable showing, but it's psychologically depressing for a band to hear that dates are being canceled due to "poor" ticket sales. They were only poor because initial estimates were too generous. The Spanish promoter had been permitted to postpone paying advances; when his ticket sales didn't meet expectations, he simply canceled the concerts in Barcelona, Málaga, Madrid, and San Sebastian, leaving an unfillable hole in the schedule. This was poor management. A strong (and unified) management team would've insisted the money be in the bank before the band left the United States, but there was an overabundance of managers representing David, Graham, and Stephen as individuals and as a group. This author joined the tour in Toulouse, France, and saw a performance in which a robust and full-voiced Crosby carried a tired Stephen and a sick Nash. After Toulouse, the cancellation of the Spanish dates forced the group to take a week's hiatus. Smokey found an empty resort hotel on the Italian Riviera (it wasn't yet high season) and the band lay in the sun for a week until the Milan and Rome concerts. David stayed in his room or drove to Rome to look for drugs.

In London, this author watched a depressed and obsessed David vegetate in his hotel. There was a shortage of drugs and Deedee showed up from California, carrying more. She was that solicitous and caring of David. Together, she and this author shopped for English clothes for David (the sport coat they bought was worn to his sentencing in Dallas in August). David had a VCR in his hotel room. He would watch the opening sequence of a Steve McQueen movie, *The Getaway*. For those unfamiliar with the film, *The Getaway* begins with some realistic footage shot at Huntsville Prison in Texas. Ranks of prisoners dressed in white cotton uniforms are being marched through the yard, run through the gates, and worked in the fields, supervised by blank-faced

guards on horseback, wearing mirrored sunglasses and carrying shotguns. The soundtrack is a carefully orchestrated ca-
cophony of slamming steel gates and the barked orders of
the guards, coupled with shouts of prisoners and barking
bloodhounds. Hell on earth. David would watch it, run it
back, and watch it again. "That's where they're going to
send me," he'd say and play it back like Howard Hughes in
his final days, watching *Ice Station Zebra* over and over
again. It was a time of deep depression and profound regrets.
Maybe it wasn't cool to have snored in front of the judge
who was going to sentence him.

We went out on tour twice during my really mashed-up base
period, at least twice. [Three times, including Europe.] I managed
to get onstage, except when my drugs didn't come through. There
were a couple of times when I was real sick from not having my
heroin and I would walk off and go backstage and throw up and
they would come and get me and drag me back onstage. It was
gross. It was gruesome. It was the death throes of that group. By
that time, if I didn't have my drugs I couldn't function. I would go
completely crazy on everybody and of course nobody could keep
me supplied all the time, so it was a real disaster. I remember
walking offstage to throw up, while Nash and Stills continued
without me. Stills left the stage during Nash's solo section, came
back, and threw a bucket of water on me. They didn't really want
to do it. I begged them. I said I could carry my weight. I was
determined to be a functioning addict. I said, "If Ray Charles can
do it, I can do it. If Coltrane could do it, I can do it." Well, sure:
Ray quit and Coltrane died.

On August 5, 1983, Judge Pat McDowell had this to say:

JUDGE MCDOWELL: *In setting punishment, the problem I have is that
. . . what happens to you ought to serve three purposes: . . . to
punish you, to rehabilitate you, and to deter others from committing
similar crimes. I think the deterrent part of that statute is the part
that ends up hitting someone like you harder because what happens
to you is going to be known by more people than if it happened to*

somebody from, say, North Dallas or South Dallas or whatever.
Those are some of the hard rules of the game . . . Mr. Crosby, it
will be the order, judgment, and decree of this Court that you be
taken by the Sheriff of Dallas County, Texas, and by him safely kept,
by him transferred to an authorized receiving agent for the Texas
Department of Corrections, where you will be confinded in F-82-
85707JL [the drug charge] for a period of five years and in F-82-
85678-NL [the weapon offense] for a period of three years . . . to
run concurrently.

Because David had managed to make his court dates on time
while out on bail, Judge McDowell allowed him to post bond
during the appeal process, notices of appeal having been filed
with the court. David went back to California while the
press reported the severity of the sentence. *People* magazine's headline said: BUSTED, DESPAIRING AND STRUNG-OUT,
FOLK-ROCK SUPERSTAR DAVID CROSBY FACES FIVE YEARS IN
PRISON. *Rolling Stone* was particularly snide and smarmy.
"The long-and-patient arm of the law has finally dealt with
David Crosby. After a year of postponements, Crosby
pleaded guilty . . . to cocaine possession and carrying a
gun into a bar, two felony raps that could've earned him
thirty years in jail." The unsigned article went on to malign
Crosby's music and recalled other, unrelated arrests. "If his
appeals are unsuccessful," *Rolling Stone* asserted, "Crosby
will have to serve a minimum of twenty months." They
might've got the facts more or less right, but on every suppo-
sition and conclusion *Rolling Stone* was wrong.

ELEVEN

B y 1983, I wouldn't look at what the situation was or what the drugs were doing to me. I didn't consider how my health was deteriorating and I refused to admit that I simply wasn't doing what I wanted to do. On a conscious level, I could articulate it clearly: "I can't do this anymore. I'm going to put myself in the hospital." Then I'd pick up the pipe and take another toke. I'm not sure which of the voices in my head said, "Let's go to the hospital," and which one said, "Let's take the next toke," but those two certainly weren't talking to each other. It's my feeling now that there are always a number of different levels of my consciousness talking to each other, a dialogue that goes on all the time. It makes me feel sane: I don't know whether I am or not, but at least I feel that way and I feel good.

I tried to quit at least six times, signing myself or Jan and myself into some sort of hospital or formal program. Five times I actually got in the door; at Coke Enders I didn't. I got to the place, but I didn't get all the way in before I went back out again. A couple of times I went in under duress; I didn't have any choice. What I got was the classic "nudge from the judge." Other times, there was nobody with a gun to my head. There were friends at the intervention who urged me to go to Scripps. My doctor urged me to go to Ross General Hospital, but nobody told me to go to Altoona, Pennsylvania, to try the "little black box" cure. I found that place by myself, with a little help from Peter Townshend, who recommended it to me via transatlantic telephone. Briefly stated, the idea is that the major problem with people addicted to heroin and opiates is that when they quit, their bodies are no longer producing endorphins, so they feel terminally awful. The device that was supposed to counteract that was a black box that a Scottish woman scientist claimed would restimulate the production of endorphins very quickly by introducing microvoltage through two EEG [electroencephalogram] pads behind your ears. So far, so good. This was at a time when the medical community and people in the hospital business were realizing that recovery was going to be a multimillion-dollar industry. I was contacted by a man who claimed to be a rabbi, supposedly from Israel. He offered to pay for me and Jan to go to a hospital in Altoona, Pennsylvania, called Cove Forge, a respected recovery facility for alcoholics and addicts. We were excited about it because it was a place that would take both of us and treat us together. The rabbi got them to bend the rules because if the black boxes worked, I'd publicly endorse them and it would be a Big Deal.

It was another horror show. I don't think anyone knows to this day if the system works. It only strengthens my belief that anything that cracks the wall of disbelief is worth trying. When you're severely addicted, you don't believe you can quit. Anything that shakes that belief, whether it's a little black box and funny microvoltage, megavitamins, massage, psychotherapy, hypnotherapy, incarceration, or a pink bunny suit, whatever gives you a chance to believe that you can beat it is what you need. The black box couldn't work on cocaine addiction because the problem is in the neurotransmitters, not in the endorphins. We know this now; it's part of the rapidly widening body of knowledge about the problem. Back then, all we could do was lie there and feel like shit.

We stayed in Altoona for less than a week. I counted the time in minutes (9,852) because that's how the time felt going by; it was absolute hell. Finally we admitted we couldn't stand it, flew to New York, and went to see somebody to get loaded. The worst thing about it was that we left both of our suitcases and my two best guitars. The rabbi took them, claiming that I owed him money, even though he said he would pay for us to be there. I lost my Martin D-18 conversion to twelve-string, which was the best acoustic twelve-string I've ever had or heard anyplace, and my best Martin D-45 six-string. If anyone ever sees my twelve-string, write to me in care of my publisher. There isn't another one like it in the world: it's a twelve-fret, twelve-string mahogany D-18 conversion with a black pick guard that comes up in front of the bridge to cover the peg holes where it used to be a six-string. It's mine and I need it. I crave it. I want it. I miss it. Those two guitars and the suitcases full of clothes are just some of our favorite things that we never got back.

Jan and I tried to help ourselves because we didn't like things the way they were. Frequently, we experienced moments of utter despair and I thank God that neither of us is suicidal. Most assuredly, there were many times when I would've committed suicide, the result of the most profound depression. The kind that hits you when you've been doing cocaine for twenty years and haven't stopped once during the last twelve months. I never stopped; I only paused. I'd hesitate only long enough to get the minimal amount of sleep necessary to enable me to pick up the pipe again. We wouldn't admit we were in trouble. Jan and I would hide in each other's arms and say, "They all just don't understand." When we realized we were totally strung out, we'd say, "There isn't anything we can do about it. We're just trying to survive. We can't live without it. We gotta have it, so we'll get it."

It never got to the point where I thought of deliberately killing myself the quick way, but I was sure as shit doing it the slow way. There was no way to avoid saying that. And it's true that you don't know when you're doing it to yourself. That's the thing that's weird. I'm sure that any of my friends, people I knew who died on drugs—Cass, Hendrix, Joplin, any of the rest of them—would tell you the same thing: "I'm not trying to kill myself." Why would Jimi Hendrix want to kill himself? He was the greatest guitar player that ever lived. Nobody could touch him. Why would Janis Joplin want to kill herself? They might have been lonely and they might have had problems working it out in their lives, but they had music! They all got nailed by junk. Junk'll do that. You score a little better than you thought and you're dead. Michael Finnegan, that paragon among musicians, has an insight into addiction which bears repeating. He says, "It's the only terminal illness that tells you you're fine." And it does. It's the most insidious goddamn trip. I knew that that guy over there was Death, in a black cloak with a scythe, but I made him look like a guy in a business suit with a briefcase and went on with what was left of my life.

People magazine interviewed David in August, while he was preparing his appeal from the conviction and sentence imposed by Judge McDowell. It was a rare public glimpse into David's life, which he usually kept secret. The strategy was to focus attention on his plight, to enlist public support against what David believed was an unduly harsh sentence, and to garner some sympathy. Instead, the article in *People* drew an unflattering picture of a disturbed man who was ill with addiction and full of self-pity.

PEOPLE: *The folk-rock star looks haggard and beaten. The choirboy face that graced the Byrds album covers in the mid-60s is now marred with open sores. His torso is bloated and heavy, his fingernails are black and bitten, and his arms are scarred with wounds and bruises. The man whose voice soared in the harmonies that made Crosby, Stills, and Nash a siren of the New Age now speaks in a despondent monotone . . . Sitting in his yard, speculating on his future, he shows fright in nervous, darting eyes and pitiful pleading words. "Please say this isn't fair, okay?" he begs. "You're in a position to help. Just say that I said, 'If anybody cares, please help me. Please write letters or call. I need your help. I need everybody's help. If there's anybody out there who loves me, please try and do something . . .' I'm strung out, but what I really need is money so that I can clean up on my own."*

Letters from fans poured in to Judge McDowell's court and were entered into the files. Shelly Roecker, who hadn't seen David in seven years, emptied her savings account and sent several thousand dollars. More formal pleas on his behalf were submitted by Graham Nash and others who knew him. Their tone was similar, a litany that restated David's personal anxiety and concern: "David needs treatment, not incarceration. Prison may make him suicidal or worse. Please don't send him to jail." In the late fall, David and Jan agreed to Dr. Robert Belknap's suggestion that they enter a recovery center. Three-South is the wing at Ross General Hospital in Marin County that handles the addicted and substance-dependent. Vasilious Choulos is an attorney in San Francisco who was a neighbor of David's in Marin, the Choulos kids were fans of David, there had been good feelings between all of them in the past, and Choulos (who is called Bill by his friends) felt kindly and sympathetic toward David. Bill had been introduced to David by the late Don Lewis, one of David's best friends. And besides all that, he was a resource that David hadn't tapped yet.

BILL CHOULOS: *He was driving a big Harley hog, dressing in that way, and he had impetigo all over him. I'd hear about strange goings-on with Hell's Angels, that dope dealers took his car away and all kinds of weird stuff. He was playing with the wrong people. Since he didn't come to me for help—except in this one instance—I made arrangements to try to get some money. He suggested a few people that I should call. I called Graham Nash, who was very sympathetic, but he'd been through this. I contacted Belknap and he was in the same position, carrying heavy unpaid bills for David and his girlfriend. When I called Bill Graham, his first response was "Goddamn son of a bitch. Why the fuck are you calling me? You're calling me to help him and when he's on his feet, he turns around, tells me that I'm ripping him off, and the next day comes to me and wants something!" Graham went on and on and after he went through this tirade I think he did send some money. He may have sent a couple of grand. I was left with people who thought they could do something for David and somehow get results, a little bit of glory, where other people had failed. They were going to be his saviors. I was the same way; he came to me and by dint of my own strong personality I was going to say, "David, do this. David, do that," and he was going to do it. At least he'd come to me rather than my going to him. We managed to get him into Ross and I got word that he was raising hell. Initially, they thought it was going to be wonderful. He wanted to bring his guitar. He was going to be great for the other patients. Well, he walked out and that was it. We didn't get any money back—obviously. We'd paid for a month, so that money was just blown.*

Dr. Belknap's admissions report on David is in the Prologue of this book. It's an accurate description of David's physical condition, but it couldn't predict his next medical problem: kidney stones. David doubled over in pain one night and Belknap made a house call to Mill Valley at three in the morning. He diagnosed the stones and David was admitted to Marin General Hospital for treatment. Jan accompanied him and slept in a chair by his side. The next day withdrawal symptoms set in, so they called a friend to bring some drugs and paraphernalia to the hospital. Irvin arrived at the same time as Dr. Belknap. The doctor recognized the drug courier for what he was and insisted David not do freebase in the hospital. Crosby was extremely cranky and there was a confrontation. David yanked the IV drip from his arm and stormed out of the hospital, blood flowing from his arm and dripping on the floor.

DR. ROBERT BELKNAP: *Jan and David kept each other going, no question about it. They kept each other addictive. On that level it was an extremely destructive relationship and whenever anyone suggested treatment, they would try to find a facility that would take them together. He would always say, "Can you admit Jan at the same time? Can you admit her to the same room?" It was a folie à deux, but I'd say, "Yes, I'll do that. I just want you guys to get treated. Let's do it." At Marin General, when he decided he was going to leave, he was raging, cursing a blue streak. I moved toward him to try to get him to calm down. I said, "Wait, wait, let me take this IV out," and he swung on me. That was shocking. We'd always maintained a good relationship and swinging on me represented the ultimate loss of control. I never provoked him—ever, not once—because that's a rule of mine. Why act like an angry father?*

Three-South at Ross General was hopeless. They didn't like me. I didn't like them. My memory is that the place wasn't run very well. But I tried. Twice. Then I went to a hospital called Gladman Memorial in Oakland. Gladman is a private mental hospital that also does detox and recovery work; it has a locked ward, which I didn't originally intend to visit. I was checked in as a voluntary patient and when I got tired of it I walked out. I went about two blocks and came back. When I returned, I made the mistake of saying that I felt tremendously depressed, even suicidal.

As a result of revised legislation prompted by patients' rights activists and civil libertarians, confining someone against his will for any length of time is almost impossible in California. Even a seventy-two-hour hold requires medical certification and a fourteen-day detention requires hearings in front of a judge. To be confined involuntarily for any longer than that requires considerable legal work and certification by independent physicians upon the request of a next-of-kin. The appearance of sanity and a lucid façade will almost guarantee a person's personal liberty. Despite this, Bill Choulos and some others got up on the stand to testify that David should be held against his will. They believed it was their only hope for effecting his recovery and the only chance for him to get free of his addiction. Paul DeGaudio is a doctor and was the administrator in charge at Gladman Memorial Hospital.

DR. PAUL DEGAUDIO: *I'm reading from his chart now. "On 12/16, the patient was placed on suicide precaution and also placed on involuntarily hold after he had made statements that he had no reason to live, that there was no pleasure in his life, and that he would blow his brains out if he were incarcerated as a result of leaving the program. When this therapist questioned him, he affirms what he has said, he says that he could make arrangements to have a gun available, and it was later learned that he did have access to guns in his house. At the seventy-two-hour evaluation it was . . . hoped that with his participation in the chemical program of this facility that he would become more hopeful, less depressed, and for this reason he was placed in a fourteen-day certification. The patient requested a writ hearing, which was denied. [He had the hearing, but he didn't win.] The patient was continued on an involuntary basis, 12/26, but his status was changed to voluntary inpatient."*

BILL CHOULOS: *I testified against him. The only way we would possibly keep him there was to assure a judge that he was a danger to himself and the community and while the danger was a bit abstract, I had to make it a little more real and I kind of stretched it a bit. I Mickey Moused it, saying things like "It wouldn't be out of the realm of speculating that he might take his own life." As I did that, David sat there and was in control enough that he was sort of laughing while I was testifying.*

I had never been suicidal, but at some point they got that word out of me and instantly they had cause to put a fourteen-day hold on me and put me in the locked ward. They knew I wasn't suicidal. They wanted to help me break the drug cycle so they put an involuntary hold on me, which is legal in California. The law also provides for a review of your holding order by a court, which I asked for, at which several people who knew me—good friends all—testified. They said things like "Hey, absolutely, he's endangering himself, are you kidding?" and "No, he's not going to blow his brains out with a gun, but he certainly is going to do it with drugs."

Gladman Memorial is a small hospital tucked onto a side street in downtown Oakland, California. Oakland is a depressed city with a high crime rate and bears the same relationship to San Francisco as Newark does to New York; it's big, you know it's out there, but there's no reason to go there. Gertrude Stein said, of Oakland, "There's no 'there' there." Again, the reader is referred to the Prologue; the psychological evaluation presented there was written by a psychologist under referral from Gladman. Dr. DeGaudio quoted from David's medical charts and histories when he recalled Crosby's short-term visit:

DR. PAUL DEGAUDIO: *We had him seen by a neurologist, a psychologist, and a psychiatrist. He was withdrawing from heroin, using methadone; he was placed on Valium because we were afraid he might have a seizure. During the first two days of hospitalization, the patient was allowed to rest and in the group session, he told us that he knew he had to deal with his drug problem; that he knew it would be difficult; that he was concerned about his career and he wanted to return to work; that he was appreciative of the support that he was getting from his friends; that he wanted to get back on his feet so that he could be more available to his daughter. He had pictures of her, which he kept in his room. David was getting healthy: as soon as he had eaten, his face began to clear, he felt physically better, and he wasn't in any pain from withdrawal. He began to question if this was the right time. He was becoming restless and was aware that he had left two other programs at about this point in his detoxification treatments. Nash spoke up for him. He said, "David really wants help. He's really going to stay here. He doesn't feel he belongs in the closed unit with individuals who are mentally ill; he'll sign in voluntary and he'll stay." David swore up and down he was okay. At that time I didn't think he was suicidal. I thought he was going to continue and so he signed in voluntarily. At no time after the sixteenth did the patient voice any suicidal thoughts. In fact, he vehe-*

mently denied he was suicidal. He stated that he had used the word "suicide" because he wanted to elicit sympathy and he regretted having done that. In talking to his attorney and one of his partners, it was learned that there was no evidence of any past suicide attempts, even though the patient had had personal tragedies in the past. For this reason and for the fact that there was no indication that the patient was, indeed, a threat to himself in terms of suicide, on the twenty-sixth, the patient was allowed to sign in. He said that he would continue in the hospital for the next four days until Friday and at that time he planned to visit another partner in Southern California. Attempts were made in therapy to motivate the patient to want to work in the program, although these were met with resistance.

I convinced a court I wasn't suicidal enough to be held against my will and I conned the psychiatrist into putting me back in a regular room. I could leave the room when I wanted and have visitors, so I took advantage of those privileges and got high inside the hospital. Twice somebody snuck me in a rock of coke and once someone smuggled some heroin in to me. I didn't want to quit and that was that, no matter what I promised the different judges and counselors and friends who still might've cared about me. I swore to Graham that I'd hang in a few more days if they let me out of that ward, but as soon as I talked my way back into the unlocked section, I broke my solemn promise to my best friend and left.

> While David was in Gladman, Jan was eking out an existence in the decaying Greenwood Way house, subsisting on the kindness of dealers and dope friends who would pity her enough to bring food or drugs and pay the delinquent utility bills. When David got out of the hospital, he started to tour with his own band; it was the only source of income and Mort was making sure there was some income.

Mort meant to help, but the overall effect of me and freebase and him basing and everybody around me basing set up the downhill slide in the people around me. By that time I was only associating with people who were loadies. I didn't have any friends anymore that were not getting whacko all the time. Carl and Graham and everybody else I knew had pretty much said, "Well, Jesus, if we can't get him in a hospital, what's the use? I don't want to watch it. This is a bad movie." They used to call my bus "the lab" and my companions on the road were a group of sleazos and one very damaged girl. The only time anybody ever saw me was when I was out prowling the halls trying to score or because I'd run out of dope or because it was time to work. The rest of the time I was hiding in my bus or hiding in my hotel room, taking copious quantities of drugs. I was a blatant, obvious druggie. Touring under those circumstances was absolute mayhem. We didn't have money for gas; I had to bail the last tour out with advance money from the CSN tour I was doing right after it, just to pay off the bus. There was one time we stopped in a truck stop and the bus driver wouldn't go any farther unless a check went to his company. We were going to get dropped right there in a truck stop on a turnpike if we didn't get a check to them. It was more than awful; it was totally awful.

Randy Hylton was a big-boned country boy who drove buses for a living. He was a test driver for Greyhound, he knew the road, and was sent by the custom coach rental company to drive on David's solo tour. Later, he'd become a road manager, but in 1984 he was the new kid on the block.

RANDY HYLTON: *When I got a call asking me if I wanted to do the David Crosby solo tour, I was excited at the chance; the thought of doing a David Crosby tour made me proud. I was at the airport on time to meet the flight and there was no David Crosby, no band. I called the office and tried to find out if there had been a change of plans and they laughed and told me to hang in and they would show up eventually, which they did. David got on the bus, looked around, and quickly went to the back with Jan. I didn't see much of her at first. We drove to the hotel and the show and the next morning I was in the coffeeshop having breakfast when David and Jan came down.*

It was the first time I really had a chance to meet and talk with Jan. I was surprised at David's choice of girlfriends: she wore her hair in a stocking cap, looked to be about ninety or ninety-five pounds, her teeth were unattractive, and she looked very unkempt; David looked exactly the same. We ordered breakfast and, right in the middle of our conversation, David leaned his head back and fell into a deep sleep. He even started to snore, with the knife and fork in his hands and food on the fork. I reached over and touched his hand and said, "Mr. Crosby," before he spilled the food on himself. The waitress caught him and said, "I wish I could sleep like that." I was confused as to why he would be up so early if he was that tired.

We started out from St. Louis and I started noticing a unique, pungent smell in the bus. I thought I had a problem; something was either burning or rubbing or something. The band members laughed and reassured me there was nothing wrong with the bus. In Chicago I was trying to help the road manager and the money was short; we did not receive as much as the promoter was supposed to give us. There was a problem almost from the very beginning. I didn't realize what David was doing in the back of the bus until I walked back and saw the pipe. Then I knew. I figured as long as I stayed away from it and stayed out of the back of the bus, there would be no problem. When we were in Ohio, Jan got an eye infection and David wanted me to take her to the emergency room at the hospital to see if there was anything that could be done about it. At the hospital, one of the nurse's aides looked at Jan and said, "Isn't it nice you have your son to bring you to the hospital?" Jan and I looked at each other in disbelief; she was thirty-four and I was a couple of years older. I said we weren't related, that she wasn't my mother. They examined Jan and came to me and said, "What's her problem? Obviously it's more than just an eye infection." They kept us there for a while, but we talked our way out. When I came back, the band asked why I didn't leave her there. They seemed aggravated that I didn't agree with them that Jan was holding David back, diminishing his supplies, and making it hard for everyone to function because she was drawing so much energy that David was unable to perform at his best level;

they put a lot of blame on Jan and it was tough. It was a very tense few days.

We did a show in Denver and left David in the hotel when we left to go to Vail. There had been a mix-up about who was taking who where . . . and when. We were in the bus a hundred miles down the road and David was asleep in his room when the maid came in. He had left all his paraphernalia spread out on the nightstand, as he usually did. He had also burned part of the nightstand, as he sometimes did. The maid was shocked. She went and got the manager, who came up with a security guard. They woke him and informed him that he was going to have to vacate the room. The promoter, by that time, sent someone over to get him. We were all very fortunate that the manager of the Holiday Inn was kind and didn't raise a stink.

Years later, when Crosby and Nash were playing in Lake Tahoe at Caesars Palace, David was wandering through the casino after a show. A blackjack dealer looked up from his cards and asked David if he remembered him. David didn't; it was the man who had been the manager at that Denver hotel. He was still a friend and fan and expressed pleasure at seeing a changed and different Crosby. The sight of his trashed hotel room and the sleeping sick man was still vivid in his memory. Anyone who experienced that tour, either as bystander or participant, has powerful recollections of it. Mark Aguilar, the lead guitar player, remembers it all too well:

MARK AGUILAR: *All of us were used to David and Jan dropping their torches because of all those ruined motel rooms. We used to move them from room to room so they wouldn't get busted; at one time we walked in their bathroom and somebody was sitting on the toilet, asleep with a lit torch right next to the wall and the toilet paper, and there was a big burn mark on the wall. Almost in flames. We were all pretty cautious about smelling smoke; we'd be sitting in the bus, smell something, and everybody would say, "Fire!" like it was a drill. We'd all run to the back of the bus and Jan and David would be pushing stuff behind them, trying to put it out, saying, "No, no*

*fire here." They'd scoot together, real close, smoke billowing up be-
hind them, just like two little kids caught playing with matches. We
all bought our own fire extinguishers, just in case, because we slept in
the bunks right outside their room. I was on the bottom bunk, on the
floor, where I could smell smoke first. We had two buses taken away:
one because of fire, the other because our management wasn't paying
the bills. Every four hours the new driver would pull over and make a
phone call and ask his dispatcher, "Hey, did the money come in for
today?" That guy was kind of friendly toward me, so he took me
aside and said, "Slick, I'm gonna keep all of David's gear, but I'll
give you your shit when we pull off to the side and unload everything." That made me feel great—here I'll be in Ohio, on the side of
the fucking interstate with my amp and guitar. Thank you. You're so
kind.*

RANDY HYLTON: *That brings to mind the time I was driving and
smelled something burning and sent someone back to check on them
and they wouldn't unlock the door, said everything was fine. The
next day I went back to clean the bus and got into the back room and
found out they had fallen asleep with one of the torches on and had
burned a massive hole in the mattress that went through a six-inch
sheet of foam rubber, plus the covering and part of their comforter.
Judging from the size of the burn hole in the mattress, I was surprised
they hadn't killed themselves. I noticed David's hands were always
burned, with big burn blisters on them, from nodding off with the
torch on. David had a knack of not wanting to turn the flame off. He
would keep the flame burning all the time; set it down on the nightstand or on the bus without turning it off. He was constantly burning
clothes, burning himself, burning furniture.*

JAY DAVID: *When we played in New York, we had a guy named Elton
who said he knew the best pizza place in Brooklyn, so we took the
whole bus down into Brooklyn and there were all these Italian people
looking, wondering, "What the fuck. Who are these people?" We
found his pizza place and we all traipsed out to go get our pizza and*

it's snowing and it's slushy and it's Brooklyn and it's early in the morning and we're walking along and Crosby says, "Hey, Jay. Look!" I look down and the fucker's got no shoes on and he's walking in his socks through the slush, like he's so stoned it was like the fuckin' Pied Piper of Pizza, walking down the street being followed by these Italians saying, "Yo, that's David Crosby."

We played the Lone Star Café and Mary Travers [of Peter, Paul, and Mary] came back to see David after the show and he kept her waiting a long time and finally stuck his head out to say, "Hi, sweetheart. Nice to see you." And she was just crestfallen. Most people that knew him in the old days were always shocked to see how he looked. When we finished our second show and Tony went downstairs to get the money, it turned out someone was saying something like "We're not going to pay you all the money" and put a gun on the table. [The Lone Star management felt that David had not done a full show, so he didn't deserve full payment.] So Tony got David and David went to get his gun. So now I had to keep these guys away because I could just see the fuckin' headlines in the Enquirer *or the* Times *because this was after Texas. It was all I could do to get David to put away that gun. I said to him, "Look, what's the best thing? What's the better part of valor? Are you going to go down there and get into a shoot-out for a couple of thousand dollars? Wake up, dummy! Leave it. Just leave it. Let's drive off winners. You didn't kill nobody. They didn't kill you. Let's just get out of here." That time we got out of there.*

That's how David spent the first half of the year. He was touring with Jan for fees that barely paid for expenses and band salaries after drug purchases and servicing the debt on drugs that had been fronted to him. Mort would generally be along for the ride and Lydia and Myrna would appear and disappear anywhere along the route. A stoned and/or hung over road crew spent every day dealing with irate hotel managers, car rental agencies, anxious promoters and club owners, and the constant parade of dealers and hangers-on who came to visit David, sell or give him drugs, and get high with him. The characteristic smell of the tour was the reek of burning freebase and propane mingled with the odor of charred furniture, scorched upholstery, and blistered paint. David spent most of the time in isolation, emerging only to do his shows, for which he was miraculously present.

MARK AGUILAR: *He would go out there and entertain them, as high as he was. He went out there like a champ every night and really pulled it off. He could still sing. The drug didn't allow him to sit around his room or his house and be creative, but he still could go out and play the tunes that he had written years ago and sing the shit out of them. There was a night where he couldn't talk because he was so coated. His windpipe and down in his lungs, man, was covered with that shit they scrape off the glass; he was out there saying, "Ahhh," and then he started singing and he was doing fine. I went to him and said, "Just sing what you want to say to them, man. Don't try and say anything." David tells the audience, "I've got an alien in my throat," and a little guy in the audience yells up, "Spit it out!" And I said, "Just sing to them, man. Don't talk." He sang "Guinnevere" beautifully that night. It was amazing. I couldn't believe it.*

Mort, speaking for David, convinced management that he could join Graham and Stephen and do a credible job on the tour that summer. The band had no new album in current release, but the previous year's showing proved they could draw an audience, so Crosby, Stills, and Nash were booked for a lucrative summer tour. The David Crosby Band had served its purpose and had played behind him for an entire horrendous season. Mark had even moved to California, with some misgivings about being so close to David and Jan.

MARK AGUILAR: *When I first met Jan, she was a beautiful young lady who was full of life. By 1984 it was a whole new movie, man. She had lost a lot of weight. Her complexion looked almost like scar tissue. A lot of times I think she burned her cheeks with the torch, smoking. She had huge spots on both of her cheeks and was wearing that knit cap over her hair, which was so stiff and solid underneath that it just stayed in place when she took it off—you could set your music up in there and play. They were seriously fucked up and got kind of dirty. They didn't bathe regularly or wash or any of that stuff. Years ago, Jan and I used to hug and kiss, she'd say, "Oh, Slick, you played so good. Give me a hug." On that tour, if she'd ask for a hug, I'd say, "Wait a minute, Jan. I got the flu." Two months later, she said, "Slick, that was so good. Come here. Give me a hug." And I said, "Jan, I'm not feeling too good. I got the flu." She says, "Still?" I think she finally copped to it, said to herself, "Hmmm, I don't think this guy wants to be too close to me right now."*

When the summer came, Crosby, Stills, and Nash went out on tour. Each member of the group traveled in his own bus. By now, Randy Hylton was David's personal road manager. Mort accompanied David on the tour, bringing his own entourage: sister Myrna and girlfriend Lydia. They deliberately left Jan behind, alone in the house. Mort ordered the utilities and phone service shut off. Jan shivered for days in an unheated, unlit house, unable to call for assistance, too shaky to go out, deprived of transportation, companionship, and any meaningful care. A drug friend named Rosita warned her that she had overheard a conversation between Mort and an outlaw biker named Big Mickey, in which Mickey had said, "Look, if you really want Jan out of the picture, I'll do it for you." Mort delegated that terrible responsibility to the unstable biker, who was one of Rosita's lovers. Working with a junkie named Robert, they conspired to drag Jan through hell.

JAN DANCE: *I didn't take her word to mean too much danger, I just thought, "Well, in a couple of weeks we'll be out on tour and it won't matter." A few days before the tour, I was given notice. Mort or someone said, "Guess what? You're not going." I was devastated. David and Mort told me, "We'll make sure you get drugs. Someone's supposed to bring you a little bit every day, so you can get by." I was alone in the Mill Valley house and I started to move from room to room. I'd let things pile up around me as I sat in one spot and when there got to be too much stuff around me, I'd go to another room. I was feeling the pain of my own situation, knowing I was starving and freezing and unable to do anything for myself. I wasn't sane enough to know how to deal with it. One night someone showed up in the darkness and got me high. He brought me some candles* and I went through all my flashlights, I had no more batteries. David thought people were keeping their promises and taking care of me. When he couldn't reach me, he figured the storm had created some problem with the line. Eventually, he called a neighbor and asked him to go check on me and news got back to him that I was in this devastation, so he set it up for a guy named Robert to bring me drugs. After I got the phone back and the heat turned on, he showed up and said, "I have the stuff, but I don't have it with me. We have to go get it." I went with him; I had no choice. I didn't like to go out. I didn't look good; I had stopped washing my hair because it was all matted and I couldn't get out the tangles. I couldn't get anyone to help me. It was such a mess that I had to wear this hat over my head constantly. It would hurt my skin to take showers, so I stopped doing that—I kind of sponged off a little bit. It was hard, knowing I was doing that to myself.

We got to a house and went in. I had my bag with me with all my stuff in it: my pan, my pipe, and an itinerary for the tour. Then Robert got weird, told me the stuff was someplace else, that he had to go get it. That wasn't what he said before. He left and I sat there getting angrier and angrier by the minute because I knew something wasn't right. I just wanted my stash and I didn't want anybody to bother me until that could be taken care of. I wasn't thinking at all. Robert came back with one gram instead of the three I was expecting. Rather than make a scene over the missing grams, I decided to do up what I had and while I was setting up my pan and stuff Robert left the room. Then there was a commotion in the kitchen. Big Mickey had come in and was saying something about keeping the door locked and I heard him punch Robert and knock him down. Then Robert was whining that he had just gotten there and didn't have time to lock anything and Mickey hit him again, hard, and I heard him fall.

I put the gram in my pocket, just as Mickey came into the dining room with this incredible power inside him. His energy filled the room. I looked at him and felt fear. He looked at me with these angry, killing eyes and said, "You sit down. We've got something to talk about." Then he threw a pair of handcuffs on the table and I got really scared and he said, "Look, bitch. It's about time you got real. You're making your old man crazy; you're killing him with your attitude and if you don't cut it out, I'll make sure you do. You're still smoking that shit, aren't you?" I said, "Yes." He said, "You're not going to smoke it anymore. If you can't stop when I tell you to stop, I'll show you how you're gonna do it." He walked around me and before I knew what he was up to, he hit me on the side of my head, just below my ear, toward the back. He hit me so hard I flew out of the chair and landed on the floor. When I tried to get up, he said, "If you make a sound, I'll hit you again." So I didn't make a sound. I felt fear for my life for the first time ever. He had a knife on one hip, a gun on the other, he was wearing only a pair of shorts, and on his fingers he had big rings with skulls and crossbones and Harley-Davidson stuff, so when he hit me, it made an imprint on my skin. He walked around the table, sat down and started to taunt me, and said, "I know Robert just came back from the house. Where's the drugs?" I said, "I haven't got any." He said, "Well, I already took the shit away from Robert, so you'd better not be lying to me." As it turns out, the other drugs that I was supposed to get were in Robert's pocket. Mickey found them when he was beating him in the kitchen. Then he sat down in front of me, put a mirror and my stash on the table, and started to snort it up—right in front of me. Later I found out he'd been up for five days, snorting enormous amounts of speed, crank, and cocaine.

Big Mickey was a maniac when he was normal, so you can imagine what that did to him. He proceeded to snort up my stash, while the anger built up in me. Robert walked in from the kitchen and he had this look in his eyes like "This motherfucker's crazy. Be careful." I said something flippant to Mickey like "How come I can't do any, but you can?" and he got to the side of my chair so fast I didn't even have time to think about it and hit me on the other side of my head, knocking me off the chair onto the floor again. He told me he was going to make sure that I never touched another drug as long as I was alive and as long as it took for me to go through withdrawal, he was going to stay there and watch me at gunpoint. He said that if he couldn't be there, he would have assistants watch me, and while all this was happening, three of his biker friends and two of their old ladies showed up and watched while he beat me up. I was scared for my life and I started to look out the window to see where I could run, trying to devise a way to bolt. The third time he hit me, I landed flat on the floor and I started to cry, because he had knocked my hat off and my tangled hair was falling out and I felt all my dignity leave; he'd done my drugs and I was in awful pain. Mickey said, "I told you not to make a sound, you bitch," and began to kick me in the side with steel-toed boots. I rolled across the room. He came over and kicked me back across the room. When he was about to kick me for the third time, I begged him to stop. I literally begged him to not kick me anymore. His answer to that was "If you shut up right now, I won't kick you . . . but I might kick you in a few minutes."

I pulled together all my energy and stopped crying and became very still and when I tried to get up I knew something was wrong with my ribs. I knew that I'd been hurt. He made me sit in that chair while he raved and did my drugs. By now, he had become a total lunatic, demanding to know where David was. He was going to tell him a story that he saw me hitchhiking out of California and that he gave me a ride across the state line and that I had told him that I was miserable and was tired of screwing up David's life, that I was leaving so that he could have a better life. He took my purse and dumped everything out. He smashed my pipe to pieces and took everything else: all my money—I had two hundred dollars in there —and the tour itinerary. Then he tried to call David, calling number after number in the itinerary because he didn't know how to read it. He didn't see that the schedule said NO HOTEL. BUS. I knew that they were on the bus and that there was no way to reach them until they got to the gig or until the next day when they got to a motel.

Mickey eventually stormed out of the house. While he was gone, Jan begged Rosita to at least help her smoke the remaining gram she had hidden when the ordeal began. Rosita was afraid of Mickey's temper if they should be caught. Jan reminded her that David had friends in every Bay Area chapter of the Hell's Angels and if word got out that Jan had been mistreated, there might be serious repercussions; not from David, but by biker friends who would do real and permanent damage to whoever molested Dave's old lady. Rosita relented, feeling some guilt over her part in the conspiracy. After the women smoked the gram, Jan's pain stopped. Jan was allowed to pass out on the couch; she wasn't permitted to go to the bathroom without one of the women accompanying her. She knew she couldn't run with her ribs injured and wondered if she was bleeding internally. She was kept prisoner for two days, watched in shifts, until Mickey finally returned and crashed on the adjoining couch.

JAN DANCE: *I woke up the third morning and Mickey was asleep on the next couch. I wanted to kill him. I wanted to hurt him as much as I hurt, but I knew I couldn't get away with it. Later, I was in the kitchen, trying to be as nice as I could, because I didn't want to provoke him—I was afraid that he would kill me. Instead, he cooked me a steak and said, "Don't you feel better now?" And of course I lied. I said, "Man, I feel great. I'm really glad you did this for me. I can't thank you enough." He said, "Well, I'm glad you feel that way because I'm going to leave my guys here to watch you. Make sure you don't try to escape. I'm going to see your old man and I'm going to tell him the story I told you I'd tell him." The next thing I knew, he and Rosita were on a plane. They caught up with David on the road. When they told him their version of events, David made them give him the number at the house where I was. The next day, early in the morning, the phone rang. I was alone with one of the biker girls because the men went to the store for more beer. She answered it and I heard her go from hip and groovy right to scared. She handed me the phone. It was David! He said, "There'll be a cab there in five minutes. I want you to get in it and go home. Get some things. Jay David will pick you up. Go to a hotel tonight. He'll bring you to where I am tomorrow."*

David told the biker girl, "If you want to stay alive, you better let my old lady leave because if she's not at another number I'm going to call in ten minutes, you can kiss your life goodbye." He instilled fear over the phone. The cab arrived and Jan left. She went straight to the house on Greenwood Way, picked a pistol from the stock of weapons in the house to defend herself against further assault, packed some clothes and a guitar, and waited for Jay David to arrive.

JAY DAVID: *Crosby, Stills, and Nash were out on the road and David called me and said, "Please, would you help Jan get packed? She needs to get out of there." So I went to fuckin' Dracula's Mansion up there; it was like one big cobweb to me. Somebody was after her or something; I don't know whether it was the pipe or what, but she had to get out of there and stay in a motel overnight. I got her a room in Mill Valley and she said, "Thank you very much." At the big house she was living on a mattress on the floor. At the motel she took the fuckin' mattress off the bed and sat down on it. It's like the chick wanted to lie on a mattress and didn't want to have anything to do with sheets. We got a few changes of clothes for her and she wouldn't wear them. She had a watch cap on and she wouldn't take it off. Lord knows what was underneath it. The next day she couldn't find her way through the airport. It was a gargantuan struggle for her.*

Jan arrived in St. Louis, bruised and shaken, suffering withdrawal. Big Mickey and Rosita had left. Mort and his friends denied any knowledge of a plot to kidnap Jan and fabricate a story about her wanting to leave David. It was suggested that she hallucinated the whole scene, that she was trying to attract attention to herself to compensate for not being taken on the tour. Randy Hylton and David took Jan to a local emergency room for X rays; they revealed two broken ribs and internal injuries. It would be three months before her ribs would heal and six months before they stopped hurting when she took a deep breath. The blows to her head had dislocated her jaw slightly and complicated an already serious set of dental problems. Jan still wouldn't take off her knit hat; her matted, unwashed hair remained hidden.

Everything that happened to Jan while I was on the road got to me secondhand or after the fact. Then I'd frantically make long-distance calls and try and straighten things out. A lot of the

time Jan would come with me. When she didn't, it was because
Mort managed to force the issue by saying, "Look, David, you
have to keep your scene together with Stills and Nash and it
makes you look three times as bad to have her out here." The
pity was that I could agree with that. When I left Jan alone, I
always had it set up so that she'd get a certain amount of money
and drugs every week and everything was supposed to be covered. When it didn't happen or when she was unhappy or afraid,
she'd call me; sometimes the problems would be real and sometimes they wouldn't. She wanted to be with me, she was lonely,
she wasn't getting as much dope as she wanted, she was being left
alone up there, and she hated it. She loved me. She wanted to be
with me, so she would make it always sound much worse than it
was. It was hard to separate crying wolf from a cry for help. It's
not that it wasn't bad; it was and I'm sorry I left her there. But
I'm sorry I got her involved in the drugs in the first place and
there isn't any good part about it. It was all screwed and after Jan
got to St. Louis, things got even worse.

RANDY HYLTON: *Jan was in a lot of pain and it was decided she
would stay with us for a few days. David didn't want her left alone
at his home in Mill Valley. We drove from St. Louis to Kansas City
and from there we'd fly to Denver for a show the next night; the bus
would catch up with us later. David said there were two bags that he
wanted to hold and we would carry them aboard the aircraft. At the
last minute, we decided they should be checked and not carried on
the plane. Unfortunately, the flight was delayed and since David
had no drugs with him, he wasn't feeling well. David and Jan were
sitting in the seats directly behind me. David asked someone for some
coke and got a few grams. Then he went through his bag and discovered he didn't have any baking soda to make base. When he asked
me for it, I told him it was in one of the two bags we checked at the
last minute. He said, "I want those bags." I called the stewardess
and said, "Is it possible to get a couple of checked bags from the
cargo hold? Mrs. Crosby needs some medication that's in one of*

them. *She needs to take her medication.*" Since the flight had been delayed, the stewardess said she'd try and get the bags brought up. It might take a while.

We waited and David was getting more and more agitated. The door to the jetway was still open and all of a sudden there's a man in a suit there with two armed guards. He calls the stewardess over and talks with her. I see her point at me. The man in the suit motioned me to come over. When I walked over to him, he said, "Sir, did you ask for some bags to be moved out of the plane?" I said, "Yes, I did." Then he said, "Is this your gun?" I was flabbergasted. I said, "No, it's not my gun." He asked, "Are these your bags?" And I said, "No. Those are not my bags." I knew that David was out on appeal and if I said that those bags were David's, everything would stop right there; the tour was over. He asked me whose bags they were. I said they were Mrs. Crosby's. They asked her if they were her bags and her gun and she said yes each time. Then the man says, "You're both under arrest for federal air piracy. Will you come with us, please?"

UNITED PRESS INTERNATIONAL: *Kansas City, Mo. A thirty-three-year-old woman who said she is the girlfriend of rock singer David Crosby has been charged in federal court with attempting to board a commercial airliner with a handgun. Jan Dance and Randall Ryan Hylton, manager of the Crosby, Stills, and Nash rock group, boarded a flight in Kansas City for Denver. She asked that her luggage be brought to the passenger section of the plane and authorities said when a flight attendant passed the bags through an X-ray machine, the attendant noticed the image of a gun. The bags were searched and authorities said they found a .22 Magnum, five rounds of ammunition, drug paraphernalia, small quantities of cocaine, hashish, marijuana, and heroin residue. In an affidavit given to the FBI, Dance said she met Crosby in 1977 and subsequently moved into his home in Mill Valley, Calif. She described the relationship as "daily live-in" for more than five years. Dance was released by the FBI after the municipal charges [for possession of drugs] were filed. U.S. Mag-*

istrate Calvin K. Hamilton issued the arrest warrant on the federal charge Thursday. Osgood said Dance's whereabouts are unknown. Dance was in Kansas City for a performance by the group the night before her arrest. Dance told authorities she carried the gun to protect herself.

JAN DANCE: *They kept me there almost a whole day. I got finger-printed. They took me to a courthouse. I met FBI agents. I was in deep shit. I thought I was in trouble for the gun and only the gun. I knew that because the bullets weren't in the chamber that that was in my favor; they were in a separate compartment of the bag, hidden in a sock. It might've looked a little funny to everybody else, but they knew that I had no intention of endangering anyone. They let me go under my own recognizance and told me I had to appear before a judge and take care of the matter.*

GRAHAM NASH: *When the policemen came down the aisle, David totally ignored what was going on. He was just looking out the window. They took Jan; she waved goodbye to him; he didn't do anything. They arrested Randy Hylton, took him off in handcuffs, the plane takes off, and David goes back to smoking freebase in first class. It absolutely amazed me that he could let his old lady take this fall for something that was obviously his. There was concern later, of course, and we got Mac Holbert and Bill Siddons to deal with it, as best we could. We couldn't let Jan be forgotten, so we tried to do whatever we could. I couldn't get over David letting her go like that.*

Randy, although arrested, was released. He gave convincing testimony that he was simply a road manager holding claim checks for more than forty suitcases, that he didn't know what was in any of the bags, and that he had simply been following instructions from his bosses when he asked the flight attendant to retrieve a couple of checked bags. David didn't react. In jeopardy because he was out on an appeal bond and, under Texas law, a convicted felon, he did nothing and said nothing as they led Jan off the plane. After even a cursory interrogation, it was obvious Jan wasn't an air pirate or hijacker—everyone agreed that it hadn't been anyone's intention to knowingly bring a gun onto the aircraft. The federal authorities agreed to release her if the local prosecuters would charge her with drug offenses, based on the residue and paraphernalia in the bag. When she left town with the band and failed to reappear, the case went back to federal court, where it stayed. Larry Lichter is the San Francisco attorney who conducted Jan's defense:

LARRY LICHTER: *She got out of town with just a municipal infraction, for possession of a tiny amount of drugs, which was the civilized way to do it. However, the FBI agent and the feds had seen her and they wanted a promise that she was going to do something medical. They weren't going to file federal air piracy charges against her or charge her with federal drug possession. They let her go with a signature and a promise to do something. When I got the problem, she had refused to do anything and they were charging her with air piracy. It's like after they got on the airplane, they went through the suitcase because the gun turns up in the X-ray machine, right? They see the gun; that gives them the right to open the suitcase. They take the gun; they take the ammunition. They see bindles [paper packets used to wrap cocaine and heroin in retail quantities], they see the blowtorch, and they see marijuana and hash in with the guitar strings. They scrape everything and get what the federal courts in the western district of Missouri consider a "measurable amount" of cocaine. I tried the wrong defense. I should have argued, "Hey, you know, if she could have measured it, she would have used it. It wouldn't have been there. So she wasn't in knowing possession. She's innocent." Nevertheless, they charged her with cocaine as the only drug offense; I think it was for four-tenths of one gram: "a measurable amount." That's the law in that part of the country. In California it's "a usable amount." They let the gun charge stand and offered probation, assuming that she would get cleaned up.*

They were wrong. Jan and David returned to Marin and holed up in the Mill Valley house, living like rats under siege. The CSN Tour had earned enough money to enable them to live a while longer and to pay for David and Jan's defense. Unfortunately, there was still the daily drug drain. Every few days David would make his way to the bank or telegraph office to collect funds. From there he'd go to a dealer's house or to a phone to arrange for a dealer to deliver drugs to the house, where he and Jan did nothing but the drugs. Personal hygiene, housecleaning, laundry, and pet care were beyond them. The gatehouse was usually occupied by a dealer or junkie gofer, but on occasion there'd be a responsible houseguest living there. Randy Hylton and Mark Aguilar were both invited to stay at the compound and each has his own depressing scrapbook of sense memories:

MARK AGUILAR: *When I stayed up there, my place would be broken into every night. It was broken into by David and Jan. I'd go buy groceries, then go out for a while and when I got back, I swear to you, it was like Hansel and Gretel. I'd walk into my place and I'd see a trail of bread, a piece of bread that fell out of the loaf. There'd be about four, five slices going down the steps to their house. I'd follow the spilled food straight to their refrigerator and, sure enough, there was all my food that I had bought. In my bathroom I would have medication that did not get you high, something for a rash that I had. One night I got home a little late and found a box of baking soda, all my capsules are opened and dumped out; somebody tried to make base out of rash medicine. I went down the hill to a pay phone and David caught me as he was coming home from somewhere. He asked me, "What are you doing?" and I said, "Man, I'm leaving." He said, "Don't leave me, man. Stay here with me. Come on. Please . . ." I still left. I couldn't take it anymore; I had been on the road away from home for almost a year. Coming in and finding that shit and my food gone—enough was enough.*

RANDY HYLTON: *I wound up staying up in his garage apartment and every other day I would drive David to Mort's house for his supplies. David had let his house go completely. There's no way I can describe the filth and the living conditions. Dirty dishes covered with food were piled so high they were almost falling off the counter. They had at least a dozen cats. None of them was neutered or spayed, so there*

were a lot of kittens running around. David was sleeping on a mat-
tress in the living room and anything that he needed was on the floor
at the edge of the mattress. There was a television at the foot of the
mattress and the dining room table was completely full. David would
spend a lot of time nude or with just a shirt on. The mattress had
burn holes in it. The master bedroom had a fire in it, which they had
put out with a fire extinguisher—that left a white powdery residue
over everything. Clothes were piled up everywhere. The cats had the
run of the house, so the stench was unbelievable. There was a long
piece of carpeting in front of the fireplace filled with cat feces and
urine. Some of the plumbing worked, some of it didn't. I spent most
of the day and part of an evening cleaning the kitchen and bath in
my little apartment because everything was just so dirty that I didn't
want to use anything unless it was sanitized. When I was done, Jan
showed up, walked into the bathroom that I had spent a lot of time
cleaning, locked the door, and took a shower. I was upset because
there were two or three showers in the main house, so I complained to
David, who told me to take it easy, to relax. He reminded me he
wasn't charging me any rent to live there. That was true, but both he
and Jan had staph infections, big sores on their bodies and faces.
Onstage we covered David with makeup, but in my bathroom I was
worried about catching something.

Randy went home, too, and Rosita moved into the gatehouse
with her new boyfriend, Billy. They were more in character
with the spirit of the Crosby compound at the time. Billy
and Rosita were active dopers, low-level dealers, unstable
personalities, and both suffered from self-delusion. Nobody
living in the Greenwood Way house admitted their condition
and as long as David could get on his motorcycle and ride
somewhere to get something, they'd get through another
day.

I was in a hospital zone on Sir Francis Drake Boulevard in
Ross [a small town in Marin County, just north of Mill Valley]. I
was going by good old Ross Hospital, where I had such good luck
kicking drugs the previous year. I was doing about sixty, crossing

over a double yellow line in the middle of the road, on a loud Harley-Davidson. I passed a long, solid line of stopped cars, stalled in traffic. I had about a gram of base and a half-gram of heroin and a double-edged dagger for self-protection. You might say I was just out for one of my little rides. Then a cop pulled me over, asked to see my license, and asked to look in my bag. I said, "Ah, you don't want to look in the bag." He said, "Yes, I do."

UNITED PRESS INTERNATIONAL: *San Rafael, Calif. David Crosby, founder of the 1960s rock group the Byrds and later the leader of Crosby, Stills, Nash, and Young, faces arraignment Oct. 23 on drug and weapons charges. Crosby, forty-three, was arrested in Ross, Calif., late Tuesday after police officers stopped him for a traffic violation. He was later ordered to appear in Marin County Municipal Court. A search uncovered a dagger, an unknown powder believed to be an illegal drug, and narcotics paraphernalia, Ross Police Chief Douglas Miller said. Crosby was booked for investigation of possessing drugs and narcotics paraphernalia, carrying a concealed weapon, and driving with a revoked license. He was freed on $5,000 bond.*

The Dallas district attorney's office kept close tabs on David's behavior; Jay Ethington opines that the zealous Knox Fitzpatrick cultivated a network of informants and cooperative police departments. Word of the Marin bust got back to Texas because David's arrest had made the wire services and was in the news. There was also an informal system of information exchange that stretched from the Marin County D.A.'s office all the way to Deputy District Attorney Knox Fitzpatrick in Dallas. Judge McDowell was not pleased when he heard the news.

The cops were cool. I have no gripe with the Mill Valley cops. They were always pretty decent to us and as a police department I would rank them real high. They were always pretty decent and there were lots of times they stopped me and hassled me but didn't make the arrest. This time it was the Ross police or the

Marin Sheriff's Department that got me and they made the arrest. That caused a rehearing of my appeal bond. We had to make another appearance before the judge in Texas and he was real clear with me. The plea I kept making was that I was sick, I had a drug problem, I was addicted, whatever I was doing wrong was a result of my illness, and I kept promising to seek help. Judge McDowell went along with that: he had seen me nod off in court, he knew I wasn't totally in control, and he also knew I hadn't made it during my brief stays at Ross Hospital and Gladman Memorial. So he said I had to go into a real serious facility. He even gave me the choice of hospitals. I could go anywhere I wanted and anywhere they'd take me, but it had to be a closed facility. Closed. Not one where I could just leave when I felt like it. We came up with Fair Oaks Hospital in New Jersey. Stephen Pittel helped me get in there.

> Pittel is a psychologist who specializes in the administration and organization of drug diversion and counseling programs. He doesn't normally see private clients, but David was a special case and required special attention. Pittel lives and works in a charming wood house on a side street in Berkeley, California, and like most professionals who dealt with David, he has mixed feelings about the time spent with his celebrity client.

STEPHEN PITTEL: *At the time that I met David I was doing an interlude as the director of a drug abuse treatment program in Marin. I had done just about everything else in the drug field from basic research to international consulting. I don't practice psychotherapy. One of David's lawyers, a man I knew, brought some cash over and said, "There's a client I want you to evaluate," and paid me in advance, which was a rarity. With Crosby it was the only time I got paid in advance and I still haven't gotten paid the balance of what he owes me. The lawyer said, "This guy is very bright, fiendishly so, very difficult, and you'll just have to meet him for yourself and form your own impressions." My mission was to evaluate David, recommend treatment as an alternative to incarceration, and then convince* the judge that was a reasonable way to go. A woman named Deedee brought him to my place and I was watching from my window as they navigated the stairs; there was this young attractive woman leading an old man up the stairs. He was creaking and groaning, he had to stop every couple of steps, and when he came into my office he looked like hell. I told David how lousy he looked and he said, "Hey, I'm beautiful. Everybody tells me how great I look." I grabbed him by the arm and took him into the bathroom. I said, "Look in the fucking mirror and tell me how beautiful you are." He was convinced he was okay. He was convinced about a lot of things. One, he was convinced that nobody knew more about freebasing than he did, which was empirically probably correct. He had probably done it more than anybody else around. Two, he was convinced that nothing that anybody knew or claimed to know about cocaine or its treatment was true with regard to freebase or valid in his case—he was the preeminent authority on everything having to do with it and if it wasn't for these people in Texas who were trying to throw his ass in jail that he was just doing fine. He didn't want treatment; he wanted maintenance. He was willing to go along with anything the court did rather than go to jail; he saw jail as death. Basically, he wanted to run a scam on the judge and do whatever he could to beat the case, which makes him just like everybody else in the same situation. He was not positively motivated.

Time was running out, so I started looking at all these fancy luxury programs in San Diego and Orange County and Boca Raton and then I started interviewing people from the places to find out what kind of services they provided and the one that emerged clearly from all this was Fair Oaks in New Jersey; in balance it was the only place I felt could do the job. John and Mackenzie Phillips had been through there and I liked the fact that they didn't treat celebrities with any particular respect—I heard a story that when a famous politician's kid was there they didn't have a bed for him, so they set up a folding cot next to the pool table in the lounge and I kind of liked that—it showed they had their priorities right. So I recommended Fair Oaks and it was accepted by the judge.

That hearing was held on December 9, 1984. On December 14, Judge McDowell issued his instructions to David and the defense attorneys. Four days later, an appellate court issued a ruling overturning the Crosby conviction. On December 18, David was rescued once again by his two best friends— the Fourth Amendment to the Constitution of the United States, which prohibits unreasonable searches without a warrant, and the "fruit of the poisoned tree" doctrine, which holds that evidence so obtained can not be considered. The trial record showed, said the court, that Crosby had a reasonable expectation of constitutionally protected privacy in his dressing room and Officer Rinebarger had no reasonable grounds and no warrant authorizing him to enter the dressing room uninvited, over the objections of a sentry placed there to prevent entry of unauthorized persons. The ruling was immediately appealed by the Dallas district attorney's office and would be tested repeatedly as it made its way up the ladder of the Texas judicial system.

David, however, believed himself to be off the hook. He began stalling his admission to Fair Oaks, putting off the date all through Christmas and New Year's and into January of 1985. After all, a court had ruled him innocent. Why should he be bound by McDowell's order to seek medical treatment in a supervised facility, a medical jail? Jay Ethington, David's Dallas defense attorney, explains the problem he was having and charts the course of the Crosby defense:

JAY ETHINGTON: *Keep in mind that Crosby was convicted, he'd left on bond, and he would screw up every three to six months or something like that. We'd have another bond hearing [to keep him out of jail]. While that was going on, we went to the appellate court. The appellate court reversed the conviction. They [the prosecution] filed a motion for rehearing; we reargued it again; the appellate court reversed themselves at the intermediary appellate level. So we argued it there twice. We got an adverse ruling the second go-around. That was at a time when Crosby had gotten a couple of sensational arrests. I told him, "You know, the more you fuck up, the harder it is for us to convince these judges that there's no heat on this case."*

Every time David had appeared in court, he had acknowledged that he had a drug problem, he was chronically addicted, and he needed help to beat his addiction. Ethington had even called an expert witness (Pittel) to confirm the assertion. McDowell sympathized, but could not countenance the dreary cycle of repeated admittances, abbreviated stays, and voluntary checkouts. David's case was still under active review; he'd win one, he'd lose one. He was out on an appeal bond only because of his repeated assurances that he was aware of his problem and actively seeking help in controlling it. After weeks of waffling, Pat McDowell finally lost his patience and issued an arrest warrant for David, effective on a certain date, to be executed if he didn't immediately enter a secure medical facility for detoxification and treatment.

STEPHEN PITTEL: *David is about as severe a case of addiction and its consequences as anybody is ever going to get to see and I personally think that it's not only inhumane but unethical and outrageous for anybody to attempt to treat him on an outpatient basis. To see Crosby and to know anything about cocaine and to recommend anything other than long-term inpatient treatment, with a healthy dose of psychiatric therapy thrown in, is just wrong. I began to see that the entire system of people around David were colluding with him—it was as if he was being victimized in the same way as very poor people are victimized. With poor people, it's simple: there's a problem family with no money and the kids have social workers and probation officers, the father's got a parole officer. Everybody's responsible for a piece: school, court supervision, medical care, this, that, the other. Nobody is taking overall case-management responsibility for the person or the system. With David, we had exactly the same thing. There were Texas lawyers and Los Angeles lawyers and the Northern California lawyers and Bill Siddons and his managers and agents, Mort and his minons, and Deedee and Jan, and on and on. Everybody was dealing with a piece of David and everybody wanted to keep the factory producing and nobody except Jan and Deedee gave a fuck about David.*

I had to go somewhere or the judge would revoke my appeal bond and order me into prison. The choice was Fair Oaks Hospital in New Jersey, a very expensive facility with restricted access and locked wards. A junkie jail for serious dopers. Mort took me there and the day I was admitted I was lying on the bed at a motel, knowing I was going to have to go in that night, smoking freebase like a fiend and making my preparations: I had premade chunks of base and some heroin all wrapped up in a balloon and tied off so I could take it in with me. I had a "cheater's pipe," which is just the stem of a base pipe with a rubber tube on it—no bowl or superfluous glassware—the minimum I needed to get high. I was still totally unwilling to give up getting loaded. As I was lying there, I looked at my ankles, which were swollen twice their size and red with cellulitis infection. I cried and took another toke. I remember getting frantically loaded in the limousine all the way there and once I was admitted, I was gross. I was totally in denial, rude to everybody, getting loaded until they caught me and took my stuff away. I remember yelling at people and swearing that they couldn't make me stop, that I was going to get out. They could only keep me so long and the minute I got out, I was going to get loaded again. I was charming.

STEPHEN PITTEL: *David was not charming for more than thirty seconds at a time at Fair Oaks. He was miserable. He was unhappy. He wanted out. The second day he was there they discovered an ounce of cocaine and a quantity of heroin he was hiding in the pouches in his cheeks, like a little squirrel. David was very sorry they confiscated it. Physically, he was a mess. He needed dental work. He had serious edema and all sorts of other medical complications, including sleep apnea and skin infections. He begged me to get him out. I said, "David, you can walk whenever you want. Anytime you decide you'd prefer to be in jail than to be in the hospital, you can walk out." There's a policy at Fair Oaks that patients agreed to when they signed in, saying you wouldn't sign out without forty-eight hours' advance notice, to keep people from making impulsive decisions.*

*There was close supervision and you had to be accompanied if you
went outdoors. David was calling Jan all the time and his manager
told me, "I don't think David can get better unless Jan does." David
prevailed upon me to call Jan and I called her, talked to her, and
went over to the house in Mill Valley and met with her. She looked
like hell and she was emaciated.*

While David was sweating it out at Fair Oaks, Jan was called
back to Kansas City to face trial in federal court on the
charges stemming from her arrest on the airplane in the
Kansas City Airport. She too had reneged on her promise to
enter a drug diversion or treatment program and the U.S.
Attorney in Kansas City took the same stance as Judge Mc-
Dowell in Dallas. He filed a misdemeanor drug charge and
ordered the case to trial. The terms of Jan's probation and
plea bargain had included a familiar promise: to seek help to
end her dependency. Larry Lichter understood the difficulty
of getting Jan to quit:

LARRY LICHTER: *I wouldn't plead her guilty to that because I knew
that she would end up locked in jail if she didn't comply with her
probation. So I fought the case the best I could to the point of
actually going there and trying it in front of a jury. I told them all
that happened was the airline employees got the wrong suitcase.
Which is, of course, a defense to the gun charge. She didn't intend to
bring a gun on the plane; she just wanted her stuff. The jury let her
go on that.*

Lichter remembers that the prosecuting team wanted nothing more than Jan's rehabilitation; her appearance was so
awful that she inspired pity in the courtroom. The prosecutor, in his summation, made an argument that Lichter successfully protested and had stricken from the record, but
once said, was irrefutable. Pointing at Jan, the prosecutor
said to the jury, "Look at this woman. Do you honestly
think that a verdict of innocent is the best thing you can do
for her?"

LARRY LICHTER: *I put her on the witness stand on the third or fourth
day; she was rational. Prior to that, she had been facedown on the*

table when I wasn't there to prod her awake, like, for example, during my opening statement. If I'd have known how to stop the scabs and stuff, it would have been good too. Jan wouldn't take her hat off. All the conventional wisdom says when you start a jury trial, first take the client to the beauty parlor. No chance of getting her to the beauty parlor; she would fight to the death rather than do anything like that. She said her hair was so tangled that she was embarrassed; I offered to have it done by the pros, any way she wanted. She wouldn't do it. The final word was in the newspaper headline: ROCK STAR'S GIRLFRIEND CONVICTED OF DRUG CHARGE. *What upset me was that the judge could have given her a chance to have a clean record and he didn't. In federal court, they have the right at sentencing—if it's a little thing—to sentence someone to rehabilitation; you can divert them into a program or for counseling, but they didn't do that for Jan. They put her on probation.*

Jan was on probation, David was on an appeal bond. Their personal liberty was becoming a fragile privilege instead of a sturdy right. Jan returned to Marin and waited while Pittel made efforts to enroll her in a treatment program in San Francisco, in an inpatient resident program that had a good reputation for managing addiction. She stalled, denied, and eventually failed to attend. Her Kansas City probation supervisor wanted to jail her, but the local federal probation officer thought she might benefit from medical attention and kept her free while lawyers and therapists tried to get her into treatment. In New Jersey, David kept on struggling at Fair Oaks, making a fuss over the fact that he wasn't permitted to play music or record; his therapists felt it was more important for him to work on his head than to work on his music. After more than a month and half in the program, David went over the wall, leaving Fair Oaks abruptly—without warning and without permission.

I ran away. I was really stupid. I had spent seven weeks straight in Fair Oaks and I actually could have beat it right then and never done any jail time at all. I can't believe how stupid I was. I was in denial, saying things like "Hey, it's not going to work. I'm going to get out of here and I'm going to get loaded and that's what I want and fuck you people. I don't care what you tell me. I don't care about any of your bullshit. You don't know what you're talking about in the first place." Somebody came with a car from New York and met me in the yard. It was a guy from Marin County, a really bad guy who came there to get me out. He used a stolen credit card. He figured that somehow I was worth money and he could get a piece of it. I rigged it so I could go out for walks; I was cooperative and expressed interest in getting some therapy, so they allowed me yard privileges. I spoke to my friend on the phone. He showed up with his car. I got in and we drove to the city, where I made another stupid mistake, kind of a compound fracture of the intelligence. I called Mort to get the number of a woman we knew in Greenwich Village. That made at least one person who knew where I went when I left the hospital. And he told someone else and they told someone else. I was in the city for less than forty-eight hours. I'd gone off to visit someone else to get loaded and when I came back to the apartment, there were New York cops and DEA guys and some guy who flew up from Texas waiting for me. Six guys in the apartment when I got there; I knocked on the door and they said, "Hi!" and took me downtown.

UNITED PRESS INTERNATIONAL: *New York, N.Y. Rock singer David Crosby was arraigned on drug possession charges Friday and the judge set bail at $15,000 and ordered the songwriter to hand over his passport. Crosby was arrested by police in Manhattan Tuesday, ending a search that began Sunday when he disappeared from Fair Oaks Hospital, a private psychiatric facility in Summit, N.J. Crosby had been ordered to undergo the drug rehabilitation by a Dallas court after he was convicted of cocaine possession and carrying a pistol in a Dallas nightclub. He was arrested Tuesday for possession of a small amount of cocaine, said Mary deBourbon, a spokeswoman for Manhattan District Attorney Robert Morgenthau. State Supreme Court Judge Stephen Crane set Crosby's bail at $15,000. Texas is*

seeking Crosby's extradition as a result of his failure to abide by the
rehabilitation program set by the court, deBourbon said.

The first place they took me was a fucking horror show: Man-
hattan Central Booking. That's a huge tank full of guys waiting to
be processed. I was there for fourteen hours or so, lying on the
floor. I was frantic, cold, and I wanted to die. Then they put me in
a place called the Tombs. The old Tombs was a terrible old place.
The new Tombs is probably the nicest jail I've ever been. I spent
the night waiting for arraignment. Finally, they took me to
Riker's Island, which is one of the biggest, baddest jails you ever
saw. Riker's Island is the New York City prison, on an island in
the middle of the East River. Fortunately, someone took pity on
me and put me in a protective custody section in one of the
hospital buildings. I was still in an old funky barred cell with a
barred space outside, but I wasn't in the general population,
which was kind of them. I was there for a couple of weeks and
when I waived extradition, Texas came and got me. A big Texan
with a ten-gallon hat and boots and a badge took me on a commercial flight to Dallas. In handcuffs. It's pretty humiliating. We
sat in the very last row in coach class and my escort turned out to
be a decent guy. He was kind enough to ask the pilot for permission to take the cuffs off.

There had been a case where a transported prisoner had
grabbed somebody's gun, shot a couple of people, and held some
guys hostage; it was a terrible scene and the result was a policy
that required prisoners who were being transported on airplanes
to be handcuffed. You could be released, but it was at the pilot's
discretion. They knew who I was and my Texas guard asked the
pilot's permission; it was granted and I made the rest of the ride
with my hands free. I was even able to eat a Reuben sandwich
and it was the best food I'd had in a long time. When airplane
food in coach class is the best food you've had in a long time, you
know you've been living a bad deal. When we got to Dallas, they
put me in the Lew Sterrett County Jail. Sterrett is a model jail,

which means lots of tile and glass and cement and steel. It had fluorescent lights that were never turned off and there were no windows. It was awful.

Because he was a celebrity, David was kept "out of population," as they say in correctional institution jargon. (Being "in population" means you're part of the community of prisoners, sharing cell space, mingling in the exercise yard and dayrooms, and eating in the main dining hall.) That can be a privilege or a terrible burden; the alternative to being in population is to be "in segregation," which means held separately, individually, and alone. Solitary confinement—or "the hole"—is euphemistically known as "disciplinary" or "administrative" segregation. David was segregated, the practical result of which was that he was kept in enforced isolation, just the same as if he had committed some breach or infraction punishable by solitary confinement. In fact, he was being held apart to prevent any "incident" that might attract the attention of the press. If there's anything prison administrators hate worse than prisoners, it's media attention directed at their prisoners, their institutions, and, by extension, themselves. Like all good career civil servants, they don't like to be in the spotlight. The net result was David's isolation while he was a Lew Sterrett inmate. It didn't help his cause when he was caught stealing bacon.

I was a trustee for a while, assigned to Food Service. I pushed a meal cart, delivering trays to prisoners. The diabetics had special diets that included stuff that regular prisoners didn't get, like bacon. Food Service detail means you can swipe little things here and there. Everyone does it. One day I had my fingers on some bacon and someone either saw me or complained about their missing a bit of breakfast and turned me in. They took away my trustee status and put me back into isolation. Then they transferred me to a place called the Government Center, which is in central, downtown Dallas, right near Dealy Plaza. It's an old, old, jail. Things were looser than Lew Sterrett and that made it a better place. I was put in a little block that had been designed for seven prisoners and there were only four guys in it, so we had a lot of room. We made friends with the trustees, who would give us an extra dinner or two every so often. We had our own TV in the little common room and we had individual cells. It was grubby and it was dirty, but there was a phone I could use. Collect calls only, but it made life a little more bearable. I could call Jan. There was a library cart that came around, so I could get books to read. I was still in denial. I did almost four months there and somehow a maneuver took place which resulted in me getting back out on my appeal bond. I had been calling Mort in California and I'm ashamed to say I did a really shitty thing to my friends.

Graham Nash and Bill Siddons flew to Dallas to put up the bail money and get me out. They had to go to some lengths to raise the fee for the bondsman, but because they were my friends and because they had a business and artistic interest in me, they got me out. Did I show any gratitude? Did I behave in any way responsibly? No. First, I told them I was grateful, then I told them how happy I was to be out of jail, and finally I told them it was genuinely nice. I said something like "I'm straight now and I like it. This is great. I'm not going to do freebase anymore." In actuality, while I was saying that to them, I already had set up a meeting with Mort in Los Angeles the very next day. I did it on the phone from the Fairmont Hotel in Dallas, where we went after I was released. We flew to Los Angeles. They dropped me at a hotel. I got in a cab and went straight to another hotel, where Mort was waiting for me. I went to the seventeenth floor, went to his room, opened the door, walked in and grabbed the pipe and the torch and got loaded—*bam!* And this is when I had a huge start on beating the habit; I was straight from enforced abstinence, I didn't do any drugs in jail, even though there was shit available, and my system was drug-free. In retrospect, it's almost impossible to believe I did it, but I did. That's pathetic and there's no defense, except to shrug and say, "All right, so I wasn't ready." I had to slide a little farther down into the pit, which I promptly did. I went back to Mill Valley, where Jan was waiting, to a life where there was no money and only one reliable source of drugs—good old Mort. And he wasn't that reliable. He was wondering when I'd start producing an income that could support both our habits, since he was getting to the point where he was doing too much and *his* life was starting to fall apart. He wasn't able to pay back what he was being advanced and his connection was starting to dump him; it was getting worse and worse.

A story appeared in *Spin* magazine that made the *People* article look like a puff piece. It was titled "The Death of David Crosby" and, in researching it, writer Edward Kiersch went to see David at an associate's house. He described meeting Jan: "An emaciated barely dressed woman eventually strolls into the kitchen, grabs a bag of potato chips, and vanishes behind a sliding door. She giggles childishly as the door slams shut." Then he reported on David's appearance: "A disheveled, unshaven figure staggers into the living room . . . His stomach is bloated, his thinning, frizzy hair leaps wildly into the air. A few of his front teeth are missing, his pants are tattered, and his red plaid shirt has a gaping hole. The most frightening thing is his pale swollen face, riddled with thick white scales, deep and encrusted blotches that aren't healing. Looking at him is painful. A fourteen-year addiction to heroin and cocaine has caused David to resemble a Bowery bum. The spiritual leader of the Woodstock Nation is now a vision of decay."

Jan and I were very lonely and full of fear. I was always afraid that I was going to have a seizure. I was always afraid that I was going die of a heart attack. I was even more fearful that I would get busted. I knew that would be the end because in some part of my mind I wasn't stupid. I was crazy, but I wasn't stupid. I was blatant. Anyone with half a brain could tell that I was fucked up and holding [possessing drugs]. Everybody knew it by that time; it was a matter of public record. It had been on magazine covers, in newspaper headlines, everywhere: COCAINE AND CROSBY. I think the DEA could have popped me for interstate transport of dope or dealing lots of times and never did because I was such a magnificent Judas goat for them, a stalking horse. If they just followed me around, they would see everyone I contacted. Then they could follow them back to whoever they knew and if they did that

repeatedly, they could've rolled up huge networks of drug dealers. They'd be blind, raging stupid if they didn't do it. They
missed a lot of great chances. It would've been like 1964, when
you could've arrested all the pot smokers in Los Angeles by having one undercover cop working in Wil Wright's Ice Cream Parlor
on the Sunset Strip. If anyone walked in with red eyes, bust him.
The same thing was true of me. Anybody with whom I had contact had something to do with dope. It was the common cord that
bound us together. Anyone who didn't have something to do with
dope had backed off. I was all alone, except for Jan, Mort, and
Mort's little circle of friends, who had lots to do with dope . . .

By the summer of 1985, Crosby, Stills, and Nash had a tour
booked again. We were in demand; each year the promoters offered us more than the year before, despite the fact we didn't
have a record out. We had a large loyal following and new fans all
the time, young people who discovered the music on their own.
It's largely a fog because there's not much to remember except for
getting high, not getting high, and worrying all the time in between. When I was onstage I would think that I was succeeding
because I had all this acceptance from the audience and all the
support of my friends. I'd feel I was getting away with it. I wasn't,
but I didn't know it. I was doing mediocre work. This is what
passed for a good time: we'd be traveling in the bus, I'd have
dope, I'd be sitting in the back with Jan and we'd be getting
loaded or we'd be in a motel room and we'd be getting loaded and
fooling around and for the moment the pressure was off.

There were times when the group played in Texas when I was
frightened to be in the state because of my legal problems.
Crosby, Stills, and Nash would play concerts in Dallas or Houston
or Austin and Stills and Nash could sleep in a hotel near the gig,
but Crosby would stay in a motel in Louisiana. That meant Mort
and Lydia, Myrna, and me and Jan—that's three motel rooms.
Then we'd charter an expensive airplane, a twin-engine turbo-
prop kind of airplane. Fly across the state line, play the gig, and
zap back to the airport, where I would jump on the plane, flip up

the stairs, and meet Mort, who'd be waiting for me with a pipe and a torch, and I would get loaded on the way back to Louisiana. We had to use that same plane to fly back to California from the last gig in Texas because nobody wanted me anywhere near them, even on commercial flights, not after the episode with the wrong bag and Jan getting busted for the gun and another episode on an earlier tour, where everybody showed up at the airport to get on the plane and the cops were there because they had intercepted a shipment of heroin that had been sent, counter to counter, hold for pickup by consignee: me. They wanted to know where Mr. Crosby was. Mr. Crosby was already out of state on the bus and everybody else was standing there at the counter with cops saying, "What about this heroin?" I was a constant risk, a perpetual embarrassment, and a massive thorn in the sides of my partners.

Chris Rankin is a young road manager and assistant who toured with CSN. He started in the music business as a sub-teen, helping his father, a singer, songwriter, and guitarist. He's spent half his life backstage and goes by the nickname Hoover, which is not a drug reference. He was a road tech with the band since the early eighties.

CHRIS RANKIN: *The crew used to call Jan: Death. "Where's Death?" we'd say because that's what she looked like. It would be ninety degrees in those outdoor gigs in the evenings, with humidity in the eighties, and Jan would be wearing a pea coat and a wool cap and long sleeves and thick pants and she'd be kind of cowering, into a shivering-in-the-corner kind of groove. She was worse than Dave, in both physical appearance and in a generally keeping-it-together mode. We were structuring the shows so that Dave could get offstage twice every set to hit the pipe: once during intermission and again during solo sections. Whenever Dave would leave we had to make sure there was some sort of private area close to the stage where the shit was and he could take a couple of hits, come back onstage, and sing. It was part of the contract, a production thing. It had to be within a certain distance of the stage because if it was too far, he couldn't make it. We also had it in the contracts that there could be no uniformed security personnel in the backstage dressing room area because Dave was paranoid. He didn't want to see any cops or uniforms.*

GRAHAM NASH: *He tried his best to do a two-and-a-half-hour show, but he couldn't make it without getting high. If he tried to stay onstage too long, he'd get sick. Physically ill, unable to work. He'd break out in a sweat, not be able to function, and have to leave. One time in Philadelphia he left the stage for fifty minutes. What could Stephen and I do? We had to totally rearrange the set, put in songs of ours that we hadn't done for years, just to keep it going. Stephen did a couple of his solo things and left and it was my turn. I did some of mine and we took an intermission before the second half of the show. I went down to the dressing room and found Crosby soaking wet. Dripping from head to fucking foot and I thought, "My God, he's not sweating that much, is he?" What happened was that Stephen took a five-gallon container of water and threw it at him in total disgust. Mac Holbert saw it and said it was one of the saddest things in his life to see David—once a proud, leonine, macho guy— just shivering and shaking and whimpering and wet through and through.*

> Jim DeLuca started as a truck driver and evolved into a transportation coordinator. He's driven for Crosby, Stills, and Nash ever since the beginning and in twenty years he's never lost a single piece of equipment and was late to the gig only once, when blizzards stopped everything else on the road. A dedicated biker, he's trucked his Harley alongside David's so they could go riding together. His company, Fly by Night, moves rock 'n' roll tours all over the continental United States and he's seen more than his share of backstage weirdness. He was in the dressing room while Graham was onstage; he watched Stephen Stills come into the room that night:

JIM DELUCA: *I'm watching Crosby lying on the couch. I'm hearing Graham and Stephen performing, then just Graham, and Stephen comes through the door. You know those big trays they fill with beer and soft drinks backstage? Stephen goes to the table, takes all the bottles out of the tray, stacks them neatly on the table. When he's got the thing empty, nothing in it but ice and water, he walks over and dumps it all on David.* Whoosh! *David comes off the couch, soaking wet, and Stephen, in all sincerity, gets on him big-time and says, "Never walk off the stage during a performance! These people paid good money to see a CSN show and they are going to see a CSN show, even if you have to die up there on the stage and if you die onstage, then they're gonna watch that too. You're going back up there!" David was still in shock from the ice water, but he walked out the door, soaking wet, hair everywhere, just like he walked out of the shower. He went right up on the stage and started hummin' and strummin'.*

I can remember sitting in a hotel in Hawaii at the end of the tour: I had my little pile of base and I had my pipe and I had my torch and I had a spare can of gas and I had a little paper of heroin and I was sitting there and there was some room service brought up. The curtains were open and I was looking out at the dawn coming up over the Pacific (because I'd been up all night smoking by myself) and I felt pretty good. I thought I was real hip stuff. I said, "Wow, look at this. I've got this all together here." That feeling would only last as long as the dope—or the propane, or the room service or until I broke the pipe—because I nodded out. That happened all the time. Or I'd burn myself with the torch because I fell asleep with it lit or I'd burn a hole in the bed and wake up with the smoke alarm shrieking and security people from the hotel banging on the door saying, "What's on fire in there?" Then I'd have to get rid of everything and hide the torch and the paraphernalia and explain to them that a cigarette burned that smoldering six-inch hole in the mattress—when I didn't even have any cigarettes or pot. I was constantly defiant because I didn't know how else to be. I was scared shitless all the time. I was constantly paranoid. I used to carry a gun because I thought people were after me, trying to rip me off, and I was constantly struggling to have enough money to score.

We had meetings where I would say, "I need five thousand a week," and we'd try and make it on that; it wouldn't be enough and I'd have to up it to seven thousand. Just for drugs. It was total absurdity because I would be keeping me high, Jan high, Mort high, and anybody in Mort's entourage who wanted to be high, usually his sister and whoever he was trying to fuck. Mort saw touring as an endless supply of money that was always going to be there. He assumed we could keep all the balls in the air as long as Crosby, Stills, and Nash kept working and we could stay high forever. It didn't work like that. A slow, inevitable degradation took place: in the quality of work, in the presentability of our front, and in my ability to stay alive.

When we got back to Mill Valley, we were lower than before —if such a thing was possible. I'd wake up and call a taxi to take me to Mort's in Novato. I'd pick up enough supplies to get me through the day or a few days—if I was lucky and had talked someone, somewhere, out of some money. Mort was starting to show signs of wear; his dealers had started to cut him off and he was using as much as I was. It wasn't so easy for him to keep up his precious front.

Then I got busted again.

UNITED PRESS INTERNATIONAL: *Mill Valley, Calif. Rock star David Crosby, forty-four, who has had several drugs and weapons scrapes with the law, was free on $5,000 bond on new charges, plus hit-run driving, officials said. Crosby is charged with possession of paraphernalia to freebase cocaine and a .45-caliber pistol. He also is charged with driving his car into a fence and fleeing, police said. He was freed on $5,000 bail after the arrest Wednesday, not far from where his car struck a fence along a road on Mount Tamalpais, police said. His companion, Jan Dance, thirty-four, also was arrested on drug and weapons charges. Crosby was sentenced to prison in Texas in August 1983 for carrying cocaine and a pistol into a nightclub* *where he was performing, but the conviction was overturned on grounds his dressing room was illegally searched. The singer is also on three years' probation for an arrest in November 1984 in Marin County for driving under the influence and with a suspended driver's license. His attorney said, "We will be entering a plea of not guilty. We deny the charges."*

Hit-and-run—and they caught me with a gun. It was my own fault. I didn't hit anything serious; I knocked one board off a guy's fence. It was because I was driving too fast and I shouldn't have had the gun and I didn't stop and that was that. The guy who owned the fence saw me do it, got my license number, and called it in. It was somebody's rented car they had gotten from somewhere and as soon as I saw the red lights flashing in my rearview mirror I knew it was all going to go to shit. There wasn't any way the court in Texas could overlook it and, sure enough, they set a date for me to come back down there and have another hearing. I knew what the judge would say before he said it: "You got busted again. You were holding again. You were high again. You had a gun again. I told you not to do that. You did it again. Okay, you're going to go to prison." Jan and I were isolated, frightened, paranoid, and broke. We sat around, waiting for the ax to fall, wondering what the hell we were going to do.

The news got back to Dallas and Judge McDowell scheduled a hearing for David to show cause as to why his appeal bond should not be revoked and why he shouldn't be remanded to custody to begin serving his sentence in the Texas Department of Corrections. David knew that if he walked into McDowell's courtroom through the big door to the public corridor, he'd surely leave through the little door to the holding cells in back. He failed to appear. It was Thanksgiving, 1985, and the holiday weekend slowed down the paperwork; on Monday the judge would issue a fugitive warrant for David Crosby and Knox Fitzpatrick would make sure the Marin Sheriff's Department got their copy. By the time the long weekend was over and deputies went to the house in Mill Valley, David and Jan were gone. They ran. In addition to all his other troubles, David was now guilty of interstate flight to avoid prosecution.

I didn't want to go to prison and there was a warrant out for my arrest. I knew I had blown my appeal bond and that I was going to be sent to jail in Texas. We wanted to get off the dope, but we couldn't cope with hospitals and treatment centers and we didn't want to get split up. So we decided to go to Florida, find the boat, and have Robbie Smith sail us to to Costa Rica, where there's no extradition treaty with the United States. We had heard that the *Mayan* was somewhere in the Bahamas, but we didn't know where, exactly. My thoughts were that we were leaving the country forever. I was giving up my friends, my future, and everything I'd done while living in the United States.

BILL SIDDONS: *It was Thanksgiving, right before he left. I took him into a hallway and begged him not to run. I said, "David, this is the major mistake of your life. You cannot live on a boat for the next thirty years. You will never perform in the United States or any of its territories. Anywhere you try to go, they will get you; you'll run out of money so fast you won't know what hit you. It's not going to work. Don't even try to do it." He said, "Right, Bill," took the money, and left town. Right after that a mutual friend who lives in Mendocino called me and told me that her house had been hit by the FBI, looking for Crosby. So I called David Vogelstein and every other attorney involved with Crosby and said, "The FBI's looking for him." I think it was Vogelstein who told him, "David, you're wasting your time. The FBI's looking for you; they're at the airport. Go to the airport; go to jail. Why don't you just turn yourself in?"*

That wasn't the plan. David sold the last tangible asset he had, a grand piano, for five thousand dollars. That was his getaway money. He called on outlaw friends for help, knowing he couldn't travel on commercial airlines. His contact was an East Bay character named Ronald Wiggins, who shared these recollections during an interview conducted inside the walls of the California Correctional Center in Susanville in the far northern corner of the state. He was confined on charges unrelated to the role described here. David caught up with Wiggins on November 23, 1985.

RONALD WIGGINS: *I demanded he come to my house and stay for a Thanksgiving dinner, because hey, this is traditional. Right? Besides all the rest of the bullshit that's going on, let's get some real values back in here. He wanted to go to his boat and he was crying in his beard. He kept saying, "I think I have this together," and it wasn't together. Nothing panned out. On Sunday morning it was drizzling and gray outside. David says, "I gotta get some help. Can you take me to see a couple of my friends at their clubhouse and I'll see if they can come up with a van to drive me down to the boat." Right. We drive to the place; David and the main guy have a little pow-wow and the long and short of it was that they didn't want any of their soldiers in a van with David, driving across the country on a three-day trip that would probably take two months, given the fact that he was a basket case and would slow down anyone, no matter how awesome, how bad, or how capable. I told him, "I'll get you a plane and a pilot and we'll fly you down to the boat." We got him one of those tried-and-true Saratoga Cherokee Sixes that's hauled many eight-hundred-pound loads for us over the years. Dave was like a beached whale and there was plenty of room for him to lie down in the back of that bird. He could just lay there, with his little pipe and Jan, and look out the windows. We scored all the human fuel and all the plane fuel necessary for him to get down there and they took off.*

We made a crazy flight across the country, me and Jan in the back of a charter aircraft, traveling from Northern California to South Florida in a single-engine plane. I was smoking heavily, since we had three or four thousand dollars' worth of dope with us. Jan and I were so happy—we were together, we were high, we were running away together. We stopped for the night twice: to eat and refuel. We stayed in cheap motels near airports in Albuquerque, New Mexico, and Little Rock, Arkansas. We gave false names. When we got to Florida, the pilot said he wouldn't take us to the Bahamas. No way we could talk him into it; he was weirded out by our behavior on the plane ride down. Luckily, at the air-port we chose in Florida, they had a courtesy car they'd lend to people who flew in without arranging ground transportation; I talked them into lending it to me, which didn't make the pilot happy because it went on his driver's license; I had lost mine. I swore to him that there was no problem, that I'd return in a day, that all I had to do was run down to Coconut Grove and see some friends to work out the Bahamas thing.

We took off in the loaner, a bronze Chevy six-cylinder four-door middle-aged car, and went to Miami to see Bobby Ingram. He said, "I love you, but you can't stay here." I said, "I know that. We're hot and I wouldn't want to stay here. I just wanted to see somebody and say hi, y'know?" He was sorry, he loved us, but it was no go. We went to another friend's house in the neigh-borhood, in Coconut Grove. This was a guy from whom we'd gotten dope, a nice man with a family. They were having a wed-ding for one of their kids the next day; they let us spend the night. That night we ran out of dope. We spent our last two hundred dollars buying grams. Some of the people there got loaded with us; others freaked out because we were doing base. One of the daughters had a screaming fight with us because her favorite thing to do was to have screaming fights with people. To get us out of their place, they took us to one of his son's places— true déjà vu. It was a place in which I lived many years ago, when I lived in Miami! All we did was lie there and be sick and try to figure out what to do. We were at a complete loss, out of money, living on pizza, and we didn't even know in what kind of shape we'd find the *Mayan*. We still thought that Robbie might help us get away and find some way to get straight, to get through this. We went to Jan's sister Annie's place and she and her husband said pretty much the same thing as the Ingrams: "We love you, but you can't stay here."

ANNE DEISTER: *I'm working at a Fortune 500 corporation, I'm a corporate officer, and I get a phone call from Jan and she says,*

"We've got a serious problem. We're running from the law because David didn't go to his hearing thing; it didn't look right. We're going to get on the boat; we're going to sail away and we need somebody to pick us up at an uncontrolled airstrip in Port St. Lucie." I called my sister Patti and told her, "I'm very worried about this." Patti agreed. We didn't know what the circumstances were. We spent the night with my sister because we didn't want to be home if Jan and David showed up. The next day, when we came back from dinner, there they were. They had parked this semi-stolen rental car across the street and left us a note saying they were asleep in the car. While I'm reading this amazing note, they wake up and see us and come running across the street. Jannie is just screaming, crying, and David is hurting and they both look as if they're going to die that night. I called our attorney, who had helped Jan in Kansas City, and he said, "Give them rest and counsel them to leave tomorrow and turn themselves in." We did that, but it took Keith, my husband, to get them to leave. They begged—first for another day, then for a few hours, then for thirty minutes. Jan finally said, "We've got to go," and they left.

We took off again. We were running out of options. We went up north to where the boat had been, hoping to find track of somebody who could take us to where it was. We knew some people who knew Robbie and we were still trying to find out where Robbie was. He said he would meet us in the Bahamas. We got to Jupiter, Florida, and found out he was still there. We finally found him and the *Mayan* and discovered, much to our dismay, that the boat was in no shape to sail anyplace. I hadn't seen the boat in years and hadn't sent much money in all that time. There hadn't been any maintenance. There was evidence of neglect and disrepair everywhere. The *Mayan* wasn't seaworthy and Robbie didn't want to sail us anywhere, anyway. He had the same insight as everyone else: "If you're on the boat, we can't be on the boat, because they're going to come for you and I don't want to get busted." I reminded him it was my boat, so he and the crew packed up and left, jumped ship and left us alone. To his credit, he came back from time to time and brought us a pizza or some cheeseburgers, a few Pepsi's or something because we were dying at that point, totally without hope. We might have overdosed ourselves on heroin—if we had any. I'm not normally suicidal, but we were out of choices. There was no place to go, no way to get there, no one to believe our stories, nobody to believe in us, and no way we could beg, borrow, or steal any money, drugs, or anything we needed. We had reached, in the classic sense, the bottom.

I went ashore and was talking to somebody when I realized where I was and I had a flash, common to a lot of people in their final moments of dissolution and despair. It was my moment of clarity—my Moment of Decision—when I realized with utter lucidity that I could not go on. There was no way to proceed any farther down this path. There was *no more path.* I had a moment's worth of courage, the strength to turn myself in. I was so afraid that I would blow it that I didn't go back and tell Jan I was going to surrender. I didn't even go back for my shoes. I got a ride to the FBI office in West Palm Beach, where I turned myself in, just as I was, barefoot, without even saying goodbye to Jan. That's how crazy I was.

UNITED PRESS INTERNATIONAL: *West Palm Beach, Fla. David Crosby surrendered to the FBI Thursday on a Texas warrant charging him with failing to appear at a bond revocation hearing. FBI agent Bob Neumann said Crosby walked into the West Palm Beach office at 3:45 P.M., EST. Crosby, forty-four, was handcuffed by local police and taken to Palm Beach County Jail to await being shipped to Texas. FBI agent Bob Neumann said Crosby, wearing a red T-shirt with the words* DAVE'S TOURS *on the back, walked into the bureau alone and offered no resistance. Asked for comment as police put him in a squad car, Crosby, his brown stringy hair tumbling on his shoulders, grinned and said, "Wish me luck, huh." He said he surrendered because it "seemed like the right thing to do." Crosby, whose dull brown, shoulder-length hair was streaked with gray, said little in court Friday. He was unshaven and wore a blue jail smock and pants as he sat among about sixty other inmates before the hearing. Crosby left behind the* Mayan, *a thirty-nine-year-old, low-slung vessel that was anchored over the weekend in the Intracoastal Waterway near Palm Beach. Its crew is waiting for the outcome of the musician's case. "We really want to spend some time cleaning her up. She's slid down—just like David," Capt. Robbie Smith said. "But David's not going to stay down. He's not going to die like you've been reading. He's got a real bad problem and he'll straighten it out. This [ship] is one of the only things in his life that he has left."*

Leaving behind the wreckage of his boat, his loved one, and his life, David began to do his time in jail. For the first time in twenty-five years, he was not looking forward to getting high later. He was going to stop. He had to. There was no other choice.

TWELVE

···························

They took me to Texas and put me back in the Lew Sterrett County Jail in the same exact cell that I had been in before, as if to say, "Get the picture, Dave?" That wasn't bad enough. They moved me back to the Government Center and this time they put me in the grubbiest, filthiest, shittiest solitary they had: a steel box, with a steel door with a slot in it, a shitter, a shower, eight or nine roaches, one dim lightbulb, peeling paint, and a lot of stink. Old human stink, shitter stink, and noise. If I have one overriding impression of jail, it's of eight radios on different stations and two television sets on separate channels, all running at the same time at full volume, with some very loud people yelling back and forth to each other over it. Things clanging, metal doors slamming. Clanging and banging all the time, while I was kicking heroin and freebase cocaine. I couldn't sleep. I couldn't eat well. I lay there and rolled over and over in my bunk. I looked like a hog on a spit. I was in a great deal of pain and that's how I spent Christmas 1985. It was during the worst and most disabling part of my withdrawal. Christmas dinner was a tamale and some beans or maybe a hot dog. It was hot, the food was cold, and I didn't even know what day it was.

The first couple of months when you're kicking heroin, after a habit as big as mine, you go through descending orders of magnitude of severe physical pain. They didn't give me anything for it, not even an aspirin. Their attitude was "*You* got yourself into this —*you* get yourself out." That was the worst. I had to beg someone in the hall for something to read—I'd settle for anything, any book, any writing at all. When I did get something, I realized my eyes were starting to go and I didn't have glasses. My teeth were rotting out of my head and I came down with severe back and neck pains, stress-related. I was depressed all the time, without hope. I was barely alive when a prison doctor finally examined me and said, "It's not cool for you to keep this guy in solitary like this." The doctor recognized the extent of my withdrawal pains, he could figure my level of addiction from my records: a quarter of an ounce of cocaine and at least half a gram of heroin a day. He moved me to a twenty-five-man dorm, a big, open space with beds and no individual cells. That was much better. I got to watch television and read books. I had people to talk to and there was a phone, for which you had to wait in a long line. But it was a telephone, a link to the outside, and I could call Jan. She was my inspiration. I owe so much of what happened next to Jan. She said, "I'm going to make it. I'm in a hospital and I'm going to recover. They're showing me how to do it!" I could hear that she was sincere, that she had found the strength to believe that she could beat it. I was encouraged to answer, "Okay, let's fucking do it. We'll make it through all this, however long it takes. We'll be back together and be alive and all right, we'll have fun and have our lives back." It was the first time that I ever really believed it, saying it to Jan on the wall phone in the jail.

After I was in the hospital section and the infirmary for a while, they said, "That's enough," and sent me back to Lew Sterrett and put me in solitary again. Fortunately, Sterrett is a modern jail, so my new solitary was better than the old-fashioned, horrible isolation cell that I had been in at the Government Center. I wrote a letter to the captain in charge of Lew Sterrett, saying, "Please, take me out of solitary, will you? Put me in population. I'm real gregarious person. I need people to talk to and I'm lonely in here and I don't get to watch TV or have books or anything." Pretty soon I had an answer. It was explained to me that they were doing it in self-defense because they didn't want to look bad. They figured that if I got in population and some great big guy broke me up or killed me, it would make the papers. They don't care if anyone gets killed; it makes no difference to them whatsoever. But if it makes the papers, that's bad. So they kept me out of population. They wouldn't even let me exercise because they thought my back pain was arthritis; I didn't get out for anything. Nothing. Zero. I didn't get out at all. They don't have yard time there because they don't have a yard. It's a county jail, so they can make their own rules. They had an exercise area which was the only social life there was and I tried to get to it, but they wouldn't let me go. And they never turned off the lights. I remember pulling the blanket over my face and lying there, listening to the weirdos freaking out.

We had people in there who should have been in some kind of psychiatric confinement. Instead, they found themselves in a special row of cells that were different: some had solid doors instead of bars, others had barred doors with glass, and some of them were just metal boxes lined with rubber—no furniture, no sink, no toilet, just rubber walls and a floor and a hole to piss and shit into. Guys who went there were put naked into rubber rooms, confined without any clothes. They were the inmates who got violent or who came in screaming crazy. If a guy came in on PCP or some other freak-out drug, he'd be stuck in one of the boxes. I've seen them hog-tie men, put them in restraints and then take one strap from their ankles and put it around their neck and say, "As soon as you calm down a little bit, we'll take that one off." These were guys who tried to punch a guard. Some skinny little black kid would swing and suddenly he'd be taking on five big football-player-size guards who'd just level the little guy and then tie him up. It was scary shit.

I didn't have any problem that way. I was reasonable. I could talk. They knew who I was. They had a handle on me. I was somebody they could relate to. Some of them even liked my music. Most of them said something like, "Gee, it's a shame you winding up like this. How come you got into all that heroin and cocaine and shit? Hell, you had money." The only addicts the jailers and deputies saw were guys off the streets; they couldn't understand how someone with a job and money could spend everything on drugs. These ol' boys were not rocket scientists. A couple of them tried to give me religion. The prison system would allow preachers to visit and it would admit little choirs to sing to us on Christmas. There's a lot of religious activity in jail; it's something to do. In Texas I saw lots of evangelical Christians, a few of whom befriended me. One or two did it out of true Christian charity and concern, but most wanted to win my soul for Jesus and score extra points in heaven.

This author visited the Lew Sterrett County Jail in Dallas and was surprised by the reasonableness of the rules for out-of-state visitors. Jail policy allowed visits outside of normal visiting hours if the visitor had identification showing he or she lived at least fifty miles outside of Dallas. A California driver's license was proof enough. On a Sunday afternoon in February 1986, after visiting hours, the writer made his way to 500 Commerce Street in Dallas, site of the Sterrett facility, and met with David for most of the afternoon. The two old friends talked for a few hours on a telephone, while looking at each other through a barrier of steel and bulletproof glass. No contact. David was puffy and bloated, the cheap polyester coveralls barely fit, and prison uniforms have no buttons or zippers or metal fastenings. The whole outfit was held together with Velcro. It was one step more chic than a hospital gown. Crosby was shaky, but sane. It was the longest conversation the two men had in five years.

I started writing letters for the first time in my life. I'd carry on a correspondence with people who'd write to me. For the first time in years, I had a public, permanent address. Anyone who wanted to write to me could send a letter, in care of the jail. I got mail from friends and a heartwarming amount of mail from people I didn't know: fans of the music or people who cared enough to express sympathy for my plight and to encourage me to continue in my struggle against addiction. There were letters from almost a dozen different guys in Huntsville. They all said, "Look, man, Huntsville is better than Dallas." I didn't want to go to prison. I had major anxiety about it—if I went there, I thought I'd die. Huntsville has a reputation as one of the worst prisons in the world; it was known for a tremendous amount of violence. But these guys said, "Come on down here, man. The food is better. You can play in a band. You get to work. You get to be out in population." I wrote them back and said, "No shit?" and they said, "Hell yes. You get to go to commissary. You can buy ice cream. It's a lot better." After a few months in solitary, I was ready for anything resembling a more normal existence, so I applied for a transfer to the Texas Department of Corrections facility at Huntsville. The transfer was approved. If Lew Sterrett could be characterized as bad, then the transfer to TDC was frightening.

REUTERS, LTD.: *Dallas, Texas. Drug-plagued rock star David Crosby was transferred from the Dallas County Jail to a state prison today and authorities said he may be permitted to join an inmate band. A spokesman for the Texas Department of Corrections in Huntsville said Crosby may be assigned to a work detail that would allow him to entertain other prisoners. "But I don't think we would set up anything special or give him any preferential treatment," the spokesman said.*

On March 6, 1986, in the middle of the night, I was called out of my cell. I turned in my stuff, rolled up my mattress, and said goodbye to my books. You're only allowed to take personal writing materials, your cheap pad, paper, pen and pencil. I was handcuffed to another inmate, we were herded in pairs to the sally port, loaded on an old Bluebird bus, and driven all night, sitting on metal benches in the bus. There was a driver and a guard with a shotgun sitting in a cage in the back of the bus. In the morning, we got to Huntsville. They moved us into a room, told us to strip, and we returned our Dallas County coveralls. Then they sent us to the showers, gave us a temporary uniform—white coat and pants and a white shirt—and some cheap, bad footwear that never fit. I can say this about prison shoes: no pair of them, no single shoe, ever fit anyone, ever, no matter what. Prison shoes are not made for human feet. You'd have to have cloven hooves to be comfortable in them. Limping along, we next got our haircuts and they made us shave our faces; no mustaches or facial hair permitted, whatsoever. After that, we were assigned cells in the Diagnostic Center, which is where you spend your first few weeks in Huntsville Prison.

Diagnostics is where you take a lot of tests to determine your level of education, comprehension, intelligence, and where they try to figure out your psychological profile and security level. It's also where they filter out the gang members. It's not too hard to do because most of the guys who do time and join a gang are identified by tattoos, usually self-applied or done with a friend and a ballpoint pen. These are markings that say I'M IN A GANG. Not literally, of course, but there are clear jailhouse tattoos with initials: TS stands for Texas Syndicate, MM stands for Mexican Mafia. Those were the two major affiliations. Then there were the Banditos, the Texas biker gang, equivalent to Hell's Angels in California. There were some people at Diagnostics who showed some compassion; trustees or cadre. They were prisoners too, but they had responsibilities and work assignments and they processed us. There was a guy who worked in the kitchen named Thomas Simanek, a poet, a songwriter, and a lyricist; primarily he was a poet. He'd written two or three books of poetry while he was inside, convicted of murder. He won't be out any time soon. The poetry's pretty good, especially *Songs from the Big House.* We still write to each other.

There was a psychologist who saw me, a nice man with a Hungarian name that escapes me; I told him what was going on with me, that I'd like to find my way out of this thing, but that I'd slid so far down into a hole that I couldn't even see ground level. By this time I had been drug-free for only a few months and I was still going through terrible withdrawal from base. I craved it all the time. I dreamed about it several times every night. I'd dream of doing it and not doing it; I'd imagine finding some and losing it. I was having nightmares. But slowly it started to get better. During the two weeks I was in Diagnostics, I started to write "Compass." That was important because when I saw the lyrics to "Compass" I realized that, even though I was still suffering and things were not fun, there was obviously more of me awake than had been in a long time. It was the turning point. It was when I realized this was actually going to happen. I was going to wake up and somehow the long nightmare was going to end. I was so proud of those lyrics. I showed them to the psychologist and he said, "These are great." With a touch of my old modesty, I said, "Yeah, they are, aren't they?" I was stunned. I showed them to my friend Simanek and he echoed the psychologist's appreciation. That was real, positive feedback because Tom knew. He was a poet. He saw the images.

Huntsville was better than Lew Sterrett on a lot of levels; the first day we walked into the mess hall I saw real eggs. I almost got down on my knees and gave thanks right there. It was the first real egg I had in a long long time. They only gave us one, but it was real. It had been in a chicken! It was a big deal. Remember, although the food was much better than it was up in the county jail, it was still bad. I mean bad, as in *bad*. I kept putting on weight because all they feed you is five kinds of starch a day. They feed you cereal, bread, rice, beans, and potatoes. If there's meat, it's some form of pork; that's the only animal protein, except for the eggs. I don't know what they did with the chickens; maybe the guards ate them. Prison pork is always the lowest, worst cut of bad pig meat from hogs raised by inmates. It's jail-meat. I don't know how I got through it, but I did.

After my evaluation time in Diagnostics, I was assigned to the

Wynne Unit. I think they did that because somebody pulled some strings and I suspect it was Mr. Gregory Gathwright. They knew I was a musician and Wynne Unit was the place that had the best band and a tradition of playing good music. In the days of the Huntsville Prison Rodeo, they used to furnish the music for the big show, which was nationally known. It was discontinued because the old prison stadium was condemned. They still had little concerts on major holidays and they staged an annual country and western music show. Wynne Unit always provided the band. Gregory Gathwright was the music teacher, an employee of the Texas Department of Education, not a prison guard or administrator. He was there on a contract basis to run a music program as part of the process of inmate rehabilitation. Wynne Unit was the only real musical scene in the Texas prison system and in Huntsville, the TDC consists of about forty thousand inmates, spread over twenty-eight to thirty different units. They're all maximum security institutions, all fenced. They all have machine-gun towers. There are no lightweight places; there are no work camps, halfway houses, or honor farms. It's all hard time.

At Huntsville, most of the inmate population works at menial and semiskilled jobs in prison farms, factories, shops, and mills. They stamp license plates, make furniture, sew mattresses, grow food, tend livestock, clear brush, and cut lumber. There is a smaller group, composed of gang members, violent cases, psychotics, and the generally maladjusted. They don't let those dudes out. They're kept in segregation, locked in their cells in special blocks or wings. If someone from segregation is moved through the general population, they're assigned two guards, front and back, and put in handcuffs. One guard keeps his hands on the handcuff chain, controlling the pace and direction, the other has a big metal club, in case there's a disagreement or policy difference between the inmate and the guards. Get the picture? I've seen guys from segregation dragged by the handcuffs into the infirmary, streaming blood, battered beyond recognition. I saw it with my own eyes and it happened repeatedly. The explanation was always: "He fell down the stairs." I didn't personally witness any deaths, but two men died while I was there: one from stab wounds, the other reportedly a suicide, who was said to have hung himself from the air vent. That's a little difficult in segregation . . . the air vents are six inches off the floor. Generally, it's safe to say that a lot of people were beaten up in fights between inmates or in fights with guards.

There was a group of guards called SORT, and they were the guys you could count on to "sort things out" if it got heavy. The initials stood for Special Operations Response Team, which I'm told has been discontinued, but while I was there, they were an elite unit dressed in all-black fatigues with big black combat boots. They'd double-time and march back and forth in close-order drill whenever they went by. They were huge ol' boys who volunteered for this because it meant a little extra pay. There were never any of them bothered with a brain; they were bad mothers who'd get sent anywhere there was trouble. There were lots of full-automatic weapons around the prison, M-16s mostly, and we even had a dog farm where they raised hounds to guard prisoners and track escapees. You could safely say it wasn't summer camp. Some farms are harder than others; Wynne was in the middle. We had plenty of murderers; we had people who were in for planting bombs. One of the men who befriended me was a guy named Murray Chappell, who was in for trying to bomb an abortion clinic. I found him to be a decent guy. He was one of the guys who wrote me a letter when I was up in county jail, saying, "Hey, it ain't so bad down here."

And it wasn't. My arrival at Wynne Unit was special, thanks to a prisoner named Billy Jones. Billy was the lead guitar player in the prison band and had one hell of a lot of time to practice and a lot of time to serve: he was in for murder. He went into the joint when he was in his late teens or early twenties and taught himself music while on the inside. When I met him, he had already done ten or a dozen years. What I found sad was that in all the concerts and public performances he played with the band,

Billy never experienced playing for women and girls, which is half the fun of playing rock 'n' roll. To this day he's never had the fun of watching an audience of both sexes enjoy his music.

GREGORY GATHWRIGHT: *This particular guy he's talking about is, in my estimation, the best guitar player I've ever seen in this setting [prison] and if he was out where he could develop his talent, there's no doubt in my mind that he'd be playing somewhere professionally. But he was convicted under the new "aggravated circumstances" law in '77, which means that he has to serve at least twenty years flat on a life sentence. So, theoretically, 1997 is when he comes up for parole, so he has a few more years to develop his talent.*

Gregory Gathwright is a devout Christian and a music teacher who guides inmates at the TDC prison in Huntsville. A former schoolteacher who taught at Huntsville High School, he transferred to the prison system because of a better pay scale and a more highly motivated group of students.

GREGORY GATHWRIGHT: *They call me a music instructor. The prison system is a system within the system. Every prison has units inside it, like a campus. They call it the Wynne Campus; I guess it sounds better on the transcript to say you're at a campus. I'm a schoolteacher; that's what it amounts to. It's almost a shame they pay much better to teach inmates than they do pay to teach high school kids, but I've had real good response 'cause there's no school counselor sticking kids in guitar class or the band. These guys want to be there. I was raised in the church and Christian music, gospel music, that's my thing. I think it kind of hurt David's feelings when he found out I wasn't all that familiar with his music.*

Billy Jones and some other guys sought me out my first night. They had snuck two cheap guitars out of the band room because they were so excited that I was there. Here was a real musician from the outside and they were thrilled. Billy got me out of my cell and got me up to the prison library. We climbed up into a loft in the library and played. It was the first night I was there and the feel of a guitar in my hands was stimulating, exciting even. I was grooved. Billy must've had the cooperation of a couple of guards who were friends of his, young guys who were equally delighted I was there. That first night I was still a celebrity, even though we had to sneak around to play music. Then I found out I had to audition to get into the band.

GREGORY GATHWRIGHT: *The guys in the band were real interested in seeing if Crosby would be transferred to the Wynne Unit from Diagnostics because that unit is supposed to have the best musicians in the prison system. I thought it would be nice to have him over here and work with the guys and show them something about harmony and help them out. David was shipped over on a Friday, my day off.*

The first chance I really had to see him was on Sunday morning. I work with the church choir and after the service I went and looked up his cell location. The first time I saw him through the cell bars, I thought, "I've got the wrong guy. I'm going to go back and get the right address." I said, "Can you tell me where they've moved David Crosby?" He said, "Hey, man." I couldn't believe it. I'd seen him in pictures with the hair and mustache and this guy had his hair cut short and he was unshaven and he said, "I've been wanting to meet you." He auditioned for the band. Usually when a guy auditions I have him sit in with the band. David sang "Wooden Ships." He'd already played with these guys over the weekend up in the education department and they had already worked on some things. I hate to call it a formality, but there wasn't any way in the world I wasn't going to have him.

There were a lot of guys who were in the church, Christians that wanted to witness to him and felt that if they could convert David, it would be a real feather in their cap. But I had a vision and I never had one before. It came to me in a dream that he would come to the unit and I was to witness to him. But I never could. I felt we communicated and I believe I communicated my ideals and faith to him. And he played good music.

There were several guys in this band who were talented. The lead singer was good and had a terrific high range; he was the lead singer of the band until I got there and he was a solid harmony singer too. There were a couple of other guys who played guitar and sang. There was a tough little cracker who played bass well and a black guy, Mike Curtis, who knew every Crosby, Stills, and Nash song better than anyone else there—he was a bright, intelligent guy and a good musician. Even though Billy Jones was younger than me, he was an older and wiser head. He taught me a lot about how to stay alive in prison.

The way you do that is by having, making, and keeping friends. I had friends. The racial trip at Huntsville was never explicitly laid out verbally, but it was obvious. There were three groups: white guys, black guys, and Mexicans. Black guys were kept with black guys, white guys were in with white guys, and Mexicans were with Mexicans. They don't mix very much. At work you can be friends. I had friends in all three camps, but I was an unusual case. Because I was a public personality, people responded to me in two ways. I had people who wanted to be my friends, like Murray, who had loved my music. But I had to deal with guys who hated their lives and hated me for making a lot of money and living what they thought was a glamorous life on the outside. Those dudes were dangerous. One of my benefactors was a little guy named Polack, who ran the cutting and measuring section of the mattress factory where I worked. When I managed to get under his wing and worked at cutting and measuring material, my work in the factory became bearable. That's when I started to mix with people and develop friends. There was an underground of the literate, people who passed books back and forth. You have to smuggle books in your socks because you're not supposed to carry anything in the halls. We'd stick a book in our socks and hope they didn't catch us. If they did, it was only a paperback, so the penalties weren't too bad. Polack was doing twenty-five years for armed robbery and was a little, skinny, scrawny, ugly, mean-looking guy with a great sense of humor and he was tough as a nail.

I was in C Block. Picture a building three stories high, with three tiers of cells, each tier thirty cells long. At one end is a common room where you can be during certain times of the day and in the evening. The common—or day room—has steel tables bolted to the floor and two television sets on the same wall, twenty feet apart, both turned up as loud as they go, tuned to different stations; noisy, but not half as noisy as the domino games. The official rules of prison domino play demand that individual players slam their pieces on the table as hard and as loud as possible, usually with accompanying curses, shouts, and threats. Spectators are encouraged to comment at the same volume level. The cells were two-man cells, about five feet wide by twelve feet deep. There was a little desk at one end with a toilet next to it. Two bunks against one of the long walls and barred doors, electrically controlled from a guard station at the end of the tier. There were a number of these buildings, each one with its own layout of cellblocks and tiers. Some were built in the thirties, in the traditional layout you see in prison movies, and others were more modern, like office blocks with steel-mesh windows. In addition, there were farm and shop and factory buildings, where we prisoners performed useful labor. There were about twenty-five hundred men in the Wynne Unit. Sometimes I'd be assigned a cellmate; other times I was alone. I roomed with a forger, a guy who played bass in the band, and some others. There was always a turnover.

There were all kinds of guys, some of them hardasses, others real dangerous. They were angry men. They all believed they didn't deserve to be there and they'd walk around enraged, like loaded bombs. They weren't just pissed off; they were ready to kill. These were the guys who would look at you and say, "What the fuck are you fucking looking at? Don't you fucking look at me again or I'll fucking kill you." I believed them and the first thing I learned was to avoid them.

As for the guards, if you knew them, you'd call them by

name, unless you were talking to a lieutenant or a sergeant. They'd be addressed by their rank or title. Between ourselves, guards were called "screws" or "fuckheads." If you didn't know a guard, you didn't call him anything. There was a warden, but we never saw him; he was an old guy close to retirement and he was on his way out. The guy we did see was the screw who ran the place: Warden Jones, who hated my ass. It wasn't personal: he hated everybody's ass. He wore a bulletproof vest, carried a six-shooter, wore a cowboy hat and cowboy boots, and had all of his suits tailored. One day he caught me outside the band room where I wasn't normally supposed to be; that day I had permission to catch a breath of air. Warden Jones took great pleasure in writing me up, putting a violation on my record, which could have extended my stay in prison. He was so happy he caught me he was absolutely gleeful: I can still hear that cracker drawl, saying, "Now I'm gonna git you, Mr. Crosby. Yessir, I'm gonna write yo' ass up." (I take it back. Maybe it *was* personal.) I requested a hearing from a board of review that considers these things and they dropped the charge. Mr. Gathwright stood up for me, told them I had permission to be where I was, which was true.

Other people there were pretty decent. The major who was the boss of the uniformed guards was a hardass, but a relatively fair man. A lot of the officers and sergeants were civilized, while others loved to give you a hard time and fuck you over. There was one sergeant who was known as the Dope Dog because it was his gig to sniff out the guys who had drugs. He was pretty nice to me; I didn't have any. I think he was trying to curry favor with me, hoping I would give him something he could use; that's how everything works inside. The core of the system is a network of informants. That's also the root cause of most injuries. Someone informs, someone else figures out who did the informing, and then there's an accident and someone gets hurt—usually the informer. It's not real hard for a person to have an accident in prison. Whenever there was violence or a bust or some other kind of problem, there'd be a lockdown. Sometimes they'd lock us down for two or three days in a row; no mess hall, no day room, no work, just endless cell time and meals of stale bread and cheese sandwiches in a paper sack.

Generally, they had the real troublemakers confined "in segregation." I don't like TDC, but I'll say this: their system works for them. It's brutal, but it's functional. The guys who would really get up in your face and stick a knife in you were kept locked up, for the most part. The guys who were in the working population were guys who wanted to be there and they understood what was at stake. There was a general undercurrent of brutality and the perpetual threat of violence, but I doubt if it surfaced more than once a week.

The routine was simple, monotonous, and tough. At five-thirty in the morning they'd ring a long, loud bell. The big lights would come on and you'd have five minutes to get dressed and ready to get out. They'd roll the cell doors open and we'd walk to breakfast. It was a long walk. We ate in a prefab thing that looked like a giant house trailer expanded in all directions. It was a couple of hundred yards from the main building. Once we were inside, we'd pick up a metal tray with compartments and get the slop they fed us. The food was terrible, but better than Dallas. You'd eat with your buddies, stand in line with your buddies, and walk with your buddies. As in any collection of primates, we'd form natural affinity groups and have a social order. You always hung with somebody because if somebody was going to get you they'd get you when you were alone. They couldn't get you if you were with other people because then there would be witnesses and they'd have to kill them, too—and it was harder to kill five people than it was to kill one. Not impossible, just more difficult. That's what they mean by "social order." Consequently, I hung out heavy with my friends. It wasn't paranoia; there were people who were angry at me. One of them was a big, mean black guy, a real son of a bitch who used to tell me regularly that he was going to do me up. Eventually, I had to deal with him. He was about six-foot-three, weighed two hundred and fifty pounds, and he wanted to do my ass. Not in a sexual sense; there was plenty of homosexuality in prison, but fortunately I was fat and not real appealing. Take a guy like me—over forty, overweight—nobody's going to want me for a shower toy. My first priority was to make friends and have some buddies to watch my back while I watched theirs.

After breakfast we'd march back to our cells until about six-thirty in the morning, when I'd go to work in the mattress factory. Huntsville made institutional mattresses for the state of Texas and sold them all over the country. At work, there'd be a head count and if it didn't come out right, everything would stay like it was until they got it right. There were three counts a day: morning, evening, and midday; if the count didn't clear, they kept us wherever we were. After morning count, we'd make mattresses all day. I'd take material from a huge bolt of cloth, run it down a long table, measure it, double back and measure it again, and repeat the process until there were thirty layers of cloth on the table, ready for cutting. The frames at the end of the table held rolls of mattress fabric that weighed several hundred pounds; it took three or four guys to mount the cloth. There were measuring marks on the long cutting table and we'd walk and cut, walk and cut. I got real good at walking and cutting. I marked the material for the right kind of corners to cut. I'd lay that material. We'd cut padding for special pads. I learned how to work vibrating cutters. It was probably the third straight job I had in my life: the first two were when I was a kid in Santa Barbara, where I worked in a Chevy agency, delivering cars, and in a drugstore. Neither of those jobs lasted as long as my employment at the mattress factory, where I couldn't be fired. I made friends in there, with a supervisor, Earl McWhorter, whose son worked for TDC in Diagnostics; both men were fair with me. The prison business is the biggest industry in Huntsville; it's like making cars in Detroit or cooking rubber in Akron. There are families there with six people from several generations working for TDC; it's the largest employer in the county.

Our mattresses went to other prisons, hospitals, and institutions all over the country. Trucks would come in, load up, and ship them out. Sometimes somebody would try to sneak in the truck and escape, but the system they used to prevent that was real simple: after a truck was loaded, they'd park it and lock it, and let it sit in the Texas sun for three or four days before they sent it anywhere. If there was an escapee inside, they'd just find a dead body when the truck got to the other end. That all happened before I got there; I just heard about it. I managed to get along okay; I learned what I could and couldn't do. There were a couple of places you could hide and sleep. That was important because I was developing adult onset diabetes and as my insulin levels changed, I'd find myself falling asleep regularly in what was approaching a diabetic coma. Medical Services should've caught it when they passed me in, but they didn't. Their primary function was to catch malingerers and repair the severely damaged; they weren't the best diagnosticians in the world. Dental Services was somehow much better.

After work, if it was one of the days that I worked all day, I would get back to my cell late in the afternoon and lie there, reading and trying to forget about everything or writing letters or song lyrics. Movement was limited; you could get about when they unlocked your cell, but there was no place to go but the dayroom and dominos and dueling televisions were not my idea of a relaxing time. And if you were in the dayroom and the cells were locked, you stayed in the dayroom until the cells were unlocked. Most times it was easier to hang out in my cell.

I gained a lot of stature in the factory as the result of a combination of luck and circumstance. The factory wasn't automated, but there were a hell of a lot of machines: a huge contraption that turned raw cotten bales into mattress stuffing, sewing machines, cutters, stretchers, packers, and the like. The machines needed a lot of maintenance and the prisoners who ran the maintenance shop were the elite. They were old-timers who had their little scene together, a little private shop space with an air conditioner and a small refrigerator: no supervisor or administrator would come back and bug them if they did their job and kept everything running and the factory met its production quotas. These wise old guys took me under their wing because I knew something they didn't expect me to know.

One day I saw one of them, the oldest and most influential, playing with a piece of specialized hardware. I said, "That's a breaker bar." His head snapped around and he looked in both directions before he spoke. He said, "How the fuck do you know?" and I answered, "I know how to pick locks." He said, "Bullshit. Don't fuck with me, hippie. You don't know shit." I maintained I knew what I was talking about, but he still didn't believe me and he said, "Check the hippie, says he knows how to pick locks." He pulled out a couple of rakes and a breaker bar and a padlock and said, "Pick this." He handed me a Master #3 lock. Fortune was smiling on me: it was the lock I knew best. The Master #3 has only four tumblers and it's a cheaply built lock. It's a snap to pick. To myself I said, "Thank you, God. Somebody loves me." He could have handed me a Shlage or something with a tricky double tumbler that would've been beyond my level, but he handed me a lock that I had picked before.

I slipped the bar in there, tensioned it, took the rake, kicked one tumbler up, kicked another tumbler up, found the third and fourth tumblers, and *spang!* It opened. The guy looked at me and said, with some respect, "Son of a bitch, you're a *criminal!*" Because I was a singer and took a dope bust, I wasn't really in the hierarchy, which considers real criminals to be guys who are robbers or burglars, that kind of offender. But because I knew how to pick locks, I was "a criminal" in the good sense of the word. I was admitted to the jailhouse fraternity, all because some doper I once knew showed me how to pick locks. Since I'd been a burglar once, I was fascinated and it was something to do when I got high; I'd sit there and try to pop a lock. As a direct result of practicing burglar skills on a Master #3 padlock while stoned, I now had some influential friends at Huntsville.

Like everyone in the joint, I carried a weapon. The guys in

the mattress factory had access to heavy metal: we used foot-long steel needles to stitch the mattress tags and we all used Craftsman razor knives, the kind that hold the trapezodial insert razor blade. I had one of those in my belt all the time. We used eight-inch-long sharp steel scissors for cutting and trimming and we sharpened them ourselves. Everybody had these things all the time, so if some shit was going to happen, it was going to be real serious, real quick. I think that's probably why there weren't more fights, even though there were plenty of animosity and grudges between people inside. The availability of weapons made it like a nuclear deterrent. If violence erupted, there was a good chance of "mutually assured destruction." It was guaranteed that if you moved on somebody, his buddies would move on you and there'd be six, eight people dead or cut inside of a minute. It was like being locked in a closet with a guy when you've both got hand grenades; neither of you is going to pull the pin.

The closest I came to confrontation was with the big black guy who never got off my case. He was the only man to put an overtly threatening move on me; he reached into my pocket and took a picture I had in there, a personal photo someone had sent me. I said, "I didn't tell you you could do that," and took it out of his hand and put it back in my pocket, just like that. I got right up in his face and said, "Don't do that. Don't fuck with me." He comes right back at me, says, "I can do whatever the fuck I want," and I answer back, "Uh-uh. No, you can't." This was a big step, but one of my good friends, one of these real bad white boys, had clued me into the truth, which is, "If they're talkin', they ain't doin'." The mean bastard was all bluster and I didn't know it. I was scared of him. My bad pal said, "Call him on it. Get up in his face. Tell him to make his best move. I'll be three feet away. Don't worry about it. He doesn't have the guts to do anything. And if he does, I'll kill him." On that note of encouragement, I confronted my tormentor. He backed down, growling and swearing, and that was the end of it. I got along great with most other people there the rest of my time inside.

Three afternoons a week, David would be excused from work in the mattress factory and would report to the band hall to work with the prison band and inmates who wanted to play or learn music.

When I was in the music room playing with these guys, I was actually happy. I started being creative. I'd write lyrics to myself in the middle of the night. I'd dream about a song and wake up to write down the lyrics. Then I'd write more lyrics. I'd try to be alone, separate from the band for a little while, so I could work on tunes, but there was no place to go. There would be fourteen men in the band room trying to learn guitar and I'd be trying to help each of them; all of them thrashing away on cheap nylon-string guitars, singing "Michael, Row the Boat Ashore," and me saying, "Change. Now change. Change back." I could get some privacy in the bathroom, but that was not a pleasant-smelling space and there were no other rooms or rehearsal spaces or anything like that. But when we got to play as a band, it was exciting and it was cool and between me and Billy and Curtis, we could make this band cook. We did a concert that was supposed to be a Big Deal, but they wouldn't let the whole prison be in one place at one time. They'd run the men through in shifts, by blocks. You'd play for one block, then you'd play for the next block, and the next, and the next, until everyone heard the music. A Block had all the real weirdos and it was also the block where they housed the gay boys and that was difficult for us. We didn't like playing for them because they'd shriek and carry on and comment on our looks and clothes. Playing for our block was great because all our friends would come in gangs, they'd go crazy and cheer, and we loved it. It was good rock 'n' roll and they got to have a break in the prison routine and see our live show, which they treasured. It got me a lot of goodwill because I was good. Guys would come up to me in the yard and say, "Shee-it, man. I thought you was just a fat fucked-up junkie, man. But you can still do it. Y'know that?" I was singing well. I looked very funny onstage, but I could sing and play and we rocked out. It was a hot little band.

GREGORY GATHWRIGHT: *It was a small band until David got in it. Then, all of a sudden, there were musicians climbing out of the woodwork, wanting to audition for the band. It was the greatest attendance booster we've ever had. Guys who played on the linoleum —that was their only instrument—wanted to come out just to be near him and I had officers and officials suddenly wanting to make inspections of the band hall. Before he got in the band, we had four or five pieces. By the last concert he played, we had eleven or twelve players, including some horns and saxes and three percussionists. It was incredible. He was fascinating to watch because whenever he would come out for class, the first thing he would do, while everybody else was setting up, would be to sit at the piano and run through these progressions. I've never heard him like that, except on his recordings. These were things he was working out and as he'd be playing he'd look over at me and grin because he was happy.*

Playing and singing straight was an unfamiliar feeling. I hadn't been onstage with a drug-free system in more than twenty-five years, since I was a kid. Even when I was a young folkie, working in Florida with Ingram and my brother, I was smoking joints and taking speed all the time. For the last fifteen years I'd been as smashed as I could get on everything I could find—all of the time. I had made innumerable public statements, often quoted, that I had been stoned for everything I'd ever done and yet here I was, playing and singing straight and sober. That was really bizarre. The two strangest things to do when you finally get straight are music and sex. You have to rethink the whole deal. It's a whole new ballgame. Sex when you're stoned is totally self-serving gratification and it's got nothing to do with making love. Not when one is as whacko as I was. That's why I was so selfish and that's why I was into such kinky stuff: I was obsessive about drugs and sex. Freud understood it; he was obsessive himself. I believe Freud explored sex because he was a cocaine head. I don't know if anyone in psychiatric circles agrees with me, but I know that cocaine makes you want to get into kinky sex. As we write this, the *New York Times* is running a story about documented studies showing that crack addicts acquired "exaggerated sexual desires and diminished inhibitions" and "engaged in sexual behavior they avoided when not using the drug." I know that's true: from personal experience and because my behavior changed when I stopped doing drugs. There wasn't any sex for me in prison and that left only music to be explored and playing and singing straight was a new adventure, a powerful experience, my salvation, and, along with Jan, my raison d'être.

What about Jan? When David went to jail in West Palm Beach, she sought shelter with her family. She had talked with David after his incarceration and promised to seek help for herself; if he could have the courage to turn himself in, she would find the inner resources to quit the addiction that had crippled them both and brought their lives to such a dismal state. Annie and Keith Deister took care of Jan.

ANNE DEISTER: *She was awful. She slept twenty hours a day and every time she would ask for food I gave it to her. She drank chocolate milk by the gallon. She ate homemade lasagne, homemade chocolate cake. I cooked for two solid weeks and fed her; it happened over the holidays, so it was perfect. We took her everywhere we went and made her feel like part of the family again. It took us three days to get her in the bathtub because she said her skin hurt, but we made her take a bath. Patti's a beautician, so she gave Jan a haircut. We all bought her clothes for Christmas because she had no clothes. The day after Christmas we took her to the airport. She was ready to change her life; I saw it in her.*

JAN DANCE: *Annie gave me the money to fly back to Mill Valley, which was my choice. I called my probation officer in San Francisco and I told him I was coming back to turn myself in to a treatment center and that I had no intention of going anywhere else. I was in trouble for running after the last Marin bust, when David was charged with hit-and-run. When we were stopped, I took responsibility for the gun he had in the car, a loaded .45 in the glove compart-*

ment; the news had gotten back to Kansas City and they wanted to put me in jail for a year for violating my probation. I went home to Mill Valley and found Mort and Lydia and their kid there; they had gone through David's house and moved all the valuables out of it to the gatehouse, where they were living. They had a Christmas tree and everything. I stayed the night and the next morning Gene Schoenfeld picked me up and he drove me to Salinas, where the hospital was, and I began my treatment, the day before New Year's, 1986.

Jan underwent detox and rehabilitation at the Steinbeck Clinic in Salinas, where David's old friend Dr. Eugene Schoenfeld was director. She made surprising progress and not only survived the process but emerged a healthy woman who was employed part-time at the clinic to counsel new arrivees and assist in the program of therapy. She lived at a halfway house for formerly addicted women called Hope Haven and gradually rebuilt her damaged personality and depleted confidence. When she went back to court in Kansas City to face the judge, her probation supervisor, Joseph Brandenburg, was amazed by the extent of her recovery and rehabilitation. Jan was spared the year in jail, but Judge Calvin Hamilton imposed a grim condition of probation.

JAN DANCE: *The judge told me this: "I had every intention of putting you in jail for a year, no matter what. But since you've made so much progress since the last time I saw you, I decided to put you on a longer probation instead of giving you a year in jail. A principal condition of that probation is that you can't see David Crosby for five years. If you break the contract, you'll be in violation of probation and I'll put you back in jail for the year I'm not giving you now." I was between a rock and a hard place.*

When I went to jail, I told Jan that we had to beat this thing and that I had to do my time. It's what we needed to do if we were ever going to have any life at all. She agreed, since that's what she had wanted all along anyway. She wasn't happy; she wanted us both to quit a long time before that and she had done her best to push in that direction, even though she was strung out. Gene

Schoenfeld is a hero; he was one of the last straight people to see us before we ran for it and he begged us both to go into hospital. I said that if we went to a hospital they'd come for us and throw me in prison. He offered to admit me under a different name—anything to get me to go—because we were in a mess. It was Gene who took Jan to the Steinbeck Treatment Center and put her in intensive care and took her through the horribles.

DR. EUGENE SCHOENFELD: *These are the notes I made during my exam of Jan in Oakland in late November of 1985, when she weighed less than ninety pounds. "Jan Dance is a very slender, Caucasian female. I had last seen her three and half years ago; she has aged a great deal during this time. She has poor dentition, notable in the front incisors in her mouth. She, like her friend, has ulcerations of the skin of her arms and her face. The ulcerations are more prominent and the scarring and the discoloration caused by the healing ulcers are more prominent in Jan Dance than they are in her companion." The skin ulcers on Jan and David were due to their scratching and picking constantly. Some high-dose cocaine addicts think they have bugs beneath the skin. Jan thought there were irritating cocaine crystals under her skin. "Ms. Dance has the same history of problems with cocaine freebase and heroin as David. When I asked her how she felt, she said that she felt fine, but she doesn't look fine. She has a grey complexion, pale. She looks 20–25 years older than her real age and complains about sore gums and loose teeth. Her gums are red, swollen, and friable. Incisors are loose. I suggested a proper diet and multivitamins daily. Diagnosis: (1) scurvy (2) heroin and cocaine addiction."*

Two months later, at about the same time as David was being transferred from Lew Sterrett in Dallas to the TDC facility in Huntsville, Jan was discharged from the Steinbeck Treatment Center in Salinas.

DR. EUGENE SCHOENFELD: *This was my discharge summary for Jan. "She took a little while to adjust to the rules of the Unit, but thereaf-*

ter became quite cooperative and helpful. She began to gain weight and with regular feeding and care began to take more care of herself, paying more attention to her personal grooming, including her dress and hair care. While in the hospital she was referred to Dr. Rocco, an oral surgeon, who began care of the patient's teeth, which had been in very poor condition as stated. The length of her stay in the hospital was a little longer than that of most other patients because of her necessity for dental care. She was transferred to a women's residential facility in Scott's Valley called Hope Haven. At the time of discharge, the patient had gained twelve pounds. Her spirits were much improved. She was alert and oriented, and will continue her care in the Hope Haven Residential Program." I continued to see her as an outpatient since that time.

I lived for the afternoons in the band room and I lived for letters. I got a ton of mail from a lot of people who were fans. I probably received more mail than anybody else in the whole prison. You lived for mail inside. I could recognize the sound of the footsteps of the man that brought the mail. I could tell a hundred feet away that it was him coming down the row of cells. Sundays were bad because they didn't deliver mail. I started writing letters when I got to Diagnostics and by the time I got into population at Wynne Unit, I was writing letters like a fool. I would write as many as eight letters in one day—to all kinds of people. Jan, Gottlieb, Nash, and Michael Finnegan were my favorite correspondents. Even Stills wrote me a couple of great letters. I wrote people and thanked them for trying to help. I told them what was happening to me and I tried to describe what it was to wake up, to regain real consciousness. Whenever I'd write a good set of lyrics, I'd send them to Jan and the others. I sent ideas for screenplays and stories to Carl.

The best part of my mail was Jan. She sent me pictures of herself, she sent me postcards with pictures of sea otters, whales, dolphins, and beautiful waves. I dressed out my cell until I had it decorated to my taste: pictures from home here, books over there, and a fan hung by some strings so it would blow on me at the right angle. There was no air conditioning and it was Texas in the summertime. We lived with our fans; we loved our fans. I was married to my fan. We could buy them in the commissary, along with candy, cigarettes, and little clip-on lights to read by at night. I had it all. I told every friend I had on the outside to buy me a ton of books and order me a truckload of magazine subscriptions. I had three towering stacks of books on my desk, at least two hundred and fifty volumes of paperbacks and hardcovers; I was the C Wing library. People would come by and trade. They'd say, "I got some good science fiction. What you got in war stories?" We'd trade and lend and swap and exchange. I had the best collection of anybody in there. Everything and anything is currency or a commodity in prison. Haircuts. Time. Work. Money. Joints. Food. Commissary stuff, primarily. Cigarettes were the generally accepted legal tender. A joint cost two packs of cigarettes; there was dope on the inside. Miraculously, I didn't want any!

I'd seen the joints. They were about the size of a toothpick and they were shitty joints. Get high? There wasn't any point to it. Something had happened to me. It started happening, I realized, even before my first day in Huntsville. It was a feeling that I'd had in the infirmary at the Government Center, talking to Jan on the phone. I was making a commitment, I had touched bottom, and somewhere deep inside I decided to try and do it straight— drug-free. When I started to write lyrics again, in Diagnostics, I knew that everything that I hoped about it being possible *was* possible. My mind could come back; I wasn't going to die on drugs; my life wasn't over. Day by day, standing on the chow line, working in the mattress factory, playing music in the prison band, reading, sleeping, writing—every moment in the present convinced me there was going to be a future. It took months, but changes were happening. I was emerging from a condition of utter hopelessness, what the book calls "complete and incomprehensible demoralization." I was experiencing little glimmers of hope and every day, as summer wore on, I found myself believing I was going to see tomorrow—and another tomorrow after that—until finally I came to knowledge that I had an entire life left to live. I had come all the way from wishing for death to believing in life.

> There was drug counseling available at Huntsville, but the sessions were group encounters held once a week and not particularly rewarding or productive for most of the prison population. Thomas Colkin is a young counselor who works for the Texas Department of Corrections; he met David in a group that was formed during David's stay at Wynne Unit.

Colkin ran an encounter session drug therapy program for a group of us. It was the only drug therapy there was and it was twice as effective as anything in the county jail because in county there was no counseling or therapy at all. This was something you could do, once a week for one hour at a time. Colkin was swimming upstream through a river of shit, trying to bring sobriety to inmates and rehabilitate them in the midst of an institution in which more than half the population was convicted of drug-related crimes. Nevertheless, he deliberately structured a group of inmates who were bright, relatively sensitive, and had histories of serious habitual drug use. We would meet and talk and somehow it was working. Tom Colkin was so sincere and direct with us that we began to express a consensus, a mutually held belief that said, "Hey, let's really try." We all promised each other we would not get loaded on anything that was in the prison and we all promised each other that when we got out, we would not get loaded on anything that was out there. Tom Colkin was a real help because he believed in us.

THOMAS COLKIN: *I had a game plan. I wanted to steer the group, but it wouldn't be steered. After the third meeting, I realized I'd just try and guide them to where they wanted to go and it worked out great. That group had so much energy in it that David went from sitting by himself to actually being some kind of leader. You could see the energy flowing out of that guy and he worked the group as if it were a concert, except that the members of the group took turns being the performer and getting feedback and strength from the others. The spirit coming out of that group made your hair stand up. It was wonderful. I think David was learning that if you really like yourself, if you're the whole, functional individual God or whatever meant you to be, there's no need to give your reality away to a chemical, to food, or even to another person, unless they are there to dance with you the rest of your life in a good and healthy marriage. If you really know yourself, then, truly that's what recovery is—going back and getting in touch with who you really are, being able to answer the question: "How well do you want to get?" The best thing David can do for anybody is to stay straight. Not that he owes me, the prison, or any drug program anything. There might be people trying to get him to do concerts and drug benefits and if it helps him, fine, but his greatest testimony is staying straight. I don't care if he doesn't write another song and you never hear another word about David Crosby. If he stays straight, that's enough for me. I like him as a musician, but any addict that goes through recovery is special to me just for that, whether he's famous again or not. Recovery's the most important thing.*

Judge McDowell had decided to credit David with all the time he had served in various facilities, including Fair Oaks Hospital and his first incarceration at Lew Sterrett. The state of Texas, faced with overcrowded facilities and a growing number of prisoners, decided to double up on "good time," giving prisoners with clean records extra days to credit against their sentences. David was going to benefit from this, since he had hopefully applied to the Texas Board of Pardons and Paroles for a parole, after completing whatever they thought was an appropriate stay at TDC's Huntsville Prison. He was coming up on his first anniversary in various confinements and friends were beginning to submit letters of recommendation to the board, requesting David's release.

To the Texas Board of Pardons and Paroles:
Having been Mr. Crosby's friend and partner for al-

most twenty years, I would like to lend my support to the earliest release of David. No one has been affected or more deeply hurt than I by the hold that drugs have had on him . . . my hope was replaced by cynicism. However, the many recent communications I have had with David clearly indicate to me he is clearer of mind and stronger of spirit than I have seen him in the past seven years. I fully realize that his imprisonment most probably saved his life . . . I feel that his release at this time would allow him to get back to the more positive side of his life and once again become the creative and sensitive human being I have so missed throughout this painful ordeal . . .

—*Graham Nash*

To Whom It May Concern:

As long as I have known David Crosby, he has been one of the most intelligent, joyous human beings I have ever had the pleasure of knowing . . . [but] drug addicts do not know how to live a sober life; they have to be taught. I was and I'm most grateful for the love and attention I received . . . I believe David should be free to become what he can be, but that takes work. Letting an addict out into the world with no program is the same as killing him . . . I have personally never heard of any other group or organization with the track record of the [anonymous groups]—give him a chance; send him to the people who know.

—*Grace Slick*

Dear Judge McDowell:

Today, for the first time in years, I believe David has made major strides toward recovery from his addiction . . . He poses no threat to society and little threat to himself . . . When he returns to the entertainment business, he will find a community that is intolerant and unforgiving of drug dependency. He will find enthusiastic support for his legitimate creative expression and he will find well-organized and well-attended group counseling among his peers. He is not the first star to destroy his life with drugs and there are many others who now offer a meaningful support structure that is new to Hollywood. I will personally extend myself in any way I can to make his transition comfortable and effective . . . David is well on his way to rehabilitation, has genuine opportunity for gainful employment in his chosen profession, and should be shown some measure of compassion as he tries to re-construct his life.

—*Carl Gottlieb*

I was told that I wouldn't make my first parole, but I applied anyway. I had an interview in July of 1986 that told me nothing; the interviewer was completely noncommittal. In August I was in the dentist's office, having some dental work done. The dentist was a contract doctor from outside. He was washing his hands when he said, "Well, did you see?" I didn't know what he was talking about. I said, "See what?" He answered with a curious look on his face: "You mean you don't know?" By now I'm starting to feel something. I said, "Know what?" That's when he handed me a newspaper with an article in it saying I had been paroled. It was the first I'd heard of it. I screamed, out loud, a yell that could've shattered steel. Sure enough, it was true; it became official when I got what we called my "Nineteen." That's a TDC Form 19 and nothing is real until that's issued to the inmate. I told Jan, she was ecstatic. Everybody was blissful. I was one happy guy. David Scott came down to visit me and told me that he had a plan for gigs for me to do; he was going to straighten up and stop drinking so that we could hang out together and work. I felt I had things to do. I was writing songs again. They had to be sung, shared, recorded. Nash and Jackson and Stills and everyone who had answered my letters was giving me positive feedback. They had every reason to be skeptical because I had done this before and always fucked up, but this time was different. I'd crossed over a line that I hadn't even approached before.

UNITED PRESS INTERNATIONAL: *Huntsville, Texas. Rock singer David Crosby could be paroled from a Texas prison in the next two weeks if the plan is approved by officials in California, where Crosby plans to go upon his release, parole officials said. Parole board spokesman Mike Roach said Crosby's release was approved by Texas corrections officials but remained subject to the approval of California authorities. In prison, Crosby works as a fabric cutter at an inmate mattress factory during the mornings and spends the afternoons playing guitar and piano with the inmate band. In the past two months, Crosby has written lyrics for nine songs and put two of them to music, ending a four-year inactivity caused by his drug addiction.*

It was the culmination of the promises Jan and I had been making to each other, long-distance. Each of us could honestly report to the other that it was working. I could say to her, "I'm getting better," and she could say back, "Me too." She weighed twenty-two pounds more than when we parted eight months earlier. I had a picture of her, showing her hair all shiny, her eyes clear and bright, and a big smile on her face. "My God," I said. "She didn't die. Look, man. Here's the girl!" I got all excited about the possibilities and my friends were checking in with messages of support and encouragement, saying, "I'll help you," "You can live with me," and "I'll help you do this." Everybody was so good I began to have belief. If there is any key to beating drugs and drug addiction, it's belief. Every other time I didn't believe I could stop, but somehow, in prison and in those letters and in the love that people showed me and held out to me, I found belief that I could make it.

The day came. I gave away all my shit. I got on another Bluebird bus and they carted me off to the walls, where they let me loose.

On August 8, a week short of his forty-fifth birthday, David walked out the downtown Huntsville unit that is the heart of the prison complex. Bill Siddons met him and drove him to Houston, an hour or so south. There, David would have to live in a place called New Directions for a few weeks, until the formal paperwork transferring his parole to California was completed; California would have to agree to accept him. Parole is a curious process. Technically, the parolee is still a prisoner of the state, which (in its wisdom and mercy) decrees that he may complete his sentence outside the walls, under varying degrees of supervision and control. The model parolee is one who gets out of prison, completes a process of reintegration into society by dwelling at a "halfway house," and goes home to live with his parents until he can get back his old job at the sawmill or factory. This satisfies the requirements for a parolee to have gainful employment, not consort with criminals, and reestablish "roots in the community." The rules and procedures were not developed to deal with people who played rock 'n' roll for a living, toured nationwide, and had substantial resources or access to money. It meant a little extra delay and complication, but it was worth it.

I stayed at New Directions, sleeping there every night. I spent every day in a hotel room, catching up on movies and ordering room service. I ate everything I couldn't get in prison, which was too much. I shopped for civilian clothes that fit me. The halfway house stretched the rules a little bit because they knew that I didn't have to go get a job. They knew that I had a job waiting for me in California. They also knew that they were only a holding station while the transfer to California came through. I went to some rehabilitation meetings and counted the days. The best part of it was when Graham Nash showed up—he deliberately changed his tour schedule to play Houston at a club called Rockefeller's. When we played and sang together, it was heaven. It was the first real sign to Graham that I might actually be serious this time, that I was going to do it. The audience was in ecstasy. I was in ecstasy. It was an extraordinary moment.

GRAHAM NASH: *David met us at the airport, which I thought was really neat. We went to a hotel, we were hanging out, and we were having a good time. David knew I was playing a show, he knew I'd ask him to join me, so we sang a couple of things, not a real rehearsal, just a little warm-up. At the point where I usually did "Wind on the Water," I'd normally play a tape of "Critical Mass," which David wrote, in the dark, then fade up the blue lights when we hit the down chord of "Wind on the Water." David opens the curtain and walks out in the dark during "Critical Mass." Everybody knows who it is and the place went bananas. We did a great show. David had that same fire that I'd loved him for in the past; he wanted to be there, you couldn't get him offstage, he was bathing in the adulation, he was loving the spotlight, he was singing with his friend, he'd done his time, and he was straight. I've talked to people that went to that show all the way from San Francisco and Philadelphia. It was a sublime night.*

On August 22, 1986, David arrived in Los Angeles and moved in with this author in a comfortable apartment in West Hollywood. The California Parole Authority required a stable environment, a residence "in the community." The apartment had been inspected by David's parole officer and the rules had been explained: no drugs or weapons on the premises, which were subject to unannounced search without a warrant. David would undergo regular drug testing and would have to be prepared to show up for a urine analysis whenever requested; failure to make a test appointment or testing "dirty" (evidence of drugs in the analysis) could be grounds for revocation of parole, arrest and reconfinement.

The transfer came through and they sent me to Los Angeles. Now there are several people to whom I owe an enormous debt for helping me to get back on my feet and back into society. It's a very difficult thing to do and I had a tremendous amount of help that other people who get out of prison and try to reenter society don't have. I feel enormous sympathy for them. I wish there were more ways for society to help released prisoners; it is extremely difficult to try and find new friends, throw away your old phone book, stay away from drug opportunities, find a job, get a place to live, somehow earn enough money after taxes to keep alive on some kind of food, and get around without the money to buy a car, taking public transportation or walking everywhere. It's not only tough, it's practically impossible. When I got out, several things happened: my friend not only said I could come stay at his apartment but he told the probation people in Northern California that Jan could come stay at his apartment and he would give her a job. That made it legal for her to come to Los Angeles. I have to say this the right way because my coauthor is sitting right across the table from me; the man did wonderful things for us. He let me and Jan stay in the spare bedroom in his apartment, he lent us his old BMW [a 1974 2002], he took me to the store and bought me every stitch of clothing I had, he fed us both three meals a day for months on end, he took us to the movies, he rented us videos, he bought us what we needed, he lent us cash, he encouraged us to go to meetings, he tried to help me go on a diet. He's secretly a probable Commie rat and a creep and certainly one of those radi- cal union writers, but he did do marvelous things for me. My old diving partner, Bev Morgan, blew my mind by laying a brand-new four-door BMW 325 on us, saying, "Pay me later." He even kept it in his name for months because I didn't have any credit and couldn't establish any; I had a new driver's license after I got out, but for a long time after that, if you punched my name into a TRW terminal, smoke would come out of the top, bells would ring, and alarms would go off. I was not a candidate for ready credit.

As for Jan, she was able to join me because of the good efforts of Joseph Brandenberg, her probation supervisor in Kansas City, a thoughtful and considerate man. He had prepared her probation report and knew the depth and extent of her rehabilitation. He works directly with the judge, who had been really angry at Jan for trying to protect me and getting herself in trouble again, on the hit-and-run charge. (She had taken the rap for the gun, which was mine, of course.) Judge Hamilton issued the probation order that prohibited Jan from seeing me for five years, the entire length of her extended probation. We appealed to Brandenberg and told him we were both trying to put our lives together. We pointed out that Jan completed her hospital and detox program, was living successfully in a rehab residence, and was such an exemplary person that she was teaching and helping as a counselor at the same hospital where she detoxed. The people in charge of her recovery had her helping other addicts. I said, "She's doing great and I've done my time. I'm being tested constantly. I'm on parole. It's absolutely provable that I'm drug-free. Can't you please get something done to have this five-year prohibition lifted? We want to get married!"

Normally, when you call up a federal institution of any kind, they say, "Call me back in three months. I'll see if I can remember your name," or "Gee, the guy you want is in the other building," or "The copying machine is broken and the computer's down," or "I'll need some time to collect the files and review your case." They don't want to hear about whatever it is you want them to do. Joe Brandenberg, on the other hand, was completely human, fully approachable, and entirely sensible. He didn't bend the rules for us, but when we asked him something justifiable, he agreed it was reasonable. He went to the judge and asked him to change the order and he did. Jan and I had permission to be together! We were not only ecstatic, deliriously happy, and profoundly in love, we were both drug-free and determined to stay that way.

Graham's wife, Susan Nash, found us a house to rent in the Valley, near them. The Nashes took us under their wing and did everything they could to help: Graham cosigned the lease for us and lent us the enormous amount of money it required for the first and last month's rent and deposit. In 1986, when I got out of prison, I was flat broke and I still owed the IRS close to a million dollars in back taxes, money that was spent on dope instead of paying Uncle Sam. One of my first acts as a responsible citizen was to declare bankruptcy; I'm still fighting my way out of that hole. But I want to point out that I had advantages—tremendous advantages—given to me by many close friends. It would require a separate chapter just to list them all. I particularly need to thank the people who are responsible for getting me to meetings. The meetings and the fellowship they offer have been tremendously helpful to me and I go to them regularly. The people I respect in the music business and in motion pictures are all coming to the same conclusion or have already come to the realization that if you want to do anything, if you want to be a creative force, if you want to write, if you want to produce, if you want to direct, if you want to write songs, if you want to play well, if you want to make records, you can either do drugs or your art. You can't do both and survive. Jan and I began attending meetings regularly. There were people in the program we had known for years; Michael Finnegan and his wife, Candy, were enjoying their newfound sobriety and Michael had been playing with CSN since the seventies. Everywhere we turned, there were old friends freed of their addictions and dependencies. Paul Kantner says cocaine is an intelligence test. If you're taking it, you fail.

Two and a half years after my last puff of dope, I still have dreams about taking drugs. I had one the night before writing this and I still have to fight the recurring nightmares. At meetings with other recovering addicts, I'll ask the whole group, "Do you guys have dope dreams?" Almost every hand in the place will go up. When I was first getting straight in prison, I would dream about dope every single night—sometimes two and three times in the course of the evening. The dreams come in all shapes and forms, but the archetypal one starts as a struggle dream where you're fighting to do something and you can't quite get it. You find yourself in a dreamscape, frantically going to people's houses in some city someplace, struggling to get some dope. There's a lot of anxiety involved and the circumstances will change, but you're always going to people, trying to get some drugs. Then you get them and sometimes I'll dream the actual act of smoking the pipe or chasing some heroin on a sheet of tinfoil and the dream switches to another kind of illusion, which is the feeling of "Oh my God, I've done it! How am I going to keep everybody from finding out?" That's a guilt dream and it's worse than the struggle dream because it's a true nightmare, one from which you wake up deeply disturbed and sometimes agitated.

There are mornings I get up truly unhappy and sick inside; it takes me a while before the real world can soak back in and ease out the bad shit. If the dreams get too bad or appear too often, I'll go directly to a meeting, hang out with somebody else, and talk about it. The dreams are a part of the psychic scar tissue from doing what I did. I don't want anybody to think that it's all Pollyanna peaches and cream because it's not. If you're an addict, you have to deal with it for an extremely long time while you're recovering and the early stages are hellishly tough. I don't want to give anybody any misleading ideas that recovery is easy. It's not easy; it's difficult, but it's worth it. That's the key: it's not easy, but it's worth it.

Being around people that do drugs or have them is one of the big no-no's. I can't totally avoid it because of the work I do. Sometimes I'm forced into contact with someone who's still holding out and still doing drugs. I'm not going to name names, but there are people who still think it's cool to take cocaine; obviously I think they're damn fools. Unfortunately, the fact that they still exist means that I'm going to be forced into contact with them sooner or later, which troubles me; there just isn't any way around it. I know exactly how their minds work. I know what they're doing. I see myself in them and it makes me acutely uncomfortable. Luckily, I'm no longer driven into a rage when someone comes up to me and offers me dope, which some people still do. Usually it's at the gigs. Some local entertainment businessman of some sort will say, "You want a little pick-me-up?" My response used to be "What the fuck is wrong with you? Don't you realize what I've been through, you asshole? How can you do that?" Nowadays, I just say, "No, no thanks, I don't do that shit anymore," and leave it at that. I can't understand what drove anyone to offer me something that could put me back in Huntsville Prison for five years. My objectives were clear and going back to jail was not one of them. For the first year after I was released on parole, I was closely supervised. All I wanted—and all that I needed to do—was work.

With the approval of his parole officer, David played a series of solo concerts, touring with an acoustic guitar and playing small clubs and venues. It was a tour that served a twofold purpose: it reaffirmed his ability to make music and play to audiences and it fulfilled two-year-old contracts that had been abrogated when he went fugitive and was sent to jail. David Scott had booked a number of dates in the winter of 1985. By 1987, they had all been played off—to sold-out houses and enthusiastic reviews.

SAN FRANCISCO CHRONICLE: *David Crosby, as evidenced by his performance Thursday night [October 30, 1986] before a packed house at the Miramar Beach Inn, has not only survived, but has emerged stronger in spirit and truer in voice than anyone might have hoped. . . . He went right into "Lee Shore," his voice oozing honey, his cheeks as rosy as those of a Scotsman, his cherubic smile warming the room. . . . He was in charming form as he ended the song to cheers. Next up was the classic "In My Dreams," his voice full and rich, the guitar true and ringing . . . Crosby left the stage, came back once to wail his way through "Long Time Coming," and departed as his fan club stood cheering for five full minutes.*

Marilyn Townsend was one of the big surprises waiting for me in Los Angeles. I walked into the local district office of the California Correctional Authority, signed up, and took my place on the wooden bench with all the other recently released guys from joints all over California. I got there expecting that my parole officer would be a surly civil service lifer who hated his job and hated me. The person I met was a bright, funny, intelligent, well-educated, cooperative, perceptive human being with whom I could talk about anything. I could discuss my recovery with her on any level. She was a veteran of eighteen years on the job and was one of the first women parole officers in the state. Marilyn turned out to be a real friend to me and Jan, an actual pal, and her existence in the system is proof that it isn't all bleak. There are good people out there. We weren't as lucky with the federal probation officer to whom Jan was assigned. That was the most vicious asshole I've run into in years—and I'm including all the dealers and low-life scum I met during the time I was addicted. He showed no hope or mercy and would reduce Jan to tears by telling her that there was no way she was going to get well. As a condition of my parole and of Jan's probation, we were both subject to random drug testing. This jerk made Jan come in and test two or three times for every time I was called and never missed an opportunity to tell her he was expecting her to test dirty and take a fall. He "knew" she wasn't going to make it! He was wrong then and he's wrong now. He's a wrong guy.

Both Jan and David were drug-free and welcomed drug testing. It wasn't fun for them to have to show up in a bleak windowless Formica-and-fluorescent government office and pee in a bottle at the whim of some civil servant, but it was a pleasure to come up negative, time after time, proving their new constancy to the state, to each other, and to the community in which they were trying to live normal lives. It was an ongoing struggle and temptations would appear at the oddest times. Once, after breakfast in a deli in the Valley, this writer and David were walking with Jan to the Crosbys' car. A passing biker on a Harley recognized David, rolled to a stop, reached into his leathers, and produced a baggie of bright green weed, offering a few buds out of appreciation. True to his word, David wasn't outraged. He politely declined. Another time, more invidious, David and Jan were searching for a cat that had strayed from the house and disappeared. Maryann Zvoleff put posters on telephone poles in the neighborhood and one of them produced a response. The Crosbys drove to check it out.

Someone had seen a flier and said they thought they might have found the cat. We went over to see it, but it wasn't ours. While we were driving home, we found ourselves on a familiar street. All of a sudden I had a realization: "If I keep going straight and cross that next intersection, I'm going to be right in front of a dope dealer's house. I even know he's still living there." Jan and I looked at each other. Both of us were crying because we were terribly unhappy about losing our cat; our depression was a perfect excuse to get loaded. We had done it thousands of times before. I even had enough cash in my pocket to pay for anything we might have wanted. We looked at each other: we knew where we were, who lived on that street, and what was in the house on the next block. We got to the corner and turned left. We never crossed that intersection and never drove past the dealer's house. We took ourselves out of harm's way and we felt good about it.

We invested a lot of time and effort getting straight. It's something anyone can do; it's just not easy. But you save your life and get back your existence as a human being. Because of that, it's a great investment. The dividend is that I'm no longer afraid all the time. I used to live in fear of getting busted, of not being able to get my next fix of dope, of being harassed by people I owed money to, of having a seizure and dying, of being unable to hustle some money to somehow stay alive for another day. Nowadays, without fear or apprehension, if I'm in some kind of trouble, I can call a cop! That's quite a novelty for a serious addict who kept some kind of dope and a gun on his person most of his adult life. Graham and I were driving along one day recently and saw our friend Don Gooch running down the street. When we stopped and asked, "What's happening?" he told us a friend of his had just been burglarized and the guy that did it was that guy over there with the purple bag on his shoulder. Don went over and stopped him and we called the cops on the mobile phone. I got to do it. I got to say, "My name is David Crosby and I want a cop." We laughed ourselves silly about it and we caught a burglar.

During that first year of living in sobriety, David was coming back to his music, testing his new songs, finding his performance skills intact, and constantly marveling at the sensation of doing it all drug-free. It was a new world he was

479

exploring. In October 1986, the Bridge School Benefit brought David back together with Graham, Stephen, and Neil for the first Crosby, Stills, Nash and Young concert in a decade. It was a legendary evening, featuring performances by CSNY, Bruce Springsteen, Don Henley, J. D. Souther, Danny Kortchmar, Robin Williams, Nils Lofgren, and others.

Robin Williams, God bless him, when I walked in backstage, said, "Good God Almighty, free at last!" and made me laugh so hard I could not believe it. All these people were supportive. Every one of them, without exception, came over to me at some point in the evening and said, "Man, I'm so glad that you're still alive and I'm so glad that you're making the effort to quit. Welcome back and stay straight." It felt fantastic and Crosby, Stills, and Nash is a well-oiled machine. We know how to do that trick really well. But when you drop Neil into it, it's like dropping nitroglycerine into the mix. He's such a powerful force as a performer and as a creative person that the soup turns explosive right away. It's either very bad or fantastic and that night it was fantastic; all I can say to anyone who didn't see that performance is "You missed a hell of a show." We played again—all four of us —at a benefit for Greenpeace in Santa Barbara and the significant thing about that evening was that at least half of the show was new material, new songs that blew everybody's mind. They were expecting us to come out and amble through some golden oldies, but we came out and nailed them with brand-new songs. Neil told people, in print, while I was in jail, that if I straightened up, he would come back and work with us. I think that he wanted to honor that commitment and I also think that he loves to work with us when we're workable. We're not without our problems still, but as we write this, our first album together in fifteen years is finished and will be released.

NEIL YOUNG: *If these guys want CSNY, then there should be four guys as strong as Graham and I are, who can handle it. We should be physically able to take on the job of setting an example for an*

entire generation that could be halfway to the fucking grave. They've
got to say, "Hey, the next twenty years could be better than the last
twenty." They have to see that; if they can't see that from CSNY, this
may be the last chance they get. They have to see that we can go
through all this shit and come back stronger and sharper than we
were before. Our audience, all the people around the country and
around the world, no matter what has happened to them in their
lives, no matter how many good friends have died, how much shit
they've piled on themselves, how many losses they've endured—what-
ever it is—if we can be so strong after everything we've endured, it
would be like fresh water running over the entire audience.

I think I can satisfy Neil's desire to see me healthy and
strong; God knows, I'm going to keep trying. I've got lots of
unfinished business and the rest of my life to get things done and
to achieve new goals. First things first, as Gottlieb says, which is
why I proposed to Jan after New Year's in 1987. At first, marriage
seemed a way to get around the judge's order that we couldn't be
together. But when I saw the look on Jan's face as we talked
about it, once I said the "m" word, I realized this woman was
totally in love with me and I was totally in love with her. I
thought to myself, "She's one of the nicest human beings I've
ever met in my whole life. We are incredibly happy together. Why
am I hanging on to my old prejudice against being married? I
don't want to be with anyone else." One night when we were
lying in bed, I said, "Hey, Jan." And she said, "Yeah?" And I
said, "Let's get married." She burst into tears; I took that to
mean "Yes." It's the smartest thing I ever did. She's a fantastic
woman. I'm incredibly lucky to be with her and I don't think she
would have ever left me, but I'm real glad we formalized the
arrangement. I couldn't be happier about it. We wrote a letter to
the judge:

Dear Judge Hamilton:
Please let me thank you for permitting Jan Dance and

myself the opportunity to resume normal lives together. We live happily in Encino, California, a suburb of Los Angeles, and we are planning to be married on May 16, 1987. My professional life as a musician and recording artist is going well and I find myself a functioning, productive, and healthy working citizen. Miss Dance and I are receiving weekly drug counseling, we attend meetings every week, and continue to report to our probation and parole officers on a regular basis; by all accounts, we believe we're doing well.

I've been especially fortunate in my professional life and have enjoyed steady concert bookings and work in the recording studio since returning to Los Angeles. Consequently, I was pleased that Miss Dance and I have been invited to go on a sailing vacation with my partner Neil Young on his yacht in the Caribbean, sailing out of the American Virgin Islands for about ten days beginning March 23. Miss Dance's probation officer informs me that he cannot give permission for Miss Dance to go outside the continental United States, that only you can grant such permission. The people with whom we will be vacationing are sober and drug-free and have been strong supporters of our recovery. The situation would be healthy and extremely beneficial to us both and it is a rare opportunity. We'd very much appreciate the chance to enjoy it. My parole officer, Ms. Marilyn Townsend, has already granted me permission to leave the continental United States for this specific purpose and I would respectfully ask you to do the same for Miss Dance.

—*David Crosby*

We got permission and had our honeymoon even before we got married. Neil and Peggy Young took Jan and I sailing in the Caribbean on Neil's schooner, the *Ragland,* which is a hundred-foot Baltic trader, rebuilt from the keel up, a real beauty. We sailed to Panama and it was heaven, catching fresh fish out of the ocean for dinner and watching sunrises and sunsets over the blue

water together. It's truly gratifying to know that everybody loves
Jan. As much as she was despised and villified and shunned
before, that's how much she is loved now.

In May, invitations were sent to seventy-five or a hundred of
David's closest personal male friends, inviting them to a
"Vulgar and Tasteless Stag Party in David's Honor." Another three hundred invitations went to wedding guests, who
would attend the nuptial ceremony the morning after the
stag party. On May 15, at the Registry Hotel overlooking
Universal Studios, the Presidential Suite (often occupied by
Michael Jackson or Nancy Reagan) was the site of a good
deal of vulgar and tasteless entertainment: a trio led by a
pianist-singer named Eddie Zip played music, there was food
and drink in abundance, a beautiful woman named Suni
Montgomery poured drinks at the bar, wearing the skimpiest
of bikinis, and the equally stunning Maryann Zvoleff
watched the door and checked invitations, almost dressed in
virginal white. Jackson Browne, Howard Hesseman, Elliot
Roberts, and many others who are in this book made rude
remarks and comedian John Farentino said that David
couldn't go swimming anymore because every time he'd walk
up on the beach, Greenpeace would push him out to sea.
There may have been some nude dancers there; this author
doesn't remember.

There were no other girls at the bachelor party. Nothing happened. The party, arranged once again by my illustrious and de-
mented friend Carl, was a lot of fun and very embarrassing. I'll
say that much. No physical contact took place. I was roasted and
toasted by my friends and family and there were nonalcoholic
beverages for the abstainers. There was even a traditional stag
video, only someone [editor Lauren Vercel and the multitalented
Ms. Zvoleff] cut the lewd images into a Crosby, Stills, and Nash
television interview and matched the editing to our music. While
our voices were singing innocuous songs like "Teach Your Children" and "Our House" and "Find the Cost of Freedom," the
screen images were absolutely lewd, triple-X-rated stag party porn
footage. Huge laughs and heavy breathing from all the guests. I
was exhausted when I got home and the wedding was at 10 A.M.

the next morning. Graham and Susan Nash joined us and renewed their vows on their tenth anniversary; it was a double ceremony. We were dressed in formal cutaway coats and striped trousers, the brides carried bouquets, and there were press cameras and television reporters covering the event. The best party was at the Nashes' house afterward, during the reception, when Susan and Graham and Jan and I jumped in the pool in the middle of the party because we were bored with just walking around, sweating in the heat. We had a great time. It was an admirable thing for Susan and Graham to share their tenth anniversary as we began our first and it was a memorable party: that's what it's like, having real friends and living real life.

> That summer Crosby, Stills, and Nash toured the United States and made more money than they had ever earned as a group before. Without a current hit record, they sold out almost every venue. Their tour was economical, David put aside money to begin repaying his debts and settling his beef with the IRS, and everywhere they played the reviews and audience responses were satisfying, encouraging, and approving. As an added bonus, on November 11, 1987, the Texas Supreme Court sustained David Crosby's appeal and concluded that the original search and seizure of his dressing room in Dallas was illegal. His conviction was finally overturned by the highest court in the state of Texas. During the winter, David played numerous concerts and some benefits —as a solo artist, in duet with Graham Nash, and with CSN and CSNY. He recorded a solo album for A&M Records, *Oh Yes I Can,* which included many of the songs he wrote in prison and after, and completed a brand-new Crosby, Stills, Nash, and Young album (recorded at Neil's ranch, with Young's wholehearted and enthusiastic participation). Promoters and the band's management had no trouble arranging another national tour for the summer of 1988. David also cowrote this book, reexamining the darkest and highest moments of his life, and the boat was rescued.

All the time I was in prison I thought about the *Mayan* and when I got out I felt like making amends to it the way I'd make amends to a person. The schooner had been a good friend to me and represented all the healthiest and best parts of my life. When I let it go downhill, spent all my money on drugs, and couldn't take care of it, I accumulated an enormous backlog of guilt about the boat. Before I went to jail, each time I saw her, she would be more trashed out than the time before. I'd hear more stories about how the *Mayan* was sitting around, going to pieces, and people were selling things off to get money. I know I left her in less than responsible hands, but nobody else would take her. No responsible person would put themselves in that position because they knew there was no money to take care of her; I'm lucky she didn't sink. I think there was some sort of nautical guardian angel watching over the *Mayan* who kept her whole and alive. As for the people who were aboard during my protracted difficulties, I bear them no ill will because they managed to keep her afloat. As I started getting back on my feet financially, I heard that the schooner had been abandoned while its crew took a delivery through the Panama Canal to the West Coast. They left the *Mayan* parked on the Inland Waterway in Florida. Bev Morgan and I went down to get her.

BEV MORGAN: *One day David says, "You know, I gotta get the boat." We had word she was in the Bahamas all this time and getting her out of there would be sticky, since David's parole limited his freedom to travel out of the United States. I'd have to be his agent and we'd need a Bahamian attorney and someone familiar with the local scene to guarantee we could clear the paperwork and get the boat out of Bahamian waters. Eventually, we started keeping a coast watch for the boat because they'd have to come in sooner or later. They couldn't stay out there indefinitely. When the boat came in, David called me to tell me she was in Jupiter, Florida. We flew down, rented a car, and rounded up a couple of folks we knew down there [including a young deckhand named Liam Ingram, Bobby Ingram's grown son]. We found the* Mayan *moored off some dinky sport-fishing dock, deserted. We rowed over and checked the whole thing out, fired up the engine, and took off. Well, pretty soon we see Robbie. He's running across the bridges, yelling, "Hey! What's going on?" We were going along at six or seven knots while he was driving his car along the bank, zigzagging over the bridges as we went through. Finally, he found a boat and some buddies and they came out and got on the* Mayan. *As it turned out, everyone was nice and worked with us, sailing her down to the yard where she was going to be repaired. It all worked out great. No problem.*

I put the *Mayan* in a first-class yard near Palm Beach and it'll take a year and a half to overhaul her, but when it's all done, she'll be completely rebuilt, structurally, from the ribs up. Bud and Cassie Hedrick are back aboard and Bud knows the boat better than anyone except the guys who built her forty years ago. Bobby Ingram is there and Billy Martinelli is building new masts for her in his shop in Sausalito. When we're done, she'll be a brand-new John Alden schooner, which is a rare and beautiful thing. I plan on having the *Mayan* for the rest of my life and I'm going to go sailing around the world, cruising with people I love. Sooner or later we'll go all through the South and Southwestern Pacific. I'd love to go to Australia and New Zealand and New Hebrides and the Seychelles, off the coast of Africa. Then there's South America to sail around and the Caribbean and I dream of sailing up the great rivers of the world: the Amazon, the Yangtze, the Irrawaddy, and the Nile as far as the Aswan Dam.

In May of 1988, around our first anniversary, Jan got a letter from Joseph Brandenberg that officially released her from further probation. On June 13, the Supreme Court of the United States denied a petition for a Writ of Certiori from the Dallas County district attorney, who carried his failed case all the way to the top, trying to keep my conviction on the books. He lost. The decision of the Texas Supreme Court stands: my conviction was ultimately overturned and the lower court directed to find the defendant (me) not guilty, even though I served a year in jails and prisons. I don't regret a minute of that time.

DAVID CROSBY

JAN CROSBY: *David and I talked about this the other day, saying how ironic it was that he was able to stop using drugs and cleaned up his life for me, while I was doing the exact same thing for him. I wanted to prove to myself and to the world-at-large and to David, in particular, that I could be strong and set a good example. I came to realize that I needed to change my behavior and that I could become more healthy as I went along. We each had it in mind for the other before it ever came to doing it for ourselves. I don't know where that came from, but I'm glad it happened at all because in our case, it saved our lives. Even when David and I weren't married on paper, we were married in our spirit and in our hearts.*

JOE WALSH: *I have to say this. The guy who was in the news a bunch and that guy who was really out there and seemed very strange, that wasn't David Crosby. He'll be the first to tell you; that was somebody else. I thank God every day that Cros is back and I want everybody to know that he's alive, he's well, he's paid his obligation for not being the Cros, and he's the foundation to an awful lot of us musicians who kind of consider ourselves as having seniority—I can be an old-timer, I suppose, at this point. We need Crosby here. He's a good guy. He's the voice you can't hear because when he sings harmony, he sings perfect. You can hear Stephen below the Cros. You can hear Graham. You can hear Stephen and Graham. But you can't hear the Cros. He's got that middle part and it wouldn't be CSN without him. He loves to sing harmony and he's one of the very, very best at his craft. And if you ever go sailing and he's on your boat, you'll be fine. Just be ready to carry groceries.*

> **I have wasted ten years**
> **in a blindfold**
> **Tenfold more than I've invested**
> **now in sight**
>
> **I have traveled beveled mirrors**
> **in a flycrawl**
> **Losing the reflection**
> **of a fight**

But like a compass seeking North
there lives in me a still sure spirit part

Clouds of doubt are cut asunder
by the lightning and the thunder
Shining from the compass
of my heart

I have flown the frantic flight
of the batwing
and only known the dark
because of that

I have seized death's doorhandle
like a fish out of the water
Waiting for the mercy
of the cat

But like a compass seeking North
There lives in me a still sure spirit part

Clouds of doubt are cut asunder
by the lightning and the thunder
Shining from the compass
of my heart

"Compass,"
Words and Music by David Crosby

The story of a life isn't over until that life is over; a biography of a living person is a human story, changing each day, added to by every moment. Selective memory's a mechanism for recalling the past to support the present in an attempt to influence the future. Real life isn't so easily manipulated. We live with the consequences of our choices, we suffer our follies, and we live to enjoy the wisdom that is in all of us. David has the last word:

If there is a God and He puts anybody anyplace for any reason, what God put me here to do is to be able to be creative, to be able to accomplish good work, to be able to come through for my friends who believe in me. In the process of writing all this, I went through an incredible catharsis, examining and realizing and dealing with everything I've done: the bad and the good. It's the reality I created, the life that I lived, and I can look at it, learn from it, and let it go. I am glad to be alive, to have shed a burden that almost killed me, and to face a future that I think I understand. For that, I can only offer thanks.

—David Crosby and Carl Gottlieb
Los Angeles, Florida, Kauai,
1987–88